# CRACKS IN TIME

# THE UNOFFICIAL AND UNAUTHORISED GUIDE TO *DOCTOR WHO* 2010

CRACKS IN TIME

THE UNOFFICIAL AND
UNAUTHORISED GUIDE TO
*DOCTOR WHO* 2010

STEPHEN JAMES WALKER

First published in England in 2012 by
Telos Publishing Ltd
139 Whitstable Road, Canterbury, Kent, CT2 8EQ

www.telos.co.uk

This edition 2021

Telos Publishing Ltd values feedback. Please e-mail us with any comments you may
have about this book to: feedback@telos.co.uk

ISBN: 978-1-84583-179-0

*Cracks in Time: The Unofficial and Unauthorised Guide to* Doctor Who *2010*
© 2012, 2021 Stephen James Walker

British Library Cataloguing in Publication Data.
A catalogue record for this book is available from the British Library.

# TABLE OF CONTENTS

# INTRODUCTION

Although I live just outside London, with its many theatres both large and small, it is only about three or four times a year that I find the time to see a live stage play. So, with hindsight, it was very fortunate that one evening in the summer of 2008 I managed to catch a performance of Polly Stenham's *That Face* at the Duke of York's Theatre in the West End. Why fortunate? Because one of the leads in that play was Matt Smith, who a mere six months later would be announced as the actor cast to succeed the hugely popular David Tennant as the star of *Doctor Who*.

In *That Face*, Smith's performance in a very demanding part was outstanding – and, I later learned, award-winning, having earned him the Best Newcomer accolade in the *Evening Standard*'s annual theatre awards – but never did it cross my mind that he could potentially be a future Doctor. The main reason for this, I suspect, was simply that he seemed too young – albeit, at 25, not actually as young as the 18-year-old character he was very convincingly portraying. This issue of his age was probably the main talking point in the press and amongst fans following the announcement of his casting as the eleventh Doctor. Would such a young actor be able successfully to portray a 900-plus-year-old Time Lord?

This was not the only question on fans' minds in the months leading up to the Easter 2010 on-air debut of Series Five.[1] Another big unknown was to what extent, and in what ways, *Doctor Who* would change now that Steven Moffat had succeeded Russell T Davies as its head writer and showrunner – the person whose creative vision drives the whole production. Moffat had proved himself to be a brilliant writer for the show with his past contributions, including award-winning episodes such as 'The Girl in the Fireplace' in Series Two and 'Blink' in Series Three, but would he be able to maintain that phenomenal standard when called upon to provide a greater number of scripts per year, while at the same time also performing all the other duties that were part and parcel of his new role? And how well would he cope with the demands of heading such a large and complex production, at a time of increasing budgetary pressures? Would he be as adept as his predecessor at negotiating the arcane administrative practices and internal politics of the BBC? To assist him in this, he would have his fellow executive producers, Piers Wenger and Beth Willis; but they too were newcomers to the show, so it was very much a case of 'all change' at the top.

These are just some of the issues addressed in *Cracks in Time*, which is the latest in Telos Publishing's series of comprehensive guides to *Doctor Who*. The first section of the book notes all the main events, news stories, promotional activities and so forth that occurred in the *Doctor Who* world in 2010, in what is designed to serve as a useful record of this time from the 'outside looking in' perspective of the

---

[1] The 2010 series was actually the thirty-first in *Doctor Who*'s long history. However, it was the fifth since the show's TV revival in 2005, and was promoted as Series Five by BBC Worldwide and, on DVD and Blu-Ray, by 2Entertain, so I will be referring to it as such in this book.

viewing public. Following this, there are capsule biographies of all the main cast and production team members who worked on Series Five. Then comes the most substantial section of the book, a detailed guide to and analysis of all 13 episodes, plus the 2010 Christmas Special, 'A Christmas Carol'. Lastly there are seven appendices, covering: the first episodes in *The Adventure Games* series of downloadable *Doctor Who* computer games; the *Doctor Who Live* stage show; Series Five of *Doctor Who Confidential*; the viewing figures and fan rankings; the first entries in BBC Books' original eleventh Doctor novels range; the first of the original eleventh Doctor comic strip stories; and other officially-sanctioned original eleventh Doctor fiction published during this period.

If you are reading this book, the chances are that you are already an avid follower of the good Doctor's adventures, but I hope that in the following pages you will find much to interest, inform and enlighten you, and ultimately to enhance your appreciation and enjoyment of the 2010 run of episodes in what is undoubtedly my favourite TV series of all time!

*Stephen James Walker*
*February 2012*

# PART ONE
# THE YEAR AS IT HAPPENED

# CHAPTER ONE
# DAWN OF A NEW ERA

2010 began with *Doctor Who* enjoying a peak of public interest and acclaim. The transmission of the tenth Doctor's swansong, Russell T Davies's 'The End of Time' Part Two, on the evening of New Year's Day saw 11.79 million viewers tuning in to BBC One, with 0.48 million more watching on BBC HD. This made it the number one rated programme of the week (although number two in the official chart, which counted figures for HD channels separately); an impressive achievement by any standards. An appreciation index figure of 89 showed that the programme had also been greatly enjoyed by those who had seen it.[2]

The special got a generally positive reaction in the press, too. Critic Mark Lawson commented on the *Guardian* website on 2 January:

> Davies's final script was typical of the depth and intelligence he has brought to the new incarnation of the show: the plot seemed deliberately to be modelled on *Hamlet*, which [David] Tennant has played triumphantly on stage and TV during his final year as the Doctor.
>
> In common with the prince of Denmark, the Time Lord from Gallifrey agonised aloud over whether it would be right to kill a man (the Master) after a painful encounter with his mother, played by Claire Bloom, whose Shakespearean roles include Hamlet's mother, Gertrude.
>
> Again like Hamlet, the Doctor died with a promise to 'sing him to his rest', although the offer in this case came from aliens – the Ood – rather than angels.
>
> The final line Davies gave to Tennant was a suddenly regretful 'I don't want to go!', and it is likely that, somewhere inside, both actor and writer feel a little like that.

Many fans also felt very sad at the passing of an era that had proved unprecedentedly popular, generated huge amounts of tie-in merchandise and seen the show winning numerous awards voted for both by industry professionals and by members of the viewing public. However, there was excitement too at the prospect of the forthcoming series of adventures, produced by a new team headed by acclaimed writer Steven Moffat and featuring a regenerated Doctor in the form of 27-year-old Matt Smith alongside his new companion Amy Pond played by 22-year-old Karen Gillan. A first trailer for this series was shown on BBC One just a

---

[2] For a full episode guide to 'The End of Time', plus full ratings information, see *End of Ten: The Unofficial and Unauthorised Guide to* Doctor Who *2009* (Telos Publishing, 2010).

couple of hours after the broadcast of 'The End of Time' Part Two, and it was due to begin its on-air run just three months later. Recording was already well under way, with reports and photographs of the location work frequently appearing in the press and on online fan forums.

The BBC's official *Doctor Who* website – at www.bbc.co.uk/doctorwho – was being revamped in preparation for the new series, and on 7 January it released a new publicity image of Smith's Doctor, plus one portraying the transition between the tenth and eleventh Doctors. It also confirmed the names of the writers for the forthcoming run of episodes: there would be six from showrunner Steven Moffat himself, two from Chris Chibnall, and one each from Mark Gatiss, Toby Whithouse, Simon Nye and Richard Curtis. The last two names on this list were particularly intriguing to many fans, as neither had contributed to *Doctor Who* before, and both were well-known for their high-profile successes on other shows, Curtis in particular being a very big name in the film and television industry.

There was a degree of confusion amongst fans as to how the forthcoming series should be referred to. News had emerged that it was being described as Series One for some production purposes, on the basis that it was the first series for the new production team and the new Doctor. Some fans, however, preferred to think of it as Season 31, taking into account the show's classic-era history as well. In the end, though, most settled on calling it Series Five, as it was the fifth full series since *Doctor Who* had returned to TV in 2005; and it later emerged that this was how it would be marketed too, notably for its DVD and Blu-Ray releases by 2Entertain.

On the evening of 20 January, further evidence of the popularity of the tenth Doctor's era came when *Doctor Who* triumphed at the National Television Awards ceremony at the O2 arena in London. The show itself won the Drama category, as it had done every year the awards had been held since 2005[3], and David Tennant took the Best Drama Performance accolade. Tennant was on hand to collect his individual award in person, and for the Drama one was joined on stage by Sarah Jane Smith actress Elisabeth Sladen and 'The End of Time' guest stars June Whitfield and Bernard Cribbins, the latter of whom gave an acceptance speech.

In early February, further titbits of advance information about Series Five continued to emerge. The production crew were spotted recording scenes at a number of locations, including the historic Stonehenge site in Wiltshire, and *Doctor Who Magazine* revealed the titles of the first three episodes – 'The Eleventh Hour', 'The Beast Below' and 'Victory of the Daleks' – plus the names of a number of the guest stars who would feature during the series. This was the first time that Arthur Darvill's role as Rory was publicly mentioned, although at this stage no indication was given that he was to be a semi-regular; and Alex Kingston's return as River Song was also announced – although this came as no surprise to fans, as she had already been spotted recording scenes with Matt Smith and Karen Gillan for the two-part story that had been first to go before the cameras but would fill the third and fourth slots on transmission. Looking further ahead, acclaimed science fiction and fantasy writer Neil Gaiman announced, in an acceptance message for a comics awards show, that he would be contributing a script to Matt Smith's second series as the Doctor.

In an interview in the 9 February edition of the *Perthshire Advertiser* newspaper,

---

[3] There were no National Television Awards in 2009.

Scottish actress Neve McIntosh revealed that she would be appearing in one of the Series Five stories, and also gave some intriguing details of the characters she would be playing:

> It's a dream come true for the sci-fi fan, who reckons the latest occupant of the TARDIS has the potential to outstrip his predecessors Christopher Eccleston and David Tennant.
>
> She said: 'I think he's going to be really good, the best yet out of the new guys.
>
> 'The stories have got a bit darker. I play twins, and they're big lizard warrior women.
>
> 'They're one of the Silurian tribes that have been undisturbed under the earth. And of course we get disturbed.
>
> 'It's the first time I've worn prosthetics but I'm still recognisable if you know me well enough.
>
> 'But there'll probably be lots of people going, "Who the hell is that?"'

Long-time fans quickly picked up on the actress's reference to the Silurians, a monster race that had appeared first during the Jon Pertwee era in the early 1970s and again during the Peter Davison era in the following decade. This was the first firm indication that they would be returning again in the forthcoming series.

An indication of how the lack of a full series in 2009 had adversely affected *Doctor Who*'s standing with children came on 11 February, when the Audit Bureau of Circulations (ABC) released figures for circulation of the *Doctor Who Adventures* magazine for younger readers. These indicated that in the six months to the end of the year, each issue had had an average circulation of around 45,000 – almost 46% down on the equivalent figure for 2008 (and a long way below the incredible peak of around 155,000 achieved in 2007, when the magazine came out fortnightly rather than weekly). Jaynie Bye, joint managing director of BBC Children's Magazines, commented: '*Doctor Who Adventures* is down year on year, as anticipated, but is still performing well given the absence of the show from the schedules for most of this period. We are confident that circulation will increase with the return of the Doctor to our screens in 2010.'

14 February saw the *Sunday Times* publish an article headed '*Doctor Who* in War with Planet Maggie', looking at the inclusion of an element of political satire in the classic era story 'The Happiness Patrol' (1988). This created a brief flurry of other media interest, most notably an item on the 15 February edition of BBC Two's *Newsnight* in which presenter Gavin Esler spoke to 1980s script editor Andrew Cartmel and Conservative MP, and *Doctor Who* fan, Tim Collins.

On 17 February, the official *Doctor Who* website released a promotional image from a forthcoming specially-shot trailer for Series Five. The trailer itself was first broadcast on 20 February on BBC One. It was one minute long and had been made by Red Bee Media and the Mill not only in a standard 2D version but also in a 3D one. Both versions would be screened in numerous cinemas up and down the country over the next couple of months. A BBC spokesperson told *Broadcast* magazine: '*Doctor Who* is the appropriate vehicle for 3D. It just fits. It's a great way to introduce and showcase the new Doctor to younger viewers.'

The trailer opens with the Doctor and Amy lying side by side on a grassy bank in a park, looking up at the stars above, with the following exchange of dialogue:

> **Amy:** 'How about that one?'
> **Doctor:** 'A bit green up close.'
> **Amy:** 'That one's flickering.'
> **Doctor:** 'Yeah, sorry, thought I'd fixed that.'
> **Amy:** 'Who are you?'
> **Doctor:** 'I'm the Doctor.'
> **Amy:** 'Doctor who?'

The ground then cracks open, pitching the Doctor and Amy into a tunnel-like vortex. The Doctor grasps Amy's hands and tells her 'Hold on tight' as monsters swirl around them, including Weeping Angels and a Dalek that demands 'State your identity!' 'Trust me!' shouts the Doctor, to which Amy replies 'What? Why?' They then become separated, with Amy spinning away into the vortex shouting 'Doctor!' while the Doctor grapples with a Weeping Angel, which disintegrates. The Doctor and Amy then come back together, and in a voiceover, the Doctor says: 'All of time and space, everywhere and anywhere, every star that ever was.' The Doctor and Amy are then shown lying back on the grassy bank, as the Doctor asks, 'Where do you want to start?' A fearsome alien face (which viewers of Series Five would later discover to be one of the Silurians' metallic visors) then bursts through from below, as an announcer intones: '*Doctor Who*. The journey begins. This Easter on BBC One.' For some screenings, the trailer was run at a faster speed, with the actors' voices pitch-corrected to compensate, and lasted only 40 seconds. Although no doubt expensive to produce, the trailer met with a mixed response from fans. Some admired its 3D effects, but others considered it rather crude in execution and lacking the impact of those seen in previous years.

17 February also saw the announcement of the outcome of a competition launched the previous October by the BBC's long-running children's show *Blue Peter* to design a different TARDIS console. The thousands of entries had been whittled down to one in each of three different age categories by *Blue Peter* editor Tim Levell, *Doctor Who* production designer Edward Thomas and showrunner Steven Moffat. The overall winner had then been chosen by Matt Smith. It was Susannah Leah from Todmorden in West Yorkshire, who had entered in the 11-12 year olds category. The prize was to have her design featured in a forthcoming episode of *Doctor Who*, although the details of this were yet to be revealed.

On 22 February, the *Sun* broke another piece of Series Five casting news, reporting that well known comic actor James Corden would be putting in an appearance:

> The larger-than-life comic was spotted learning lines while on a train to the *Who* set in Cardiff.
> When quizzed by a fan, excited James – Smithy in the award-winning sitcom [*Gavin & Stacey*] – blurted out the secret.
> A show insider said: 'We normally keep our guest stars under wraps but you can't hide a bloke like James.
> 'And now he's not coming to Wales for *Gavin & Stacey* any

more, it's pretty obvious why he is here.'

Pals say James, 31 – who filmed much of *Gavin & Stacey* in Welsh resort Barry Island – is a huge *Doctor Who* fan.

And he jumped at the chance of appearing in the new BBC One series, which starts at Easter.

Published on 10 March, Issue 194 of the popular science fiction media magazine *SFX* featured a special 3D lenticular cover photo showing the Doctor and Amy in a forest, with two Weeping Angels and the TARDIS behind them. This was produced specially for the magazine in co-operation with the *Doctor Who* production office.

On 25 February came the news that the first episode of Series Five would have its debut US broadcast on BBC America on 17 April. This was reported in the trade paper *Variety* and confirmed on BBC America's own website. At the beginning of March, Canadian broadcaster Space followed suit by announcing that the episode would also go out on 17 April in that country. Strong rumours were meanwhile circulating that the series' start date in the UK would be 3 April, with the show back in its traditional Saturday evening weekly slot, but at this point there was no official word from the BBC. ABC in Australia were also keeping their plans under wraps for the time being, although they confirmed that the series would begin airing sometime in April.

Issue 419 of *Doctor Who Magazine*, which went on sale on 4 March, revealed the titles for the fourth, fifth and sixth episodes of the forthcoming series to be 'The Time of Angels', 'Flesh and Stone' and 'Vampires in Venice'.[4]

On 8 March, the BBC Press Office put out a press release headed 'The 11th Doctor embarks on his maiden voyage … with a whistle-stop tour presenting five regional premieres across the UK'. This read in part:

> *Doctor Who* will begin an exciting national tour across the UK in March, introducing the new Doctor to fans of the series in five different locations spanning the length and breadth of the British Isles.
>
> The tour will introduce the eleventh Doctor, Matt Smith, and his companion, Karen Gillan, to fans of the show and offer them a unique chance to meet the stars.
>
> Each location will also host a regional premiere of episode one, 'The Eleventh Hour', for pre-selected local school children, working alongside BBC Outreach to enable kids to get a first look at the new Doctor in action. The screenings are not open to members of the public.
>
> Matt and Karen will travel around the UK on a specially themed *Doctor Who* tour bus, featuring the new TARDIS logo and iconic imagery.
>
> BBC Outreach proactively takes the BBC into specific communities and sections of society, and has been integral in organising and supporting the tour.

---

[4] The latter title would be amended slightly to 'The Vampires of Venice' prior to the episode's transmission.

The focus of the tour is targeting hard to reach and relatively under-served communities by the BBC.

The Doctor's maiden voyage will commence on 29 March in Belfast, and then travel to Karen Gillan's home town, Inverness, for a screening on 30 March.

The bus will then move on to Sunderland that afternoon and Salford on Wednesday 31 before finishing later that day in Northampton – Matt Smith's home town.

Following the tour, from 1 April to 3 April, the BBC will also hold events for three days at selected BBC Big Screens across the UK, giving *Doctor Who* fans in London, Manchester, Edinburgh, Plymouth and Swansea the chance to interact directly with the show in their home towns.

The events will feature exclusive footage – including the chance to see the *Doctor Who* trailer in 3D – and giveaways, and fans can also get their photo taken tumbling through the giant vortex.

Visitors will also be able to meet some of the scariest monsters that have had viewers watching from behind their sofa for generations as well.

About the tour, Piers Wenger, executive producer and Head of Drama, BBC Wales, said: 'This is a great opportunity for the new Doctor and his companion to interface directly with the people who matter most to *Doctor Who*: the fans. The chance to visit them in their home towns will ensure that the eleventh Doctor's maiden voyage is an utterly magical one.'

Another accolade for the final year of Russell T Davies's tenure came on 9 March when *Doctor Who* won the annual Television and Radio Industries Club (TRIC) award for Best TV Drama Programme. Bernard Cribbins attended to accept on behalf of the show.

Australia's leading TV blog, TV Tonight, reported on 10 March that 'The Eleventh Hour' would be shown there on ABC1 on the evening of 18 April, although it would be made available to watch online a day earlier – the same day as it debuted in the USA and Canada – on the channel's iView service.

On 14 March, the BBC's regular online listing of advance programme information finally confirmed the scheduled UK transmission date of 'The Eleventh Hour' as 3 April. However, there was still some confusion in evidence as to how the series should be identified: the listing originally referred to it as 'Series Five', but this was quickly amended to say simply 'New Series'.

The issue of *Radio Times* for 20 to 26 March, which went on sale on 16 March, carried a Steven Moffat interview headed 'Policing the darkness', in which he addressed, amongst other topics, the show's capacity to deliver behind-the-sofa thrills: 'It's not *The Exorcist*. If you'd seen [Series Three episode] "Blink" at 10.00 pm you wouldn't have said it was frightening – it's mostly Carey Mulligan [who played Sally Sparrow] looking winsome in an old house – but at 7.00 pm it's surprising. Sometimes kids have nightmares, but kids have nightmares anyway. *Doctor Who* just juggles their dreams around a bit.'

18 March was a red-letter day for the new *Doctor Who* team as it saw 'The Eleventh Hour' being unveiled to members of the public for the first time at a press screening held that evening at the Cineworld cinema in Cardiff. The TARDIS police box was stationed outside the venue – initially lying prone on the ground in a simulation of a crashed state, similar to that seen near the start of the episode, and later upright – and Matt Smith and Karen Gillan were both present, along with members of the show's production team and some celebrity fans. Executive producer Piers Wenger took the opportunity to announce that *Doctor Who* would have its usual Christmas special in December and then return for a further series, again starring Matt Smith, in 2011.

To coincide with the screening, the BBC Press Office released an extensive press pack of information about Series Five. This included extensive interviews with Steven Moffat, Matt Smith and Karen Gillan. On the subject of the casting of the show's new lead actor, Moffat said:

> 'I had a clear idea, which actually turned out to be the absolute opposite of what we ended up doing – which always happens when you get the casting right. I actually remember at the beginning of the process when I got a little bit cross whilst looking at the list of actors as it was full of people in their twenties. I said to everyone that we couldn't have a Doctor who is 27. My idea was that the person was going to be between 30 and 40 years old, young enough to run but old enough to look wise. Then, of course, Matt Smith comes through the door and he's odd, angular and strange looking. He doesn't come across as being youthful at all, in the most wonderful way.'

Asked what made Karen Gillan perfect for the role of the new companion, Moffat commented:

> 'The challenge with casting the companion is that there are only so many people that would actually go through those blue doors. It has to be someone that loves adventure and doesn't quite feel at home with where they are. They have to be a feisty, fun-loving and gutsy person – and now we've got Karen Gillan. She was just exactly right for the role despite inhabiting Amy Pond in a way that was quite different from how I originally wrote the part.'

Another question put to the new showrunner was how his *Doctor Who* would differ from what had gone before. He said:

> 'I've never done anything differently, at least not deliberately, I just try and think of all the best and maddest *Doctor Who* stories I want to watch, and get them made – there are worse ways to make a living. You could say that I'm more into the clever plots; I like the big twists and the sleight of hand. I like playing around with time travel but I don't think it should be at the

front of *Doctor Who* in every episode. However, I do think it should happen more often and reinforce the fact he has an odd relationship with time. For example, no one is ever dead to him. He can't say "I knew Winston Churchill", he'd say "I know Winston Churchill". Everyone in the whole universe is still alive to him and he has no sense of time passing. I find that all fascinating. If you look at the stories I've written so far, I suppose I might be slightly more at the fairytale and Tim Burton end of *Doctor Who*, whereas Russell is probably more at the blockbuster and *Superman* end of the show.'

Asked about being cast as the Doctor, Matt Smith responded:

'It was quite weird news to receive. I mean, at that point it was a piece of information I couldn't share with anyone, so it didn't feel tangible, but needless to say I was very pleased. I actually ended up walking around London listening to Sinatra on my iPod. Funnily enough my mum had texted me to say she thought I should play the Doctor a week before my agent asked me to audition, so she was delighted I got the part. I was also abroad when it was announced on the BBC, and my phone went mad – the bill was enormous!'

On the challenges of the role, Smith said:

'I think these things are only as intimidating as you allow them to be. It's a real privilege to join such a successful show; it's a bit like [a football player] joining Manchester Utd. It's good to be part of something strong, and long may it continue. Plus, I couldn't have inherited the role from a nicer man. I guess it's like anything really; the more you do something the less daunting and intimidating it becomes.'

Smith admitted, however, that his first day of recording on location – on Southerndown Beach in Ogmore Vale, for 'The Time of Angels'/'Flesh and Stone' – had been difficult:

'It was very tough because we were up against the tide and could only film until 3.00 pm. It felt like being in a twilight zone because there were so many people watching and dozens of paparazzi around! It was nice that Karen was there as well though, because we were both going through the same experience. We were also surrounded by *Doctor Who* fans and every time I had to nip to the toilet they followed me. I've now learnt this is the norm on *Doctor Who*!'

As for what viewers could expect from the eleventh Doctor, the actor commented:

'He is still the same man, but I think my Doctor is a bit more reckless; he's a thrill-seeker and addicted to time travel. He is the mad buffoon genius who saves the world because he's got a great heart, spirit and soul, but he also doesn't suffer fools. I hope all of these things come across, but I think I've also injected a bit of my own personality into the role. I also helped choose the Doctor's costume, which was great fun. Steven Moffat was very keen the outfit isn't seen as the overriding factor of the Doctor's personality, but we still needed to find something that felt right. We tried on lots of things but kept reaching a dead end, and we dismissed a number of items including a long leather coat, a long blue coat and some short punky stuff! But then one day I brought in my braces and a tweed jacket and it went from there. Soon we had the whole outfit, although something still felt like it was missing, and I asked if I could try on a bow tie. At that point the execs all bowed their heads in concern, but luckily when I tried it on we agreed it worked, and it has sort of become the signature of my Doctor now.'

Recalling how she was cast as Amy Pond, Karen Gillan said:

'I found out on the day of my second audition with Matt, so at least I didn't have a really long wait. It just didn't feel real, and I couldn't believe it! I knew that the audition was for the part of the companion, but I wasn't allowed to tell anyone about it. They even had a code name for the role, because it was so top secret. The code name was Panic Moon, an anagram of companion, which I thought was really clever. I wasn't allowed to tell anyone that I'd got the part, but my boyfriend was with me when I found out so there was rather a lot of screaming! I decided not to tell my parents as I didn't want to spoil the surprise, but when I finally did tell them I made a special day of it and my mum took a day off work. She just couldn't believe it when I told her. She was doing the dishes and she literally stopped in her tracks and cried. She's a huge fan of the show, has been a fan for years. She even has Dalek bubble bath at home!'

Asked how she thought Amy would differ from previous companions, Gillan replied:

'Well, for a start Steven Moffat has written a brilliant character. I do think Amy is different from previous companions because she's very equal to the Doctor. She doesn't take his word as gospel and she's always happy to challenge him. If he tells her to do something then she won't necessarily do it, she might go

off and do her own thing, which can sometimes create a rift
between the two of them! They are best pals though and it's a
very up and down relationship, because they are both very
passionate people. The Doctor is definitely an alpha male and
Amy is an alpha female, so when they meet, they combust.
They have quite a turbulent relationship, but it's also really
passionate and they care about each other. Amy can really hold
her own against him, and Steven's written some great one-
liners. It's a great relationship.'

Of her costumes, Gillan said:

'I think it's quite important that I feel like her when I wear the
clothes. So I worked quite closely with the costume designer,
Ray [Holman], and also the producers, to come up with the
signature Amy look. They were generally vintage clothes, but
we tried to incorporate high street styles as well, because Amy
is young. I think naturally there is going to be some of me in her
style, as I relate to Amy and we are the same age as each other.'

The press pack also contained quotes from the two people who had joined
Steven Moffat as the show's new executive producers, Beth Willis and Piers
Wenger, the latter of whom was also Head of Drama at BBC Wales. Willis said:

'It has definitely been a big challenge taking on this show,
because we love it so much, and why tinker with something
that has been as popular, successful and brilliant as it has been?
But at the same time we are terribly aware we have to look
forward and work out how the show is going to survive in the
future. In 2005 the team looked at what was fresh and new then
and we have to do a bit of that ourselves. Looking at the
episodes we've filmed so far, we're starting to see the impact of
those changes; what the team has managed to achieve is pretty
thrilling.
    'The fact we have Steven Moffat writing it and Matt Smith
starring in it gives the show an inevitable element of change.
However, the one thing that hasn't made us scared about this
change was reading Steven's scripts. I felt deeply honoured and
excited to be in a position to be working with such great scripts.
It doesn't really matter what colour you use, where the camera
is or how you position a light; Steven and Matt are brilliant,
which has made my and Piers' jobs much easier.
    'There have been loads of challenges, but let's face it, it's
been a really exciting show to work on. We've got a fantastic
cast, we've got a fantastic writer and a fantastic team and we've
just kind of dived in at the deep end and had a ball!'

Wenger noted:

CHAPTER ONE: DAWN OF A NEW ERA

'It is the biggest show on British TV in terms of the level of technical expertise everyone has to be versed in. There were new challenges for Beth and me, as we had limited experience in dealing with prosthetics and complex CGI. However, I think the biggest challenge was to move everything forward and make the right calls on what to change and what not to.

'*Doctor Who*'s audience is an incredibly loyal and passionate one, and one of the show's biggest advantages is that it takes you to new worlds every week. Bringing it back with a new writer and leading man after all its success so far, we couldn't be modest in our ambitions to find new ways for the show to thrill people.

'I've always been a fan and I was even accused at the age of eight of shoplifting a copy of *Doctor Who Magazine* from my local newsagents – completely wrongly I hasten to add. I was accused of it probably because I was in there all the time reading them!'

The press screening generated a large amount of coverage for the show. Simon Gaskell of the *Western Mail* reported on the event the following day:

Fans of sci-fi series *Doctor Who* queued in the rain last night to catch a glimpse of the stars of the show at the premiere of the first episode of the new series in Cardiff.

Scores waited outside Cardiff's Cineworld cinema near a crashed TARDIS to catch sight of the new Doctor, Matt Smith, his sidekick Karen Gillan, and writer Steven Moffat.

The episode was aired to a packed fifth-floor theatre and received rapturous applause at its conclusion.

In a question-and-answer session afterwards, the 27-year-old star of the show said his favourite Doctor was Patrick Troughton, who was the second actor to play the role.

He said advice from previous cast members included a lengthy conversation with his immediate predecessor David Tennant, while former assistant Billie Piper sent him a text wishing him good luck.

...

Asked what kind of Doctor he was, Smith said: 'I hope there's a recklessness and sense of adventure and sense of risk.

'But to be honest, I take it day by day.'

Jody Thompson wrote on the *Daily Mirror*'s website:

New Doctor Who Matt Smith said the new series will offer 'madness, tenderness and recklessness with adventure and risk' at its launch last night.

Matt, who is the eleventh Doctor after taking over the role

21

from David Tennant, was joined by the cast and crew at the bash in Cardiff.

Smith, 27, is the youngest Time Lord yet and said he was inspired by his predecessors.

'For the first week or month you are completely aware the show has had great success, but it's something that inspires me, it's not a burden or a weight.

'I'm proud that it is one of the most popular shows in Britain.'

Steven Moffat, who replaced Russell T Davies as lead writer for the series, said the prospect of romance between the Doctor and his new companion Amy Pond, played by Karen Gillan, was not out of the question.

'You take two attractive people and they will probably be a bit romantic about each other,' he said.

'It is a complex story between Amy and the Doctor, it is not simple.

'It is not a story you have ever seen between the companion and the Doctor before.'

On the BBC News website, entertainment correspondent Lizo Mzimba said of 'The Eleventh Hour':

> As a story it veers between witty and creepy, and speeds along as well as the best episodes of the past few years.
>
> Matt Smith's Doctor is quirky and energetic, perhaps bringing the most alien interpretation to the role.
>
> He is frequently clumsy and uncoordinated in his physical approach, while mentally firing off ideas in all directions.
>
> The episode is not instantly accessible to non-*Who* fans as it's just too complex, but as the series continues it may prove ultimately more satisfying.

The episode seemed to be equally well received by other reviewers. Simon Gaskell of *South Wales Echo* commented:

> Comedy is frequently replaced and interchanged with gripping suspense and a level of scariness not been seen in the show before.
>
> In between a quantum leap through time and a final rooftop scene in which [Matt] Smith finally gets a change of clothes, the Doctor displays the same level of ingenuity, and wit, as ever before.
>
> And if the action in the first episode – merely a set-up for the rest of the series – is anything to go by then it will be the most adventure-filled series yet.
>
> Smith's performance is encouraging and he brings both playful wit and serious guardianship to his role.

As excitement grew for the start of the series, 21 March saw a new trailer debut on BBC One, consisting of a selection of clips from the forthcoming episodes. In the USA, BBC America had started showing its own trailer too, composed of a different selection of clips. Both trailers could also be found online, and over the next couple of days BBC America updated its *Doctor Who* website to include, in addition, profiles of the Doctor and Amy and a photo gallery from 'The Eleventh Hour'.

The 22 March edition of the *Guardian* featured an interview with Steven Moffat, conducted by journalist Gareth McLean. This was wide-ranging in subject matter, even venturing into the area of politics, with Moffat commenting that he hoped the Conservatives would not win the forthcoming General Election. Of *Doctor Who*, McLean wrote:

> The precise worth of the brand is a closely guarded secret, but according to BBC Worldwide the drama has been sold to over 50 territories and has shifted more than 3.3 million DVDs, more than 7 million action figures and, in 2009 alone, around 300,000 books. And then there are the pencil cases and folders, Cyberman and Dalek masks and the deal, reputed to be worth £10 million, to bring *Doctor Who* to Nintendo DS and Wii. Meanwhile, David Tennant's final outing as the Doctor secured BBC America's highest primetime rating and *Doctor Who* is BBC Worldwide's top-selling download on iTunes in the US.
>
> In short, it's a behemoth of a brand. The burden Moffat bears, therefore, is quite different from that shouldered by Davies in 2005, and it's something of which he's very conscious. 'To me, a "brand" sounds evil,' he says, 'reminiscent of men in tall hats running factories and beating small children; but you have to be across it. All those things should be joyous – those toys should be terrific – because the active creative engagement of children with *Doctor Who* is unlike any other show that they watch. When *Doctor Who* is over, they get up, invent their own monster, their own planet, their own Doctor and play. I know, because my son recently designed a new TARDIS control room. If anyone said to me "invent a new monster so we can sell more toys", I'd kick them out of my office.'
>
> Moffat says he doesn't have an agenda for how his *Doctor Who* will differ from Davies's but 'these things happen as a matter of instinct' and his instinct led him towards a more 'storybook quality'. 'For me, *Doctor Who* literally is a fairytale. It's not really science fiction. It's not set in space, it's set under your bed. It's at its best when it's related to you, no matter what planet it's set on.'

The edition of *Gay Times* magazine that went on sale on 24 March had a cover photograph of Matt Smith as the Doctor and extensive coverage of the show inside, including quotes from actors Smith, Karen Gillan, Arthur Darvill – his first ever press interview about his role as Rory, which was now revealed to be a semi-regular one – and, from the behind-the-scenes team, executive producers Steven Moffat and Piers Wenger, writers Mark Gatiss and Gareth Roberts and costume designer Ray Holman. There were also short interviews with Russell T Davies-era guest stars Tracy-Ann Oberman (Yvonne Hartman in 'Army of Ghosts'/ 'Doomsday' (2006)) and Tom Ellis (Thomas Milligan in 'Last of the Time Lords' (2007)) and a competition to win various prizes, including signed photos of Smith and Gillan. In his interview, Moffat said of Smith that he was like famous TV astronomer Patrick Moore 'in the body of an underwear model', to which Smith responded: 'I'll take Patrick Moore, fine. But I definitely haven't got an underwear model's body, no way, not on this schedule. All my gym's gone out the window. God no, I take that as a gross over-compliment to be honest. And also! When the hell has Steven Moffat seen me in my pants alone?'

Also on 24 March, the official *Doctor Who* website was updated to give the 3 April start date for the new series, and also to confirm that BBC Three's accompanying behind-the-scenes show *Doctor Who Confidential* would be returning for a further run.

Amongst a flurry of coverage in the UK press and media in the run-up to the start of the series was an article in the *Femail* section of the 25 March edition of the scandal-mongering *Daily Mail*, in which columnist Allison Pearson took issue with Karen Gillan's costumes:

> The 6ft-tall former model claims she will be the sexiest companion in the show's history, wearing skirts too teeny to blow your nose on.
>
> 'Initially, they wanted me in trousers, just because of the practicality of running around,' explains Karen.
>
> 'But I wanted the miniskirt because I think it really suits Amy's sassy character.' Matt Smith describes her as 'the sexiest companion that's ever lived'.
>
> Since when was *Doctor Who*'s assistant supposed to be sexy? They're meant to be one of the boys, running around saving distant worlds.
>
> Is it too much to ask that family TV remains the one universe yet to be invaded by *Nuts* magazine?
>
> What next – K-9 as a pit-bull and Cybermen become Cyberchicks with metal boobs? *Doctor Whooarr*? No thanks.

Fans of the show were quick to ridicule this article, pointing out that the Doctor had had other sexy companions in the past – one of whom, Leela in the mid-1970s, had been far more scantily-clad than Amy – and that there had already been a sexy female Cyberman in the *Torchwood* episode 'Cyberwoman' (2006).

26 March saw Matt Smith appear on the BBC One/BBC HD talk show *Friday Night With Jonathan Ross* – on which both of his predecessors had also guested to promote their respective debut series. In this interview, recorded the previous day, Smith showed Ross the new sonic screwdriver his Doctor would use. He confirmed that a new TARDIS interior set would be seen, and that the police box exterior had also been given a make-over in a different tint of blue. A clip from 'The Vampires of Venice' was shown, which had a temporary music soundtrack different from the

one that would be heard on the episode's eventual transmission.

On 27 March, a sneak preview of the opening scene of 'The Eleventh Hour' was made available to view on the BBC's Red Button interactive TV service. This would continue to be accessible on the service at various times up until the episode's transmission.

BBC Radio 2's Paul O'Grady show on 28 March featured an exclusive, specially-recorded audio trailer for the new series. This began with O'Grady introducing the Abba song 'Super Trouper', only for the music to be interrupted by snatches of the TARDIS materialisation sound. Matt Smith's voice was then heard delivering the following lines, over the background hum of the TARDIS interior:

> **Doctor:** 'Woah! Oooh … Ah. Feel like I'm still falling. Talk about crashing through the stars! Ouch. Got to think. Who am I? Who am I? Come on. I know this. There's the TARDIS. So, I'm the Doctor. Yes. The Doctor. Where am I? Ooh. Looks like a radio station. Made of bakelite. And, is that a mouse in the corner? Am I meant to be here? Don't thinks so. Not yet. It's not Saturday. Gotta go, gotta go, gotta go, gotta go, gotta go. Ahhh …!'

The TARDIS dematerialisation noise was briefly heard, before the Abba track resumed. O'Grady then came back on, marvelling over what had apparently just happened in his studio.

The edition of *Radio Times* for 3 to 9 April, which went on sale on 30 March, boasted a fold-out cover featuring a photo of the Doctor and Amy in the TARDIS interior – the first time the new set had been revealed to the public – and the headline 'All New Who'. Inside, the magazine contained more photos – including a different one from the session that had produced the special *SFX* cover shot – and interviews with Matt Smith and Karen Gillan, as well as a brief preview of all 13 episodes of the new series. This amongst other things confirmed that the sixth episode was called 'The Vampires of Venice' and revealed the previously-undisclosed title of the seventh as 'Amy's Choice'.

Also on 30 March, Steven Moffat was a guest on BBC Radio 4's early evening arts show *Front Row*, talking about his work as *Doctor Who*'s new showrunner.

The 31 March edition of CBBC's *Blue Peter* saw Matt Smith making a guest appearance, and also presented some clips from 'The Eleventh Hour' and other Series Five episodes. Interviewed by presenter Helen Skelton in a greenhouse while helping her to make a TARDIS birdfeeder, Smith said that he regarded the Doctor as 'the greatest part in British TV history, really', that he enjoyed working with Karen Gillan, who was 'as mad as a box of cats', and that the things he would most like to have in the TARDIS were a piano and a football pitch.

On 1 April, Issue 420 of *Doctor Who Magazine* went on sale. Making its own contribution to publicising the new series, this featured a choice of two covers – one of the Doctor, one of Amy – and extensive preview material on the forthcoming episodes.

Matt Smith also made another promotional appearance on 1 April, this time on BBC One's early evening topical programme *The One Show*. Smith emerged from the TARDIS police box to be interviewed by presenters Adrian Chiles and Christine

Bleakley. He again showed off the new sonic screwdriver prop and expressed his admiration for Patrick Troughton, and also spoke briefly about the promotional bus tour that had been announced on 8 March. This tour had concluded the previous day, Smith and Gillan having dropped in to various schools around the country to introduce preview screenings of 'The Eleventh Hour' and answer children's questions. The three days of Big Screen events now followed, with audiences treated not only to advance screenings of the episode itself but also to live appearances by various monsters including Cybermen and Scarecrows.

The morning of 3 April saw 'The Eleventh Hour' being accorded recommended viewing status in a number of the national newspapers' programme listings for the weekend. There were also more substantial pieces in some, including an A-Z of *Doctor Who* facts in the *Daily Telegraph*, a piece on Karen Gillan in the *Sun* and an interview with Matt Smith in *The Times*.

Then, at just after 6.20 pm, came the event that all this pre-publicity and promotional activity had been leading up to: the debut transmission of 'The Eleventh Hour' on BBC One and BBC HD. Some 15 months after Matt Smith was first announced as the actor chosen to play the eleventh Doctor, the new era for *Doctor Who* was finally under way.

# CHAPTER TWO
# COME IN NUMBER ELEVEN

It quickly became apparent that 'The Eleventh Hour' had got Series Five off to a flying start. Overnight ratings – not as accurate as the final ones that would be released some 10 days later, but nevertheless a good indication of how many viewers had watched the episode 'live' – showed that there had been an audience of 7.7 million on BBC One and a further 0.3 million on BBC HD, making 8.0 million in total. This represented a 36.8% share of the total TV audience at that time, and made *Doctor Who* the most watched programme of the day. These figures were very much on a par with those for the opening episodes of David Tennant's three series as the Doctor, and suggested that the level of public interest in the show remained undiminished, despite the 'gap year' in 2009 and the change of leading man.

The press, too, gave the new Doctor's debut episode an overwhelmingly favourable reaction. The *Daily Mail*'s review by Sinclair McKay, published on 4 April, typified the positive response:

> This deft first episode … was packed with one-liners and an even more fantastical feel than of late. But it had that old reassuring combination of intense Britishness, quirkiness and a sense of the macabre.
>
> The new Doctor was hurled straight into the complex, time-hopping business of meeting his new companion, Amy – first as a young girl a few years back, then, in the winning form of Karen Gillan, a thoroughly grown-up Amy.
>
> It was a clever and occasionally rather moving way of getting into the age-old set-up, that of the Doctor and his glamorous Dr Watson. Unlike previous *Doctor Who* companions, Amy is a kissogram.
>
> To the Doctor's amusing bewilderment, it transpires that Amy also has a French maid, a nurse and a nun outfit in her repertoire.
>
> But when the Doctor spirits her away to the stars at the end, he is not aware that she is to be married the next day. There is a spark between the two of them – but of what? It all bodes intriguingly well for the next 12 weeks.
>
> And Smith seems to have caught it all effortlessly – the sudden leaps of inspiration, the mobile face, the geeky yet implacable squaring up to terrible monsters.
>
> By the end of the episode, in his tweed jacket and bow tie, like an Indie-band Professor Quatermass, you have forgotten all about his illustrious predecessor.
>
> Indeed, Smith might turn out to be one of the best Time Lords of the lot.

5 April brought the news that the episode had scored a very good Appreciation Index (AI) figure of 86 – one of the best of any of that weekend's TV programmes.

All in all, 'The Eleventh Hour' had received a terrific reception; and Steven Moffat and his team could scarcely have hoped for a better start than this.

On 6 April, a trailer for the series' second episode, 'The Beast Below', was made available to view on the official *Doctor Who* website. It also started to appear in selected programme breaks on BBC One. It consisted of a dramatic montage of clips from the episode, ending with a voiceover stating: '*Doctor Who*. The journey continues. Saturday at 6.15 on BBC One, and catch up on BBC iPlayer'. Similar trailers for the subsequent episodes would be released on a weekly basis from this point on, accompanied by online video introductions to the episodes by members of the cast and production team, although their use on TV would gradually decrease as the series progressed.

An exciting innovation was revealed on 8 April when the BBC announced that over the coming months the official *Doctor Who* website would be making available, free to download in the UK, a series of interactive computer games, called *The Adventure Games*, for PC and Mac.[5] Four games were planned initially, all featuring the Doctor and Amy, voiced by Matt Smith and Karen Gillan. They had been commissioned by BBC Vision's Multiplatform team and were executive produced by Steven Moffat, Piers Wenger and Beth Willis, plus Anwen Aspden of BBC Wales Interactive and videogaming consultant Charles Cecil. The animation was being produced by Sumo Digital, with scripts being provided by two of the TV series' writers, Phil Ford and James Moran. The stories would feature appearances by various popular monsters, including the Cybermen, and music by the TV show's composer Murray Gold. The titles of the four games were being kept under wraps for the time being, but it was promised that more information would be revealed at a press event in Sheffield on 21 April, prior to the first game going online on 5 June. Simon Nelson, head of BBC Vision Multiplatform, was quoted as saying:

'A few years ago, we couldn't have dreamt of commissioning such an innovative form of drama. By integrating the creation of these "interactive episodes" with the development of the TV series, we've been able to create amazing two-hour dramas, in which you control the action. We've all imagined what it would be like to come face to face with some of the universe's most terrifying monsters – now, viewers can find out for themselves.

'Establishing new forms of drama is exactly what the BBC should be doing. By aiming these "interactive episodes" at the broad audience of the TV show – unique in British television, in that it encompasses at least three generations – we're aiming to encourage the family to gather round the PC or Mac in the same way they do the television. Driving computer literacy is a keystone of the BBC's public service remit and we expect *Doctor Who – The Adventure Games* to be hugely popular in the homes of Britain this year.

'Only the BBC could produce such an innovative slice of

---

[5] See Appendix A for further details of these games.

new drama. We're offering two-hour original *Doctor Who* episodes to production standards on a par with the TV series, working with the very best creatives within the UK. We're hugely proud of *Doctor Who – The Adventure Games*, which will establish new standards in interactive drama and allow families the country over to enjoy *Doctor Who* stories in unique and innovative ways.'

Meanwhile, Matt Smith, Karen Gillan and Steven Moffat arrived in New York to promote the imminent debut of the eleventh Doctor's adventures on BBC America. They answered questions at an industry screening of 'The Eleventh Hour' at the Paley Centre for Media on 12 April; attended another screening of the episode at the Village East Cinema on 14 April; and gave numerous interviews to newspapers and local TV stations.

Just a fortnight after its last *Doctor Who* cover, *Radio Times* again accorded the show this coveted position on its 17 to 23 April edition, which went on sale on 13 April. In fact, the magazine came in a choice of three covers. These all featured an identical shot of a Dalek in the left foreground with the Houses of Parliament in the background, but with the Dalek in one of three different colours – red, blue and yellow – reflecting the signature colours of Britain's three main political parties, who were about to contest a General Election on 6 May. They thus had the effect of promoting not only the Daleks' return to *Doctor Who* but also the BBC's extensive coverage of the run-up to the General Election. They intentionally recalled the similar *Radio Times* cover for the week of 30 April to 6 May 2005, which had served the same twin purposes and had later been voted best British magazine cover of all time in a 2008 poll organised by the Periodical Publishers Association. This time, though, there was a major difference: whereas the Dalek seen on the 2005 cover was of the traditional design, in the bronze livery used during the Russell T Davies era, this one was much bulkier, with an odd humped back, and had a plastic look to it. Many fans initially assumed that this was due to *Radio Times* having used a badly-made model when putting its cover image together. Soon, however, it became apparent that this new design would actually be featured in the forthcoming Dalek episode, 'Victory of the Daleks', itself; and, moreover, that the bold, garish colours pictured on the trio of covers had not been used just to represent the three political parties but, again, would actually be seen in the episode, along with white and orange ones. The fans' reaction to this news was overwhelmingly negative, with many expressing horror that one of *Doctor Who*'s greatest icons had been tampered with in such a way. No other development since the show returned to TV in 2005 had been as poorly received as this.

Inside this *Radio Times*, Mark Gatiss, the writer of 'Victory of the Daleks', contributed a piece about the appeal of the Daleks, and there was an article about the audience reaction to some of the classic era Doctors, drawing on information from the BBC's written archives – which coincided with a few of these documents being made available to view online, in the Archive area of the BBC website. A *Doctor Who*-related question even sneaked into an interview with Prime Minister Gordon Brown: he was asked to pick a favourite out of Jon Pertwee, Tom Baker, David Tennant and Matt Smith, and named fellow Scot Tennant.

Still in New York, Smith, Gillan and Moffat took part in a Meet the Cast event at the Apple SoHo store on 16 April. Their on-stage interview by *TV Guide*'s Matt Roush was subsequently made available as a free-to-download podcast on iTunes.

Also on 16 April, it was revealed that 'The Eleventh Hour' had received as many as 1.27 million views on the BBC's iPlayer service within the week after its TV debut – a record number for the service.

17 April saw 'The Eleventh Hour' make its long-awaited debut on both Space in Canada and BBC America in the USA, at 21.00 ET in each case. In the one-hour slot prior to this, both channels aired a documentary called *Doctor Who: The Ultimate Guide*, introducing new viewers to the Doctor's world. It was later reported that on BBC America 'The Eleventh Hour' had gained 1.2 million live or same day viewers, one of the channel's best ever figures. On Space it had been seen by an average of 0.47 million, with nearly one million watching at least part of the broadcast, making it the highest-rated non-sports programme of the day. *Doctor Who* was also currently standing as the top-rated TV show in the US and Canadian iTunes store. With press and media interest in the show remaining strong as well, it seemed that *Doctor Who*'s profile in North America had never been higher.

On 18 April, Australian viewers got their chance to see 'The Eleventh Hour' on ABC1. Subsequent reports indicated that it had gained an exceptional 1.03 million average viewing figure in the five major capital cities, despite strong competition from other networks. It had also performed very well on the online iView service. As in North America, there was much accompanying media interest, and Matt Smith gave a number of interviews, including one with Michael Idato of the *Sydney Morning Herald*, who wrote:

> The changing of the guard includes a new executive producer, Steven Moffat, who replaces Russell T Davies. Smith says Moffat has given him enormous freedom to find the personality of the Doctor.
>
> 'We had a series of conversations about the Doctor, about the world, the general dramatic arc but, to a certain extent, he said, "There you are, kid, there's the palette, paint it",' Smith says. 'But he has such an ingenious mind and *Doctor Who* is, literally, in his blood. He knows it inside out and I think he has brought an element of the fairytale to it, and that's something that, to me, feels very exciting.'
>
> ...
>
> Smith describes his relationship with [Karen] Gillan as, 'the heartbeat of the show, the Doctor and the companion, and it's definitely something that evolves.
>
> 'It's not something that is immediate on the first day, because you're two people and you're placed in this peculiar situation but, thankfully, Karen and I get on famously. I don't know if it's fate or luck or whatever but we make each other laugh.'

On 19 April the BBC Press Office announced that the eleventh Doctor would soon be making a guest appearance in a forthcoming two-part story in the CBBC spin-off show *The Sarah Jane Adventures*, starring Elisabeth Sladen as the title character. This story, written by Russell T Davies, would also feature the third Doctor's one-time companion Jo Grant, played by Katy Manning. The show's executive producer Nikki Wilson was quoted as saying:

'We are absolutely thrilled to be introducing Sarah Jane and the gang to both the eleventh Doctor and Jo Grant, and to have a script penned by Russell T Davies is the icing on the cake!

'Viewers are in for a real treat, with an action-packed story full of Russell's usual wit and warmth, which takes the gang inside a secret base beneath Snowdon and introduces brand-new vulture aliens, the mysterious Shansheeth. All this, plus a trip to an alien planet – a first for *The Sarah Jane Adventures*.'

The launch event for *Doctor Who – The Adventure Games* took place as scheduled on 21 April outside Sheffield's main railway station. The white, yellow and red new-style Daleks from 'Victory of the Daleks' patrolled the area, with Nicholas Briggs on hand to provide the voices, keeping passers-by entertained with a stream of amusing banter. Also present was a new type of special weapons Dalek dubbed Dalek Storm, made by fan Alan Clark, which actually received a more positive reaction from members of the public than the BBC's own redesigned props. Promotional postcards, pens and posters were handed out by BBC representatives. Some lucky children also had a chance to test out the first of *The Adventure Games*, with a number of journalists trying their hand at it as well, and the general consensus was that it was great fun, although a few bugs were spotted that would hopefully be corrected by the time it went online – at this point, it was still at the 'alpha testing' stage. The event ended with a question and answer session for which Briggs was joined by five other panellists: Charles Cecil (executive producer), Barnaby Edwards (Dalek operator), Ian Tweedale (interactive editor at BBC Wales, responsible for getting the game commissioned), Sean Willard (creative director at game designers Sumo Digital) and Phil Ford (writer). Matt Smith and Karen Gillan had originally been due to attend as well, but as things turned out they were still in the USA, having been stranded there by flight disruption caused by ash from the recent eruption of the Eyjafjallajökull volcano in Iceland.

The following day, the title of the first game was officially confirmed by the BBC as 'City of the Daleks'. A brief synopsis was provided, which read: 'The TARDIS materialises in 1963 – and London is in ruins. The Daleks have seized control of time and the only chance of saving Earth lies in a desperate quest to Skaro, the Daleks' home planet – before time catches up with Amy, the last survivor of the human race!' Phil Ford was quoted as saying: 'This is quite a series opener. We destroy London even before the credits roll – so you can only begin to imagine where we travel to from there. "City of the Daleks" is as big-budget as you can imagine: from London we head to Kaalann, the capital city of the Daleks, one constructed from pure anger and hate. And these new Daleks don't like to be messed with, so players are about to enjoy a new interactive episode which is as heart-pulsing as anything you've seen before.'

Also on 22 April, it was announced that this year's BBC Proms series at London's historic Royal Albert Hall would include another *Doctor Who*-themed concert, following on from the hugely successful one staged in 2008. This would have two performances, on 24 and 25 July, with a full orchestra playing selections from Murray Gold's incidental music from the show, plus a number of classical pieces.

Like Smith and Gillan, Steven Moffat was still stuck in the USA at this point. From his hotel in Los Angeles, he told the press that he was delighted with the immediately positive reception the new series had gained. He also wrote a BBC website blog entitled 'The return of the Weeping Angels', which appeared online on 22 April. In this he previewed 'The Time of Angels'/'Flesh and Stone' and discussed how he had given the Weeping Angels a new twist for their second appearance in the show. He also recalled the first day of recording for Series Five:

> First walking onto a big, grand, typical *Doctor Who* location and seeing the bright blue [police] box waiting was so odd for me. We'd been so careful up to that point, and not put the *Doctor Who* name on any of our signs, but still the paparazzi and fans found us within about 20 minutes!
>
> I was stood on set with my phone, looking at pictures of myself that fans had taken, already on the web. On one occasion I saw a photograph of myself watching the filming, which had been uploaded so quickly that I hadn't moved from the position I was in by the time it was on the web!
>
> My other memory is of this day ending early because the tide came in unexpectedly. I did slightly wonder if this would be the shape of things to come.
>
> That scene on the beach was about three pages longer originally. The rain on the second day of filming was so torrential that I suggested I could cut three pages, provided I could relocate them in a new TARDIS scene.
>
> I ended up adding the scene that sits immediately after the credits, with River flying the TARDIS better than the Doctor. That's a lovely scene, and a much better start to the show, but it's all a consequence of torrential rain and the tide coming in.

Also while stuck in Los Angeles, Moffat worked on his script for the 2010 Christmas special, the title of which had yet to be revealed at this point, getting himself in the right mood by playing Christmas carols.

*Radio Times* continued its fine run of *Doctor Who* content by including in its 1 to 7 May edition, which went on sale on 27 April, an interview with Alex Kingston about her return to the role of River Song. Speaking to Benjamin Cook, a regular *Doctor Who Magazine* contributor, the actress said that she was pleasantly surprised to be invited back to the show, as she had assumed her appearance in 'Silence in the Library'/'Forest of the Dead' (2008) would be a one-off. She also commented on the speculation that River might be the Doctor's future wife: 'The flirtation between them still indicates they have a much more intimate relationship further down the line – and I sort of hope it is that. I hope they're married. Otherwise, if she's his mother, the flirtation isn't quite appropriate!'

At the end of April, it emerged that later in the year, during the break in production between series of *Doctor Who*, Matt Smith would be playing a very different role: that of the gay writer Christopher Isherwood in a BBC Two drama entitled *Christopher and His Kind*, set in 1930s Berlin. This would be directed by Geoffrey Sax, who back in 1996 had gained a *Doctor Who* credit on the Paul McGann-starring TV movie.

With the UK's General Election now only days away, the Green Party placed a Dalek-themed promotional video on its official YouTube page. This featured red, blue and yellow Daleks – their colours representing those of the three main political parties, as on the *Radio Times* covers a couple of weeks earlier – being zapped by laser beams fired from the eyes of a green-coloured rabbit, to the soundtrack of the song 'One of These Things is Not Like the Others' from the US children's show *Sesame Street*. This video was quickly removed, however, after complaints were made that it was in breach of copyright.

Meanwhile, a 30 April report headed '"More interesting" than *Doctor Who*' on the website of the polling organisation YouGov claimed that 29% of people considered the recent televised pre-Election debates between the Labour, Conservative and Liberal party leaders 'the most interesting thing on TV over the past two weeks', well ahead of *Doctor Who* at 17%.

Also on 30 April, the *Daily Telegraph* ran an article headed '*Doctor Who* prompts surge in popularity of bow ties'. A spokesperson for the Topman chain of stores was quoted as saying: 'Since the new *Doctor Who* aired we have seen a dramatic rise in bow tie sales. In the last month our sales have increased by 94%. Last week alone they accounted for 14% of all our tie sales – whereas over the last six months they have been only taking around 3% of our tie sales.' It seemed that, as the Doctor liked to claim in the show, bow ties were indeed becoming cool!

The 3 May edition of BBC One's *The Graham Norton Show* saw the host make reference to a recent controversy sparked by the fact that, when 'The Time of Angels' had its debut transmission on the channel, an animated trailer for one of his other shows, *Over the Rainbow*, had been superimposed over the cliffhanger scene at the end – an intrusion about which over 5,000 viewers had subsequently made complaints, arguing that it spoiled the drama. As Norton spoke, a revised version of the same trailer appeared at the bottom of the screen, showing his animated figure being exterminated by a Dalek! Later on the same programme, Karen Gillan appeared as a guest. She described how she had been cast as Amy, and again recounted how her second audition had been carried out in secret, supposedly for a show called *Panic Moon* – in fact an anagram of 'companion'. When another of Norton's guests, American singer Nicole Scherzinger, seemed unfamiliar with the term 'kissogram', the host joked that it was 'an anagram for stripper'.

On 4 May, tickets for the two forthcoming *Doctor Who Prom* concert performances were released to the public – and sold out within just a couple of hours, to the disappointment of the many who missed out. A small allocation of around 500 additional tickets would be made available to buy from the venue on the day of each performance, but big queues were expected.

In a 5 May article headed 'Scantily-clad vampires and a pass at Doctor Who ... the BBC's idea of family viewing' the *Daily Mail* also revisited its earlier gripe about the show being 'sexed up':

> Dozens have complained about an 'overtly sexual scene' in last
> Saturday's episode, which saw the Time Lord being

propositioned by his new assistant Amy Pond.

Karen Gillan's character was shown lying seductively on a bed, before lunging at the Doctor, trying to undress him against the TARDIS and kissing him.

She then joked about how long it had been since the 907-year-old Time Lord, played by 27-year-old Matt Smith, last had sex and claimed she didn't mind if they had a one-night-stand.

Afterwards, a trailer for a forthcoming episode, to be screened on Saturday, revealed the plot centres around a group of young women vampires, scantily dressed in low-cut nightdresses.

Last night, fans reacted angrily to what they claim is the 'sexualisation' of the show, saying the material was 'totally inappropriate' for a family drama.

The article also included quotes from pressure group MediaWatch – which, as Mary Whitehouse's National Viewers and Listeners Association, had been a frequent critic of *Doctor Who* back in the 1970s – who felt the seduction scene in 'Flesh and Stone' had been 'slightly out of place' and 'sailed pretty close to the wind'. However, a BBC spokesman revealed that only 43 complaints had been received, and commented 'Millions of *Doctor Who* fans watched and enjoyed last Saturday's episode, including the lighthearted and humorous scene in which Amy kissed the Doctor.'

By mid-May, 'The Eleventh Hour' had racked up a further half million views on the BBC's iPlayer service, taking the total to 1.78 million – which meant that it now overtaken a 2009 episode of the motoring show *Top Gear* to become the most requested programme ever on the service.

On 14 May, the *Scotsman* newspaper ran an intriguing story about a forthcoming *Doctor Who* stage show:

Doctor Who, the stage show, will come to Scotland in October as part of a nine-city UK tour, the BBC announced yesterday.

The arena show, which will play at the SECC in Glasgow, marks the latest touring adaptation of a BBC television hit, on the heels of live versions of *Strictly Come Dancing* and *Top Gear*.

While the show will boast special effects, and video scenes shot with the new Doctor, Matt Smith, it will not have live performances by him or his co-stars, who include Scot Karen Gillan.

Contrary to the article's claim, there had at this point been no official announcement by the BBC about the stage show – early plans for which had first been reported by the *Sun* as long ago as 16 February 2009. However, that announcement was soon forthcoming, on 17 May, when the following description was issued:

Developed in association with *Doctor Who*'s executive producer and showrunner Steven Moffat, *Doctor Who Live* promises the same excitement, adventure and suspense that viewers have come to expect from the TV programme and will feature specially filmed new video scenes.

Opening in wartime London and concluding in an epic on-stage battle, audiences should expect the unexpected as the Doctor's arch-enemies the Daleks are joined by some of the best-loved and most terrifying monsters from the TV series including the Cybermen, Weeping Angels, Judoon and Oods to name but a few.

*Doctor Who Live* will feature special FX, optical illusions and spectacular pyrotechnics building to an epic finale. Specially edited video clips, drawn from the TV programme, will be shown on a massive screen and accompanied by the music of long-time *Doctor Who* composer Murray Gold. These iconic scores will be brought to life by a 16 piece orchestra live on stage.

Steven Moffat was quoted as saying, 'This is everything I ever wanted since I was 11. A live show, with all the coolest *Doctor Who* monsters, a proper story, and brand new screen material for Matt Smith's Doctor! I'll be writing scenes for it, and probably attending every single night!' The show was due to open at London's Wembley Arena on 8 October and then to move on to Sheffield, Glasgow, Birmingham, Manchester, Nottingham, Cardiff, Liverpool and Belfast, with 25 performances in total, concluding on 7 November.

18 May saw the *Daily Star* run an erroneous story headed 'Joanna Page is Being Lined Up as the Next Star of *Doctor Who*'. This read in part:

Sizzling *Gavin & Stacey* babe Joanna Page is being lined up as the next star of *Doctor Who*.

The move comes after the Welsh beauty scooped a part in the latest series.

The blonde actress is set to play a long-lost relative of the Time Lord in two episodes.

And bosses hope she will stay on to become a major star of the hit BBC One sci-fi show.

Like Freema Agyeman, who initially landed a role as a scientist before becoming the Doctor's assistant, bosses hope Joanna, 32, will have a 'big future' in the show.

They see the babe, who helped *Gavin & Stacey* to a BAFTA and Best TV Comedy Award, as a huge ratings draw.

An insider said: 'Joanna could be massive for the show.

'She's been offered two episodes and if that goes well the sky's the limit

'She'll start off as a long-lost relative of the Doctor but may then become a major player.'

Asked about this report in a Press Association interview a few days later, the actress denied that there was any truth to it.

On 22 May a new *Doctor Who* exhibition opened in the Centre for Life in Newcastle upon Tyne. This would run until 31 October, and would feature an array of original props and costumes from the show, including Daleks, Cybermen, Sontarans, Ood and Judoon.

The 28 May edition of BBC One's *The One Show* featured Karen Gillan as a guest. Interviewed by Matt Baker and Christine Bleakley, she spoke about the importance of her having an input into Amy's style, and about her mother's enthusiasm for *Doctor Who* and other science fiction shows. A clip from the following day's episode, 'Cold Blood', was also aired.

The 5 to 11 June edition of *Radio Times*, which went on sale on 1 June, carried an interview with Richard Curtis in which he explained how he had come to write for *Doctor Who*: 'My kids absolutely love it. We all watched the Christmas special two years ago and my children said I had to do one. Scarlett, our eldest, pointed out that while I'd always promised I would write a children's movie, by the time I do, she won't be a child any more. And the great thing about telly is how swift it is by comparison with films.'

With Series Five now more than half-way through transmission, a special preview screening of Curtis's episode, 'Vincent and the Doctor', took place at the BFI Southbank in London on the afternoon of 2 June. It was followed by a question and answer session with Curtis, executive producer Piers Wenger, director Jonny Campbell and Karen Gillan. A five minute video clip of their discussion was subsequently made available to view on the BFI's website.

On 5 June, the PC version of 'City of the Daleks', the first story in *The Adventure Games* series, was officially launched in the UK. (A commercially-marketed international version would become available in July.) It had in fact been made available to download three days earlier, but that advance release was intended by its designers as a final test to try to pick up any remaining glitches in the programming. The launch of the Mac version was delayed until a couple of weeks later.

Ever keen to sniff out a possible scandal, two of the national tabloids, the *Daily Mirror* and the *Daily Star*, reported in their 14 June editions that Series Five's eleventh episode, 'The Lodger', may have revealed rather more of Matt Smith than viewers had bargained for. The *Daily Star* said:

> As Matt [Smith], 27, rushed from a bathroom, a blue towel covering his modesty slipped.
>
> It was a 'blink and you'll miss it' moment that lasted a fraction of a second in the 6.45 pm show.
>
> But, within minutes, fan sites and forums were buzzing with claims that Doctor Who could boast of being Doctor Huge.
>
> Cheeky fans posted the exact time of 15 minutes and 10 seconds into the show that the Doctor's lunchbox appeared and urged others to freeze-frame.
>
> *Who* fan Rich Johnston, who posted details on a website, boasted: 'It is true, you can clearly see. Yes, while millions were watching the football I really did see the Doctor's willy.'
>
> Another fan added: 'Amazing, it leaves little to the imagination.

'The Doctor may have two hearts but he appears to be a typical human male in other areas.'

...

A BBC spokesman said: 'Fans might speculate about what they saw.

'But I can assure them that Matt wasn't totally naked when he filmed these scenes.

'He was sporting an item to protect his modesty.'

Smith himself later confirmed in interviews that he had been wearing a pair of flesh-coloured shorts when the scene in question was recorded.

For the third time during Series Five, *Doctor Who* graced the cover of *Radio Times* when the issue listing programmes for 19 to 25 June – including the series' penultimate episode, 'The Pandorica Opens' – went on sale on 15 June. The cover depicted Amy standing in a dramatic pose with the Doctor behind her and Stonehenge with Roman centurions in the background, and carried the headline 'Thoroughly Modern Amy'. Inside, Karen Gillan was interviewed. She spoke about acting alongside Matt Smith and about her approach to playing Amy, saying: 'The one thing I never wanted to do with Amy was to base her on any kind of formula, to conform to what works – or what has worked – in a companion; you know, the whole likeable, girl-next-door business. Amy is likeable, I hope, but she's not ordinary. She's quite complicated and there are layers to explore. So I was taking a few risks with her, and I think it works.'

Also of interest to *Doctor Who* fans in this issue of *Radio Times* was an interview with ninth Doctor actor Christopher Eccleston, in which he made some rare comments about his time on the show and even referred obliquely to the disagreements with the production team that had led to his departure after only one series: 'I was open-minded but I decided after my experience on the first series that I didn't want to do any more. I didn't enjoy the environment and the culture that we, the cast and crew, had to work in. I wasn't comfortable. I thought "If I stay in this job, I'm going to have to blind myself to certain things that I thought were wrong." And I think it's more important to be your own man than be successful, so I left. But the most important thing is that I did it, not that I left. I really feel that, because it kind of broke the mould and it helped to reinvent it. I'm very proud of it.'

On 16 June, another preview screening was held, this time of 'The Pandorica Opens', at BAFTA's Princess Anne Theatre on London's Piccadilly. The screening was introduced by BBC Head of Drama Commissioning Ben Stephenson, and audience questions were answered by Steven Moffat, Matt Smith and Karen Gillan. Arthur Darvill had also been due to attend, but was unable to make it. Amongst those in the audience were BBC One Controller Jay Hunt, who was called upon to field a question about the impact on ratings of new viewing technologies such as hard-disk recorders and the iPlayer service, and Waris Hussein, the director of the very first *Doctor Who* story back in 1963, which Moffat warmly praised. In response to one question, the showrunner also took the opportunity to disagree with widely-reported comments made the previous day by well-known actor, writer and presenter Stephen Fry to the effect that *Doctor Who* was evidence of the infantilisation of television. Moffat commented: 'Let's be fair to Stephen Fry, he's the biggest *Doctor Who* fan in the world; he's just trying to sound grown up. *Doctor Who* was designed, as Waris Hussein will tell you, specifically to be a family programme. That's what it's for. It's a junction between the children's programmes and the adults' programmes. It's the one that everybody sits and watches. It is for adults, it is for children. It's a rather brilliant idea: why don't we make a programme that everybody wants to watch? We should do that more often.'

On 17 June, an article on the computer and video games website MCV reported on the huge success being enjoyed by 'City of the Daleks':

> Half a million consumers downloaded *Doctor Who – The Adventure Games* in its first two weeks.
>
> The free downloadable game was the first of its kind from the BBC, and the broadcaster hopes its success will inspire the games and TV industries to work closer together.
>
> 'The result is a lot more than I was expecting,' Simon Nelson, controller of portfolio and multiplatform at BBC Vision told MCV.
>
> 'We had set ourselves some fairly stretched targets on this and we've blown them away.
>
> 'The credit goes to the *Doctor Who* and marketing teams, who are among the best in the BBC at creating integrated campaigns, messages and interactive spin-offs. This has been part of the *Who* planning process rather than just a bolt on at the end, which too many interactive things have been.'

On 22 June, a launch event was held for the second of *The Adventure Games*, 'Blood of the Cybermen', the PC version of which would become available to download in the UK on 26 June and the Mac version on 30 June. Writer Phil Ford, executive producer Charles Cecil and Dalek and Cyberman voice artist Nicholas Briggs discussed the game with fans from around the country in a question and answer session streamed live on the official *Doctor Who* website. Two script extracts from the story were also released online.

A further promotional event for 'Blood of the Cybermen' was held on 25 June at the Hayes in Cardiff, hosted by BBC newsreader Jason Mohammed – who had made guest appearances in several Russell T Davies-era episodes of *Doctor Who* plus *The Sarah Jane Adventures*. Scenes from the game were played on a big screen, and fans could pick up free promotional postcards and posters.

Also on 25 June, ITV's breakfast show *This Morning* featured a pre-recorded piece in which Matt Smith spoke to interviewer Alison Hammond about, amongst other things, the imminent transmission of the series finale 'The Big Bang'. This was made the subject of a report on the *Sun*'s website later that day, which read in part:

> *Doctor Who* is coming to an end – but will the Time Lord survive for another series?
>
> The season finale, 'The Big Bang', sees the Doctor, played by Matt Smith, trapped in the Pandorica by his enemies.
>
> But will he get out alive?

Speaking on *This Morning* today about the episode, Matt said: 'There's an important character coming back but I can't say who but it is very significant – it's a cracker!'

And he admitted he felt 'emotional' when he watched it back with Karen Gillan, who plays the Doctor's assistant Amy Pond.

He explained: 'I watched it and was quite emotional probably because it was the end of the series and we'd worked so hard and we'd got there.

'I watched it with Karen and we were like "Woo hoo!"'

On 26 June, a number of newspapers and media outlets previewed that evening's transmission of 'The Big Bang'. Picking up on Smith's comment on the previous day's *This Morning* about an important character returning, the website of the *Metro* free newspaper indulged in some wild speculation, apparently prompted by discussions on online fan forums:

Plot details have been kept tightly under wraps, but the rumour mill has been in overdrive about the return of some famous faces.

One widely reported story is that old school Time Lord villain Omega will make an appearance, while there have been hints that David Tennant could even come back in the guise of the 'Doctor-Donna' – whose personality was a mix between the eponymous hero and his sidekick played by Catherine Tate.

As fans discovered that evening, these theories were all well wide of the mark – the returning character was actually Amy's younger self, Amelia, played by Karen Gillan's cousin Caitlin Blackwood, who had first been seen in 'The Eleventh Hour' at the start of Series Five.

With the transmission of 'The Big Bang', Matt Smith's first run of episodes as the Doctor drew to a close. In the UK, the show had attracted perhaps a little less media attention than in previous years, and there also seemed to have been a slight downturn in promotional activity by the BBC – notwithstanding an excellent run of coverage in *Radio Times*. One development bemoaned by many fans was the discontinuation of the previous practice of releasing weekly podcast commentaries on the episodes, leading some to wonder if Steven Moffat was less keen than his predecessor to support this more peripheral kind of activity. This disappointment was compounded when it became apparent that the Complete Fifth Series DVD/Blu-Ray box set release from 2Entertain would also have fewer episode commentaries than usual; and many fans were baffled and upset by the bizarre decision, apparently taken at executive level in Cardiff, that all the commercial releases of the episodes should presented them in edited form, without the exciting 'Next Time' teasers – a move that prompted dozens of customer complaints. On a more positive note, however, the box set did include two specially-shot 'Meanwhile in the TARDIS' scenes, the first set in the gap between 'The Eleventh Hour' and 'The Beast Below', the second in that between 'Flesh and Stone' and 'The

Vampires of Venice'.[6] More importantly, the show's public profile remained extremely high – and in the USA, had risen to a previously unparalleled level. And with exciting events such as another Prom concert and the *Doctor Who Live* shows on the horizon, and the advent of *The Adventure Games*, it seemed that there would still be plenty going on in the *Doctor Who* world to keep fans entertained during the six month wait till the annual Christmas special.

---

[6] See the Episode Guide entries on 'The Eleventh Hour' and 'Flesh and Stone' for further details.

# CHAPTER THREE
# THE LONG WAIT TILL CHRISTMAS

On the evening of 27 June 2010, the day after 'The Big Bang' was transmitted, evidence of how fashionable *Doctor Who* had become in recent years was provided when Matt Smith made a surprise appearance on stage at the famous Glastonbury music festival, with the group Orbital. The Gigwise website reported the following day:

> The British actor introduced the electronic duo's rendition of the TV show's theme on the Other Stage.
> 'So Glastonbury, this is the last song of the evening, people, if you're lost ... Let's make this one count,' he said.
> 'For Orbital, they're back! For Glastonbury, we're back! Let me hear you cheer, let me hear you roar, for Glastonbury!'

In fact, not only did Smith introduce Orbital, but he also played additional keyboards on their rendition of the *Doctor Who* theme!

29 June brought the release of further information about a rather different stage project, the *Doctor Who Live* touring show. This was in the form of a promotional image revealing the monsters it was planned to feature: Judoon, Smilers, Clockwork Men, Silurians, Weeping Angels, Ood, Cybermen, Saturnyne vampire girls, Daleks and Scarecrows. Rather incongruously, the monsters were shown on a football pitch background with the tag line 'Monsters First 11' – tying in with the fact that the FIFA World Cup was currently in progress.

On 12 July, the BBC Press Office revealed some details about the 2010 Christmas special, production on which officially commenced that day. The press notice read, in part:

> In the grand tradition of *Doctor Who* Christmas specials, this year the show has once again attracted stellar guest stars as veteran actor Michael Gambon (*Harry Potter*, *The Singing Detective*) and opera diva Katherine Jenkins, in her first acting role, join the Time Lord for what might be his most Christmassy adventure yet!
> Arriving on set for her first day of filming, Katherine Jenkins said: 'I'm over the moon to be involved in the *Doctor Who* Christmas special – I can't quite believe it as it's a part of the family tradition at the Jenkins household. I heard the news that I got the role on my thirtieth birthday and it was the best birthday present ever!'
> About the [special], lead writer and executive producer, Steven Moffat, commented: 'Oh, we're going for broke with this

one. It's all your favourite Christmas movies at once, in an hour, with monsters and the Doctor and a honeymoon and – oh, you'll see. I've honestly never been so excited about writing anything. I was laughing madly as I typed along to Christmas songs in April. My neighbours loved it so much they all moved away and set up a website demanding my execution. But I'm fairly sure they did it ironically.'

The Christmas special follows on from Matt Smith's first series as the Doctor, which attracted huge critical acclaim for Smith, his companion, Gillan, and lead writer Moffat, from press and legions of fans alike.

Ben Stephenson, Controller, BBC Drama Commissioning, said: 'Matt Smith and Karen Gillan captivated audiences in their debut series and *Doctor Who*'s clever twist on the much loved *A Christmas Carol* will thrill BBC One viewers this year with special guest stars Sir Michael Gambon and singing sensation Katherine Jenkins joining Amy and the Doctor for an unforgettable present!'

In Issue 424 of *Doctor Who Magazine*, on sale from 22 July, Steven Moffat revealed that Piers Wenger and Beth Willis would be remaining as his fellow executive producers on Series Six, but that Sanne Wohlenberg would take over from Tracie Simpson as producer on the first two production blocks, following Simpson's departure to work on the new BBC Wales drama *The Fabulous Baker Boys* (later renamed simply *Baker Boys*). The show's long-standing production designer Edward Thomas had also moved on, to join the production of a new BBC One science-fiction drama *Outcasts*, and had been succeeded by Michael Pickwoad.

The *Radio Times* for 24 to 30 July, published on 20 July, had a special 'school holidays' theme, and included a short Matt Smith interview conducted by a 13-year-old named Jack. Asked what his favourite food was, Smith replied: 'Spaghetti bolognese, banana sandwiches. I love biscuits with tea and am partial to a chocolate muffin or two.' Steven Moffat was also interviewed in this issue, but mainly about *Sherlock*, a new BBC One project on which he had been working with Mark Gatiss alongside *Doctor Who*. The first episode of this modern-day adaptation of Sir Arthur Conan Doyle's famous Sherlock Holmes stories (after an unbroadcast pilot made in 2009) was scheduled for transmission on 25 July.

On 24 and 25 July, the two *Doctor Who Prom* concert performances took place as scheduled. Matt Smith, Karen Gillan and Arthur Darvill all appeared on stage, and Smith also played the Doctor in a Steven Moffat-written segment in which he interacted with audience members and enlisted the aid of one surprised young boy in saving the Royal Albert Hall from imminent destruction. The music for the shows came courtesy of the BBC National Orchestra of Wales, with vocal support from the London Philharmonic Choir. Ben Foster conducted the orchestra for the Murray Gold-composed selections from *Doctor Who*, which were set to montages of clips shown on screens around the auditorium. Grant Llewellyn meanwhile took over the baton for the classical pieces, featuring works by John Adams, Gustav Holst, Carl Orff and Richard Wagner. Daleks, Judoon, Cybermen, masked Silurians and Saturnyne vampire girls took turns to menace the audience at various points during each performance. The concert was very positively received, as the *Guardian*'s classic music reviewer Michael Hann noted in a piece published on 25 July, in which he also wrote:

> One has to feel a little sorry for the musicians at Prom 10 – the BBC National Orchestra of Wales, conducted by Ben Foster and Grant Llewellyn, and the London Philharmonic Choir, plus solo singers Mark Chambers and Yamit Mamo. For everyone in the Albert Hall knew they were the supporting cast to the stars of *Doctor Who*, who introduced each piece, and the monsters, who appeared during many of them.
>
> It was a Trojan horse of a Prom, a handful of dramatic pop-classics thrown in among Murray Gold's music for the TV series, in the hope, presumably, that some of the young audience might leave as enthused by Wagner as by seeing the Supreme Dalek warn Foster of his conducting responsibilities. In truth, though, the attention of much of the audience wandered during the classical interludes, all of which were conducted by Llewellyn, returning when Karen Gillan, the Doctor's assistant, Amy, took to the stage to introduce something of Gold's conducted by Foster.

The *Daily Telegraph*'s Robert Colvile was also enthusiastic about the concert in his four-star review published on 26 July:

> The atmosphere was fevered – the TARDIS parked by the bust of Sir Henry Wood, the sound baffles dangling overhead like flying saucers, and monsters from the show marching through the packed auditorium as the BBC National Orchestra of Wales and London Philharmonic Choir expertly synchronised their playing (under conductor Ben Foster) to scenes from the show. Even the Daleks were back, offering the Prommers tea and biscuits.
>
> In the end, however, it was all about the Doctor – witness the rock-star welcome that greeted Matt Smith's second-half appearance. Smith's Doctor gave his customary manic performance, enlisting the help of a mini-me audience member in braces and bowtie to save the Albert Hall from a 'wibbly-wobbly, explodey-wodey thing'. Arthur Darvill (Rory Williams) also pitched in, but the bulk of the hosting was ably handled by co-star Karen Gillan (Amy Pond).

The 24 July performance was broadcast live on BBC Radio Three from 7.30 pm to 9.45 pm, with the 20-minute interval at 8.20 pm being filled by a Matthew Sweet-presented documentary entitled *Dance of the Daleks*, looking at the history of the TV show's incidental music. A TV broadcast of the concert was also promised for later in the year.

In a 30 July-published interview with Simon Brew of the Den of Geek website,

Steven Moffat spoke about his hectic schedule combining his work on *Doctor Who* with that on *Sherlock*. He said that in addition to the 2010 Christmas special he would be writing five further episodes for Series Six:

> 'Yeah. I'm basically following what Russell [T Davies] did. Having worked out the sums and worked out how he does it, I thought that's a perfect way of doing it.
> 'But there is no way of balancing this. The last year has been extraordinary. I've had about four days off, and that includes Christmas Day. I work every weekend, I get up early in the morning, I go to bed late at night. There is no way of balancing it.
> 'It's extraordinary, but it's great fun too! Great fun, so long as it doesn't kill me.'

The official *Doctor Who* website continued to make available a range of exclusive content relating to the show. Released in the first week of August was a new game called 'Amy's History Hunt' (also referred to as simply 'The History Hunt'), requiring players to decipher a series of clues in order to find the Doctor's 'favourite painting' in a sealed vault. This was notable for including a number of specially-recorded segments featuring Karen Gillan as Amy. Most of these were audio only, but there were also four videos recorded on the TARDIS set: an introduction to the game (duration 1' 42"); a piece about the life of Winston Churchill, including clips from 'Victory of the Daleks' (2' 14"); a similar biographical piece on Vincent van Gogh, including clips from 'Vincent and the Doctor' (2' 26"); and a short conclusion at the end of the game (0' 14"). Players who succeeded in finding the combination to unlock the vault were able to access the short story *The War of Art*, specially written by Paul Cornell, revealing what the Doctor had been doing while the search for the painting – *The Pandorica Opens*, from the episode of the same name – had been going on.

Although the eleventh Doctor's era was well under way now, accolades for his predecessor's final batch of specials were still accumulating. His work on 'The Waters of Mars' having been judged the Best Male Performance in a 2009 Science Fiction Television Episode in Canada's Constellation Awards a couple of weeks earlier, David Tennant picked up another title on 1 August when he was named Best Actor – Television in the Airlock Alpha website's prestigious Portal Awards for science fiction, having gained no less than 68% of the participating fans' votes. *Doctor Who* itself won the Portal Award for Best Series – Television, receiving 65% of the votes, with the spin-off show *Torchwood* taking second place. The Best Supporting Actor – Television category went to Bernard Cribbins for his role as Wilf Mott in 'The End of Time'. Coming more up to date, Alex Kingston was named Best Special Guest for her portrayal of River Song in 'The Time of Angels'. However, Karen Gillan lost out in the Best Actress – Television category to *Torchwood*'s Eve Myles. The special Gene Roddenberry Award for lifetime achievement was given to Russell T Davies for his stewardship of both *Doctor Who* and *Torchwood*.

The latest ABC circulation figures for *Doctor Who Adventures* showed that during the first six months of 2010 its average number of readers each week was 53,559 – up by about a fifth on the equivalent figure for the last six months of 2009, but still below that for the first six months of 2009. For the first time, figures were also published for *Doctor Who Magazine*, which had not previously participated in the ABC certification process. Its circulation for the first six months of the year was an impressive 35,374, with 73% of readers being in the UK or Republic of Ireland.

Matt Smith and Karen Gillan made further guest appearances on BBC One's *The One Show* on 20 August, this time together. They were interviewed by Alex Jones and new host Chris Evans – ex-husband of Billie Piper, of Rose Tyler fame – and discussed amongst other things the scene in 'Flesh and Stone' where Amy kisses the Doctor. A first promotional photograph from the Christmas special was unveiled, showing Matt Smith recording a snowy scene of the Doctor standing by the TARDIS police box.

Further information about the forthcoming *Doctor Who Live* shows was released on 26 August. The biggest piece of news was that the star of the shows would be Nigel Planer, an accomplished actor still probably best remembered for his role as the hippie Neil in the anarchic early-1980s BBC Two sitcom *The Young Ones*. His character in *Doctor Who Live* was named as the space-travelling showman Vorgenson, who journeys the galaxy with a Minimiser device containing many of the Doctor's foes held captive in a miniaturised state – a scenario recalling that of the classic-era story 'Carnival of Monsters' (1973). Planer was quoted as saying: 'I'm incredibly excited to be joining *Doctor Who Live* and this role is something of a boyhood dream come true. My character Vorgenson, who has been developed specially for the show by Steven Moffat, is the Greatest Showman in the Galaxy, and using his incredible invention, the Minimiser, he can make any *Doctor Who* character appear on stage as part of his travelling show dedicated to his hero.' Other details disclosed were that Matt Smith's Doctor would be seen via some specially-shot video sequences; that renowned illusionists the Twins would be devising special effects for the show, including one in which a Dalek would seem to fly; and that Nicholas Briggs would be not only taking on his usual role as monster voice artist but also appearing in person as the Doctor's old friend Winston Churchill.

On 27 August, the third of *The Adventure Games* series was made available to download in the UK. This one was called 'TARDIS' and was written by James Moran. Steven Moffat was quoted on the official *Doctor Who* website as saying: 'Since 1963, kids have wondered what it would be like to control the TARDIS. Now we're handing complete control of the most powerful ship in all of space and time to a generation of children. Everybody duck. "TARDIS" is a brilliant, brilliant adventure. It's funny, touching, terrifying, amazing – everything a *Doctor Who* episode should be.' Supporting material accessible via the BBC website included a video introduction to the game by Karen Gillan and a PDF of a short story by Moran entitled *Wish You Were Here*, which served as a preview mini-adventure.

On 28 August, Gillan made a personal appearance at the Hamleys toy store in Glasgow to sign copies of the new Amy Pond action figure from Character Options. This generated a minor controversy, as Gillan could see only 250 fans in the time available, and about 400 had turned up. The *Herald* newspaper quoted a BBC spokesperson as saying:

> 'Karen is an extremely popular star and we were pleased to see
> her fans out in force to cheer her on. It would have been

impossible to meet and greet everyone who came, so to manage the event fairly we worked together with Hamleys to allocate on a first-come-first-served basis 250 wristbands. This was advertised clearly in advance both in-store and online and staff were speaking to people in the queue for the bands to keep them updated and aware of how quickly these were going. Karen very kindly stayed for an hour longer than we had asked to ensure that fans had a good amount of time with her and overall the event was very positive with fans excited to see Karen in person.'

Immediately after this event, Gillan joined Steven Moffat at the Edinburgh International Television Festival to take part in a masterclass and answer questions about *Doctor Who* and, in Moffat's case, *Sherlock*. Videos of their sessions were subsequently made available to view online on the Festival's website. For *Doctor Who* fans, the most significant announcement made at the Festival was that, in a surprising departure from past practice, the show's 2011 series would be split into two blocks for transmission, with seven episodes in the first block and six in the second, and a 'game-changing' cliffhanger in between. The BBC Press Office issued a press notice on 29 August that read in part:

> The split transmission is the result of a request from Steven Moffat to write a new *Doctor Who* story arc that involves a big plot twist in the middle of the series. By splitting the series Moffat plans to give viewers one of the most exciting *Doctor Who* cliff-hangers and plot twists ever, leaving them waiting, on the edge of their seats, until the autumn to find out what happens.
> Steven Moffat said: 'The split series is hugely exciting because viewers will be treated to two premieres, two finales and more event episodes. For the kids it will never be more than a few months to the next *Doctor Who*! Easter, Autumn, Christmas!'

By the beginning of September, excitement for the debut of the *Doctor Who Live* shows – now only a month away – was really starting to grow. In an interview with *SFX* magazine, published on its website on 1 September, the show's director, Will Brenton, was reported as saying:

> 'When I first came aboard this project, it was … very akin to the Prom offering. And what I thought we needed to do was bring this space alive a lot more, by making it a narrative that takes place in real time, in that arena at that moment. Which is what we've done.
> 'So we've created a brand new *Doctor Who* character, called Vorgenson, but it is a character who grows out of a previous *Doctor Who* story called "Carnival of Monsters". All of its genealogy grows out of that episode. And the fans who spotted

that reference will enjoy how it happens. It's taken what happened in that episode and moved it on, and updated it and had some fun with it as well.

'And that's the kind of collaboration that we've been having. I sat down with Steven [Moffat] and said, "I've got this *Jurassic Park* kind of feel, with a character who's reeling out these characters," and he immediately said, "Well, 'Carnival of Monsters'! Let's let it grow out of that."'

In other promotional activity for the stage show, the next few days saw appearances being made by assorted groups of Cybermen, Clockwork Men, Silurians and Scarecrows in Sheffield, Nottingham, Birmingham, Liverpool and Belfast.

The winners of this year's prestigious Hugo Awards for science fiction were announced on 5 September, and the Best Dramatic Presentation, Short Form category went to *Doctor Who*'s 'The Waters of Mars'. This was the show's fourth success in the same category, but on the previous three occasions the winning story had been a Steven Moffat-scripted one – 'The Empty Child'/'The Doctor Dances' (2005), 'The Girl in the Fireplace' (2006) and 'Blink' (2007)[7] – whereas 'The Waters of Mars' was written by Russell T Davies and Phil Ford.

6 September was a notable date for *Doctor Who*. Behind the scenes, it marked the start of recording on Series Six. First to go before the cameras this time were the episodes intended to fill the third and fourth slots on transmission, written by Neil Gaiman and Mark Gatiss respectively.[8] This production block marked the return of director Richard Clark, who had last worked on the show on the Series Three episodes 'Gridlock' and 'The Lazarus Experiment'.

The same evening, at the Dorchester Hotel in London, the 2010 *TV Choice* Awards were presented, and *Doctor Who* was announced as the winner in the Best Family Drama category. Karen Gillan and Steven Moffat both attended the event. Gillan was quoted as saying: 'It's great. This is the first award we've ever received for this generation of *Doctor Who* – so it means a lot.' Moffat added: 'We feel incredibly relieved and pleased that we're carrying on winning awards. That's what the show is for, frankly. Big audiences and big awards.'

Also on the evening of 6 September, at 8.30, immediately after a repeat of 'The Big Bang', BBC Three presented the promised TV broadcast of the *Doctor Who Prom* concert from the end of July. The programme had only an hour-long slot, and so omitted all of the classical music, as well as a few of Murray Gold's *Doctor Who* pieces. For a limited time from the same date, an accompanying behind-the-scenes programme, *Backstage at the Doctor Who Prom*, was made available to view on the BBC's Red Button service.

7 September saw another award go to *Doctor Who*, or more specifically to its leading man, Matt Smith, who was named Best Actor in *GQ* magazine's Men of the Year show at London's Royal Opera House. Smith travelled up from Cardiff to attend the event, along with his then girlfriend, model Daisy Lowe. He emerged

---

[7] In each case, the Award was given in the year after the episode's debut transmission.

[8] Gatiss's episode would ultimately be moved back to ninth in the running order.

from the TARDIS police box to collect the award, presented by noted artist Tracey Emin.

At 7.00 pm on 10 September, BBC Three went one better than with its first broadcast of the *Doctor Who Prom* by presenting an extended, 90-minute version, with all of Murray Gold's compositions and some of the classical pieces reinstated.

A final significant award for the 2009 run of specials came on 19 September when *Doctor Who* was named Best TV Programme at the annual FantasyCon event of the British Fantasy Society. The award was collected on behalf of Russell T Davies by writer Rob Shearman.

Another notable piece of news broke on 20 September, when the gaming website MCV reported that *The Adventure Games* had been recommissioned for a second run:

> To date the first three [of] *The Adventure Games* have been downloaded over 1.6m times, with a fourth release due out later this year.
>
> The new games will once again be produced by Steven Moffat, Piers Wenger [and] Beth Willis, along with Anwen Aspden, and be developed by Sumo Digital. Screen stars Matt Smith and Karen Gillen will also return in digital form.
>
> 'Given the success of the first series, we'd be daft not to recommission,' BBC's Head of Multiplatform in Vision Simon Nelson stated.
>
> 'But it's not just about the numbers; the feedback we've had has been overwhelmingly positive. Our audience has been introduced to a new form of drama – and, for many, these have been the first computer games they have downloaded. We've set new standards in audience participation – and we think we've really helped push the concept of families actively playing together. I can't wait to see what the team does next.'

September may have been a relatively quiet month for *Doctor Who* in terms of media coverage, but production of the 2011 series was still proceeding apace in Cardiff. On 23 September, the official *Doctor Who* website announced a significant piece of casting news: the series' third episode – the one written by Neil Gaiman – would see a guest role taken by Suranne Jones. Jones was best know to the general public for playing Karen McDonald in the ITV soap opera *Coronation Street* between 2000 and 2004, and had previously featured in the story 'Mona Lisa's Revenge' (2009) in *The Sarah Jane Adventures*. She was quoted as saying: 'As an actor, it's hugely exciting to be cast in *Doctor Who*. I'm a massive fan of the show and I was blown away when I read Neil's script and uncovered what's in store for my character. I'm sworn to secrecy, so viewers will just have to wait until next year to find out any other juicy details!'

On 29 September, the BBC issued a 'showreel' presenting clips from its next six months' worth of drama output, including a number from the 2010 *Doctor Who* Christmas special. This was the first time that any clips from the special had been publicly released. Matt Smith was also seen in his role in *Christopher and His Kind*, while former Doctors Christopher Eccleston and David Tennant could be spotted in their latest BBC parts, in the series *Accused* and the play *Single Father* respectively.

Word on the fan grapevine was that advance ticket sales for the *Doctor Who Live* shows had been less healthy than the organisers had hoped. The prices – ranging from £25.00 minimum to £38.50 maximum, or £42.50 maximum in Belfast – were cited as a possible reason. Although these were not atypical for an arena-style show, a family of four would need to spend a considerable sum – at least £100, plus extra for travel and refreshments – in order to attend. Suggestions that all was not well with the show appeared to be confirmed when, on 30 September, one of the three Glasgow performances, scheduled to take place on 14 October, was cancelled for what were described as 'logistical reasons'. Ticket holders were offered refunds or seats at a different performance. Nevertheless, the show's opening night, on 8 October at Wembley Arena in London, went off without a hitch. There were a number of notable celebrities in the audience for this performance, including Matt Smith himself, former companion Catherine Tate, writers Richard Curtis and Gareth Roberts and incidental music composer Murray Gold.[9]

Attendees at the *Doctor Who Live* shows were able to pick up an intriguing flyer for something called *The Doctor Who Experience*, due to be mounted in London in 2011. Although no further details were made available at this stage, it seemed that this was to be a major new *Doctor Who* exhibition, which would serve as a successor to the existing ones in Newcastle, Land's End and Cardiff, all of which were due to close over the next few months. A new Cardiff exhibition had also been promised for some point in the future.

On 10 October, BBC America broke an exciting piece of news: the 2011 series would see *Doctor Who* having its first major location shoot in the USA. The BBC America press release read, in part:

> The BBC announced today that [Series] Six of *Doctor Who*, [a show that] delivered record ratings for BBC America earlier this year, will open with a spectacular two-parter set in the US and penned by '*Who* supremo' Steven Moffat.
>
> Production on episodes one and two of the new season starts in Cardiff this month and Matt Smith, Karen Gillan and Arthur Darvill will then travel to America in mid November to shoot pivotal scenes. They will also be joined by Alex Kingston who reprises her role as River Song.
>
> Showrunner and lead writer, Steven Moffat, said: 'The Doctor has visited every weird and wonderful planet you can imagine, so he was bound get round to America eventually! And of course every *Doctor Who* fan will be jumping up and down and saying he's been in America before. But not for real, not on location – and not with a story like this one! Oh, you wait!'
>
> Piers Wenger, Head of Drama BBC Wales and executive producer, added: 'Steven's scripts generally inspire us to go that extra mile – this time we're going that extra four thousand.

---

[9] See Appendix B for further details of *Doctor Who Live*.

Thanks to our friends at BBC America and to the continuing ambition of our lead writer and production team, the first two episodes of Matt Smith's second season as the Doctor are going global and look set to become *Doctor Who*'s most action-packed and ambitious season opener yet.'

2010 has been a breakthrough year for the *Doctor Who* franchise across all platforms since BBC America became the official home of the series.

However, not all of the location recording for the episodes that would form Series Six's opening two-parter would be carried out in America, as fans soon discovered when the crew were spotted out and about in Cardiff on 18 October. During the afternoon, shots of extras in 1960s clothing were taped in St Mary Street and in Cardiff University's Glamorgan Building. Then, that night, Alex Kingston and guest actor Mark Sheppard were seen recording a scene that ended with River Song appearing to fall backwards off a building – a piece of action performed by a stunt woman, in just a single take. Further recording took place the following day, at the American-themed Eddie's Diner on Mermaid Quay. Matt Smith, Karen Gillan, Arthur Darvill and Alex Kingston were all present this time. More location work was seen being done on 26 October, with Crockherbtown Lane and the adjoining Park Place apparently being transformed into 44th Street in New York circa 1969.

At the beginning of November, further details of *The Doctor Who Experience* were released. This exhibition was set to open at London's Olympia on 20 February 2011.[10] It was being designed by a specialist company called Sarner and would include both a walk-through adventure section with a narrative, featuring specially-recorded video clips of Matt Smith as the Doctor, and a more traditional display of props and costumes from the show. Steven Moffat was quoted as saying:

'*The Doctor Who Experience* is a fan's dream come true – a fully interactive adventure that will allow viewers of the show to get as close as possible to some of the scariest monsters from the series. It will also be the first time that *Doctor Who* artefacts from all the show's 47-year history – classic and new – will be on display together, many of them being seen for the first time. And never mind that, this is the day the Doctor teaches you how to fly the TARDIS through time and space, and takes you into battle with all his deadliest enemies in a brand new adventure.

'So steady your nerves and bring your own sofa – the Doctor needs you.'

On 8 November, Matt Smith and Karen Gillan took part in various activities to promote the release that day of the Series Five DVD and Blu-ray box sets from 2Entertain. The pair first appeared on the ITV1 breakfast show *Daybreak*, and then

---

[10] As things transpired, the exhibition's official opening was preceded by three public preview days on 17, 18 and 19 February 2011.

guested on BBC Radio 1's *Fearne Cotton Show*. In the afternoon they visited the HMV store on London's Oxford Street to sign copies of the box sets for 300 lucky fans who had queued up for entry wristbands earlier in the day.

Two days later, Smith and Gillan were joined by Arthur Darvill at a ceremony at the Cardiff Civic Centre to switch on the city's annual Christmas lights. Smith had earlier been reported as saying: 'It's a real honour to be asked to switch on Cardiff's Christmas lights, because the city has become like a second home to not only me, but the rest of the *Doctor Who* production team. We love filming here in Wales and we even managed to get into the festive spirit extra early this year when filming the *Doctor Who* Christmas special in August. Cardiff is a great city and I'd like to thank all of its residents for being so welcoming and accommodating.' The ceremony concluded with a spectacular firework display.

12 November saw the release of the first of the two *Doctor Who* video games from Nintendo that had been announced back in March. This was 'Evacuation Earth', for the Nintendo DS platform. The official product description was as follows:

> This is your chance to be the Doctor and guide him and Amy Pond on a thrilling new adventure.
>
> Arriving on Earth only hours before a solar storm is due to wipe out all life on the planet, the Doctor and his companion discover the last group of humans preparing to evacuate. No sooner have they arrived then the TARDIS disappears and they embark on a mission to recover it, encountering Silurians and Daleks along the way.
>
> Starring the voices of Matt Smith and Karen Gillan, this brand new official *Doctor Who* storyline includes over 100 puzzles, plus over 60 exciting locations to explore.
>
> - Authentic *Doctor Who* story written by *Doctor Who* author Oli Smith.
> - Opportunity to guide the Doctor and Amy Pond through a colourful puzzle adventure.
> - Beautifully drawn characters to interact with and over 60 varied, colourful locations to explore.
> - Over 100 puzzles including three types of mini-games.
> - Features items to collect, use and combine to progress the story.
> - Fully recorded dialogue by Matt Smith and Karen Gillan throughout cut scenes.

12 November saw one other piece of news being released, when the official *Doctor Who* website announced the title of the forthcoming Christmas special as 'A Christmas Carol' – after the Dickens classic previously noted as its inspiration.

Just prior to taking part in the US location recording for the opening story of Series Six, which was scheduled for 17 to 19 November in Utah, Matt Smith was a guest on the 16 November edition of CBS's late night talk show *The Late, Late Show with Craig Ferguson*. Ferguson, a long-time *Doctor Who* fan, had intended to open the show with a humorous performance of specially-composed lyrics and choreographed dance moves set to Orbital's version of the *Doctor Who* theme, culminating with an appearance by Smith himself. However, although recorded, this sequence had to be dropped prior to transmission, much to the host's annoyance, as it was realised that the rights to use the music had not been obtained in advance.[11] A nervous-seeming Smith spoke to Ferguson about visiting Las Vegas; taking his involvement in *Doctor Who* one year at a time; and looking forward to the forthcoming location work in Utah's Monument Valley. At the end, he joined Ferguson and fellow guest Chris Hardwick, presenter of the Nerdist Podcast, in trying to play a brief section of the *Doctor Who* theme on harmonicas. Smith also recorded a segment with Hardwick for inclusion in his next podcast.

The second of Nintendo's *Doctor Who* games, 'Return to Earth', to be played on the Wii console, was released on 19 November. In this case, the official product description read:

> Young fans can play the role of the Doctor and Amy Pond in this gripping 3D action adventure to help the starship *Lucy Gray* return to Earth.
>
> Unravel a sinister plot by the Cybermen and prevent the Daleks from retrieving a dangerous Time Axis as your explore the deserted starship *Lucy Gray*. Avoid and outsmart your enemies using stealth, distraction devices and target-shooting elements found around the ship.
>
> Starring the voices of Matt Smith and Karen Gillan, this brand new official *Doctor Who* storyline includes two types of mini-game; the Gravity Gun and Sonic Screwdriver Game, which specifically make use of the Wii technology.
>
> - Authentic *Doctor Who* story written by *Doctor Who* author Oli Smith.
> - Opportunity to explore an incredible starship in this action adventure as it returns to Earth playing as either the Doctor or Amy Pond.
> - Interact with and manipulate the environment.
> - Aim and fire sonic beams with the Wii remote at coloured targets dotted around the levels that move platforms, turn on and off hazards, open doors and more.
> - Sneak past Daleks and Cybermen.
> - Use the Wii remote as the sonic screwdriver to progress through the game.
> - Fully recorded dialogue by Matt Smith and Karen Gillan throughout cut scenes.

Both of the Nintendo games were aimed primarily at 7 to 11 year olds. A

---

[11] This 'cold open' sequence was later made available to view on the show's website, after the rights issues had been resolved.

company called Blue Ocean Accessories was licensed to produce items to go with them, including sonic screwdriver-design DS styluses and Wii remotes.

19 November was also the date when – in what was now becoming something of an annual tradition – BBC One's *Children in Need* telethon presented an exclusive minute-long trailer for *Doctor Who*'s forthcoming Christmas special. This presented a host of previously-unseen clips and incorporated the caption 'Time Can Be Rewritten', with the additional word 'Christmas' gradually fading in at the start, to the accompaniment of the TARDIS materialisation noise, so that it then read 'Christmastime Can Be Rewritten'.

Three days later, the BBC Press Office released brief details of programmes for the Christmas week, including the following on the *Doctor Who* special:

> Amy and Rory are trapped on a crashing space liner, and the only way the Doctor can rescue them is to save the soul of a lonely old miser, in a festive edition of the time-travelling adventure, written by Steven Moffat. But is Kazran Sardick, the richest man in Sardicktown, beyond redemption? And what is lurking in the fogs of Christmas Eve?

On 24 November, to promote *The Doctor Who Experience* exhibition due to open the following February, a troop of six Cybermen descended on London, recreating their appearance on the streets and steps near St Paul's Cathedral in 'The Invasion' (1968) and marching across the Millennium Bridge toward the Tate Modern. They even took a ride on a tube train, to the surprise of other travellers! This provided some excellent photo opportunities and generated stories in a number of newspapers, including the *Metro*, the *Daily Telegraph* and the *Daily Mail*.

The following day, it was announced that the Mill's work on 'The Pandorica Opens' had won them the award for Best Digital Effects in the Royal Television Society's annual Craft and Design Awards. A spokesperson commented: 'The judges were impressed by some beautifully integrated effects [achieved] by green screen. "This is about as good as it gets on TV" they said.'

The *Radio Times* edition for 11 to 17 December, which went on sale on 30 November, sported another *Doctor Who* cover, this one showing the Doctor seated with Michael Gambon's and Katherine Jenkins' characters in an open carriage, apparently being pulled across the sky above an alien city by a flying shark, somewhat in the manner of Father Christmas being towed in his sleigh by a team of reindeer. The tagline read: 'Christmas Exclusive – Join the Doctor – Michael Gambon and Katherine Jenkins take the trip of their lives'. Inside the magazine, the transmission time of 'A Christmas Carol' was confirmed as 6.00 pm on Christmas Day, and there were interviews with both Matt Smith and Katherine Jenkins. Smith said of the special: 'It was a great privilege to do it. It's something I've always wanted to do since I started the show. I love Christmas, plus I've always wanted to film something in July that has got snow in, *loads* of snow ... It's very Christmassy.' Jenkins meanwhile recalled the trepidation she had felt approaching her role: 'It was *far* worse than any nerves I've ever had for any performance. I spent a lot of time thinking about it. It's such an iconic show, and it's one that we watch as a family. I just thought, "I'd love to give it a try." But I'm the first to say that I really don't consider myself an actress. So I asked if I could go in and read to them, and I thought, "Well, if I'm rubbish they won't give it to me, will they?" So I read to them, and they called me on my thirtieth birthday and offered me the part.'

On 1 December, the official *Doctor Who* website began its traditional daily countdown to the transmission of the Christmas special, in the form of an online advent calendar. Every day, fans could uncover a new item of interest, including games, publicity photos and promotional video clips.

2 December saw the BBC Press Office put out a full press release for 'A Christmas Carol'. This repeated the material from the one issued on 12 July when production on the special started, but also gave additional credits, a brief plot synopsis, and extensive quotes from both Matt Smith and Katherine Jenkins. Smith praised the imaginative quality of Steven Moffat's writing and spoke about working with the special's guest stars:

> 'It was a real privilege to work with Michael [Gambon],' explains Matt. 'I had a great time with him and he was really naughty! He's so crafty and when I asked him about working with iconic actors such as Olivier and Bates he said the one thing they all had in common was they were naughty – and he's exactly the same. He was very mischievous, constantly telling jokes and getting into the spirit of play.
>
> 'With Katherine [Jenkins], I was astounded by her professionalism. Considering it was her first acting experience I thought she handled it with real craft and diligence,' continues Matt. 'It's exactly the type of casting we want; someone fresh, exciting and new.'

The Christmas double issue of *Radio Times*, covering the period 18 to 31 December, went on sale just a few days after the previous one, and although *Doctor Who* did not feature on the cover this time, the magazine did contain a piece written by Moffat, in which he recalled working on his script for the Christmas special in a Los Angeles hotel room in April, and another interview with Smith. The main illustration for Moffat's article was another photo from the same shoot that had produced the previous issue's cover image.

By the second week of December, BBC One had begun showing trailers for its Christmas programming, under the theme 'Everyone's Home for Christmas'. *Doctor Who* was naturally one of the shows covered, although the clips used had all been seen before in the trailer aired during *Children in Need*. Also shown were a number of trailers was a new, airport-based comedy, *Come Fly With Me*, from David Walliams and Matt Lucas of *Little Britain* fame. One of these trailers, running 30 seconds, featured the white Supreme Dalek from 'Victory of the Daleks' checking in at an airline desk and receiving a boarding pass; another, running ten seconds, showed the same Dalek gliding through the airport carrying bags of duty free shopping and eyeing up some passing stewardesses.

On 10 December, BBC America made available on their website a two-minute-long 'Exclusive Inside Look' video for 'A Christmas Carol', in which Matt Smith, Karen Gillan and Arthur Darvill gave their thoughts on the special and on working with Michael Gambon and Katherine Jenkins.

The evening of 13 December saw 'A Christmas Carol' being given its first public screening, at a special British Film Institute event on London's South Bank. This was followed by an on-stage question-and-answer session with Matt Smith, Katherine Jenkins and Steven Moffat, an eight-minute clip of which was later made available to view on the BFI website. Karen Gillan was also present in the audience, but did not join her co-stars on stage. Members of the press were in attendance, and reports appeared the following day in a number of the national newspapers. The *Daily Mail*'s Sarah Bull wrote:

> Matt Smith said he was satisfied with his first series as the Doctor, but thinks there is room for improvement.
>
> Speaking at a preview screening at London's BFI South Bank, he said: 'I have been very pleased and proud of the people I have worked with and alongside. I think we achieved something – I don't know what that is – I hope people have enjoyed it.
>
> 'I think we're going to get better. I think we know the areas we can improve and the ways in which we want to improve.
>
> 'It's been a learning curve. A very brilliant and informative journey for me professionally and personally. It's something I shall not forget.'

The *Guardian*'s Vicky Frost reported:

> When Doctor Who lands in the nation's living rooms on Christmas Day it is traditional for a succession of baddies to follow. This year, however, his foe won't be Daleks and Cybermen – but an extremely hungry, flying shark.
>
> And if that isn't unlikely enough, the shark features in an adventure that takes Charles Dickens' *A Christmas Carol* for its inspiration and involves the Doctor trying to save a ship of 4,000 passengers from certain death.
>
> 'If you're going to do a Christmas Day episode, which is based on the principle that the audience have had a selection box for breakfast and are probably drunk, then you have to move it on a bit – because a normal episode of *Doctor Who* wouldn't be enough,' joked lead writer Steven Moffat after a special preview screening last night.

Katherine Jenkins made a further promotional appearance on 14 December when she visited her old school, Alderman Davies Primary School in Neath, to give the pupils a preview screening of the special. This was later the subject of a report on BBC Wales News. Jenkins said: 'Well, we filmed it over about three to four weeks, in Wales of course, and so that was lovely, because I was able to come home and see the family. It's challenging in so many ways, because I'd never done any green screen stuff either, so all the sleigh/carriage stuff, the flying scenes … When you're just in a room with a fan and having to scream on tap, you know, it was sometimes quite weird. But lots of fun, 'cause I was in the carriage sometimes with Matt, and sometimes with Michael Gambon, and so we had a really good laugh.'

16 December saw the release of yet another *Doctor Who* video game, 'The Mazes of Time', this one developed by Dundee-based mobile games company Tag Games for Apple's iPod, iPhone and iPad devices.[12] Like the two Nintendo games, this was written by Oli Smith, although this time it was aimed at players aged six and upwards. Tag Games' Head of Games Technology Robert Hemming gave the following quote: '*Doctor Who* is the UK's number one science fiction property, and I think it is in the BBC's top three for worldwide sales, so it is great to bring it to Dundee ... Since we were established we have never done a game for ordinary retail – it has always been digital distribution. The digital model allows us to talk directly to our customers, so it is quite different from the traditional games model. We can get feedback from our customers and change and adapt things.' The game involved the Doctor and Amy trying to rescue an innocent family from the fall-out of a Dalek attack, and also featured appearances by Cybermen and Silurians.[13] However, unlike in the case of the Nintendo games, neither Matt Smith nor Karen Gillan contributed their voices to the soundtrack; all the dialogue was given by way of written captions instead. The game did, though, use audio samples from the TV show and some of Murray Gold's music.

On 18 December, the *Sun*'s weekly TV listings magazine insert, *Buzz*, featured a photo of Matt Smith and Karen Gillan on its cover. Inside, a conversation between the pair was reported, with Smith saying of his friendship with Gillan: 'We'll go to the supermarket every night, get a sandwich, and trot home to learn lines. Sometimes we'll phone each other and say: "How's it going? Really badly? Me too. Do you want to come over and practise?" I'm terribly fond of Karen – we're good pals. I've learnt how to make her laugh during filming. I can say a word in a silly voice, and she'll go. Karen can do it to me too. It's that old Smith-Gillan banter – it's become quite famous on set.'

From 21 December, the BBC's Red Button service offered a series of four daily *Doctor Who Confidential*-produced behind-the-scenes preview videos for the Christmas special, presented by video blogger Charlie McDonnell. These could be viewed by Sky and Virgin Media digital TV customers and (at different times) via Freeview, and were also placed on the BBC's official YouTube channel. The four videos had the titles 'Charlie and the Runner' (3' 32"), 'Charlie and the TARDIS' (2' 55"), 'Charlie and the Christmas Lunch Bus' (2' 53") and 'Charlie and the Doctor's Badger' (6' 08"). The contents of these were fairly self-explanatory, except for the last one, which involved McDonnell buying Christmas presents for some of the show's stars. Matt Smith made an eccentric request for either a badger or some gloves, and McDonnell managed to combine both by getting him a badger glove puppet. He gave Arthur Darvill some unusual musical horns, and Karen Gillan some bars of the organic chocolate she had asked for.

On 22 December, three days earlier than scheduled, the fourth and last in the initial series of *The Adventure Games* was released in the UK. Entitled 'Shadows of the Vashta Nerada', this was written by Phil Ford, and as usual was available in both PC and Mac versions. The publicity blurb read:

---

[12] A version for the Android platform would be made available in August 2011.

[13] Further levels to the game would be released in 2011, involving Autons and Weeping Angels.

Kicking off immediately after the cliff-hanger ending of episode three, the latest [release in] *The Adventure Games* picks up the story of the Doctor and Amy who've materialised just south of London (and about 1000 miles to the left), inside a sea-bed colony called Poseidon. 'Shadows of the Vashta Nerada' features a cracking plot that surrounds a real-world conspiracy and, of course, it takes place at Christmas.

Steven Moffat, executive producer and lead writer for *Doctor Who*: 'We've gone all-out for the season finale. "Shadows of the Vashta Nerada" takes place entirely underwater – something that would be impossible for the TV series, as water is so expensive. It's thrilling, terrifying, educational and fun. Just steer clear of those shadows ...'

According to figures released by the BBC on 23 December, the eleventh Doctor's debut episode, 'The Eleventh Hour', was still the most requested programme of the year on the iPlayer service, having had an impressive 2.2 million hits. The other episodes of Series Five had averaged 1.5 million apiece.

At 8.00 pm on Christmas Eve, Matt Smith and Karen Gillan could be heard on BBC Radio 1 presenting an hour-long selection of their favourite music tracks of the year; one of a run of *Top 10s of 2010* programmes featuring different celebrities.

Later the same evening, at 10.30 on BBC One, Matt Smith could be seen making a guest appearance on *The Graham Norton Show*. Amongst the topics discussed were his *Doctor Who* fan mail, which he said his mother helped him to sort out.

Christmas Day brought the long-awaited transmission of 'A Christmas Carol' itself; and, as usual, BBC Three accompanied it up with an edition of the behind-the-scenes show *Doctor Who Confidential*. In the US, BBC America also showed 'A Christmas Carol' on the same day. They preceded it with a broadcast of the *Doctor Who Prom* programme, and followed it with a special trailer for Series Six, consisting of a montage of clips not yet seen in the UK.

In Australia, fans had to wait just a little longer to see 'A Christmas Carol', which ABC1 had scheduled for Boxing Day. As in the US, it was preceded by the *Doctor Who Proms* concert.

By this time, initial overnight viewing figures for the BBC One/BBC HD debut transmission of the special were available, and they indicated that it had won an audience of 10.3 million – almost identical to the previous year's 10.4 million figure. This was an impressive result that looked certain to see *Doctor Who* capturing a top five place in the Christmas viewing chart once the final figures became available in just over a week's time.

As usual, the special was reviewed in a number of the national newspapers. In a piece published on the *Guardian*'s website on Christmas day itself, Dan Martin was highly enthusiastic:

'A Christmas Carol' riffs magnificently and faithfully on the beauty and simplicity of its source material. At Christmas people always talk about the Greatest Story Ever Told in other terms, but this is a sumptuous triumph from start to finish.

If you thought the *Who* specials were Christmassy in the

past, then even discounting the Dickens stuff this was off the scale. The Doctor pops into Kazran's house down the chimney. There's a shark-powered sleigh ride through the chimneys of Sardicktown. There's a wonderful peasants' Christmas dinner where the Doctor proves himself hopeless at card tricks. And, of course, Father Christmas is real and our hero is mates with him. I just hope that for next year's special we get to meet Jeff for ourselves.

Most of the other press reviewers were similarly impressed. An exception, however, was the *Telegraph*'s Chris Harvey who, in a piece also published on Christmas Day on the newspaper's website, wrote:

Phew, that was a bit rich, wasn't it? I think I've eaten too much. I'm not sure if it was that festive sleigh-ride across the rooftops in a carriage pulled by a giant fog-breathing shark that had been tamed by the sweet song of a cryogenically frozen maiden that did it, but I actually feel rather queasy.

Of course, Matt Smith's first Christmas special as the Doctor had been written with the word 'Christmassy' in mind, [so] it's not really for old curmudgeons like me, who got more of a kick out of Michael Gambon's miserly Kazran Sardick when he was sneering and snarling at the beginning of the episode than when he had been thoroughly heartwarmed by the end.

But there was just something so overblown about the whole thing, it reminded me of the worst excesses of the Russell T Davies era, when everything just kept getting bigger, louder, more operatic ... feebler.

The special's ratings in the main overseas territories were just as strong as in the UK. Its first airing on BBC America drew an average of 727,000 viewers, while in Australia it beat off some tough competition to come out top in its time slot, with an average of 880,000 viewers in the five major capital cities.

Closing the year on another positive note, the *Northampton Chronicle & Echo* reported on 30 December how Matt Smith had made one young fan's Christmas:

A young boy from Northampton who spent last Christmas in hospital fighting cancer has had his dream of meeting Doctor Who come true, thanks to the *Chronicle & Echo* and the star of the hit show.

Alfe Game was diagnosed with non-Hodgkin lymphoma when he was just five and spent Christmas 2009 at Northampton General Hospital.

The seven-year-old, from Duston, went into remission from the illness in July and has since dedicated hours of his time to helping children in a similar position to him ...

To say 'thank you' to Alfe for his hard work in the

community, [we] arranged for *Doctor Who* fan Alfe to have a surprise Christmas Eve visit from the eleventh Doctor himself, Northampton-born Matt Smith.

…

Matt Smith said: 'My mum mentioned this to me and as I was going to be around in Northampton, I thought "Why not?" It was my pleasure to do it. I'm really pleased we came. Alfe was lovely and they're such a nice family.

'We talked a lot about *Doctor Who* and what he wanted for Christmas, and then he showed me his presents, but we were just hanging out really.

'It's nice to see how inspired children are by *Doctor Who* and how much of a difference it can make sometimes, when you hear about them meeting in hospital, talking about it and bonding over it.

'This has been a wonderful experience.'

# PART TWO
# BIO-DATA

# CHAPTER SIX
# MAIN CAST

<u>MATT SMITH (THE DOCTOR)</u>

Matt Smith was born in 1982 in Northampton. He initially hoped to have a career as a professional footballer, and played for the youth teams of Northampton Town, Nottingham Forest and Leicester City, but a back injury forced him out of the sport. Encouraged into acting by his school drama teacher, he joined the National Youth Theatre in London. Then, after leaving school, he studied drama and creative writing at the University of East Anglia. His first notable role as a professional actor came at London's National Theatre in a production of the Alan Bennett play *The History Boys* (2005-2006). He made his TV debut in the Billie Piper-starring BBC One dramatisations of Philip Pullman's books *The Ruby in the Smoke* (2006) and *The Shadow in the North* (2007), and appeared opposite Piper again in an episode of the first series of ITV2's *Secret Diary of a Call Girl* (2007). However, his first major TV role came in the BBC Two political drama series *Party Animals* (2007). He also made a successful return to the theatre, taking a leading role in the Polly Stenham play *That Face*, initially at the Royal Court Theatre Upstairs in Chelsea in 2007 and then at the Duke of York's Theatre in London's West End the following year. The play was critically acclaimed, and Smith's performance won him the *Evening Standard*'s Best Newcomer award. Smith was one of the first actors to audition for the role of the eleventh Doctor, and was quickly recognised by showrunner Steven Moffat as an ideal candidate.

<u>KAREN GILLAN (AMY POND)</u>

Karen Gillan was born in 1987 in Inverness in Scotland. She became interested in acting from a young age, and performed in plays at her school and in local youth theatres. She studied drama at Telford College in Edinburgh from age 16, and at the Italia Conti stage school in London from age 18. However, she dropped out of the Italia Conti course to begin working professionally, both as an actor and, for a time, as a fashion model. Her first notable TV work was as a regular performer in the Channel 4 comedy sketch vehicle *The Kevin Bishop Show* (2007-2009). Another minor TV role at that time was under heavy make-up as a Soothsayer in the Series Four *Doctor Who* episode 'The Fires of Pompeii'. She then successfully auditioned to play Amy Pond, which was her first leading TV role. She has gone on to make her professional theatre debut in *Inadmissible Evidence* (2011) at London's Donmar Warehouse, and to star as 1960s supermodel Jean Shrimpton in the BBC Four TV movie *We'll Take Manhattan* (2012).

CRACKS IN TIME

## ARTHUR DARVILL (RORY WILLIAMS)

Thomas Arthur Darvill was born in 1982 in Birmingham. His mother was involved in the theatre and his father was a professional keyboard player, so he was introduced to the performing arts from an early age. He joined the Stage2 youth theatre company in 1991, and remained with them until 2000, when he gained a job doing in-vision links on the ITV children's programming strand CITV. He studied acting at London's RADA from age 18. His professional stage debut came in the play *Terre Haute*, initially at the Assembly Rooms during the Edinburgh Festival Fringe in 2006, then on tour, and finally at the Trafalgar Studios in London in 2007. Another notable stage role came alongside Matt Smith in *Swimming with Sharks* at London's Vaudeville Theatre, also in 2007. He made his TV debut in a minor role in the ITV1 crime drama *He Kills Coppers* (2008). He then appeared as Edward 'Tip' Dorrit in a BBC One serialisation of Dickens' *Little Dorrit* (2008). However, *Doctor Who*'s Rory Williams is his most major TV part to date. In addition to his acting work, Darvill is an accomplished musician and award-winning composer, having worked in this capacity on shows including *Frontline* (2008) at the Globe Theatre and *Been So Long* (2009) at the Young Vic. He has the unusual hobby of collecting taxidermy.

## ALEX KINGSTON (RIVER SONG)

Alex Kingston was born in 1963 in Epsom, Surrey. She became interested in acting while at school, and performed for the Surrey County Youth Theatre. Later she trained at London's RADA. She went on to become a member of the Royal Shakespeare Company, but it is for her long and distinguished film and TV career that she is best known. Her earliest screen appearances came in 1980, when she had a small, uncredited part in the movie *The Wildcats of St Trinians* and played a character in three episodes of the long-running BBC One children's show *Grange Hill*. More notable film roles came in *The Cook, the Thief, His Wife & Her Lover* (1989), *A Pin for the Butterfly* (1994), *Croupier* (1998), *Essex Boys* (2000) and *Crashing* (2007). However, her greatest success came on TV, as Dr Elizabeth Corday in some 160 episodes of NBC's medical drama series *ER* from 1997 to 2004. Her performances in this hit US show gained her numerous awards and widespread public recognition. It led on to many other memorable roles, on both sides of the Atlantic, including as *Doctor Who*'s River Song, who was introduced in the Series Four story 'Silence in the Library'/'Forest of the Dead' and then brought back as a semi-regular from the start of Series Five. Other notable TV credits include *Lost in Austen* (ITV1, 2008), *Hope Springs* (BBC One, 2009), *FlashForward* (ABC, 2009), *Law & Order: Special Victims Unit* (Universal, 2009), *Marchlands* (ITV1, 2011) and *Upstairs, Downstairs* (BBC One, 2012).

# CHAPTER SEVEN
# PRINCIPAL CREATIVE TEAM

## STEVEN MOFFAT (SHOWRUNNER, EXECUTIVE PRODUCER, LEAD WRITER)

Steven Moffat was born in 1961 in Paisley, Scotland. He had gained a degree in English and begun working as a teacher when a chance encounter between his father and a TV producer led to him being commissioned to write the children's series *Press Gang* (ITV, 1989-1993), which quickly acquired cult status. He went on to create and write the sitcom *Joking Apart* (BBC Two, 1993-1995), which was inspired by the breakdown of his first marriage and won the Bronze Rose of Montreux award, and the less-well-received *Chalk* (BBC One, 1997). One of his biggest successes came with the sitcom *Coupling* (BBC Two/BBC Three, 2000-2004), which was also the subject of a short-lived American remake (NBC, 2003). Later he wrote the acclaimed drama *Jekyll* (BBC One, 2007) as a modern take on Robert Louis Stevenson's *Strange Case of Dr Jekyll and Mr Hyde* (Longmans, Green & Co, 1886). He scripted the spoof *Doctor Who* story 'The Curse of Fatal Death' for BBC One's *Comic Relief* telethon in 1999 and has contributed a number of short stories to various *Doctor Who* collections. He was the only writer other than Russell T Davies to contribute episodes to each of the first four series of the new *Doctor Who*, and these scripts earned him numerous Hugos, BAFTAs and other awards. He took over from Davies as *Doctor Who*'s showrunner in 2009. His other projects around that time included scripting the movie *The Adventures of Tintin* (2011) for director Steven Spielberg; he was due to write a follow-up as well, but declined that opportunity in favour of working on *Doctor Who*. He co-created with Mark Gatiss the BBC One show *Sherlock* (2010- ), a modern-day retelling of the Sherlock Holmes stories, the first run of which he worked on at the same time as Series Five of *Doctor Who*.

## PIERS WENGER (EXECUTIVE PRODUCER)

Piers Wenger was born in 1972. He was producer of the Victoria Wood-starring ITV drama *Housewife, 49* (2006), which won two BAFTA awards, and of the BBC One TV movie *Ballet Shoes* (2007). He trailed and worked alongside the out-going BBC Wales Head of Drama Julie Gardner during 2008, then took over from her at the beginning of 2009. Later that year he also succeeded her as executive producer on *Doctor Who*, and was involved with Steven Moffat in casting Matt Smith as the eleventh Doctor. Other executive producer credits for the BBC came on the third series of *The Sarah Jane Adventures* (2009), *Ashes to Ashes* (2010), *Upstairs, Downstairs* (2010), *Eric and Ernie* (2011) and the Matt Smith-starring *Christopher and His Kind* (2011). In 2011, after completing work on Series Six of *Doctor Who*, he left the BBC to become senior commissioning executive of Film4 Productions.

# CRACKS IN TIME

## BETH WILLIS (EXECUTIVE PRODUCER)

Beth Willis was born in 1978 and is the grand-daughter of Ted Willis, creator of the fondly-remembered BBC police series *Dixon of Dock Green* (1955-1976). She was educated in Blackheath and Dulwich in south London. She worked as a script editor on the ITV shows *William and Mary* (2005) and *Agatha Christie's Poirot* (2005-2006) and on BBC One's *The Amazing Mrs Pritchard* (2006) before becoming a producer. Her first job in the latter capacity was for the production company Kudos working on BBC One's *Ashes to Ashes* from 2007 to 2009. She then joined Steven Moffat and Piers Wenger as one of *Doctor Who*'s three executive producers. In 2011, after the completion of work on Series Six, she left the BBC and returned to Kudos to take on new projects.

## TRACIE SIMPSON (PRODUCER)

Tracie Simpson started her TV career as a production co-ordinator on BBC Wales shows including *Tiger Bay* (1997), *Jack of Hearts* (1999) and *Care* (2000). She was associate producer on another BBC Wales show, *The Bench* (2001), before becoming production manager on *Doctor Who* from the start of Series One until mid-way through Series Four. She returned to the show to produce the specials 'Planet of the Dead' and 'The End of Time' and was then appointed as one of the producers for Series Five. She left part-way through its run to take on another BBC Wales show, *Baker Boys* (2011), before moving on to produce BBC One's long-running series *Casualty* (2011- ).

## PETER BENNETT (PRODUCER)

For most of his career, Peter Bennett has worked as a second or first assistant director. His initial credits in those capacities came in the late 1970s and early 1980s, on films including *International Velvet* (1978) and *Moonraker* (1979) and TV shows such as *Minder* (1979) and *Hart to Hart* (1983). Many similar assignments followed over the next 30 years, including as first assistant director on hit blockbuster movies such as *The Mummy* (1999) and its sequel *The Mummy Returns* (2001) and on numerous episodes of *Doctor Who* during Russell T Davies's time as showrunner. His first foray into producing came on the *Torchwood* mini-series 'Children of Earth' (2011). It was on the strength of this that he was chosen to be one of the producers on Series Five of *Doctor Who*. He has since returned to his more familiar first director role, including on the *Sherlock* episode 'The Hounds of Baskerville' (2012).

## PATRICK SCHWEITZER (PRODUCER)

Patrick Schweitzer started out in TV in 1995 as a location manager. Amongst the many shows he has worked on in that capacity are the BBC's *The Mrs Bradley Mysteries* (1998-2000), *The Inspector Lynley Mysteries* (2001-2002), *Silent Witness* (2002), *Spooks* (2003), *Hustle* (2004) and *Blackpool* (2004), and ITV's *Primeval* (2007). He gained his first *Doctor Who* credit on the 2006 Christmas special 'The Runaway Bride', which led to him working as production manager on a number of episodes

# CHAPTER SEVEN: PRINCIPAL CREATIVE TEAM

of Series Three. He then became a line producer, serving as such on *Spooks: Code 9* (BBC Three, 2008) and *Ashes to Ashes* (BBC One, 2009) before joining the team on Series Five of *Doctor Who*. He has since also been line producer on *The Hour* (BBC Two, 2011) and *Call the Midwife* (BBC One, 2012).

## SANNE WOHLENBERG (PRODUCER)

Sanne Wohlenberg was born in Germany in 1968. She produced her first TV shows in the UK in the early 2000s, when she was generally credited under her married name Sanne Craddick. These included episodes of the Northern Ireland-made BBC One series *Murphy's Law* (2003). More recently she has produced episodes of *Funland* (BBC Three, 2005), *The Whistleblowers* (ITV1, 2007) and *Wallander* (BBC One, 2010-2012), as well as of Series Five of *Doctor Who*

## LINDSEY ALFORD (SCRIPT EDITOR)

Lindsey Alford studied Psychology and Zoology and joined the BBC's Natural History Unit as a researcher on wildlife programming. She then transferred to BBC One's *Casualty*, progressing from researcher to storyliner to script editor over a period of several years. Moving to BBC Wales in 2006, she gained further script editor credits on *Doctor Who* ('Daleks in Manhattan'/'Evolution of the Daleks' (2007) and 'Human Nature'/'The Family of Blood' (2007)), the whole of the first series of *The Sarah Jane Adventures*, and the *Torchwood* episode 'Adrift' (2008). She then became the principal script editor on Series Four of *Doctor Who*, and has continued in that job since.

## BRIAN MINCHIN (SCRIPT EDITOR)

Brian Minchin was born in Aberystwyth, Wales, in 1987. He worked for several Welsh independent production companies and served as assistant producer or producer on a number of low-budget films, mainly for Sgrin Wales and ITV Wales, including *Down* (2003), which he also co-wrote, *Work in Progress* (2004) and *Dead Long Enough* (2005). He was script editor on BBC Wales's *Belonging* in 2005 before moving on to work in the same capacity on *Torchwood* Series One and Two in 2006 and 2007. He gained his first *Doctor Who* script editor credits on Series Four in 2008. He was assistant producer on the *Torchwood* mini-series 'Children of Earth' (2009) and UK producer of the follow-up 'Miracle Day' (2011). He also produced Series Four and Five of *The Sarah Jane Adventures* (2010-11).

## MARK GATISS (WRITER)

Mark Gatiss was born in 1966 in Sedgefield, County Durham. He was a *Doctor Who* fan from a young age. In the 1990s he authored a number of original novels based on the show for Virgin Publishing and BBC Books and scripted and acted in the *P.R.O.B.E.* series of independent video dramas from BBV featuring Caroline John as the Doctor's former companion Liz Shaw. Also in the same decade he got together with fellow performers Reece Shearsmith, Steve Pemberton and Jeremy Dyson to form the League of Gentlemen comedy team. They made their first stage

67

appearances in 1995, with Gatiss and Dyson writing most of their material. In 1997 they were given their own show on BBC Radio 4, and in 1999 this transferred to TV on BBC Two. Later they made the movie *The League of Gentlemen's Apocalypse* (2005). Throughout this period Gatiss gained many further credits both as a scriptwriter and as an actor. He contributed two stories – 'Phantasmagoria' (1999) and 'Invaders from Mars' (2002) – to Big Finish's range of audio *Doctor Who* dramas, and then scripted the TV episodes 'The Unquiet Dead' (2005) and 'The Idiot's Lantern' (2006). He also appeared in the show, as Professor Lazarus in 'The Lazarus Experiment' (2007). His other accomplishments included writing a trilogy of Simon and Schuster-published novels about a bisexual British secret agent called Lucifer Box: *The Vesuvius Club* (2004), *The Devil in Amber* (2006) and *Black Butterfly* (2008). He co-created and produced with Steven Moffat the BBC One show *Sherlock* (2010- ), and has written some of the episodes and appeared in the role of Mycroft Holmes. Series Five of *Doctor Who* marked his return to the show as a writer, after a script he drafted for Series Four, involving Nazis and the British Museum, was unused.

## TOBY WHITHOUSE (WRITER)

Toby Whithouse hails from Southend. He began his career as an actor, and had a regular role in the BBC One drama *The House of Eliott* (1991-1994). He also appeared in the theatre – including in a 1996-1997 Gene Wilder-starring production of *Laughter on the 23rd Floor* in London's West End – and worked as a stand-up comedian. Frustrated by what he saw as a lack of quality in the scripts he was being offered, he took to writing in his spare time. He gained his first TV commission on a 1999 episode of ITV's *Where the Heart Is*, and his play *Jump Mr Malinoff* was performed as the opening production at London's Soho Theatre in 2000, winning him that venue's annual Verity Bargate Award. He then became involved with the independent production company World Productions, and developed for them the successful Channel 4 hospital drama *No Angels* (2004-2006). He scripted the episode 'School Reunion' for Series Two of new-era *Doctor Who* and 'Greeks Bearing Gifts' for Series One of *Torchwood*, both transmitted in 2006. Perhaps his most notable achievement to date has been devising and writing the hit BBC Three supernatural drama show *Being Human* (2008- ), on which he also serves as executive producer. He still makes occasional appearances as an actor, but is now focused primarily on his writing career, which saw him script a further *Doctor Who* episode for Series Five.

## SIMON NYE (WRITER)

Simon Nye was born in 1958 in Burgess Hill, Sussex. He studied French and German at London's Bedford College, and his first professional writing work was translating a number of foreign-language books into English in the late 1980s. He then authored two original novels, *Men Behaving Badly* (1989) and *Wideboy* (1991). He was asked by producer Beryl Vertue (later to become Steven Moffat's mother-in-law) to adapt the first of these into the TV show of the same title, which debuted on ITV in 1992 and then transferred to BBC One from its third series, eventually ending in 1998 after a very successful run. Nye also adapted *Wideboy* for ITV, as

*Frank Stubbs Promotes* (1993-1994). Other popular comedy shows he has written include *Is it Legal?* (ITV, 1995-1997; Channel 4, 1998), *Wild West* (BBC One, 2002-2004), and *Reggie Perrin* (BBC One, 2009-2010). His episode 'Amy's Choice' for Series Five of *Doctor Who* was a rare foray into drama.

## CHRIS CHIBNALL (WRITER)

Chris Chibnall was raised in Lancashire and began his TV career as a football archivist and occasional floor manager for Sky Sports. He then took a succession of administrative jobs with different theatre companies including, between 1996 and 1999, the experimental group Complicite. He subsequently became a full-time writer, initially for the theatre, with credits including *Gaffer!* – a single-actor piece about homophobia in football, first staged in 1999 – and *Kiss Me Like You Mean It* – which premiered at the Soho Theatre in 2001 and has also been staged in a number of European venues, including Paris under the title *Un Baiser, Un Vrai*. On the strength of his play scripts, he was invited by the BBC to develop a period drama series for them. This became *Born and Bred* (2002-2005), which he not only created but also contributed to as consultant producer and lead writer throughout its four seasons. His other TV writing credits include episodes of *All About George* (2005) and *Life on Mars* (2006). During 2005, he was charged with developing the fantasy show *Merlin* for BBC One, but this was ultimately farmed out to the independent company Shine Productions. He was lead writer on Series One and Two of *Torchwood* in 2006 and 2007, and in the latter year also gained his first *Doctor Who* script credit on the Series Three episode '42'. He became showrunner on the first series of the ITV1 show *Law and Order: UK* (2008), helped Russell T Davies to storyline the *Torchwood* mini-series 'Miracle Day' (2011) and then took on the showrunner role on the Starz historical fantasy drama *Camelot* (2011).

## GARETH ROBERTS (WRITER)

Gareth Roberts was born in 1968. He studied drama at college and worked as a clerk at the Court of Appeal while also pursuing an interest in writing. In the 1990s he authored seven acclaimed *Doctor Who* novels, plus novelisations of two episodes of *Cracker* (ITV, 1993-1996), for Virgin Publishing. He also wrote for *Doctor Who Magazine* and for Big Finish's tie-in audio CD drama range. After *Doctor Who* returned to TV, he wrote the digital mini-adventure 'Attack of the Graske' (2005) and the 'Tardisode' teasers for Series Two before scripting three episodes during Russell T Davies's time as showrunner: 'The Shakespeare Code' (2007), 'The Unicorn and the Wasp' (2008) and (with Davies) 'Planet of the Dead' (2009). He has written the new series novels *Only Human* (BBC Books, 2005) and *I Am A Dalek* (BBC Books, 2006) and several *Doctor Who* short stories, plus the novelisation *Shada* (BBC Books, 2012) based on Douglas Adams' scripts for the abandoned 1980 TV story. In addition, he scripted numerous episodes of *The Sarah Jane Adventures*. His other TV credits include: storylines for *Springhill* (Sky One, 1996-1997); episodes of *Emmerdale* (ITV1, 1972- ) in 1998; episodes of *Brookside* (Channel 4, 1982-2003) over a four year period from 1999; and co-written episodes of *Randall and Hopkirk (Deceased)* (BBC One, 2000-2001) and *Swiss Toni* (BBC Three, 2004-2004).

## RICHARD CURTIS (WRITER)

Richard Curtis was born in 1956 in Wellington, New Zealand. He has lived in England since the age of 11, and gained a first class honours degree in English Language and Literature from Christ Church, Oxford. It was while at Oxford that he met Rowan Atkinson, with whom he then appeared in a show at the Edinburgh Festival Fringe and scripted a BBC Radio 3 series entitled *The Atkinson People* (1979). This led on to him becoming a frequent scriptwriter for radio and TV comedy shows, including notably BBC Two's *Not the Nine O'Clock News* (1979-1982), for which he also composed humorous songs. With Atkinson and later Ben Elton he wrote BBC One's hugely popular *Blackadder* (1983-1989), in which Atkinson starred. In 1985 he founded the Comic Relief charity, which is the subject of an annual BBC One telethon. A further successful collaboration with Rowan Atkinson came on the latter's ITV show *Mr Bean* (1990-1995). In addition, he co-created and wrote for the multiple-award-winning BBC One show *The Vicar of Dibley* (1994-2007), starring Dawn French. By this point, he had also broken into writing feature films, beginning with *The Tall Guy* (1989). Two of his biggest successes were *Four Weddings and a Funeral* (1994) and *Notting Hill* (1999), both of which broke the record for the highest-grossing British movie ever. Further hits were *Bridget Jones's Diary* (2001); *Love Actually* (2003), which he not only wrote but also directed; and the multi-award-winning BBC/HBO TV movie *The Girl in the Café* (2005). Another charitable venture came with Make Poverty History, which he founded in 2005. In 2007 he was presented with the BAFTA Fellowship Award in recognition of both his screen successes and his charity work. *The Boat that Rocked* (2009) was his second movie as both writer and director, but was less well-received than his earlier work. He went on to write the final draft of the script for the Steven Spielberg-directed *War Horse* (2011). His Series Five *Doctor Who* episode, 'Amy's Choice', was only his second script contribution to an ongoing drama show, following a 2007 episode of BBC One's *Casualty*.

## ADAM SMITH (DIRECTOR)

Adam Smith's first notable credits as a TV director came on several episodes of the first series of Channel 4's *Skins* in 2007. He then directed a 2008 BBC dramatisation of Dickens' *Little Dorrit*, which featured former *Doctor Who* regular Freema Agyeman and future regular Arthur Darvill. He followed this up with his three episodes for Series Five of *Doctor Who*. He has also directed numerous music videos for bands including the Chemical Brothers and the Streets.

## ANDREW GUNN (DIRECTOR)

Andrew Gunn was born in Staffordshire and grew up on Tyneside. He attended film school in Surrey and Dorset, and his graduation film, *Mermaids*, won the Young Filmmaker award at the Tyneside International Film Festival of 1987. He then made several more short films, mostly shot in and around Newcastle upon Tyne, two of which, *Café au Lait* (1994) and *Half a Shave* (1996), won Royal Television Society commendations, with the latter also gaining a Certificate of Merit at the Chicago International Film Festival. Gunn worked as a focus puller for a number of years while trying to break into directing mainstream film and TV projects. In 2004 he was involved in setting up and formulating the style of the Channel 4 comedy-drama series *Green Wing*, and was an uncredited director on certain sequences in its first episode. He then gained notable credits on two episodes of BBC One's *Life on Mars* (2007) and two of Channel 4's *Cape Wrath* (2007). The following year he directed for BBC One the dramatisation of David Almond's novel *Clay* and the first two episodes of the remake of Terry Nation's *Survivors*, and for ITV1 two episodes of *Primeval*. Since his two episodes for Series Five of *Doctor Who*, he has gained further directorial credits on BBC One's *Waterloo Road* (2011) and ITV1's *Wild at Heart* (2012).

## JONNY CAMPBELL (DIRECTOR)

Jonny Campbell – usually credited during the early part of his career as Jonathan Campbell – started out as a researcher on the ITV magazine show *This Morning*. He then turned to directing, initially on some documentary projects. He got his first real break on the short film *Two Minutes* (1996), an introductory vehicle for comic actor Peter Kay that was transmitted in a number of ITV regions. This led on to assignments later the same decade directing episodes of shows such as Sky's *Dream Team* and ITV's *The Bill* and *Peak Practice*. Campbell then reunited with Peter Kay to direct the whole of the first series of the latter's Channel 4 sitcom *Phoenix Nights* (2001). Numerous further directing credits followed, on shows such as *Judge John Deed* (BBC One, 2001-2002), *Born and Bred* (BBC One, 2002), *Spooks* (BBC One, 2004) and *Ashes to Ashes* (BBC One, 2008). A notable success came on the award-winning Channel 4 sitcom *Shameless*, for which he directed some key early episodes, including the Christmas special that opened the second series, in 2004. He made his debut as a feature film director on the Ant and Dec-starring *Alien Autopsy* (2006). After his two episodes for Series Five of *Doctor Who*, he directed the acclaimed BBC Two drama *Eric and Ernie*, transmitted on New Year's Day 2011. He has also directed numerous TV commercials, for brands including Sainsbury's, Knorr, Irn-Bru and Morrisons.

## CATHERINE MORSHEAD (DIRECTOR)

Catherine Morshead worked from 1984 to 1991 as a researcher and occasional producer for Yorkshire TV current affairs programmes, including *Seven Days*, *Write On* and *First Tuesday*. This led on to her becoming a staff director at the same company, handling episodes of a number of ITV shows, including *Emmerdale* (1991) and *Haggard* (1992). She then went freelance, and amongst the may shows for which she directed were: *Heartbeat* (ITV, 1994), *Casualty* (BBC One, 1994-1996), *The Bill* (ITV, 1995-1998), *Silent Witness* (BBC One, 1997), *Playing the Field* (BBC One, 1998), *Cutting It* (BBC One, 2002-2004), *Shameless* (Channel 4, 2006), *Mutual Friends* (BBC One, 2008), *Ashes to Ashes* (BBC One, 2008), *Silk* (BBC One, 2011), *Above Suspicion: Silent Scream* (ITV1, 2012) and *The Hour* (BBC Two, 2012). Her two Series Five episodes, 'Amy's Choice' and 'The Lodger', were her first *Doctor Who* credits.

CRACKS IN TIME

## ASHLEY WAY (DIRECTOR)

Ashley Way was born in Cardiff in 1971. He started working as an assistant director on a number of largely-Welsh-based film projects. These included *The Proposition* (1997), *Hooded Angels* (2000) and *Berserker* (2001) and a series of fantasy-orientated subjects directed by David Lister: *The Fairy King of Ar* (1998), *Dazzle* (1999), *The Meeksville Ghost* (2001), *Askari* (2001) – for which he also co-wrote the script and acted as associate producer – and *The Sorcerer's Apprentice* (2002). He wrote and directed the 2003 movie *Hoodlum and Son*. His TV credits include the South African-produced children's puppet series *Filligoggin* (2000) (co-directed with David Lister) and episodes of *Belonging* (BBC Wales, 2000- ) and *Casualty* (BBC One, 2005-2006). His first contact with the *Doctor Who* world came when he directed the digital mini-adventure 'Attack of the Graske' (2005). He then went on to direct the 13 online 'Tardisode' teasers for Series Two. He directed six episodes across *Torchwood*'s Series One (2007) and Series Two (2008) and four across *The Sarah Jane Adventures*' Series Four (2010) and Series Five (2011). 'The Hungry Earth'/'Cold Blood' was his first directorial assignment for *Doctor Who* itself.

## TOBY HAYNES (DIRECTOR)

Toby Haynes is a graduate of the National Film and Television School. He gained his first TV directing credit on a 2004 episode of *Coming Up*, a Channel 4 strand showcasing the work of newcomers to the industry. He went on to direct episodes of, amongst others, *Hollyoaks* (Channel 4, 2007), *M.I. High* (CBBC, 2007-2008), *Spooks: Code 9* (BBC Three, 2008), *Being Human* (BBC Three, 2009) and *Five Days* (BBC One, 2010). Since directing his Series Five episodes and 'A Christmas Carol' for *Doctor Who* – of which he is a long-time fan – he has handled an episode of *Wallander* (BBC One, 2012) and the *Sherlock* instalment 'The Reichenbach Fall' (BBC One, 2012).

## EDWARD THOMAS (PRODUCTION DESIGNER)

Edward Thomas took a foundation course in art and design after leaving school, and then studied at the Wimbledon School of Art, from which he graduated with a BA (Hons) degree in 3D Design, specialising in theatre. He began his career as a designer on a wide variety of commercials and a number of theatrical productions, including *Turandot* for the Royal Opera Company at Wembley Arena, *Under Milk Wood* for the Dylan Thomas Theatre Company and Shakespeare's *Twelfth Night* and *Cymbeline* for the Ludlow Festival. This was followed by work on numerous feature films, including over a dozen South African productions in the early 1990s and *The Mystery of Edwin Drood* (1993), *Resurrection Man* (1998), *Darkness Falls* (1999) and *The Meeksville Ghost* (2001). He also gained credits on a wide range of TV shows including, for BBC Wales, *Jones, The Coal Project* and, of course, *Doctor Who* (2005- ), *Torchwood* (2006- ) and *The Sarah Jane Adventures* (2007-2011). He has sometimes been credited as Edward Alan Thomas or simply as Ed Thomas. He left *Doctor Who* toward the end of production on Series Five to be production designer on the new BBC One science fiction drama *Outcasts* (2011).

# PART THREE
# CREDITS

# DOCTOR WHO

CREDITS[14]

Producer: Tracie Simpson (5.01, 5.04, 5.05, 5.06, 5.07, 5.10, 5.11), Peter Bennett (5.02, 5.03, 5.08, 5.09, 5.12, 5.13), Patrick Schweitzer (5.06, 5.10), Sanne Wohlenberg (6.00)

MAIN CAST

Matt Smith (The Doctor)
Karen Gillan (Amy Pond)
Arthur Darvill (Rory Williams) (all except 5.02, 5.03, 5.04, 5.05, 5.10, 5.11)
Alex Kingston (River Song) (5.04. 5.05, 5.12, 5.13)

PRODUCTION TEAM

1st Assistant Director: John Bennett (5.01, 5.06, 5.10), Steve Robinson (5.02, 5.03), Dan Mumford (5.04, 5.05), Kiaran Murray-Smith (5.07, 5.11), Marcus Catlin (5.08, 5.09, 5.12, 5.13), Mick Pantaleo (6.00)
2nd Assistant Director: James DeHaviland
3rd Assistant Director: Heddi-Joy Taylor-Welch
Assistant Director: Janine H Jones (6.00), Michael Curtis (6.00)
Runner: Nicola Eynon Price (all except 6.00), Laura Jenkins (all except 6.00)
Location Manager: Gareth Skelding (all except 6.00), Paul Davies (5.01, 5.02, 5.03, 5.04, 5.05), Christian Reynish (5.08, 5.09), Iwan Roberts (6.00)
Unit Manager: Rhys Griffiths
Assistant Unit Manager: Geraint Williams (5.02, 5.03)
Production Manager: Holly Pullinger (5.01, 5.04, 5.05, 5.06, 5.10), Steffan Morris (5.02, 5.03, 5.08, 5.09, 5.12, 5.13, 6.00)
Production Co-Ordinator: Jess Van Niekerk (all except 5.04, 6.00), Claire Hildred (6.00)
Assistant Production Co-Ordinator: Helen Blyth (6.00)
Production Management Asst: Claire Thomas (all except 6.00)
Production Runner: Sian Warrilow (all except 6.00)
Production Secretary: Scott Handcock (6.00)
Production Assistant: Charlie Coombes (6.00)
Asst Production Accountant: Carole Wakefield (all except 6.00), Rhys Evans (6.00)
Script Editor[15]: Lindsey Alford (5.01, 5.04, 5.05, 5.08, 5.09, 5.11, 5.12, 5.13, 6.00), Brian Minchin (5.02, 5.03, 5.06, 5.07, 5.10)

---

[14] Where an episode number (or more than one) appears in brackets after a person's name in the listing, this means that they were credited only on the episode (or episodes) indicated. Otherwise, the person concerned was credited on all episodes. Some production roles were credited only on certain episodes. The 2010 Christmas special, 'A Christmas Carol', is denoted as 6.00, as it was effectively made at the start of production on Series Six.
[15] Role credited on 6.00 as 'Script Executive'.

CRACKS IN TIME

Script Supervisor: Phillip Trow (6.00)
Continuity: Non Eleri Hughes (all except 6.00)
Camera Operator: Joe Russell (5.01, 5.04, 5.05), Martin Stephens (5.02, 5.03), Ian Adrian (5.06, 5.08, 5.09, 5.10), Richard Stoddard (5.07, 5.11), Rob Arrowsmith (5.12, 5.13, 6.00[16])
B Camera Operator: Matthew Poynter (5.06, 5.07, 5.10), Ian Adrian (5.11)
Focus Puller: Steve Rees, Matthew Poynter (5.01, 5.08, 5.09, 5.11, 5.12, 5.13), Shirley Schumacher (5.02, 5.03), Anna James (5.04, 5.05), Simon Walton (6.00)
Grip: John Robinson (all except 6.00), Gary Norman (6.00)
Camera Assistant: Tom Hartley (all except 6.00), Jon Vidgen (all except 6.00), Simon Ridge (6.00), Svetlana Miko (6.00)
Camera Trainee: Darren Chesney (5.07, 5.08, 5.11, 5.12, 5.13)
Boom Operator: Dafydd Parry (all except 6.00), Laura Coates (6.00)
Sound Maintenance Engineer: Jeff Welch (all except 6.00), Dafydd Parry (6.00)
Gaffer: Mark Hutchings
Best Boy: Pete Chester
Electrician: Ben Griffiths, Steve Slocombe (all except 6.00), Bob Milton, Alan Tippets (all except 6.00), Gareth Sheldon (6.00), Peter Scott (6.00)
Stunt Co-Ordinator: Crispin Layfield
Stunt Performer: Stewart James (5.03), Gordon Seed (5.06, 5.07, 6.00), Belinda McGinley (5.07), Dani Biernat (5.07), Helen Steinway-Bailey (5.07)
Supervising Art Director[17]: Stephen Nicholas
Assistant Art Director: Jackson Pope (5.07, 5.11)
Associate Designer: James North (all except 5.07, 5.11, 6.00)
Art Department Co-Ordinator: Amy Pope/Amy Oakes/Amy Pope Oakes[18] (all except 5.01, 6.00)
Production Buyer: Ben Morris
Set Decorator: Keith Dunne (5.01, 5.06, 5.07, 5.10, 5.11), Arwel Wyn Jones (5.02, 5.03), Julian Luxton (5.04, 5.05, 5.08, 5.09, 5.12, 5.13, 6.00)
Props Buyer: Sue Jackson Potter (5.01), Catherine Samuel (5.02, 5.03, 5.06, 5.07, 5.10, 5.11), Adrian Anscombe (5.04, 5.05, 5.08, 5.09, 5.12, 5.13, 6.00)
Standby Art Director: Ciaran Thompson (5.01, 5.04, 5.05, 5.12, 5.13, 6.00), Dafydd Shurmer (5.02, 5.03), Tristan Peatfield (5.06, 5.10), Ellen Woods (5.07, 5.11), Arwel Wyn Jones (5.08, 5.09)
Set Designer: Rhys Jarman (5.01, 5.08, 5.09), Ben Austin (5.02, 5.03, 5.04, 5.05, 5.06, 5.10, 5.12, 5.13), Al Roberts (5.07, 5.11)
Storyboard Artist: James Iles (5.01, 5.06, 5.07, 5.08, 5.09, 5.10, 5.11, 5.12, 5.13), Rod Knipping (5.02, 5.03, 6.00), Matthew Savage (5.04, 5.05)
Concept Artist: Richard Shaun Williams, Peter McKinstry (all except 6.00)
Graphic Artist: Jackson Pope (all except 5.07, 5.11, 6.00), Christina Tom (6.00)
Model Maker: Julia Jones (6.00)
Petty Cash Buyer: Kate Wilson (6.00)
Standby Props: Phill Shellard (all except 6.00), Tom Evans (all except 6.00), Silas

---

[16] Credited on 6.00 as 'Robert Arrowsmith'.
[17] Role credited as 'Art Director' on 6.00.
[18] Credited as 'Amy Pope' on episodes up to 5.05, as 'Amy Oakes' on 5.06, 5.07, 5.10, 5.11, 5.12 and 5.13 and as 'Amy Pope Oakes' on 5.08 and 5.09.

Williams (6.00), Katherine Archer (6.00)
Standby Carpenter: Will Pope (all except 6.00), Justin Williams (6.00)
Standby Rigger: Keith Freeman (all except 6.00), Bryan Griffiths (6.00)
Standby Painter: Ellen Woods (5.01, 5.02, 5.03, 5.04, 5.05, 5.06, 5.08, 5.09, 5.10), Clive Clarke (5.07, 5.11), Kate Meyrick (5.12, 5.13), Helen Atherton (6.00)
Store Person: Jayne Davies (6.00)
Props Master: Paul Aitken
Props Chargehand: Matt Wild (all except 5.09, 6.00)
Dressing Props: Martin Broadbent (all except 6.00), Rhys Jones (5.01, 5.02, 5.03, 5.04, 5.05, 5.06, 5.08, 5.09, 5.10), Philip Everett-Lyons (5.07, 5.11, 5.12, 5.13), Stuart Mackay (6.00), Kristian Wilsher (6.00)
Art Department Driver: Tom Belton (5.07, 5.11, 5.12, 5.13)
Props Fabrication Manager: Barry Jones (5.07, 5.09, 5.10, 5.11, 5.12, 5.13)
Props Makers: Penny Howarth, Nicholas Robatto
Props Driver: Medard Mankos (6.00)
Practical Electrician: Albert James
Construction Manager: Matthew Hywel-Davies
Construction Chargehand: Scott Fisher
Construction Workshop Manager[19]: Mark Hill (5.06, 5.07, 5.11, 5.12, 5.13)
Scenic Artist: John Pinkerton (5.01, 5.03, 5.04, 5.05, 5.06, 5.07, 5.10, 5.11, 5.12, 5.13), John Whalley (5.01, 5.03, 5.04, 5.05, 5.06, 5.07, 5.10, 5.11, 5.12, 5.13)
Graphics: BBC Wales Graphics
Title Sequence: Framestore (all except 6.00)
Roaming Eye SFX Directors: Anthony Dickenson (5.01), Dan Lowe (5.01)
Assistant Costume Designer: Samantha Keeble (6.00)
Costume Supervisor: Bobbie Peach (5.01, 5.04, 5.05, 5.06, 5.07, 5.10, 5.11, 6.00), Lindsay Bonaccorsi (5.02, 5.03, 5.08, 5.09, 5.12, 5.13)
Crowd Supervisor: Lindsay Bonaccorsi[20] (5.06, 5.10)
Costume Assistant: Sara Morgan (all except 6.00), Maria Franchi (all except 6.00), Jason Gill (6.00), Yasemin Kascioglu (6.00)
Costume Trainee: Nikki Lightfoot (5.07, 5.08, 5.11, 5.12, 5.13)
Make-Up Supervisor: Pam Mullins
Make-Up Artist: Abi Brotherton (all except 6.00), Morag Smith (all except 6.00), Allison Sing (6.00), Vivienne Simpson (6.00)
Unit Driver: Sean Evans (5.11, 5.12, 5.13), Wayne Humphreys (5.11, 5.12, 5.13), Darren Crowlegroves (5.11, 5.12, 5.13)
Thanks To: Temple Clark & Alastair Siddons (5.01)
Casting Associate: Andy Brierley (all except 5.07, 5.11, 6.00), Alice Purser (5.01, 5.02, 5.03, 5.04, 5.05, 5.06, 5.08, 5.09, 5.10, 6.00)
Assistant Editor: Cat Gregory (5.01, 5.02, 5.03, 5.04, 5.05), Becky Trotman (5.06, 5.07, 5.08, 5.09, 5.10, 5.11, 5.12, 5.13, 6.00)
VFX Editor: Ceres Doyle (5.01, 5.02, 5.03, 5.04, 5.05), Cat Gregory (5.06, 5.07, 5.08, 5.09, 5.10, 5.11, 5.12, 5.13, 6.00)
Senior Visual Effects Artist: Craig Higgins (6.00)
Post Production Supervisor: Samantha Hall (5.02, 5.03, 5.04, 5.05), Chris Blatchford

---

[19] Role credited as just 'Workshop Manager' on 5.06.
[20] Surname misspelt as 'Bonacorssi'.

(all except 5.01, 5.07, 6.00), Ceres Doyle (5.06, 5.07, 5.08, 5.09, 5.10, 5.13), Nerys Davies (5.07, 5.11, 5.12, 6.00)
Post Prod Co-Ordinator: Marie Brown
Dubbing Mixer: Tim Ricketts
Supervising Sound Editor[21]: Paul McFadden
Dialogue Editor: Matthew Cox (5.07), Darran Clement (5.08, 5.09, 5.11)
Sound Effects Editor: Paul Jefferies
Foley Editor: Helen Dickson (5.01, 5.02, 5.03, 5.04, 5.05, 5.06, 5.09, 5.10), Jamie Talbutt (6.00)
Colourist: Mick Vincent (all except 5.07, 5.08, 5.11), Jon Everett (5.07, 5.08, 5.11)
On-Line Conform: Matthew Clarke (5.01, 5.02, 5.03, 5.04, 5.05, 5.06, 5.08, 5.09, 5.10), Mark Bright (all except 5.07, 5.11), Geraint Parri Huws (5.07, 5.11), Jeremy Lott (5.07, 5.11)
Lead 3D Artist: Matt Mckinney (5.12, 5.13)
Lead Animator: Neil Roche (5.12, 5.13)
3D Artist: Jeff North (5.12, 5.13), Darren Byford (5.12, 5.13), Wayde Duncan-Smith (5.12, 5.13), Adrian Bell (5.12), David Jones (5.12), Ruth Bailey (5.12, 5.13), Serena Cacciato (5.12, 5.13), Andy Guest (5.12, 5.13), Dominic Anderson (5.12, 5.13), Nick Bell (5.12, 5.13), Zahra Al Nabib (5.12), Nick Webber (5.13)
Lead Digital Matte Painter: Simon Wicker (5.12, 5.13)
Digital Matte Painter: Ron Bowman (5.12, 5.13), Alex Fort (5.12, 5.13), Charlie Bennet (5.12, 5.13)
2D Supervisor: Izzy Barber (5.12, 5.13)
Compositors: Greg Spencer (5.12, 5.13), Joe Courtis (5.12, 5.13), Arianna Lago (5.12, 5.13), Bryan Bartlett (5.12[22], 5.13), James Moxon (5.12, 5.13), Lyndall Spagonletti (5.12, 5.13), Grainne Freeman (5.12, 5.13), Tim Barter (5.12, 5.13), Rosemary Chester (5.12, 5.13), Frank Hana (5.12, 5.13), James Etherington (5.13), Sarah Bennett (5.13)
VFX Co-ordinator: Alex Fitzgerald (5.12, 5.13), Lorna Dumba (5.12, 5.13)

With Thanks To: The BBC National Orchestra of Wales
Conducted and Orchestrated by Ben Foster (5.07, 5.08, 5.11, 5.12, 5.13, 6.00)
Mixed by Jake Jackson (5.07, 5.08, 5.11, 5.12, 5.13, 6.00)
Recorded by Gerry O'Riordan (5.07, 5.08, 5.11, 5.12, 5.13, 6.00)

With Special Thanks To: Nikki Wilson (5.01)
With Thanks To: Martha Freud (5.10)
Script Editor: Emma Freud (5.10)

Original Theme Music: Ron Grainer
Casting Director: Andy Pryor CDG
Production Executive: Julie Scott
Production Accountant: Ceri Tothill (all except 6.00), Dyfed Thomas (6.00)
Sound Recordist: Bryn Thomas
Costume Designer: Ray Holman (all except 6.00), Barbara Kidd (6.00)
Make-Up Designer: Barbara Southcott

---

[21] Role credited as 'Sound Supervisor' on 5.07, 5.08, 5.09, 5.11, 5.12, 5.13, 6.00.
[22] Credited twice on this episode in the same capacity.

CREDITS

Visual Effects: The Mill (all except 5.05, 5.07, 5.11, 5.12, 5.13), BBC Wales Graphic Design (5.07, 5.11)
On-set Visual FX Supervisor: Dave Houghton (5.12, 5.13)
Executive Visual FX Producer: Will Cohen (5.12, 5.13)
Visual FX Producer[23]: Jenna Powell (5.12, 5.13), Beewan Athwal (6.00)
Special Effects: Real SFX (all except 5.07)
Prosthetics: Millennium FX (all except 5.01, 5.07, 5.10, 5.11)
Music: Murray Gold
Editor: Jamie Pearson (5.01, 5.06, 5.07, 5.10, 5.11), John Richards (5.02, 5.03), Will Oswald (5.04, 5.05), David Barrett (5.08, 5.09), Mat Newman (5.12, 5.13), Adam Recht (6.00)
Additional Editing: Mat Newman (5.02)
Production Designer: Edward Thomas (all except 5.07, 5.11, 6.00), Tristan Peatfield (5.07, 5.11), Michael Pickwoad (6.00)
Director of Photography: Owen McPolin (5.01), Graham Frake (5.02, 5.03), Damian Bromley (5.04, 5.05), Tony Slater Ling (5.06, 5.10), Erik Wilson (5.07), Mark Waters (5.08, 5.09), Simon Archer (5.11), Stephan Pehrsson (5.12, 5.13, 6.00)
Line Producer: Patrick Schweitzer (all except 6.00), Diana Barton (6.00)

Executive Producer: Steven Moffat, Piers Wenger, Beth Willis

BBC Wales

---

[23] Role credited as 'VFX Producer' on 6.00.

# PART FOUR
# EPISODE GUIDE

The durations quoted in the episode guide below are for the transmitted versions of the episodes, complete with the 'Coming Soon'/'Next Time' trailers that were edited out of the DVD and Blu-Ray releases.

Readers who have yet to see the episodes may wish to bear in mind that this guide is a comprehensive one that contains many plot 'spoilers'.

# 5.01 – THE ELEVENTH HOUR

Writer: Steven Moffat
Director: Adam Smith

<u>DEBUT TRANSMISSION DETAILS</u>

BBC One/BBC HD
Date: 3 April 2010. Scheduled time: 6.20 pm. Actual time: 6.22 pm.

Duration: 64′ 34″

<u>ADDITIONAL CREDITED CAST</u>

Caitlin Blackwood (Amelia Pond), Nina Wadia (Dr Ramsden), Marcello Magni (Barney Collins), Perry Benson (Ice Cream Man), Annette Crosbie (Mrs Angelo), Tom Hopper (Jeff), Arthur Cox (Mr Henderson), Olivia Coleman (Mother), Eden Monteath (Child 1), Merin Monteath (Child 2), David de Keyser (Atraxi Voice), William Wilde (Prisoner Zero Voice), Patrick Moore (Himself).

<u>PLOT</u>

The TARDIS crash-lands in the garden of a house in Leadworth, England, where the newly-regenerated eleventh Doctor meets a young girl, Amelia Pond. Amelia is scared by a crack in her bedroom wall, and the Doctor realises it is actually a crack in the universe. A shapeshifting alien criminal known as Prisoner Zero has escaped through the crack into Amelia's house, where he is hiding from his Atraxi captors. The Doctor has to take a flight in the damaged TARDIS in order to stabilise its engines, and when he returns, it is 12 years later, and Amelia has grown into the adult Amy. The Atraxi hover above Earth in their spaceships and threaten to incinerate the planet if Prisoner Zero does not vacate it. Prisoner Zero attempts to elude his pursuers by taking on the forms of coma patients in a nearby hospital where Amy's 'kind of' boyfriend, Rory Williams, works as a nurse. The Doctor uses a computer virus to draw attention to Prisoner Zero, and the Atraxi recapture him and leave.

<u>QUOTE, UNQUOTE</u>

- **Doctor:** 'You're Scottish; fry something.'
- **Doctor:** 'If you knocked this wall down, the crack would stay put, because the crack isn't in the wall.'
  **Amelia:** 'Where is it then?'
  **Doctor:** 'Everywhere. In everything. It's a split in the skin of the world. Two parts of space and time that should never have touched, pressed together,

right here in the wall of your bedroom.'

- **Amy:** 'You're worse than my aunt!'
  **Doctor:** 'I'm the Doctor; I'm worse than everybody's aunt! And that is not how I'm introducing myself.'
- **Doctor:** '*Who da man?* … Oh, I'm never saying that again.'
- **Prisoner Zero**: 'Poor Amy Pond. Still such a child inside. Dreaming of the magic Doctor she knows will return to save her. What a disappointment you've been.'
- **Doctor:** 'Bow ties are cool.'

## CONTINUITY POINTS

- The Doctor, as usual, takes time to recover fully from his regeneration. He is initially somewhat disorientated; he expels some 'regeneration energy' from his mouth; and on this occasion his taste buds are also affected, causing him to be uncertain about which foods he likes.
- As Amy's 'present' year is revealed in later episodes to be 2010, the chronology of the Doctor's encounters with her in 'The Eleventh Hour' appears to be as follow:

  o Easter 1996: The Doctor meets young Amelia in her garden, and goes indoors to examine the crack in her bedroom wall. Amelia is seven years old (as revealed in the next episode, 'The Beast Below'), so she was born in 1988 or 1989.
  o 2008: The Doctor returns, 12 years late, and thwarts the escape of Prisoner Zero.
  o 2010: The Doctor returns again, after taking the TARDIS on a 'test flight' to the moon and back, and invites Amy to join him on his travels.

- Leadworth is half an hour's car journey from Gloucester, the nearest city.
- Prisoner Zero knows the origin of the cracks in the universe, and seems surprised that the Doctor doesn't, telling him 'The Pandorica will open. Silence will fall'.
- After being damaged by the energy of the Doctor's regeneration at the conclusion of 'The End of Time' Part Two, the TARDIS gradually repairs itself, adopting a slightly different police box exterior, with a brighter shade of blue, and reconfiguring its interior into a modified design. The TARDIS key materialises in the pocket of the Doctor's newly acquired jacket, and the control console produces a new sonic screwdriver, also of a modified design, to replace the old one destroyed during the course of the action.

## PRODUCTION NOTES

- 'The Eleventh Hour' was made as Block Three of Series Five's production schedule.
- Studio recording for this episode was done at the show's usual Upper Boat studios on Treforest Industrial Estate, Pontypridd, on 24 and 25 September and

18 November 2009, and consisted principally of TARDIS interior scenes. The main location recording took place between 26 September and 19 October 2009. First to be done were the shots of the Royal Leadworth Hospital exterior, actually St Cadoc's Hospital in Caerleon, Gwent, and of the Doctor's approach in the fire engine. The roof of the Dupont factory on Mamhilad Park Industrial Estate doubled for the roof of the hospital on 28 September. The following day, the crew relocated to Llandaff in Cardiff, which was used as the location for Leadworth. The Vicarage in Rhymney, Gwent, was transformed into Amy's house, both exteriors and interiors being taped there on 30 September, 8-10 October and 12-15 October. Abertillery Hospital was the venue for recording of the hospital interiors on 1, 16 and 19 October. An extra, pick-up day was done on 20 November on the Cathedral Green in Llandaff for retakes of some of the village green action.

- The opening, pre-titles sequence of the Doctor hanging from the TARDIS doorway as the ship careers over London was produced by Nikki Wilson and directed by Johnny Campbell during production of the later episode 'The Vampires of Venice'. The aerial shots of London were taped on 1 January 2010, and the TARDIS interiors 11 days later.

- The new opening and closing title sequences for Series Five were created to a tight schedule and completed relatively late in the production process. The new theme music arrangement was also still being worked on at a late stage; the opening music was adjusted just prior to transmission of 'The Eleventh Hour' to add 'thunderclaps' coinciding with the lightning bolts seen in the visuals. An earlier version without this adjustment was included, apparently in error, on the episode's initial 'vanilla' DVD release in June 2010; the only place where this version can be found. Following transmission of 'The Eleventh Hour', the opening music was again remixed, both to tone down the 'thunderclaps' and to try to give the sequence more impact, and this new version was used for all subsequent Series Five episodes, plus the version of 'The Eleventh Hour' on the Complete Fifth Series DVD/Blu-Ray set.

- Steven Moffat wrote his script for this episode before Russell T Davies wrote his for the tenth Doctor's swansong, 'The End of Time'. He liaised with Davies to ensure continuity across the two stories.

- The idea of the sinister crack in the universe was inspired by a crack in the bedroom wall of Moffat's son Louis. The Doctor requesting, and then rejecting, various different foods from young Amelia was based on a story involving Tigger in A A Milne's classic children's book *The House at Pooh Corner* (1928).

- Although this was the first Adam Smith-directed *Doctor Who* episode to be screened, he had previously been responsible for 'The Time of Angels'/'Flesh and Stone', which would be transmitted as the fourth and fifth episodes of Series Five.

- Monsters featured in the montage of clips toward the end of the episode are Cybermen (from 'Rise of the Cybermen'), Daleks ('Doomsday'), the Empress of the Racnoss ('The Runaway Bride'), Ood ('The Satan Pit'), a Sycorax ('The Christmas Invasion'), a Sontaran ('The Sontaran Experiment'), a Sea Devil ('The Sea Devils'), a Reaper ('Father's Day'), Hath ('The Doctor's Daughter').

- A new TARDIS police box was constructed for the eleventh Doctor's era and is seen for the first time in this episode, after the ship repairs itself. (The earlier

scenes feature the old police box prop.)
- Before the closing titles, there is a 'Coming Soon' teaser of clips for the remaining episodes of Series Five, lasting almost two minutes. (This was edited out of the episode for the DVD releases, as were all the 'Next Time' teasers on the subsequent episodes.)

## OOPS!

- In the opening sequence of the Doctor hanging out of the TARDIS door, holding on by his fingertips, in some shots the door frame has a ledge, in others in doesn't.
- In the 2008 scenes, Rory's hospital identity badge states that it was 'Issued 30/11/1990' – almost 18 years earlier. (Perhaps his date of birth was mistakenly entered into the 'Issued' field on the badge? If so, this would make him a year or two younger than Amy.)
- The Doctor states that the mathematician Fermat was killed in a duel. This is incorrect (at least, in our universe – possibly the circumstances of his death were different in the *Doctor Who* universe!).
- In the scene on the hospital rooftop, a red jacket on top of the pile of clothes that Rory is holding moves to the ground and back again between shots. Also, the Doctor reaches into his pocket for the TARDIS key twice.
- Similarly, in the TARDIS interior scene at the end, the Doctor is seen putting his sonic screwdriver into his pocket twice.

## PRESS REACTION

- 'Moffat's story was built from elements familiar from the scripts he supplied to his predecessor, Russell T Davies: a hospital ward packed with twitching coma patients; a monster that hides in the peripheral vision of its victims; a portal to another world concealed in a child's bedroom. But this was more territory-marking than self-plagiarism: a signal that this programme is entering a more uncanny phase. As last night's principal monster emerged from its secret room in an ordinary house, taking the form of a blank-eyed man and a vicious-looking dog, everything felt creepily right.' Matthew Sweet, *Independent* website, 4 April 2010.
- 'He's good isn't he, this Rumplestiltskin Doctor? Tennant's time in the TARDIS now feels like it ended lot longer than three months ago. Smith inhabits the role from the moment he pops up asking young Amelia for an apple – and as fun as the kitchen scene is, the story wisely doesn't waste too much time with an unstable regeneration. The crack in the wall needs dealing with right away, and with 20 minutes to save the world, he has just as long to work out who he is. Smith is a fan of Troughton, and he dances around the crotchety-loveable-mad axis from the off.' Daniel Martin, *Guardian* website, 3 April 2010.
- 'Saturday night ... the dawn of a brave new era. David Tennant is but a golden memory. And – unknown newcomer Matt Smith has taken over TV's most iconic role. Everyone is nervous. To millions of fanatical fans, changing the

Time Lord is far more important than changing the Prime Minister. Parliaments are temporary ... the universe goes on forever. So the good news is ... you can all relax. After a fine performance in an encouragingly expensive and slick special-effects packed opening salvo, it's crystal clear that Mr Smith is certain to be a sensation. The Beeb's best franchise is in safe hands. Phew!' Kevin O'Sullivan, *Mirror* website, 4 April 2010.

- 'Gallifrey be thanked, Smith is a man who could have been born with a stripy scarf round his neck. It's there in his physiognomy – his face is made up of as many disparate workings as the TARDIS. He has a redoubtable cartoon chin offset by a hyperactive quiff, deep-set eyes and an almost Neanderthal brow. Essentially, the Doctor is meant to be a mad alien, and Smith looks like one before he even opens his mouth. By the end of episode one he was bedizened in a suitably daft public-school geography-teacher ensemble of bow tie and tweed jacket. It was ridiculous but it felt right: mad, alien, brand new but very old. A+ to the casting director. A+ to Smith.' Benji Wilson, *Telegraph* website, 3 April 2010.

## ANALYSIS

Although not actually the first episode of Series Five to go before the cameras, 'The Eleventh Hour' ushers in a new era of *Doctor Who* on screen. It marks Matt Smith's full debut as the eleventh Doctor, introduces Karen Gillan as his companion Amy Pond and Arthur Darvill as her boyfriend Rory Williams, and gives viewers the first taste of what they can expect during the tenure of new showrunner Steven Moffat, who joins fellow incoming executive producers Beth Willis and Piers Wenger and many other new contributors – alongside many established ones – behind the scenes.

The opening sequence of the TARDIS careering out of control and narrowly avoiding crashing into the Big Ben clock tower may not boast the best CGI ever featured in *Doctor Who* – it is certainly less convincing than, for instance, the shots of the police box speeding after the taxi along the Chiswick flyover in 'The Runaway Bride' – but it cleverly symbolises the show bypassing the iconic London landmarks that featured so prominently during Russell T Davies's time in charge, *en route* to the type of setting that will prove far more typical of Steven Moffat's approach; an idealised 'sleepy English village', specifically Leadworth.

Before Series Five began, there was much talk of Moffat aiming to give the show a 'dark fairytale' quality, with films such as Guillermo del Toro's *Pan's Labyrinth* (2006) and the works of Tim Burton being cited as possible reference points. There are clear indications of this in the next sequence, of the TARDIS crash-landing on a garden shed and the Doctor meeting young Amelia Pond. This has a definite fairytale quality to it, created in part by some sumptuous, filmic night shooting that looks absolutely gorgeous – a quality of camerawork that will also, happily, prove a typical feature of the Moffat era. The Doctor asking Amelia for an apple, a fruit often associated with tales of myth and magic, adds further to the 'storybook' feel.

Between these two sequences, however, comes the first indication that Series Five will not be entirely without its problems: the debut airing of the show's new title sequence and accompanying new theme music arrangement reveals them both to be distinctly disappointing. It comes as no surprise to learn that the title sequence was (for some reason) put together very quickly, as it looks rushed and lacks the impact of the one used during the ninth and tenth Doctors' eras. The new theme arrangement by Murray Gold is worse still, sounding distinctly weedy, with the driving bass-line of earlier versions almost completely absent. It is – as ever – not a patch on the brilliant original arrangement by Delia Derbyshire that was used with various tweaks throughout the 1960s and 1970s and that should never have been replaced, and does not even match up to Gold's own previous versions. Perhaps a different arranger should have been assigned the responsibility on this occasion; it seems that Gold had already given it his best shot some five years earlier.

Thankfully a much better early impression is made by the show's latest star, Matt Smith. Viewers are understandably always keen to see how each new Doctor will fare in his debut story, even though the initial characterisation and performance rarely serve as good indicators of how that incarnation will be depicted in the long run, and Smith gets off to a strong start. Any lingering concerns that he might be too young an actor to portray the Doctor are quickly extinguished here, as his age never proves an issue. He effortlessly pulls off the trick of depicting an old man in a young man's body, aided no doubt by his own rather 'old fashioned' manner and natural quirkiness – as with most of his predecessors, he clearly brings a lot of his own personality to the role. He also has appealingly distinctive features, with his prominent chin and floppy quiff of dark hair, and an amusingly awkward physicality, with his air of clumsiness and slightly bow-legged gait, famously likened by Steven Moffat to that of a drunken giraffe. In short, he quickly confirms himself to be an excellent choice to take on the mantle of the last of the Time Lords.

In fact, so good is Smith in the role that the script occasionally seems to be trying just a bit too hard to establish this new Doctor's eccentricity; something the actor is quite capable of achieving simply through his own performance. The incident where the Doctor walks straight into a tree in the garden works well enough, given his state of post-regenerative confusion; but, as someone who finds messy eating distasteful at the best of times, I could really have done without the sequence where he tries and then spits out various different foods in Amelia's kitchen. It all seems a bit too self-consciously 'wacky'. The fact that he eventually settles on 'fish custard' as his favourite is admittedly amusing, though, and provides the first trademark eleventh Doctor foible.

The spooky, dark fairytale atmosphere continues here, with the scenes in the dimly-lit and eerily empty house, where the Doctor examines the scary crack in Amelia's bedroom wall. The effectiveness of these early scenes is also due in no small part to the excellent performance of Caitlin Blackwood – Karen Gillan's cousin – as Amelia; all the more remarkable given that it was her first professional acting work. She serves as an excellent foil to Smith's Doctor, and the interaction between the pair is utterly charming.

The grown-up Amy, when the Doctor eventually meets her after returning to the house 12 years later than planned, proves harder to warm to. Moffat's decision to make her a professional kissogram, complete with micro-skirted policewoman's outfit and handcuffs, represents a surprising sexualisation of the companion character – particularly given that, in practice, 'kissogram' is these days virtually synonymous with 'strippogram'. This is emphasised in the scene toward the end of the episode where Amy refuses to avert her eyes as the Doctor strips naked to change his clothes, and obviously enjoys what she sees. (Similarly, although not in this case involving Amy, the scene where the character Jeff is clearly implied to have been looking at internet porn on his laptop brings another unusually sexual note to the show.) The later revelation that Amy's childhood encounter with the 'raggedy Doctor' caused her to become fixated on him and led to her receiving treatment from no fewer than four psychiatrists, while it perhaps excuses a rather detached performance by Karen Gillan, is also an unexpected departure. While it undoubtedly offers the potential for some unusually complex characterisation, one has to wonder to what extent that potential will actually be realised in subsequent episodes. Previous attempts to present companions with some kind of character 'twist' – such as Turlough in the 1980s, starting out with a mission to kill the Doctor – have invariably fallen flat, as early good intentions have fallen foul of the overriding need to get on with telling an exciting story.

Rory doesn't make a particularly strong impression in his debut appearance. His relationship to Amy seems similar to that of Mickey Smith to Rose Tyler back at the start of Series One: a rather clueless boyfriend-of-convenience who acts as a kind of gooseberry to the Doctor and companion pairing. However, just as Mickey developed a great deal in later episodes, clearly there is room for Rory to come more into his own as the series progresses.

As for the actual plot of 'The Eleventh Hour', this follows the approach of several other Doctors' debut stories in including an array of familiar elements, thereby reassuring viewers that although many things have changed, it is still essentially the same show that they are watching. So just as, say, Patrick Troughton's debut story featured the Daleks and Tom Baker's had the established UNIT set-up and characters, so Matt's Smith's has a number of ideas reprised from David Tennant-era episodes. The central premise, of an intergalactic 'police force' arriving in a spaceship and threatening to destroy Earth in the course of tracking down a shapeshifting alien criminal hiding in a hospital, is borrowed wholesale from the Series Three opener 'Smith and Jones'; the Doctor dropping in on Amy at different points in her life mirrors his periodic visits to Reinette in Steven Moffat's own 'The Girl in the Fireplace' in Series Two; the laptop video conference between experts is like the sub-wave network link-up in Series Four's 'The Stolen Earth'; the guest appearance by astronomer Patrick Moore follows the many celebrity cameos seen during Russell T Davies's tenure; the defeat of Prisoner Zero using a computer virus delivered via a mobile phone recalls the use of a mobile phone to thwart the Cybermen in 'The Age of Steel' in Series Two; and the Doctor's ploy of scaring off the Atraxi by invoking his fearsome reputation for defeating monsters is essentially a repeat of the way his former incarnation repelled the Vashta Nerada in Moffat's 'Forest of the Dead' in Series Four. The sonic screwdriver is used, the psychic paper puts in an appearance, and the Shadow Proclamation is cited. The Doctor putting together his new outfit from clothes discarded in a hospital also follows the pattern of two of his previous incarnations: the third in 'Spearhead from Space' (1970) and the eighth in the TV movie (1996).

The scene of the Doctor warning off the Atraxi ship from the hospital rooftop also recalls his predecessor's similar message to the Sycorax ship in 'The Christmas Invasion', and works very well in establishing his credentials as the latest incarnation of the Time Lord. Matt Smith just seems to 'get' the role of the Doctor right from the word go, as demonstrated by the significant input he had into his costume: whereas the production team initially favoured a piratical look, Smith's preference for a tweed jacket and bow tie – surely influenced by him having seen a DVD of 'The Tomb of the Cybermen' (1967) and admired Patrick Troughton's Doctor – is absolutely right for his portrayal of the character. The inspired use of a montage of clips of the previous ten Doctors and of various established monsters again serves to emphasise that this new era of the show is very much a continuation of what has gone before. It is marred only slightly by the rather odd selection of monsters chosen for inclusion in the montage: the Sea Devils come from Earth, and so cannot be properly described as alien attackers; and neither the Ood nor the Hath have posed any threat to Earth (at least, not in any of the televised stories).

Returning to the subject of the plot, it must be noted that there are several aspects of it that remain unexplained at the end of the episode. Now, this is where things get tricky for the reviewer, because it is clear that throughout Series Five Steven Moffat has intentionally left a number of plot points unresolved, to be returned to later in the unfolding of a story arc far more ambitious than any of the running themes that Russell T Davies included in his stories (most notably with the repeated references to Bad Wolf in Series One and to Torchwood in Series Two). This means that where a particular point in the narrative is left unexplained, it is sometimes difficult to tell whether a) this has been done deliberately, as part of the ongoing story arc, or b) it is simply, and more prosaically, an unintended plot hole. In the case of 'The Eleventh Hour', however, it seems that all the unexplained points fall into category a). These include the mystery of the distinctively-shaped crack in the universe first seen on Amelia's bedroom wall and then, at the end of the episode, replicated in an image on the TARDIS scanner screen; and the puzzle of why young Amelia's parents and Aunt Sharon are absent from her house, leaving her to fend for herself.

One lingering curiosity is the seemingly undue emphasis placed on the lack of ducks on the duck pond on Leadworth village green – an aspect of the story to which Steven Moffat obviously attached some significance, as it required the production crew to go to the trouble and expense of actually constructing the pond on location, where none was present. On first watching the episode, I felt sure there must be some connection between the duck pond and Amy Pond, given that her name is so unusual (and explicitly likened by the Doctor to one in a fairytale). Would there be a scene later on, I wondered, where the Doctor gives Amy the instruction, 'Duck, Pond'? Sure enough, there is just such a scene, in the hospital, when the Doctor sends Amy a text message telling her 'Duck!', just before he comes crashing through the window with a fire engine ladder. At this point, I was mentally congratulating myself on having deciphered a cryptic clue in Moffat's script. Would it turn out that the village was some sort of virtual reality, I wondered, with features such as the duck pond retrospectively constructed from Amy's memories of the things she experiences during the action? In the event, of course, I realised I was mistaken, as it appears that the pond/Pond conjunction is just a bizarre coincidence. But that's the thing about Moffat's writing: he has proved himself to be such a clever, tricksy weaver of tales that one is always expecting him to throw some 'wibbly-wobbly, timey-wimey' curve-ball into a script, taking it off in a completely unforeseen direction; and sometimes that expectation is confounded.

Perhaps, though, such a head-spinning twist would have been too much for the eleventh Doctor's introductory story, which really needs to be a relatively straightforward adventure, allowing the viewer to get to know the new team of regulars without the distraction of an overly convoluted plot. And a relatively straightforward adventure is just what is delivered here, to excellent effect. The idea of the Doctor having just 20 minutes to save the world (giving the title 'The Eleventh Hour' a pleasing double meaning – referring both to the eleventh Doctor and to the urgency of the crisis[24]) works very well in generating suspense and keeping the action moving at a good pace. There is some superbly unsettling imagery, too, when Prisoner Zero adopts the forms of some of the hospital coma patients and gets their voices wrong; appearing first as a man who barks and snarls like his dog, and then as a woman who speaks through one of her two children rather than through her own mouth. The CGI work when Prisoner Zero appears in its true, snake-like form – referred to in production, though not on screen, as the Face Tendril – is again not quite up to the show's usual high standards; but the realisation of the Atraxi ship, nicely designed with a huge eyeball at the base, is much better.

Director Adam Smith does a fine job of translating script to screen and gets good performances from a guest cast that includes some notably high-profile names: in particular, Nina Wadia, an *EastEnders* regular, as Dr Ramsden; the distinguished Scottish character actress Annette Crosbie as Mrs Angelo; and Olivia Coleman, probably best known for her roles in the Channel 4 comedies *Peep Show* and *Green Wing*, as the female coma patient. One slightly odd inclusion is the scene where, after the sun is dimmed by an Atraxi force field, the Doctor mentally reviews what he has seen on the village green, as depicted via a novel 'roaming eye' effect whereby a sequence of still images are flashed up on screen in rapid succession. Given that it has never been seen in the show before, the viewer's initial assumption is that this 'photographic recall' is a new ability particular to the eleventh Doctor, and will be a regular feature of his era – something that seems to be confirmed when, later in the episode, the Doctor holds the unconscious Amy's head and causes her to search back through her own memories, as depicted with a similar effect. Now that we know, with the benefit of hindsight, that its use in this episode is a one-off, it comes across as rather random and gratuitous. All things considered, though, 'The Eleventh Hour' is a very polished and impressive production.

Sadly, however, the episode ends with a big disappointment, as the redesigned TARDIS interior is unveiled. Prior to transmission, there were rumours on the fan grapevine that the new set was to be an updated version of the 1960s original: a bright white chamber with serried ranks of roundels on the walls and an elegant hexagonal console with an array of futuristic controls on its panels and a gleaming cylindrical time rotor at its centre. What an exciting prospect! In the event, the scene where the new interior is revealed is, to say the least, a damp squib. The new set, while it does give some nods to the original, has a chaotic and in parts almost

---

[24] Although not intentional, the title could also perhaps be seen as referring to the episode's extended, hour-and-a-bit running time.

unfinished look, and the latest control console is in essence just a more outlandish version of the previous one – memorably described by original Dalek designer Raymond P Cusick, in a *Doctor Who Confidential* interview, as 'a dog's breakfast'. It incorporates an even more absurd jumble of incongruous household items and other pieces of junk than before, and the time rotor looks disconcertingly like a big glass dildo thrusting up and down inside the central column. In short, the whole set is just terrible. It seems that, as with Murray Gold and the theme music arrangement, it was a mistake for production designer Edward Thomas to be given a second crack at something he first attempted, and did far better, back in Series One.

Some commentators have argued that the new TARDIS interior simply reflects the eleventh Doctor's 'mad professor' persona. If so, however, this is another case of the production trying too hard to convey an eccentricity that should emerge simply from Matt Smith's portrayal of the character. This continues to be a problem with the script, too. Does the Doctor really need to declare himself self-consciously to be 'a mad man with a box' in order for the audience to get the point? Would it not be better if he were simply to demonstrate his character through his actions?

To be fair, though, the biggest disappointments here – the new title sequence and theme music arrangement, and the new TARDIS interior set – are series-spanning issues rather than ones specific to this episode. Judged purely on its own merits, 'The Eleventh Hour' gets Series Five, and the era of the eleventh Doctor, off to a flying start.

# 5.02 – THE BEAST BELOW

Writer: Steven Moffat
Director: Andrew Gunn

DEBUT TRANSMISSION DETAILS

BBC One/BBC HD
Date: 10 April 2010. Scheduled time: 6.15 pm. Actual time: 6.20 pm.

Duration: 42' 02"

ADDITIONAL CREDITED CAST

Sophie Okonedo (Liz 10), Terrence Hardiman (Hawthorne), Hannah Sharp (Mandy[25]), Alfie Field (Timmy), Christopher Good (Morgan), David Ajala (Peter), Catrin Richards (Poem Girl), Jonathan Battersby (Winder), Chris Porter (Voice of Smilers/Winder), Ian McNeice (Churchill)

PLOT

The TARDIS brings the Doctor and Amy to Starship UK, where the nation's population are living after fleeing Earth due to solar flares. The Queen, Liz 10, is trying to uncover a dark secret at the Starship's heart, while her government runs a totalitarian regime enforced by scary automata known as Smilers and sinister robed figures called Winders. All the Starship's adult citizens are periodically allowed to see a video explaining the terrible thing that has been done to ensure their survival, but afterwards must decide whether to forget or to protest, and most choose to forget. With Liz 10's help, the Doctor and Amy discover that the Starship does not have any engines; it has been built on the back of a huge Star Whale, the last of its kind, which is forced to propel the vessel through space by being repeatedly tortured with electric shocks. This has been sanctioned by Liz 10, who is actually around 300 years old. Every ten years, she investigates the mystery, but when she discovers the truth, she always chooses to forget rather than abdicate. Amy realises that the Star Whale is carrying the Starship voluntarily, and does not need to be tortured to make it co-operate. She gets Liz 10 to press the 'Abdicate' button, freeing the creature from its painful slavery.

QUOTE, UNQUOTE

* **Amy:** 'What are you going to do?'
  **Doctor:** 'What I always do. Stay out of trouble. Badly.'

---

[25] Surname given in dialogue as 'Tanner'.

- **Doctor:** 'Once every five years, everyone chooses to forget what they've learned. Democracy in action.'
- **Liz 10:** 'I'm the bloody queen, mate. Basically, I rule.'

## CONTINUITY POINTS

- In a notable innovation, the Complete Series Five DVD/Blu-Ray box set, released by 2Entertain on 8 November 2010, contained two specially-recorded extra scenes featuring Matt Smith as the Doctor and Karen Gillan as Amy on the TARDIS interior set. These 'Meanwhile in the TARDIS' scenes were written by Steven Moffat, directed by Euros Lyn and produced by Annabella Hurst-Brown. The first (duration 3' 17") was intended to bridge the gap between 'The Eleventh Hour' and 'The Beast Below'. It begins with Amy, still recovering from the shock of seeing the TARDIS interior, gabbling a string of questions at the Doctor. The Doctor explains to her what a police box is and why his ship looks like one. He also confirms that he is an alien. He opens the TARDIS doors and shows her the vista of space outside. When Amy expresses scepticism that it is real, he pushes her out through the doors. This leads directly into the opening scene of 'The Beast Below', where she is seen floating outside. (For details of the second 'Meanwhile in the TARDIS' scene, see the entry on 'The Vampires of Venice'.)
- The Doctor states that Starship UK dates from the 29th Century, when the Earth was ravaged by solar flares and the population left until conditions improved. This is in accord with suggestions in 'The Ark in Space' (1975) that the Earth was temporarily abandoned due to solar flare activity in the 29th or 30th Century.
- At the time of 'The Beast Below', Starship UK has been travelling for around 300 years. This suggests that the story is set in the 32nd or 33rd Century – the latter of which appears to be confirmed when Amy's age is given in the voting cubicle as either 1306 or 1308 (see 'Oops' below).
- When the Doctor tells Amy, disingenuously, that he follows the rule of never interfering in the affairs of other peoples or planets, he is referring to what was described in 'The War Games' (1969) as the Time Lords' 'most important law'.
- Amy asks the Doctor if he is a parent, and he avoids answering. (It has been established in previous stories that he is indeed a father.)
- There is a large 'Magpie Electricals' sign by a hole in the road in the Dean Street section of the Starship. This (fictional) electrical goods company was first mentioned in the Series Two episode 'The Idiot's Lantern' and has been referenced several other times since.
- Scotland is not represented on Starship UK as the Scots wanted their own ship.
- Amy's middle name is Jessica.
- Liz 10 is Elizabeth X, the Queen at this point in history. She notes that she and her whole family were brought up on stories of the Doctor. She says that he was an 'old drinking buddy of Henry 12' and had 'tea and scones with Liz 2'. She also mentions that 'Vicky' – Queen Victoria – knighted and exiled him on the same day, as seen in the Series Two episode 'Tooth and Claw'. She adds, 'And so much for the Virgin Queen – you bad, bad boy', referring to the tenth

Doctor's relationship with Elizabeth I, as previously revealed in the special 'The End of Time' Part One.

- There were once millions of Star Whales and, according to legend, they guided early human space travellers through the asteroid belt. However, the one supporting Starship UK is believed to be the last of its kind.
- The Doctor is an old acquaintance of the wartime British Prime Minister Winston Churchill.
- The side of Starship UK bears one of the same cracks in the universe as seen on young Amelia Pond's bedroom wall.

PRODUCTION NOTES

- 'The Beast Below' was made with, and mostly after 'Victory of the Daleks', the two stories forming Block Two of Series Five's production schedule.
- The first scene to be taped for this story was actually the cliffhanger, with the West Cross Anti-Aircraft Operations Room in Swansea being used as Churchill's office on 24 August 2009, during production of 'Victory of the Daleks'. On 9 and 10 September, the crew recorded the Tower of London dungeon scenes at Neath Abbey, also in Swansea. The Dupont factory on Mamhilad Park Industrial Estate – the roof of which had been seen in 'The Eleventh Hour', and which had been used as a location in a number of previous stories – was transformed into London Market and other areas of the Starship UK interior for recording on 11-12 and 14-18 September. The final location used was the Orangery of Margam Country Park, which became Liz 10's bedroom on 22 September. Studio recording at Upper Boat took place on 8, 21 and 23 September and 4, 5, 12 and 16 November 2009. The ITV studios in Culverhouse Cross, Cardiff, were also used for one day, 7 September, for the scenes of the work tent around the hole in the road, and the Star Whale's mouth.
- Sophie Okonedo had previously provided the voice for the Doctor's companion Alison in the 2003 animated webcast Doctor Who story 'Scream of the Shalka'.
- A Doctor Who story involving a Space Whale – a concept often featured in science fiction tales in all media – was first mooted in 1980, when writers Pat Mills and John Wagner proposed one entitled 'Song of the Space Whale'. After going through a number of rewrites, this was eventually rejected in 1985, by which point Mills was the sole writer attached to the project. In 2008, a creature of this kind – although less attractive-looking than the one in 'The Beast Below' – was featured in the episode 'Meat' in Series Two of 'Torchwood'.
- The theme music arrangement for the closing credits of this episode is different from that used on all other episodes of Series Five. However, the standard version was substituted for the episode's DVD and Blu-Ray releases.

OOPS!

- When the young boy Timmy enters the Vator in the opening pre-titles sequence, the wide shot shows that to the right of the Vator there is a large window looking out onto space, but the close-up shows the corridor continuing with no window.

- The computer voice in the voting cubicle gives Amy's age as 1306, but the screen displays it as 1308.

## PRESS REACTION

- 'An immensely satisfying episode that manages to marry several traditional *Who* elements with Moffat's fresh, child-centric take. Ingenious ideas are teased out of the many mysteries (loved the glass of water bits), which are pleasingly free of heavy brooding – the reveals don't uncover stereotypical baddie behaviour, quite the opposite. The lighter, less angsty tone than of late is like a breath of fresh air and well suited to this story … The final solution ties in with what is looking like one of this season's key themes, that of the behaviour and influence of children. (Also, little Mandy in her red coat instantly reminds you of young Amelia Pond.) But Amy redeeming herself is due to her insight into human nature that the Doctor has helped give her, so he's indirectly to thank for the happy resolution.' Russell Lewin, *SFX* website, 10 April 2010.
- '"The Beast Below" was very good indeed. It worked on more than one level too. At heart, it often felt like a traditional old-style *Doctor Who* episode, with corridors to explore, an enemy observing the Doctor investigating the strangeness around him, and the constant feel of a greater threat waiting to be discovered. Long time followers of the show have seen that kind of build up many times before, and it was fun to see it again here. But while the structure may have felt familiar, the flesh put on the bones was really something quite special.' Simon Brew, Digital Spy website, 9 April 2010.
- '"The Beast Below" looks for all the world like a [Russell T Davies] story: a Technicolor morality play light on intricate plotting and heavy on modern moral parallels. But Moffat still conjures some magical ideas and takes the characters exactly where they need to go – rather than simply going in the Starship UK and putting the bad thing right, relationships are tested and solidified by differing reactions to what's going on in there. With echoes of Donna Noble's "Sometimes I think you need someone to stop you," it's only Amy who works out that once again (and this is becoming a Moffat trope) nobody has to die. Amy's not nearly as badass this week – although you wouldn't be, would you?' Daniel Martin, *Guardian* website, 10 April 2010.

## ANALYSIS

More than any other writer in *Doctor Who*'s long history, Steven Moffat uses his stories to explore themes relating to childhood and to children as characters; as for instance with the gasmask boy in 'The Empty Child'/'The Doctor Dances' in Series One, Reinette in 'The Girl in the Fireplace' in Series Two and Charlotte Abigail Lux in 'Silence in the Library'/'Forest of the Dead' in Series Four. In 'The Eleventh Hour', he gives the Doctor and Amy the following exchange of dialogue:

**Amy:** 'You told me you had a time machine.'
**Doctor:** 'And you believed me.'
**Amy:** 'Then I grew up.'
**Doctor:** 'Oh, you never want to do that.'

Toward the end of the episode, as if to emphasise the point, he includes the following virtual repeat:

**Doctor:** 'You wanted to come [with me] 14 years ago.'
**Amy:** 'I grew up.'
**Doctor:** 'Don't worry, I'll soon fix that.'

Then, after Amy agrees to go with the Doctor, the viewer sees that she has kept in her bedroom all the models and drawings of herself and her 'invisible friend' that she created as a child, and that there is also a wedding dress hanging up in the room – revealing that she was due to get married the following day. What this suggests is that Amy was on the point of putting aside her long-time fixation with the 'raggedy Doctor' and entering into an adult relationship, but that she has now chosen to postpone that transition, for who knows how long, while she indulges her childhood fantasy of going off on adventures in the TARDIS. Without even realising it, the Doctor has 'fixed' the problem of her growing up. It is fitting therefore that throughout 'The Beast Below' she wears only her nightie and dressing-gown, which gives her a childlike appearance and reflects how she was dressed when, as young Amelia, she first encountered the Doctor. In keeping with Moffat's initial dark fairytale vision for the show, this recalls J M Barrie's creation Peter Pan, a boy who refuses to grow up – a comparison that the showrunner makes explicitly in the accompanying instalment of *Doctor Who Confidential*. Just as Peter Pan's friend Wendy is often depicted wearing nightclothes and flying through the sky with him, so Amy is effectively shown 'flying' through space at the start of 'The Beast Below', while the Doctor holds on to her ankle from the TARDIS doorway.

After the TARDIS arrives on Starship UK, it is again the Doctor's affinity with children that comes to the fore when he claims that he never gets involved in the affairs of other peoples or planets, but then immediately leaves his ship and starts to investigate on seeing a young girl, Mandy, crying.

**Amy:** 'So this is how it works, Doctor? You never interfere in the affairs of other peoples or planets, unless there's children crying.'
**Doctor:** 'Yes.'

Children are in fact the first people that the viewer sees on board Starship UK, as the action opens in a classroom where the departing pupils are receiving praise, and in one case admonishment, from one of the sinister Smilers. What strikes the viewer most about this scene, though, is the incongruous mid-20th Century look of the pupils' clothing and the classroom furniture, which jars with the CGI images of the Starship exterior with its futuristic skyscrapers bearing the names of English counties. This incongruity continues as other areas of the Starship are revealed. Just as 'The Eleventh Hour' featured an idealised 'sleepy English village' setting, so the

Starship interior is bedecked with stereotypical English imagery that looks as if it has been taken from a series of picture postcards aimed at foreign tourists: elevators like those on the London Underground, complete with an almost identical logo; a red telephone box, like the one seen on Leadworth village green; a 'lollypop lady'; a bowler-hatted gent; Union Jack flags festooning the streets; and so on. While this is also consistent with the dark fairytale idea – and Moffat has cited Roald Dahl's fantastical stories as another influence – it is a pity that no explanation is given for it in the script. The Doctor's observation that the Starship's inhabitants have gone 'back to basics', in reference to them riding bikes and having washing lines and wind-up streetlamps, doesn't really cover it. What was needed, perhaps, was a line of dialogue indicating that they had consciously given the Starship a 'retro' look, turning it into a kind of theme park celebrating the UK's history. As it stands, it just comes across as a rather odd design choice by the production team, which tends to undermine the believability of the setting and take the viewer out of the action.

Liz 10's Cockney accent, out of keeping with how we hear other characters on the Starship speak, can perhaps be seen as another exaggerated homage to England's past – particularly as she seems to use it only in certain scenes. The gun-toting future monarch is given some great lines, too, and Sophie Okonedo's spirited performance in the role is excellent; certainly one of the highlights of the episode. The *mise-en-scène* when she is introduced, seated by a grand fireplace with her head turned away from the viewer, her body draped in rich red robes, a stylised white facemask by her side and an array of water-filled glasses set out on the tiled floor before her, is really quite beautiful; although, again, there is an incongruity here, as this looks nothing like the rest of the Starship. The same is true of the Tower of London setting toward the end of the episode, which likewise doesn't really make any sense in the context of a 29th Century spaceship – unless, again, one assumes, without any positive indication to this effect in the script, that it has been constructed as a heritage centre-type recreation of the historical original. It makes one wonder if this episode was actually discussed in the tone meeting prior to Block Two of production; it seems as if the designers couldn't quite decide what visual style they ought to be aiming for, and ended up pulling in several different directions at once.

Matters are not helped by the fact that, in a rare occurrence since *Doctor Who* returned to TV in 2005, this is an episode that is really rather poorly directed. Certainly Andrew Gunn, another newcomer to the show, does not get maximum value out of the disused factory location that the crew elaborately dressed as London Market, or Oxford Street as it is also referred to in the script. There are areas and aspects of this, including even a market stall with several crates of live chickens, plus many extras dressed in vintage clothing, that are seen clearly in *Doctor Who Confidential* but glimpsed barely, if at all, in the episode itself! A very wasteful use of resources.

More seriously, there are a number of scenes where Gunn's direction leaves the viewer uncertain what has actually happened. The first of these comes at the start of the episode, when one moment the TARDIS is floating in space, then the next it is inside the Starship, with no indication of it having materialised there in between. This does admittedly allow for a good visual gag – Amy is talking to the Doctor as they see Mandy crying on the TARDIS scanner screen, then suddenly the Doctor appears on the screen himself, having rushed outside without Amy noticing – but this is at the expense of the credibility of the action. Another instance is when the Doctor and Amy are trapped in the Star Whale's mouth and the Doctor causes the creature to vomit so that they can escape. The next we see, confusingly, they are in an 'overspill pipe', without any clue as to how they actually got from one place to the other. The most glaring example, though, comes after Amy presses the 'Forget' button in the voting cubicle, having watched the information video revealing the dark secret at the heart of the Starship. She sees on the screens that she has a message waiting for her, then discovers that this is a video she has sent to herself, tearfully insisting that she get the Doctor away from the Starship at all costs. Logically, it would seem that she must have recorded this video, using the 'Record' button on the voting console, before pressing the 'Forget' button. However, the way the scene is directed, there would appear to be no gap in the action to enable her to do this; she presses the 'Forget' button immediately after watching the information video. The visual grammar of this scene is badly amiss, and consequently the viewer is left completely bewildered. It is just possible that this was done intentionally, to try to engender empathy with Amy's own disorientation; but if so, it doesn't come off.

To be fair to Gunn, some of the blame for these confusions undoubtedly lies in Steven Moffat's script. In fact, overall, this is definitely the weakest episode that Moffat has contributed to *Doctor Who* to date. The parallel he draws between the Doctor and the Star Whale – both the last of their own race, ancient and kind, unable to stand by and do nothing when they see children crying – is a good one, but is really sledgehammered home. There is a degree of awkwardness, too, in the fact that the story wouldn't work at all if it were not for the fact that the TARDIS happens to arrive in space above the Starship, where the Star Whale cannot be seen, rather than by the side of it or below it, where the creature would be immediately visible. The discovery that the Starship's government have, for hundreds of years, been feeding adult protesters to the Star Whale (along with the food waste that it will presumably have to be content with in future), and using children as slave labour, is rather uncomfortably glossed over in the end, with the culprits apparently going unpunished. It doesn't seem quite right, either, that it is Amy who works out the truth of the Star Whale's motivation, while the Doctor, having seemingly given the matter little consideration, rushes ahead with (as he himself recognises) a completely uncharacteristic plan to turn the creature into a mental vegetable, which would have been a huge blunder. It is good to see the companion being depicted as perceptive and resourceful, but surely this should not be at the expense of making the Doctor seem clueless and inept. Perhaps, though, we can put this down to him still suffering the after-effects of his regeneration; and it is at least shown that Amy finds the solution to the problem by following the advice he gave her – 'Use your eyes, notice everything' – when they first arrived on the Starship and he deduced, in veritable Sherlock Holmes mode, that it was a 'police state'.

The agents of this state, the Smilers and the Winders, are pleasingly creepy creations. The former look like antique sideshow or funfair automata – the type of thing to which Rod Serling's *The Twilight Zone* specialised in giving a sinister twist back in the early 1960s – and the fact that they are seen to have, seemingly impossibly, not two but three different faces when their heads rotate through 180°

makes them even more disconcerting. The scene where it is revealed that they can emerge from their booths and come stalking after recalcitrant citizens provides a good scary surprise. The Winders, ultimately shown to be half human and half Smiler, are also nicely menacing, with their dark, hooded robes like monks' habits, and slightly recall the Clockwork Men from Moffat's 'The Girl in the Fireplace' (although it may be other things on the Starship that they are responsible for winding, rather than being clockwork themselves). Terrence Hardiman, previously best known for playing the titular character in the BBC children's series *The Demon Headmaster* from 1996 to 1998, gives a particularly good performance as Hawthorne, who appears to be the chief Winder, although in this case fully human.

The underlying message of the story, about the way humans use and abuse animals, is one well suited to *Doctor Who*. The basic idea of the voting cubicles, where the citizens have to choose whether to forget or to protest about the Starship's exploitation of the Star Whale, is very ingenious too (although the logic of allowing voters to record messages to themselves – or presumably others – is less clear …), and was given added resonance at the time of transmission by the fact that, whether by serendipity or design, this episode went out when a General Election campaign was in full swing in Britain.

This, though, is really where the positives end. Prior to this point, Moffat seemed to be a man who could do no wrong where his *Doctor Who* scriptwriting was concerned, but 'The Beast Below', while by no means a bad episode, is not up to his usual standard. This rings some alarm bells for the future: will the burden of his new responsibilities as showrunner cause him to be less attentive to his own scripts? But perhaps it is premature to be worrying about this. While going through an extra draft or two would doubtless have benefited 'The Beast Below', it is surely unreasonable to expect every Steven Moffat episode to attain the dizzy heights of 'The Girl in the Fireplace' or 'Blink'. All things considered, this is a solid and entertaining follow-up to 'The Eleventh Hour', giving the viewer a good opportunity to get further acquainted with the eleventh Doctor and his new companion.

# 5.03 – VICTORY OF THE DALEKS

Writer: Mark Gatiss
Director: Andrew Gunn

DEBUT TRANSMISSION DETAILS

BBC One[26]
Date: 17 April 2010. Scheduled time: 6.30 pm. Actual time: 6.30 pm.

Duration: 41' 46"[27]

ADDITIONAL CREDITED CAST

Ian McNeice (Churchill[28]), Bill Paterson (Bracewell[29]), Nina de Cosimo (Blanche),
Tim Wallers (Childers), Nicholas Pegg (Dalek 1), Barnaby Edwards (Dalek 2),
Nicholas Briggs (Dalek Voice), Susannah Fielding (Lilian[30]), James Albrecht (Todd),
Colin Prockter (Air Raid Warden).

Daleks Created by Terry Nation.

PLOT

Responding to a telephone call from Prime Minister Winston Churchill, the Doctor
and Amy arrive in the Cabinet War Rooms during the London Blitz in the early
1940s. The Doctor is horrified to see that there are Daleks present, masquerading as
secret weapons dubbed 'Ironsides', supposedly created by the scientist Professor
Bracewell. The Doctor insists that they are alien Daleks; which is just what they
wanted him to do when they set this elaborate trap. On their spaceship, they use
his confirmation of their identity to activate a progenitor device containing pure
Dalek DNA, which would not respond to them previously because they themselves
have impure DNA. The progenitor produces five superior, 'new paradigm' Daleks,
which exterminate the others. The Dalek ship is attacked by three Spitfires, flying
through space using gravity bubble technology that Bracewell learned of from the

[26] Unlike the other episodes of this series, 'Victory of the Daleks' did not have a
simultaneous transmission on BBC HD. The BBC HD transmission was later the
same evening, at 8.27 pm.
[27] However, see 'Production Notes' for a discussion of the duration of this episode.
[28] Full name given in dialogue as 'Winston Spencer Churchill'.
[29] Full name given in dialogue as 'Professor Edwin Bracewell'.
[30] Surname given in dialogue as 'Breen'. (This is a homage by writer Mark Gatiss to
the character Colonel Breen in Nigel Kneale's famous BBC serial *Quatermass and the
Pit* (1958/59).)

Daleks themselves. In response, the Daleks threaten to destroy the Earth using Bracewell, who is really a robot and also, because he contains an 'oblivion continuum', a bomb. The Doctor and Amy manage to disarm the bomb by convincing Bracewell that he is more human than robot, but the Daleks escape into the future in their ship.

## QUOTE, UNQUOTE

- **Doctor:** 'I've defeated you time and time again. I've defeated you. I sent you back into the Void. I saved the whole of reality from you. I am the Doctor, and you are the Daleks!'
- **Bracewell:** 'You are my Ironsides!'
  **Dalek:** 'We are the Daleks.'
  **Bracewell:** 'But I created you!'
  **Dalek:** 'No.' [Dalek blasts off Bracewell's robotic hand.] 'We created *you!*'
- **Doctor:** 'All right, it's a jammie dodger, but I was promised tea!'

## CONTINUITY POINTS

- Winston Churchill knows the Doctor of old, and always tries to take the TARDIS key from him, so that he can use the ship in the war effort. However, this is the first time he has met the Doctor's eleventh incarnation. Previous encounters with Churchill were described in the novels *Players* (BBC Books, 1999), featuring both the sixth Doctor and the second, and *The Shadow in the Glass* (BBC Books, 2001), featuring the sixth Doctor.
- Amy is, for some reason, unable to remember the Daleks, despite their recent activity on Earth in the Series Four story 'The Stolen Earth'/'Journey's End'.
- Professor Bracewell appears to be akin to one of the Dalek replicants seen in earlier stories such as 'Resurrection of the Daleks' (1984). His positronic brain has been implanted with the memories of the real Bracewell, whose fate is unknown.
- The new paradigm Daleks are grown from pure Dalek DNA contained in a progenitor – the only one of these small capsules to have been found, out of thousands originally created as a means of preserving their race. The other Daleks who bring about this restoration have impure DNA, presumably because they are some of the ones created after the Time War by Davros using cells from his own body, as explained in 'Journey's End'. The Doctor says, 'When we last met, you were at the end of your rope, finished.' A Dalek replies, 'One ship survived.' The Doctor then adds, 'And you fell back through time, yes. Crippled. Dying.'
- The five new paradigm Daleks have different functions, as denoted by their predominant colours: Supreme (white), Drone (red), Scientist (orange), Strategist (blue) and Eternal (yellow).
- When the TARDIS departs at the end, the wall behind it is revealed to bear another of the mysterious cracks in the universe seen in the previous two episodes.

## 5.03 – VICTORY OF THE DALEKS

PRODUCTION NOTES

- 'Victory of the Daleks' was made with, and mostly before, 'The Beast Below', the two stories forming Block Two of Series Five's production schedule.
- The West Cross Anti-Aircraft Operations Room in Swansea – which once served as a war room for West Glamorgan County Council and as a major incident command centre for Swansea County Council but is now a training facility – was used for taping of the interior scenes in the Cabinet War Rooms and Churchill's office on 21 and 24-26 August 2009. The roof of Cardiff University's Glamorgan Building became the roof of the Cabinet War Rooms on 27 August. The scenes in Bracewell's laboratory was taped in Jacob's Antique Centre on West Canal Wharf, Cardiff, on 28 and 29 August. Brackla Bunkers in Bridgend doubled for a corridor and storage area with the Cabinet War Rooms on 31 August. The final location was the J F Freeman Cigars factory in Cardiff, used for the Dalek spaceship interior from 2 to 4 September. Only two days' studio recording at Upper Boat were needed to complete the story, on 8 and 23 September.
- The shot of four helmeted soldiers and an air raid warden raising a Union Jack flag on the roof of the Cabinet War Rooms was intentionally framed to mirror a black and white photograph by Joe Rosenthal of US marines raising the Stars and Stripes on Iwo Jima on 23 February 1945; one of the most famous images of the Second World War.
- Barring special mini-episodes such as 'Time Crash', 'Victory of the Daleks' is arguably the shortest *Doctor Who* episode since the show returned to TV in 2005, running to just 41' 46". However, on its original BBC One transmission, it was immediately followed by a 45" trailer for 'City of the Daleks', the first of the *Doctor Who* Adventure Games: a new series of interactive computer games available to download for free from the show's official website. As this trailer was edited in before the final BBC Wales credit, it could be argued that it was actually part of the episode itself. In that case, the duration of the episode, including the trailer and the final credit, would be 42' 34". ('City of the Daleks' would be released on 5 June 2010.)

OOPS!

- There are a few shot continuity mistakes in the episode. For instance, in the corridor scene shortly after the Doctor and Amy arrive in the Cabinet War Rooms, as Churchill receives a report of an incoming formation of Stuka aircraft, the Doctor's hands move from being in his pockets to being clasped in front of his chest, and then back again, between shots. And when Churchill says goodbye to the Doctor and Amy toward the end, he lights a cigar and puts it in his mouth in one shot, but in the next shot it has vanished.
- Despite Nazi propaganda to the contrary, Stukas could not carry enough fuel to be able to reach London from Germany, and had been withdrawn from operational use against Britain before the London Blitz began. (Possibly the report that Churchill received was simply incorrect about the type of aircraft approaching.)
- The Doctor says that he has 'taken out all the alien tech that Bracewell put in' –

presumably referring to the gravity bubble and weapons installed in the one surviving Spitfire that attacked the Dalek ship – as he does not want Churchill to be able to use anachronistic technology in the war effort. However, in the following scene in Bracewell's workshop, there is still a Dalek gun plainly visible on the bench.

PRESS REACTION

- 'The concept – Churchill vs the Daleks! – is so good you want to like the episode more than you actually do. There's a disappointing lack of quotable dialogue (though there are a few gems) and the Doctor's distrustful manner for the first half means there's less of the playful banter and wacky mannerisms the season has excelled in so far. Despite these reservations, however, the episode is still rollicking good fun. The *Star Wars*-inspired space battle is the highlight, easily this season's most impressive visual effects sequence, even if it's a little on the short side (must be where they spent the budget meant for the set of the Dalek ship). Both guest stars also put on a jolly good show. Ian McNeice especially emerges from behind the comedy cigar and clichés as a lovably bumbling Churchill.' Jordan Farley, *SFX* website, 17 April 2010.

- '[This] is a story that moves along at a frenetic pace, rarely slowing to catch its breath. After a year of extra-long specials and padded out stories, I found myself wishing for a moment we had a bit longer for the Doctor to suspect the Daleks and possibly begin to doubt himself in his questioning of their motives or to have some time for things to sink in. Instead, we get a story that moves from big moment to big moment in the first half hour before settling down with a quiet finale that still left some huge plot threads hanging (and I'm not just talking about the crack in the wall that is following the TARDIS crew).' Michael Hickerson, Slice of Sci-Fi website, 19 April 2010.

- 'It's a story that could … have been so much better, even with a lot of the same elements. A wartime adventure where the Doctor finds that Daleks are being used and has to side with the Nazis to destroy them … or even more of a skit on "The Power of the Daleks" [1966], with the Daleks plotting to destroy and no-one listening to the Doctor so he has to use his wits to get him through it all … And the new Daleks – woeful. They're too big, wobbly and brightly coloured. Daleks should be tight, small bundles of power and threat and paranoia. If these were "pure" Daleks, then we should have seen original 1963 versions, or those from "Genesis of the Daleks" [1975] … but then maybe this is all part of this parallel world/whatever it is thing going on with Amy here … maybe this is what the Daleks looked like in her world … maybe they were kids' toys that took over when the time was right … who knows. All in all a very disappointing third episode, which perhaps tried to do too much but ended up collapsing due to the weight of the requirements put on it, and the need to try and bring the Daleks back as "new and improved". Why try and improve something that just doesn't need it … we shall never know.' David J Howe, Howe's Who blog, 24 April 2010.

- 'Angry *Doctor Who* fans claim a shock redesign has turned the Daleks from cold, menacing, metallic killers into brightly coloured *Teletubbies*. Others say the new breed look like Fisher-Price toys – or Ikea kitchenware. The new, bulkier exterminators, which made their debut on Saturday, have also been accused of looking fat. A fan called DiscoP wrote on a web forum: "Why have they got such huge backsides?" Aneechick added: "They looked like disabled toilets." Others claimed their coloured panels make the Doctor's armoured foes appear *spongy*. One wrote: "It's a padded Dalek. A soft toy Dalek. It looks like it's half marshmallow and half plastic." Another added: "What a shame to see a genuinely menacing Dalek design scrapped."' *Sun* website, 19 April 2010.

## ANALYSIS

Back when *Doctor Who* began in the mid-1960s, it was usual for each story to end with a cliffhanger leading into the next. 'The Beast Below' marked a rare return to that practice as, even before the 'Next Time' teaser, it included a closing scene in which the Doctor received a telephone call for help from Winston Churchill, apparently having trouble with the Daleks. This was a nice touch, neatly setting the scene for 'Victory of the Daleks' and helping to fuel the viewer's anticipation for the latest return appearance of the Doctor's greatest foes.

The episode opens well, too, with a pre-titles scene in the Cabinet War Rooms that quickly and effectively establishes the Second World War setting. The BBC is justly renowned for its skill in mounting period dramas, and this is no exception, as the attention to historical detail in the way this location is dressed, and in the cast's costumes, is superb, giving the whole thing a very authentic air.

Once we get to see more of Winston Churchill, however, we find him being depicted in a rather less authentic way. The Churchill presented here is not the shrewd politician and complex character of historical fact but a jovial caricature who talks in stirring speech soundbites, reflecting the same kind of patriotic, tourist-friendly view of Britain as infused 'The Beast Below'. Strangely, one of the few concessions to a more down-to-earth realism is the inclusion of his habitual maxim 'Keep buggering on', which jars somewhat and seems inappropriately coarse for a teatime family show. We do witness some of Churchill's pragmatism, when he declares himself willing to use any weapon, however terrible, in the fight against the enemy – 'I will grasp with both hands anything that will give us an advantage over the Nazi menace,' he says – but this is still, all things considered, a pretty superficial portrait. Actor Ian McNeice, taking his cue from the script, gives an endearing, larger-than-life performance in the role, coming across as a sort of lovable old uncle figure, but it would perhaps have been better if he had brought a bit more steel to his portrayal.

Interviewed for *Doctor Who Confidential*, writer Mark Gatiss said, '*Doctor Who* is not the place, really' to examine the more contentious aspects of Churchill's wartime leadership. To hear such a misguidedly narrow view of the show's potential being expressed by someone who is a self-confessed fan is really quite surprising. Admittedly the 'celebrity historical' stories that have become something of a staple ingredient of *Doctor Who* since 2005 have always tended to trade on and reinforce popular perceptions of their chosen subjects, but that is not to say that the show is incapable of or unsuited to presenting more sophisticated representations of historical figures and situations. As Gatiss must be aware, it was doing so even back in the 1960s, in stories such as 'The Crusade' (1965) and 'The Massacre of St

Bartholomew's Eve' (1966); and if there was any doubt that it was still up to the challenge, this would be dispelled later in Series Five in 'Vincent and the Doctor', with its brilliant depiction of the troubled Vincent van Gogh.

To be fair, though, Gatiss made no bones about the fact that what he wanted to present here was the legend of Churchill – the man as pictured on the posters – and of the British war effort more generally, rather than the historical reality. The inspiration he drew from classic British war films such as *The Dam Busters* (1955) and *Where Eagles Dare* (1968) is readily apparent. Most obviously, the 'Broadsword to Danny Boy' radio messages between the Cabinet War Rooms and the chief Spitfire pilot – a role voiced, uncredited, by Gatiss himself, in a rather exaggerated plummy accent – use call signs taken directly from the latter movie (apparently a favourite of Gatiss's father); but really the whole feel of 'Victory of the Daleks' is that of a piece of rousing wartime propaganda, and on those terms it works quite well.

Another significant source of inspiration, for the early part of the episode at least, was the second Doctor's debut story 'The Power of the Daleks' (1966). The infiltration of Bracewell's Ironsides into the British command centre shows the Daleks using their cunning in a way that has not really been seen before in 21st Century *Doctor Who*, and strongly recalls their stealthy takeover of the human colony on the planet Vulcan in that earlier story; their chant of 'We are your soldiers' here is an obvious homage to their 'We are your servants' in the latter. It is amusing, too, to hear them offering cups of tea and see them done up like soldiers, with their kit belts and military khaki livery. The Daleks are actually very well suited to being featured in a Second World War setting, their creator Terry Nation having partly based them on the Nazis. The viewer really feels the Doctor's frustration as he tries to convince everyone of the danger the creatures pose, while they continue to act in a polite and subservient manner. This is easily the most enjoyable aspect of the episode, and it's a pity that its potential isn't exploited more fully, as the script has the Daleks reverting to type rather too quickly.

But what this is really all leading up to, of course, is the dramatic introduction of the redesigned 'new paradigm' Daleks. On the plus side, the basic idea of the restoration of the Doctor's perennial foes from pure Dalek DNA is a good one, neatly getting around the problem encountered in the Russell T Davies-era Dalek stories that, following the Time War, the creatures seemed to be permanently on the brink of extinction. There is, though, no logical reason why Daleks with different DNA should require different casings, and when the new Daleks actually emerge from the progenitor unit on board their ship … oh dear, oh dear, oh dear.

The original Daleks, as designed by Raymond P Cusick in 1963, are one of *Doctor Who*'s greatest icons and, beyond the show itself, a *bona fide* British design classic; one of the most memorable products of that incredible outpouring of creativity that was the 'swinging '60s'. Over the subsequent 40-odd years, their image has become ingrained on the British public consciousness. When *Doctor Who* returned to TV in 2005, Russell T Davies ensured that its greatest monsters were brought back in a way that was lovingly faithful to the past, with only minor, cosmetic modifications to update their look for a modern audience. The new paradigm Daleks of 'Victory of the Daleks' are, by contrast, a complete travesty of the original design: considerably larger, plastic-looking, with an ugly humped back, and painted in a variety of horribly garish colours. Small wonder that they were soon being ridiculed in YouTube videos consisting of montages of clips arranged to the theme tunes of the similarly-multicoloured toddler-appeal characters of *Power Rangers* and *Teletubbies*. 'Eh-oh! It's the Teletubby Daleks!' – with the emphasis on the 'tubby'. It wasn't long before TV comedians were getting in on the act too, acerbic commentator Charlie Brooker likening them to 'furious crayons'. Clearly, the dark fairytale idea has gone completely by the board here.

At one point when the *Doctor Who* TV movie of 1996 was being planned, the idea was mooted of introducing multi-legged 'spider Daleks'. Well, now it seems that we have 'camel Daleks'; Daleks designed by committee, presumably. It is not completely beyond the bounds of possibility that the Daleks could be given a cool modern makeover (there have even been one or two good fan-made attempts), but these certainly don't fit that bill. They look like life-size versions of some of the misshapen Dalek toys that fans used to shake their heads over in wry amusement in earlier decades; or perhaps Daleks constructed using only a young child's poorly-proportioned and crudely-coloured drawing for a blueprint.

One just has to ask: *what on earth were Steven Moffat and his team thinking?*

Amongst the justifications put forward by Moffat and Gatiss, in their *Doctor Who Confidential* interviews and elsewhere, are that they simply felt like doing something that hadn't been done before (very true, but hardly a compelling reason!) and that they wanted to give the new paradigm Daleks a look similar to the 'larger, more colourful' ones seen in the two 1960s movie adaptations, *Dr Who and the Daleks* (1965) and *Daleks – Invasion Earth 2150 AD* (1966). There are, though, a number of misconceptions wrapped up in that latter motivation. For one thing, despite the statements of Moffat and Gatiss to the contrary, the movie Daleks were actually in most respects no larger than the ones in the classic-era TV show. They were made by the same company to the same dimensions, but just had raised fenders, like those featured on TV in 'The Dalek Invasion of Earth' (1964). So, in other words, they were *exactly the same size* as the ones in what was, at the time of the first movie being made, the Daleks' most-recently-transmitted TV story. Secondly, the movie Daleks had a metallic look, not a plastic one as given to the new paradigm Daleks. Thirdly, most of them had a colour scheme similar to those on TV at that time – silver and blue – with only a few, more senior ones having a limited range of relatively subtle distinguishing colours – red, black and gold – all of which have also been used to denote senior Daleks in the TV show at one point or another. So, in fact, the movie Daleks were scarcely 'more colourful' at all. And besides all that, the two big-screen adaptations have never been as popular with *Doctor Who* fans as Moffat and Gatiss seem to believe. I well recall being dragged along to the cinema to see them several times when they were released in the 1960s, and finding them to be a terrible caricature of the TV show, not even featuring the 'proper' Doctor and his companions. Discussions with my school friends revealed that many of them felt the same way too. Similarly, since organised *Doctor Who* fandom began in the mid-1970s, the predominant attitude toward the two movies has been lukewarm at best. That these dumbed-down interpretations are now being cited as a supposed source of inspiration for the TV show itself seems a completely cockeyed situation.

The idea that making the Daleks bigger gives them greater menace is another complete fallacy. The relatively short stature of the original Daleks was part of their appeal. It created the impression that they had the monster equivalent of 'short man syndrome', or that they were like vindictive, out-of-control children; and, as Raymond P Cusick had intended, it helped to disguise the fact that there was a human operator within. The hulking new paradigm version is so big that it seems almost as if there could be two or three people inside! One can only hope that the Daleks' inventor Davros never reappears in the same type of casing, or he will look like the wartime graffiti character Chad peering out over the front edge ('Wot, no Daleks!').

This redesign is the same kind of wrong-headed folly as when the Coca-Cola company disastrously reformulated the flavour of its world-famous drink in 1985, resulting in a huge public backlash and ultimate reversal of the change. Imagine the outcry if the manufacturers of the Mini car suddenly decided to give it a huge rear-end bulge. It would be bigger, certainly, but would it be better? No. To put it more bluntly, messing around with a pop culture design classic like the original Daleks is simply stupid. As *Doctor Who* diarist Jackie Jenkins astutely observed[31], it is the televisual equivalent of defacing a monument.

In the list of worst design mistakes ever made by *Doctor Who* production teams, this has to rank as one of the top two, arguably matched only by the appalling look conceived for the sixth Doctor's costume back in 1983. In fact, what Moffat and his team have given us here is the Dalek equivalent of that costume: garish, tasteless, over-the-top and utterly inappropriate. And just as that costume blighted the whole of Colin Baker's era in the show, it seems likely that every time Matt Smith's Doctor comes to battle the Time Lord's oldest and most iconic foes – and every time that they now feature in tie-in merchandise – it will have to be these horrendous new Teletubby versions. The Hunchbacks of Upper Boat.

This is not the only problem with 'Victory of the Daleks'. Sadly, from the point when the action moves away from the Cabinet War Rooms and out onto the Dalek ship in space, the episode rather falls apart. The stand-off with the jammie dodger biscuit, claimed by the Doctor to be a TARDIS self-destruct device, goes on too long, so that the viewer's initial amusement turns to irritation. Then, after his ruse is rumbled, the Doctor is allowed to wander around for what seems like an age before the new paradigm Daleks finally try to exterminate him. These scenes on the Dalek ship are not helped by the fact that the location used for them is absolutely terrible, being very obviously part of a factory floor, complete with what looks like a sprinkler system or similar piping suspended from the ceiling above. Given that the CGI shots of the Dalek ship exterior show it to be of the same type as seen in stories like the Series One finale 'Bad Wolf'/'The Parting of the Ways', surely the interior should be of the same design as well? Did the production team waste so much money on having the new paradigm Daleks constructed that they couldn't afford a decent set in which to present them? That is certainly the impression given.

To have the Dalek ship being attacked by Spitfires in gravity bubbles is a fun idea, and – like the earlier images of the London skyline dotted with wartime barrage balloons – well realised with some excellent CGI work. However, the implication that Bracewell has been able to put this plan into effect in a matter of minutes, working from only a few notes and blueprints on his desk, is totally ludicrous, and completely ruins the credibility of the sequence. The frustrating thing is that this could have been easily avoided with just a few tweaks to the

---

[31] In her book *Single White Who Fan* (Hirst Books, 2011).

script, to indicate that Bracewell had already spent some weeks experimenting with the gravity bubbles and training the Spitfire pilots in flying within them – as a way of reaching Germany without being detected by radar, perhaps – but was forced to put them into effect more quickly than intended in order to target the Dalek ship. As it stands, this climactic sequence can only be viewed as a piece of pure fantasy.[32]

There are other issues with the script, too. For instance, apart from Churchill and Bracewell, none of the other characters in the Cabinet War Rooms really gets a chance to make an impression. This means that when, toward the end of the episode, the young WAAF Lilian Breen learns that her boyfriend Reg has been killed in action, it appears a rather tacked-on and tokenistic acknowledgement of the casualties of war. What was really needed was for Amy to be given some conversations with Lilian earlier on, enabling the viewer to get acquainted with her first. (We don't even get to learn her first name in the dialogue of the episode; it is given only in the closing credits. The same is true also of the other speaking WAAF character, Blanche.)

Then there is the convoluted nature of the Daleks' plan, which involves them somehow knowing that Churchill is acquainted with the Doctor; correctly predicting that he will telephone the TARDIS and that the Doctor will respond; and hoping that the Doctor will just happen to say something like 'I am the Doctor, and you are the Daleks!' and thus provide the 'testimony' they need in order to activate their progenitor device. All highly improbable.

More seriously still, the resolution of Bracewell's plot strand is distinctly unsatisfactory. The Doctor's attempt to disarm the bomb by evoking the memories of the real Bracewell, and thereby getting the robot to think of itself as human, is a bit hackneyed to start with. What makes matters worse, though, is that it doesn't actually work until Amy takes over and – with a sideways glance at the Doctor, possibly betraying her own feelings – asks if Bracewell ever fancied someone he shouldn't. As when she saved the day in 'The Beast Below', this is good for her character – although it is really just lucky guesswork on her part that Bracewell did indeed have such an experience – but has the unfortunate effect of making the Doctor seem completely ineffectual. Then, compounding that impression, instead of deactivating the robot, the Doctor leaves him free to return home and seek out his – or rather, the original Bracewell's – long-lost love Dorabella. No doubt the idea behind this was to show the Doctor's compassion, but actually, given that the robot still has within it a bomb that could destroy the entire Earth, it just strikes the viewer as recklessly irresponsible. What if Bracewell fails to find Dorabella, or is rejected by her, or succumbs to depression and decides to 'kill' himself, as he contemplated doing earlier in the episode? Again, this is something that could have been readily addressed with a small amendment to the script, to make clear that the bomb was *permanently* disabled. But there is no such indication in the programme as transmitted.

---

[32] Mark Gatiss apparently realised this shortcoming himself later on, as in one of a series of fictitious Churchill diary entries he contributed to *Doctor Who – The Brilliant Book 2011* (see Appendix G for further details) he indicated that Bracewell had been 'converting the aeroplanes for some time, using this "gravity bubble" method'. However, this is difficult to reconcile with what is seen in 'Victory of the Daleks' itself.

CRACKS IN TIME

Andrew Gunn's direction on this episode is better than on 'The Beast Below', but still nothing to write home about. In the TARDIS scenes toward the end, he actually seems to have angled the camera off the back of the set entirely at one point. In fact, this is due to the set being so downright awful that one section of it looks just like a row of spare scenery panels left standing against the studio wall, but Gunn certainly doesn't show it to its best advantage. The supporting cast also seem uncertain at what level they are supposed to be pitching their performances – although Bill Paterson is excellent as Bracewell – and Matt Smith gives his least sure-footed showing as the Doctor.

Even without the introduction of the appalling new Daleks – or Fatleks, as many fans derisively dubbed them – this would have been quite a weak episode. With it, it sadly becomes, in this author's eyes, the first out-and-out disaster of an episode since *Doctor Who*'s 2005 revival. Not so much 'Victory of the Daleks' as 'Trashing of the Daleks'.

# 5.04 – THE TIME OF ANGELS

Writer: Steven Moffat
Director: Adam Smith

## DEBUT TRANSMISSION DETAILS

BBC One/BBC HD
Date: 24 April 2010. Scheduled time: 6.25 pm. Actual time: 6.24 pm.

Duration: 41' 42"

## ADDITIONAL CREDITED CAST

Simon Dutton (Alistair), Mike Skinner (Security Guard), Iain Glen (Octavian), Mark Springer (Christian), Troy Glasgow (Angelo), David Atkins (Bob), Darren Morfitt (Marco)

## PLOT

In the 51st Century, a Weeping Angel causes the star-liner *Byzantium* to crash on the surface of the planet Alfava Metraxis. This is in an attempt to rescue many others of its kind that are trapped there in a dormant and degraded state, having been starved of energy for many years, in a Maze of the Dead built by the native Aplans. River Song, having enlisted the Doctor's aid to escape from the liner while it was still in space, pilots the TARDIS to the crash site, to rendezvous with a group of military clerics led by their Bishop, Father Octavian. Together, the party make their way through the Maze of the Dead to reach the hull of the crashed *Byzantium*, while around them the previously-dormant Weeping Angels, feeding on radiation released from the stricken liner, start to revive …

## QUOTE, UNQUOTE

- **River:** 'Ha, I'm going to be a professor someday, am I? How exciting! Spoilers!'
- **Bob:** 'I didn't escape, sir. The Angel killed me too.'
- **Doctor:** 'There's one thing you never put in a trap. If you're smart, if you value your continued existence, if you have any plans about seeing tomorrow, there's one thing you never, ever put in a trap.
  **Bob:** 'And what would that be, sir?'
  **Doctor:** 'Me.'

## CONTINUITY POINTS

- River Song can write in Old High Gallifreyan, the lost language of the Time

111

Lords, in which she burns the message 'Hello Sweetie' into the *Byzantium*'s home box – the star-liner's equivalent of an aircraft's black box flight recorder, which flies home with all the data in the event that something happens to the ship. The box is found 12,000 years later (i.e. sometime around the 63rd Century) by the Doctor in what he tells Amy is the Delerium Archive, 'the biggest museum ever' and 'the final resting place of the Headless Monks', situated on an asteroid. He adds that there were days when words in Old High Gallifreyan could 'burn stars and raise up empires and topple gods'.

- River Song is younger here than when first seen in 'Silence in the Library'/'Forest of the Dead', and is not yet a Professor; she is addressed by Octavian as 'Dr Song'. She has met the Matt Smith incarnation of the Doctor before, in his future, but this is his first meeting with her. When River encountered the David Tennant incarnation in 'Silence in the Library', she asked him, 'Crash of the *Byzantium*, have we done that yet?' – referring to the situation seen in 'The Time of Angels'. Having deduced, from his blank expression, that he did not know what she was talking about, she must have realised that the David Tennant incarnation was earlier than the Matt Smith one. However, after flicking forward a few pages in her diary, she then went on to ask, 'Picnic at Asgard. Have we done Asgard yet?' Assuming she was not just getting completely confused, this would seem to suggest that she believed the picnic at Asgard took place, or could have taken place, at an earlier point in the Doctor's life than the crash of the *Byzantium*. There would appear to be two possible explanations for this:

  a) She had the picnic at Asgard with another, later incarnation of the Doctor, but for some reason failed to establish at that time whether he came before or after the Matt Smith incarnation, so there was still a possibility in her mind that he, and the picnic, might have come between the David Tennant and Matt Smith incarnations.

  b) She had the picnic at Asgard with the David Tennant incarnation, in an unscreened encounter at a later point in his life than when he visited the Library, but for some reason failed to establish at that time whether he came before or after the Matt Smith incarnation, hence the need for her still to ask him the question about the crash of the *Byzantium*.

On balance, b) would seem the better of the two explanations. River immediately recognised the David Tennant incarnation on arriving in the Library, without having to be told that he was the Doctor, and was shocked when she discovered that he did not know her. She also said, 'You're younger than I've ever seen you.' Since the Matt Smith incarnation appears younger than the David Tennant one (even though he is not), this would seem to confirm that she was referring to having met the latter before, when he was older. She had not previously met his companion Donna Noble (though she knew about her), so it is most likely that she first encountered the tenth Doctor at some point in his life between the end of the Series Four finale 'Journey's

End', when he parted company with Donna, and his regeneration at the end of 'The End of Time' Part Two. It would have been then that they shared the picnic at Asgard, and quite possibly had other adventures too – and (although this was not a point that needed to be considered when he wrote the episode) Steven Moffat confirmed in Issue 442 of *Doctor Who Magazine* that this is his own interpretation. However, it would seem that the Doctor with whom River spends most time, and whom she regards as 'her' Doctor, is the Matt Smith incarnation. It was doubtless he who took her to Darillium to see the Singing Towers and who gave her his sonic screwdriver – as recounted in 'Forest of the Dead' – on their final meeting before she saw his previous incarnation again in the Library, where she died. In 'The Time of Angels', the encounter at Darillium is still of course in the eleventh Doctor's future. Consulting her diary, River refers to one other such encounter, asking 'Have we done the Bone Meadows?'

- There is, though, another possible explanation as to why River recognised the Doctor straight away in 'Silence in the Library'. When, in 'The Time of Angels', he asks her how she knows who he is, given his changing appearance, she says, 'I've got pictures of all your faces. You never show up in the right order though. I need the spotter's guide'. This suggests, in addition, that she may have met incarnations other than the tenth and eleventh. If so, though, they would have to have been later incarnations rather than earlier ones, as he was in his tenth incarnation when he met her for the first time. This could be thought to lend some credence to explanation a) in the point above.

- River states that the TARDIS is not supposed to make its familiar materialisation noise on landing and does so only because the Doctor '[leaves] the brakes on'. On first consideration, this seems strange, because in past stories other TARDISes, not just the Doctor's, have been heard to make the same (or a similar) noise on materialising or dematerialising. However, River may well mean simply that the noise should not be heard *inside* the ship. In the classic era stories, the materialisation noise was generally heard only outside the TARDIS, not inside; instead, sometimes (though not always) an electronic tone sounded in the control room to alert the occupants to the fact that the ship had reached its destination. This same tone is indeed heard when the TARDIS arrives on the planet in 'The Time of Angels'. (This may also explain why no materialisation noise was heard inside the ship when it materialised on Starship UK in 'The Beast Below'; possibly the Doctor, for once, did not 'leave the brakes on'.)

- The Doctor states that he has met the Weeping Angels 'once, on Earth, a long time ago, but those were scavengers, barely surviving'. This is a reference to the events of the Series Three episode 'Blink'.

- The Aplans were two-headed creatures, but they died out around the 47th Century. Their planet has since been terraformed and become home to six billion human colonists.

- The Doctor learns from an antique book found by River Song, 'That which holds the image of an Angel becomes itself an Angel'. This seems at odds with the fact that Sally Sparrow had several photos of Angels at the end of 'Blink' but they did not themselves become Angels. However, those were all photos of the Angels in the basement of the Wester Drumlins house, which were 'quantum locked' and dormant by that point, so possibly images of quantum locked Angels are themselves quantum locked.

- The book discovered by River Song also cautions against looking into the eyes of an Angel, as they are not the windows to the soul but the doors. This advice comes too late for Amy, who has already looked into the Angel's eyes, as a result of which she is 'infected' by the creature.

PRODUCTION NOTES

- This episode and 'Flesh and Stone' were made as Block One of Series Five's production schedule.
- Principal recording for the eleventh Doctor's era got under way on 20 and 21 July 2009 on Southerndown Beach in Ogmore Vale, Bridgend (previously used at the location for Bad Wolf Bay in episodes such as the Series Two finale 'Doomsday'). This was for the scenes of the *Byzantium* crash site. Many press and fan photographers were in attendance for this momentous occasion. Further planet exteriors were taped on 22 and 23 July at Aberthaw Quarry in Fonmon, South Glamorgan. The ancient iron works in Clearwell Caves, Coleford, Gloucestershire were transformed into the Maze of the Dead from 3 to 8 August. The crew then moved into the studio at Upper Boat, recording scenes for this story on 12-14 August, 19 August and 24-25 September. Back on location on 29 September, Bute Park was used for the opening sequence of the *Byzantium* security guard hallucinating that he was in a park. The following day, Brecon Cathedral was the location used for the museum scenes. A pick-up shot of the Doctor biting Amy's hand (to prove to her that she was not turning to stone) was taped on 14 October at the Vicarage, Rhymney, Gwent, during production of 'The Eleventh Hour'. Another pick-up shot was recorded in studio, on 12 November.
- Some of the shots in the Clearwell Caves location were taped by a second unit under the uncredited direction of Alice Troughton, who had previously handled full episodes of *Doctor Who*, *Torchwood* and *The Sarah Jane Adventures*.
- 'The Time of Angels' features an unusually long pre-opening-titles section, lasting 4' 56".
- The *Byzantium* security guard tricked by River Song was played by Mike Skinner, best known for his work as a rap artist performing under the name the Streets. He was given this cameo role as he is a *Doctor Who* fan.
- The original BBC One transmission of this episode gave rise to some controversy, as the channel's presentation department superimposed over the dramatic cliffhanger scene a caption advertising the following programme, the theatrical talent contest *Over the Rainbow*. This caption (which was not seen in some BBC One regions such as Northern Ireland, and did not feature on the BBC HD transmission) incorporated an animated figure of the latter programme's presenter, entertainer Graham Norton[33], and was one of a set of

---

[33] This was the second time that Graham Norton had inadvertently impinged upon the debut transmission of a *Doctor Who* episode; his voice had briefly intruded over the opening minutes of 'Rose' at the start of Series One, having been relayed live

new idents, including some depicting the eleventh Doctor, made for BBC One by Ardman Animations, the company behind the hugely successful *Wallace and Gromit* productions. Having received a huge number of public complaints – reportedly over 5,000 in total – that the cliffhanger had been marred by this unwarranted intrusion, the BBC issued an unreserved apology and changed its policy so that in future such captions would not be used over the closing scenes of drama productions.

OOPS!

- The CGI images of the TARDIS in space in the early part of the episode show a (slightly modified version of) the old police box from the tenth Doctor's era, not the reconstituted one introduced in 'The Eleventh Hour'.

PRESS REACTION

- 'The Maze of the Dead might have had the familiar clichés of dark, sinister labyrinthine tunnels containing horrors that a few plucky heroes have to face, but the suspense was maintained well and the revelation that all the statues were Angels was genuinely shocking. Matt Smith again showed that his is likely to be the most subtle portrayal of the Doctor since Patrick Troughton, leading this viewer to wonder [if] this could be his "The Tomb of the Cybermen"! His spiel to the Angels that you should never put him in a trap was a great way to close the episode, even if his shooting of the anti-gravity globe was a slightly curious twist on the cliffhanger, and one is left genuinely curious as to exactly what will happen next week.' Gavin Fuller, *Telegraph* website, 24 April 2010.
- 'You can't help thinking that when fans first heard that Steven Moffat was the new showrunner, they half-hoped that *Doctor Who* would be like this every week. Of course, that was never going to happen. The show thrives on variety. Moffat couldn't churn out "Blink" week after the week. That's not to say that the lighter, more fantasy-tinged stories are some irritating necessity we have to put up with. They can be classics too (they often are), and they're a vital part of the show's space warp and weft. But it just seems that with Moffat back on familiar ground, the show feels more confident, strident and self-assured.' Dave Golder, *SFX* website, 24 April 2010.
- '"The Time of Angels" starts off heavy on River, then shifts more into the terror of the Angels in its second [section]. It's not as scary as "Blink", but by telling two repeat stories in one, it manages to keep each part feeling fairly fresh. Right now, I'm more interested in the Doctor/River relationship. "Silence in the Library" had them on wildly disparate footing – it was his first time meeting her, and her last time seeing him – and his memories of her death (and inability to tell her about it) are at least part of what makes him so uncomfortable around her. (The other part, of course, is that the Doctor … likes to be the smartest one in the room and doesn't appreciate being in the company of someone who knows more about his life – and his ship – than he

from one of the BBC's studios by mistake.

does.) Here, they're on slightly more equal terms, in that they at least know something of each other when they meet.' Alan Sepinwall, Hitfix website, 8 May 2010.

- 'This was what we were waiting for! Steven Moffat in full flow with a great little horror tale that just builds and builds. To be honest, this episode wiped the floor with the [previous ones in this series]. The standard suddenly jumped up a notch, and everyone seemed to be well into their stride with it all. Of course, the Weeping Angels were one of the success stories of earlier years – a genuinely original monster that was creepy and scary into the bargain. I wasn't sure though about bringing River Song back into it. I liked her in the Library story, and of course she was always a cert to return, but it all seemed a little bit like "the best of Steven Moffat" – all we were missing was a kid wandering about in a gasmask and a clockwork robot to make it complete.' David J Howe, Howe's Who blog, 1 May 2010.

ANALYSIS

As the first story to feature the spine-chilling Weeping Angels since their introductory appearance in Steven Moffat's brilliant Series Three episode 'Blink' – regarded by many as one of *Doctor Who*'s greatest classics – 'The Time of Angels'/'Flesh and Stone' had a lot of expectations riding on it. Not only that, but it also marked the return to the show of the very popular River Song from Moffat's Series Four contribution 'Silence in the Library'/'Forest of the Dead' – something that some fans doubted would ever be possible, given what a high-profile and in-demand actress Alex Kingston is. Would this latest story from Moffat be able to match up to those distinguished antecedents?

Thankfully, the answer to that question is a resounding yes. After 'The Beast Below' and particularly 'Victory of the Daleks', it seemed that the series might be in danger of going off the rails, but any such fears are quickly dispelled here. The opening sequence of 'The Time of Angels' is simply terrific, as River Song escapes from the *Byzantium* by kissing a guard with hallucinogenic lipstick – an idea possibly inspired by Captain John Hart's use of paralysing lip-gloss on Gwen Cooper in the *Torchwood* episode 'Kiss Kiss, Bang Bang' – and then ejecting herself into space, to be rescued by the Doctor in the TARDIS. Admittedly, the way she gets the Doctor to come to her aid, by leaving him a message that he stumbles across in a museum 12,000 years later, seems hardly foolproof – what if the message never reached him, or was found by one of the Doctor's earlier incarnations who didn't know her? – but the idea is so clever and amusing that any slight implausibility can be easily forgiven.

The younger River Song we see here is a touch sassier than the one we – and the Doctor – first met in the Library, as immediately signalled by a close-up shot of her fabulous red Christian Louboutin shoes as she struts along one of the *Byzantium*'s walkways. That the Doctor has previously witnessed her death doesn't seem to faze him much, and this makes sense really, as on his travels through time he must frequently encounter people of whose lives, and deaths, he has foreknowledge. River remains wonderfully enigmatic, too, as Moffat continues to tease the viewer with hints that she and the Doctor may have had an intimate relationship, or even been married, at some point in her past and his future. It is even revealed that River is able to fly the TARDIS better than the Doctor can himself. When Amy asks her about this, she claims that she had 'lessons from the very best' – although it seems that she does not mean the Doctor! The fact that River acts like the Doctor's wife is something that the obviously slightly jealous Amy quickly picks up on, but when she quizzes first him and then her about it, they both avoid either confirming or denying it – in the Doctor's case, presumably because he is not even sure himself. As Father Octavian intriguingly says to River, 'He doesn't know yet, does he? Who and what you are.' Adding to the mystery, River then tells him, 'I won't let you down. Believe you me, I have no intention of going back to prison.' In short, River is a brilliantly written character; and, as in her debut appearance, Alex Kingston does the role proud, delivering a bravura performance.

Fortunately, Matt Smith and Karen Gillan also rise to the occasion, giving their best accounts yet as the series' new leads. Their apparent assurance is all the more remarkable for the fact that, although transmitted fourth and fifth, the episodes of this story were really the first of Series Five to be recorded, and thus saw the pair making their on-camera debuts in their respective roles – a challenge that actually saw Smith suffer something of a crisis of confidence, as he has since admitted in interviews. Gillan is particularly impressive in the deliciously scary sequence where Amy finds herself trapped inside the clerics' drop-ship and – recalling similar conceits from horror movies such as *The Ring* (1998) – being menaced by a video-recorded image of a Weeping Angel that takes on a life of its own and emerges from the screen. Her performance is also notably strong when, later, Amy slowly realises that, by looking into the eyes of the Angel, she has become 'infected' by it, causing her to believe that she is starting to turn to stone – a clear nod to the Greek myth of the Medusa.

The role of the Doctor is not only very well played in this story, but also very well written, with none of the rather forced wackiness or apparent ineptitude seen at times in the previous three episodes. This is just as well, as it would be hard to envisage River Song having a romantic relationship with a Doctor who was prone to bouts of clowning and cluelessness (something that was never an issue with the David Tennant incarnation). The eleventh Doctor really seems to have got his act together now. From the viewer's perspective, this comes across as a well-thought-out strand of character development across the first four stories; but, given that they were actually made out of sequence, it must remain open to question at this stage whether that was in fact intentional or whether Moffat was simply experimenting with and refining the writing of the new Doctor's character as he went along. Whatever the case, Smith certainly seems very much at home in the part, even in his first-recorded appearance.

Some of the credit for getting such great performances from the cast – including also Iain Glen's understated turn in the guest role of Octavian – must surely go to director Adam Smith, whose high-quality work was previously seen in 'The Eleventh Hour' but who does an even more outstanding job on this, his debut contribution to the show. In plot terms, not a great deal actually happens in 'The Time of Angels'; it is an episode that relies very much on atmosphere and suspense, and Smith serves these up in abundance. Particularly memorable are the very tense – and beautifully-lit – gothic-horror-infused scenes where the characters make their way through the catacombs of the so-called Maze of the Dead surrounded by dozens of eerily-eroded stone statues, which the Doctor eventually determines to be dormant Weeping Angels. Steven Moffat has described the relationship between this story and 'Blink' as being akin to that between the movies 'Aliens' (1986) and 'Alien' (1979), and one can certainly see the validity of that analogy here. The shots of Octavian and his armed force of camouflage-suited clerics making their way through the Maze, nervously eyeing the previously-dormant but now-awakening Angels, strongly recall those in 'Aliens' of the space marines infiltrating the alien-infested atmosphere-processing plant on the colony planet LV-426. When Octavian's men Christian, Angelo and Bob are each in turn lured to their doom at the hands of an Angel that suddenly appears out of the darkness, this similarly mirrors the way that individual marines are picked off one by one by the aliens in the movie. The fact that the clerics use a 'drop-ship' to reach the planet from orbit, as do the marines in 'Aliens', is another parallel between the two.

The clerics are a novel creation by Moffat, and it seems only right that it should be a militarised Church group that is given the task of dealing with Angels. Rather less original, though, is the idea of the dead Bob's voice being used by one of the Angels to communicate with the Doctor by radio, which is similar to the gasmask boy's disembodied voice eerily emanating from disconnected telephones and inactive tape recorders in 'The Empty Child'/'The Doctor Dances' and even more so to the 'data ghost' notion in 'Silence in the Library'/'Forest of the Dead'; another example of Moffat recycling and adapting successful aspects of his earlier stories.

It is certainly fantastic to see the Weeping Angels brought back for a rematch with the Doctor. The public reaction to them when they first appeared in 'Blink' was, deservedly, absolutely phenomenal, and while it was never going to be possible for them to generate quite the same buzz of interest and excitement again – there is almost inevitably an element of diminishing returns when a monster that proves hugely popular on its debut is given another outing – they clearly held a good deal of untapped potential ripe for exploration in further stories. They fit in very well, too, with Moffat's initial vision for Series Five, seeming like creatures from the creepiest of dark fairytales. Surprisingly, though, Moffat does rather throw away what 'Blink' established as one of their unique defining characteristics as monsters: that they do not kill people as such, but rather displace them in time and then feed off the potential energy of their lost lives. In 'The Time of Angels', by contrast, the Angel from the *Byzantium* simply breaks the luckless clerics' necks, which is far less interesting. Moffat does at least address this in the script, by having the Doctor speculate that the dead clerics' bodies are needed for some purpose (which proves to be correct, in Bob's case at least, when it is revealed that the Angel's use of his voice has involved stripping his cerebral cortex from his body and reanimating a version of his consciousness), but it still seems a pity that such a great idea from the Series Three episode is sacrificed for the sake of a fairly inconsequential plot convenience.

It is always a little difficult to assess the first episode of a two-part story in isolation from the second, but 'The Time of Angels' is superbly written and produced, full of great dialogue, and has all the hallmarks of a classic in the making. The strongest episode of Series Five thus far.

# 5.05 – FLESH AND STONE

Writer: Steven Moffat
Director: Adam Smith

DEBUT TRANSMISSION DETAILS

BBC One/BBC HD
Date: 1 May 2010. Scheduled time: 6.25 pm. Actual time: 6.27 pm.

Duration: 42' 42"

ADDITIONAL CREDITED CAST

Iain Glen (Octavian), David Atkins (Bob), Darren Morfitt (Marco), Mark Monero (Pedro), George Russo (Phillip).

PLOT

The Doctor manages to get himself, Amy, River and the Church group on board the *Byzantium*. Pursued by the Weeping Angels, they gain access to the ship's oxygen factory – a chamber containing a forest of technologically-enhanced trees. A crack in the universe appears, the same as the one on Amy's bedroom wall when she was a girl, and each of the clerics that goes to investigate it is erased from time, so that his fellows no longer remember him. Amy has to wait with her eyes closed in order to save herself from being killed by the Angel that has infected her. The Doctor and River meanwhile make their way to the primary flight deck, but Octavian is killed by one of the Angels. River gets the ship's teleport working, and uses it to rescue Amy from the forest. The Angels want the Doctor to sacrifice himself to the crack, to prevent them from being absorbed by it. However, their draining of the *Byzantium*'s power eventually causes its artificial gravity to fail, and they all fall into the crack. The Doctor, River and Amy – now freed from her infection – save themselves from the same fate by hanging on to the flight deck consoles, and the crack then closes.

QUOTE, UNQUOTE

* **Amy:** 'So, what if the gravity fails?'
  **Doctor:** 'I've thought about that.'
  **Amy:** 'And?'
  **Doctor:** 'And we'll all plunge to our deaths. See, I've thought about it.'
* **Doctor:** 'A forest, in a bottle, on a spaceship, in a maze. Have I impressed you yet, Amy Pond?'
* **Doctor:** 'Bob, why are they making her count?'
  **Bob:** 'To make her afraid, sir.'

**Doctor:** 'Okay. But why? What for?'
**Bob:** 'For fun, sir.'

- **Doctor:** 'I wish I'd known you better.'
**Octavian:** 'I think, sir, you know me at my best.'
- **Doctor:** 'I look forward to it.'
**River:** 'I remember it well.'
- **Amy:** 'What are you thinking?'
**Doctor:** 'Time can be rewritten.'

## CONTINUITY POINTS

- The Doctor says that the crack in the universe contains 'pure time energy'. He adds, 'That's the power, that's the fire at the end of the universe'. He also describes the crack itself as 'the end of the universe'. When River asks how this can be, he says: 'Here's what I think. One day there'll be a very big bang, so big that every moment in history – past and future – will crack.' He later identifies the date of the explosion as 26 June 2010. This is also now confirmed as the day after Amy left Leadworth to join him on his travels, i.e. the day she was due to get married.
- The Doctor explains that when things fall into the crack in the universe, they are taken out of existence, so that only time travellers can remember them and everyone else forgets. He implies that this is what erased people's memories of the CyberKing in 'The Next Doctor' (2009) and Amy's memories of the ducks on Leadworth duck pond and of the Dalek invaders in 'The Stolen Earth'/'Journey's End' (2009).
- The Doctor says of the Weeping Angels, 'We stare at them to stop them getting closer, we don't even blink, and that's exactly what they want, 'cause as long as our eyes are open, they can climb inside.' He adds that they enter the visual centres of the brain: 'It's like there's a screen, a virtual screen inside your mind, and the Angel is climbing out of it, and it's coming to shut you off.' The only way to 'starve' the Angel of sustenance is to close your eyes.
- After the Doctor leaves the incapacitated Amy in the forest to accompany River to the ship's primary flight deck, he appears to return briefly, to tell her that it is important for her to trust him, and for her to remember what he told her when she was seven. Curiously, however, he is wearing his jacket at this point, whereas when he left with River he was in his shirtsleeves, having earlier abandoned his jacket when escaping from the Weeping Angels. Could this prove to be significant later on …?
- Octavian tells the Doctor: 'Dr Song is in my personal custody. I released her from the Stormcage containment facility four days ago and I am legally responsible for her until she has accomplished her mission and earned her pardon.' He later explains why River was in the Stormcage: 'She killed a man. A good man. A hero to many.' River later confirms this herself, describing the man she killed as 'The best man I've ever known'. The Doctor appears to suspect that Octavian and River are referring to him, but neither of them will confirm the man's identity. It is uncertain whether or not River does in fact earn her pardon after this incident with the Weeping Angels, particularly as none of the clerics actually remembers the creatures.

PRODUCTION NOTES

- This episode and 'The Time of Angels' were made as Block One of Series Five's production schedule.
- The recording dates and locations for the beach scenes and the Maze of the Dead scenes were as noted in the entry on 'The Time of Angels'. Those of the forest were taped in Puzzlewood, a large woodland area within the Forest of Dean in Coleford, Gloucestershire, on 24, 25 and 27-31 July 2009. The closing sequence in Amy's bedroom was recorded on 12 and 14 October in the usual location of the Vicarage, Rhymney, Gwent.
- The title 'Flesh and Stone' was suggested by Steven Moffat's son Joshua, who thought his father's initial idea of having another title including the word 'Angels' would be boring.

OOPS!

- In the final scene, in Amy's bedroom at night, the time on her digital clock changes from 11.59 to 12.00, and the date also changes, from 06/25 to 06/26, so clearly it is midnight. However, the 'AM' indicator changes to 'PM', when it should be the other way around.

PRESS REACTION

- 'From start to end, "Flesh and Stone" was a spell-binding blend of smart, recklessly inventive sci-fi and pure high fantasy. Moffat's always been a big ideas man when it comes to *Doctor Who*, but "Flesh and Stone" didn't so much shift the show up a gear as stick a rocket up its bum and run away laughing. As well as maintaining the Weeping Angels as a credible – and deadly – menace we got a story that tied up all niggling uncertainties of the first half of the series, from missing ducks to missing memories, and dished out a dizzying amount of intrigue for the rest of its run.' Matt Wales, IGN website, 4 May 2010.
- 'I'm just going to come right out and say it. "Flesh and Stone" can lay credible claim to being the greatest episode of *Doctor Who* there has ever been. That's better than "Genesis of the Daleks" and better than "City Of Death" and better than "The Tomb Of The Cybermen" and, yes, better than "Blink". It's just ridiculously good – so much that there's scarcely any point in picking out moments because there was an iconic sequence every couple of seconds. Amy's creepy countdown; "I made him say comfy chairs"; the oxygen factory; the clerics being erased one by one; "I think the Angels are laughing"; the moment when the Angel starts to move … You literally have to keep catching your breath.' Dan Martin, *Guardian* website, 1 May 2010.
- 'Apparently it doesn't matter anymore if you are actually *looking* at the Weeping Angels, in order to "freeze" them; it's enough to whistle cheerily with your eyes shut and *pretend* that you can see them – which gets Amy out of Moffat's forest-centred writer's block in an even clumsier manner than the reprise of the glowing fissure from "The Eleventh Hour". There's no backing out of this grafted-on weakness now, greatly reducing the effectiveness of the

core concept of the creatures. It depends on the ratings, but I think Moffat will not return to his stony monsters until he has a smaller and more intimate tale to tell with them. This one started promisingly with "The Time of Angels", but exited on a desperate note, and in a positive flurry of lucky chances.' Leo Porter, Shadowlocked website, 1 May 2010.

## ANALYSIS

Steven Moffat has sometimes commented in interviews that, when writing a two-part story, he likes to introduce a sudden shift of location or some other unexpected twist early in the second episode in order to keep things fresh and exciting. He manages to achieve this admirably in 'Flesh and Stone' by moving the action inside the *Byzantium* and, in a particularly imaginative and surprising development, revealing that the ship contains an oxygen-producing forest. This serves as a fantastic backdrop to the action, as the Weeping Angels pursue the Doctor's party through the trees – or 'treeborgs', to be more precise – in a deadly game of cat-and-mouse. Adam Smith's direction is again superb here; and as is so often the case in this series, these scenes are beautifully lit and shot, giving them a very creepy quality. This is the closest yet that Series Five has come to presenting a traditional fairytale setting – albeit inside a spaceship! – and one can now appreciate the reasoning behind the costume designer's selection of a bright red hoodie for Karen Gillan to wear in this story: Amy becomes a veritable Little Red Riding Hood, stumbling through the forest with danger lurking on all sides. The fairytale theme is touched on again toward the end of the episode, when River tells the Doctor that he will see her next 'when the Pandorica opens'. 'That's a fairytale,' he whispers in her ear. 'Oh, Doctor, aren't we all?' she replies.

Steven Moffat again fills the episode with sparkling dialogue, and the wonderfully inventive quality of his writing is very much in evidence, as he throws in one new idea after another. The notion of a Weeping Angel being able to creep into the visual centre of your brain if you look into its eyes for too long, ultimately killing you unless you keep your eyes closed, is a good innovation. So too is the suggestion that the creatures take a gleeful pleasure in their killing, even at one point 'laughing' as they attack – although again this does seem a little at odds with the tenth Doctor's description of them in 'Blink' as 'The only psychopaths in the universe to kill you nicely'. Other highlights include the infected Amy slowly counting down from ten, made to do so by the advancing Angels simply to frighten her for their own amusement, and the cleric Marco losing all memory of each of his comrades in turn as they go off to investigate the crack in the universe and never come back.

At times, though, one can't help but wish that Moffat had shown a little more self-restraint in his efforts to ring the changes. Having already in 'The Time of Angels' abandoned the superb idea of the Weeping Angels killing people by displacing them through time (as confirmed here when one of them breaks Father Octavian's neck instead), he now unfortunately undermines two of their other unique selling points as monsters. Whereas previously it was said to be essential to keep looking at an Angel in order to stop it moving – an idea encapsulated in the famous 'Don't even blink!' line from their debut story – now it is apparently sufficient merely to *pretend* to be looking, as Amy does when she edges her way through a group of the creatures with her eyes closed, guided only by a proximity detector. Moffat tries to slide around this a little in the script by having the Doctor note that the Angels are distracted by the crack in the universe, but really this is a highly regrettable departure from what was previously established. Then there is the fact that in this episode, for the first time ever, the viewer actually sees a number of the Weeping Angels move. This is also a great pity as, while it affords an instant frisson of fear, it completely negates the rather pleasing illusion previously created that even the viewer's own observation of the creatures served to keep them quantum locked. Sadly, it seems that the Weeping Angels' originality as monsters is being repeatedly compromised in this story simply for the sake of generating a few quick scares.

There are two other problems with 'Flesh and Stone' that prevent the story as a whole from attaining the classic status promised by 'The Time of Angels'. The first is that it doesn't really have a proper ending; it just sort of peters out. The crack in the universe appears out of nowhere, and the Weeping Angels eventually fall into it, having failed to realise that their draining of the *Byzantium*'s power will cause its artificial gravity to fail. There is a suggestion that it is the Doctor's presence here, or more specifically Amy's, that causes the crack to appear in the first place; but other than that, the time travellers have no involvement in the story's resolution. The other problem is that, just five episodes in, there are already some significant illogicalities and inconsistencies starting to emerge in the ongoing story arc; not so much cracks in the universe as cracks in the plot.

In this episode, the Doctor warns Amy that if the time energy from the crack catches up with her, 'It will erase every moment of your existence. You'll never have been born at all.' Later, he tells her, 'The Angels all fell into the time field. The Angel in your memory never existed. It can't harm you now.' The first difficulty with this is that it seems to be completely at odds with the properties of the crack as established in 'The Eleventh Hour'. In that instance, the crack on young Amelia's bedroom wall seemed to act as a kind of cell, inside which Prisoner Zero was initially trapped by its Atraxi guard. Subsequently, both emerged from the crack; and Prisoner Zero's escape was indeed what drove the whole story. There was no mention of 'time energy' then, or of things within the crack being erased from existence. The second difficulty is that if the Weeping Angels on Alfava Metraxis never existed, following their disappearance into the crack, why is the wreck of the *Byzantium* still on the planet, and why are the clerics still there to carry out their mission? Why, also, has Father Octavian not returned from the dead, given that he was killed by one of the Weeping Angels that now supposedly was never there?

The intended implication seems to be that, while the Weeping Angels themselves are erased when they fall into the crack, the effects of any actions they took before that still remain; it is just that no-one, except the time travellers, can remember what caused those effects – as the Doctor indicates to Amy when, in response to her question as to why she can remember, he tells her, 'You're a time traveller now, Amy. Changes the way you see the universe forever.' Time has been rewritten, but only to a certain extent. This just about works as an theory. It would also account for the fact that in 'The Eleventh Hour' there was a duck pond in Leadworth even though there were never any ducks, as the Doctor seems to suggest here that that anomaly was likewise caused by the crack in the universe (although that in itself is rather strange, given that in Leadworth the crack was on Amelia's bedroom wall, not on the village green). In short, it would seem that the Weeping Angels have been erased not so much from existence as from memory. Steven Moffat's apparent equating of these two things is, though, confusing to say the least; and one has to say that the explanations in the script are rather garbled.

Moving on from all this, the episode ends with a coda in which the Doctor takes Amy back to her bedroom in Leadworth on the night before her wedding; a scene that has proved to be one of the story's biggest talking-points, as it basically involves a suddenly lustful Amy trying to cajole the nonplussed Doctor into having sex with her. Some fan critics have argued that this revelation of Amy being sexually attracted to the Doctor comes completely out of the blue, and consequently seems tacked on and gratuitous. That isn't really the case, though; the clues have been there for all to see in the previous episodes: in 'The Eleventh Hour', Amy refused to look away when the Doctor stripped naked to change his clothes; in 'Victory of the Daleks', she cast a telling sideways glance at him when asking Bracewell if he had ever fancied someone he shouldn't; and in 'The Time of Angels', she was clearly jealous of River Song's apparent future relationship with the Doctor, and effectively positioned herself in the role of his girlfriend by asking him 'Do I look that clingy?' when she thought he was prepared to die rather than leave her to the Weeping Angels' mercy.

It was made clear right from the outset that she had been fixated on her 'raggedy Doctor' since the age of seven, and had even got Rory to dress up as him when they were playing together as kids (and perhaps as grown-ups too ...). At the end of 'The Eleventh Hour', this led to her running away from her imminent wedding, and also incidentally from her distinctly adult work as a kissogram, by going off with the Doctor in the TARDIS, in what amounted to an attempt to revert to her childhood. Now, she is still balking at the idea of marrying Rory, but displaying her competing preoccupation with the Doctor in a more carnal way, by attempting to seduce him. Significantly, this comes immediately after the life-threatening incident where she is effectively placed in the role of Little Red Riding Hood, whose story is often interpreted as a metaphor for a young woman's sexual awakening; an angle notably explored in Neil Jordan's film *The Company of Wolves* (1984), based on the Angela Carter short story.

What the closing scene of 'Flesh and Stone' does, in effect, is to show us that Amy now recognises the need for her to accept her adulthood, but remains torn between her feelings for Rory and her feelings for the Doctor. What it doesn't do, on the other hand, is to make her any more likeable as a character. The implication that she has been more or less toying with Rory's affections, and that she apparently feels under no obligation to remain faithful to him, makes her seem rather cold and selfish; and certainly in these early episodes Karen Gillan brings little warmth to her portrayal.

In my Analysis of 'The Eleventh Hour', I wondered if Steven Moffat would be able to sustain the complex characterisation of Amy set up in that introductory episode. It would be fair to say that he has succeeded in doing so, at least thus far; and that is very much to his credit. It could in fact be contended that, of all the Doctor's companions over the years, Amy is actually one of the most believably depicted, in the sense of her coming across like a real person, with some deep-seated psychological issues. There are, though, two arguable downsides to this.

First, her emotional detachment means that she fulfils less well what has traditionally been one of the companion's main functions within the show's format: that is, of being someone the audience admires and can identify with as their reference point in the stories. Secondly, it raises some uncomfortable questions about the detrimental effect that the Doctor has had on the psyche of this young woman (and perhaps of others he has travelled with) by rather carelessly dropping in and out of her personal timeline. She may have become 'the girl who waited' – as the Doctor described her at the end of 'The Eleventh Hour' – but only because he *made* her wait.

Admittedly, this is not the first time that the Doctor has been shown to have had a less than wholly positive impact on the life of a companion. One recalls, for instance, Tegan parting company with him at the end of 'Resurrection of the Daleks' (1984) because she was sick of seeing so much killing. A few have even lost their own lives in the course of their adventures – most notably Adric in 'Earthshock' (1982). There was, though, much to be said for Russell T Davies's philosophy that travelling with the Doctor should be seen as a life-enhancing experience for the companion – even if perhaps he did not always stick to that in practice, especially in the case of Donna Noble, who was ultimately deprived of all her memories of her sojourn with the Time Lord (although, on the plus side, she did get given a winning lottery ticket!) To have the Doctor actually causing psychological harm to one of his companions, albeit inadvertently, arguably takes the show into new territory. However, it would seem that, particularly in the wake of the 'Time Lord victorious' plot strand at the end of the David Tennant era, it is now a rather outmoded and unrealistic viewpoint to expect the Doctor to be depicted as a straightforwardly heroic character. A testament, perhaps, to the increasing sophistication of modern audiences. If nothing else, it will certainly be fascinating to see where Steven Moffat and his fellow writers take the story of the Doctor, Amy and Rory over the course of the coming episodes …

# 5.06 – THE VAMPIRES OF VENICE

Writer: Toby Whithouse
Director: Jonny Campbell

DEBUT TRANSMISSION DETAILS

BBC One/BBC HD
Date: 8 May 2010. Scheduled time: 6.00 pm. Actual time: 5.59 pm.

Duration: 48' 11"

ADDITIONAL CREDITED CAST

Helen McRory (Rosanna[34]), Lucian Msamati (Guido), Alisha Bailey (Isabella), Alex Price (Francesco[35]), Gabriella Wilde, Hannah Steele, Elizabeth Croft, Sonila Vieshta, Gabriela Montaraz (Vampire Girls), Michael Percival (Inspector), Simon Gregor (Steward[36]).

PLOT

The Doctor takes Amy and her fiancé Rory to Venice, 1580, for them to have a romantic date. This is interrupted when they learn that girls entering a school run by the House of Calvierri are apparently being turned into vampires. Signora Rosanna Calvierri and her son Francesco are actually fish-like creatures from the planet Saturnyne who are converting the girls into others of their kind in an attempt to save their race from extinction. Their vampire-like characteristics are produced by the perception filters that they use to disguise their true forms. The Saturnynes want to submerge Venice in order to create a habitat suitable for themselves. The vampire girls are killed in an explosion caused by a boatman named Guido, whose own daughter Isabella was converted and then executed by being thrown to the Saturnynes' male offspring swimming in the canal. The Doctor saves Venice from destruction, Amy kills the Saturnyne previously disguised as Francesco, and Signora Calvierri commits suicide in the canal.

QUOTE, UNQUOTE

* **Doctor:** 'I like the bit when they say "It's bigger on the inside". I look forward to it.'
* **Doctor:** 'Pale, creepy girls who don't like sunlight and can't be seen in ... Am I

---

[34] Full name given in dialogue as 'Signora Rosanna Calvierri'.
[35] Full name given in dialogue as 'Francesco Calvierri'.
[36] Name given in dialogue as 'Carlo'.

thinking what I think I'm thinking?'
- **Doctor:** 'She was frightened, I was frightened, but we survived, you know, and the relief of it, and ... So, she kissed me.'
**Rory:** 'And you kissed her back.'
**Doctor:** 'No, I kissed her mouth.'
**Rory:** 'Funny.'
- **Doctor:** 'The people upstairs are very noisy.'
**Guido:** 'There aren't any people upstairs.'
**Doctor:** 'D'you know, I knew you were going to say that. Did anyone else know he was going to say that?'

CONTINUITY POINTS

- The second extra 'Meanwhile in the TARDIS' scene (duration 3' 54") included on the Complete Series Five DVD/Blu-Ray box set, released by 2Entertain on 8 November 2010, was intended to bridge the gap between 'Flesh and Stone' and 'The Vampires of Venice'. (For further details of the 'Meanwhile in the TARDIS' scenes, see the entry on 'The Beast Below'.) Following on from the sequence at the end of 'Flesh and Stone' where Amy kisses the Doctor, she argues that he has given clear signals of being sexually attracted to her. The Doctor counters that he is 'not like that'. Amy says: 'You are a bloke, and you don't know it. And I am here to help'. She tries to kiss him again, but he fends her off, telling her that the real reason he took her with him in the TARDIS is that he can see the universe afresh through her eyes. Amy realises that he must have had other companions previously, and asks how many of them were girls, and if they were young and hot. The Doctor tries to avoid the issue, but Amy tricks him into getting the TARDIS to display images of many of his previous female companions, including Leela in her 'leather bikini'. The Doctor determines to go and find Rory. Amy says he is at a stag night, and the Doctor replies: 'Well then, let's make it a great one.' This leads directly into the opening scene of 'The Vampires of Venice', where the Doctor interrupts Rory's stag night.
- The Doctor says that he owes the 18th Century womaniser Casanova a chicken, following a bet.
- The Doctor has in his pocket an old library card, for 'Shoreditch Library', bearing an identification photograph of his first incarnation. The card gives his address as '76 Totter's Lane, Shoreditch, London, EC1 5EG' – the address of the junkyard where the TARDIS was first seen in the show's opening episode, 'An Unearthly Child' (1963), and to which the Doctor returned in 'Attack of the Cybermen' (1985) and 'Remembrance of the Daleks' (1988). The name given on the card is 'Dr J Smith'. This suggests that the Doctor adopted his habitual 'John Smith' alias much earlier than previously indicated. Prior to this, its earliest use seen in the show was an accidental one in the story 'The Wheel in Space' (1968) during his second incarnation.
- Rory mentions that he and Amy have paid a deposit to book the village hall and hire a salsa band for their wedding reception.
- Signora Calvierri implies that there are 10,000 Saturnyne male offspring in the waters of Venice. She later reveals that the Saturnynes are on Earth because

they 'ran from the Silence'. She adds that there were 'cracks' in the universe: 'Some were tiny. Some were as big as the sky. Through some we saw worlds with people, and through others we saw Silence, and the end of all things. We fled to an ocean like ours, and the crack snapped shut behind us. Saturnyne was lost.' The Doctor theorises that only the male offspring survived the journey, and that the vampire girls are now being created to serve as their mates.

- As the Doctor and Amy have not been to Saturnyne, it appears that not *all* of the cracks in the universe are linked to their, and specifically Amy's, presence in a specific place and time, as the Doctor appeared to suggest in 'The Time of Angels'/'Flesh and Stone'.
- Signora Calvierri seems to know something of the Doctor's involvement in the Time War, referring to him as 'the same man that let an entire race turn to cinders and ash'.
- At the end of the episode, Silence falls, literally, on the Venice waterfront, and it is implied that the TARDIS keyhole is in the same shape as the cracks that have been appearing in the universe.

PRODUCTION NOTES

- This episode and 'Vincent and the Doctor' were made as Block Five of Series Five's production schedule.
- Earlier titles considered for this episode included 'Blood and Water', 'The House of Calvierri' and 'Vampires in Venice'. 'Vampires of Venice' was suggested by 'Victory of the Daleks' writer Mark Gatiss, and given an initial 'The' to form the final title.
- Location recording got under way on 25 November 2009 at the Bowls Inn, Bowls Terrace, Trecenydd, Caerphilly, for the pub scene of Rory's stag do. The crew then moved overseas to Croatia, where sequences for this story and 'Vincent and the Doctor' were taped over the two-week period 30 November to 13 December. The towns of Trogir and Pantana both stood in for 16th Century Venice. Atlantic College in St. Donat's Castle, Llantwit Major, Vale of Glamorgan became the interior of the Calvierri school between 16 and 18 December. Llancaiach Fawr Manor in Gelligaer Road, Nelson was used for the interior of Guido's house on 7 and 8 January 2010. The following day, shots of the tunnels under the Calvierri school were taped at Caerphilly Castle in Caerphilly. The courtyard of Castell Coch in Cardiff was used on 11 January for the night scene of the Doctor and Rory breaking into the school. Lastly, some plate shots were taken in the real Venice on 13 February. A small amount of studio recording, primarily for the TARDIS interior scene, took place on 25 November 2009 and 13 January 2010.

OOPS!

- When the Doctor first grasps hold of the rope in the Calvierri school's bell tower to begin climbing to the top, one of the windows behind him has a stormy sky visible beyond, courtesy of a CGI effect, but the other has a clear, bright sky.

PRESS REACTION

- 'It was the script that kept the Doctor's vampires (which in any case turned out to be fish from space) rolling merrily along. That and the fact that [Matt] Smith has so quickly inhabited the character it's now a case of David Who? [Toby] Whithouse was playing with all sorts of demons, my favourite line being Fish Vampire Son to Fish Vampire Mater: "Mummy, what's wrong with your perception filter?" It takes a dark, bloody heart to write a line like that.' Keith Watson, *Metro*, 10 May 2010.
- 'If "The Vampires Of Venice" proved anything, it was that this series has significantly raised standards for *Doctor Who*. It was beautifully shot, and there was plenty to pick apart: the way every part of the vampire mythos was explained away by *Who* pseudo-science was delightful; the stand-off between the Doctor and Rosanna was beautifully played; the dialogue as cracking as you'd expect from Whithouse; the Doctor and Amy getting over-excited about there being vampires was cute; and the climactic shot of the Doctor scaling the tower in the rain was just the correct level of broad brushstroke. Not "horse-jumping-out-of-a-mirror", but good nonetheless.' Dan Martin, *Guardian* website, 8 May 2010.
- 'There was dramatic potential in some of the scenes with Helen McRory's villainess Rosanna and her flamboyant son Francesco (Alex Price), but the overly trivial tone of the episode never made the most of this. Worst was the sheer derivativeness. The opening scene was very similar in concept to [that of] writer Toby Whithouse's previous *Doctor Who* script "School Reunion" (girl is taken to office of evil alien posing as human), and Whithouse also pillaged the whole aliens-posing-as-humans idea from there as well.' Gavin Fuller, *Telegraph* website, 7 May 2010.
- 'I loved the title and concept of this from the start. Being a massive horror fan, I have always advocated that *Doctor Who* works well when it's being scary, which is why most of Steven Moffat's previous stories were so well received: spooky gasmasked kids, tick tock clockwork robots, blinky angel statues, walking skeletons and something nasty hiding in the darkness … all tap into buried fears. So to see vampires back on *Who* was a treat indeed. Such a shame then that they turned out not to be vampires at all, but alien fish creatures … who would have thought.' David J Howe, Howe's Who blog, 31 May 2010.

ANALYSIS

'The Vampires of Venice' marks the return to *Doctor Who* of writer Toby Whithouse, whose superb 'School Reunion' was one of the highlights of Series Two, memorably reintroducing Sarah Jane Smith and K-9 to the show. In the interim, he has contributed the excellent 'Greeks Bearing Gifts' to the first series of *Torchwood* and, perhaps most notably, created BBC Three's very popular supernatural comedy-drama series *Being Human*. Expectations for this episode are consequently high. Sadly, though, it gets off to a shaky start with a dreadful pre-opening-titles scene in which the Doctor bursts out of a cardboard cake at Rory's stag do and announces to all and sundry that Amy has tried to kiss him; and, what's more, that she is 'a great kisser'. Obviously this is intended to be funny – an attempt at *Doctor Who* in sitcom mode, perhaps – but it falls as flat as a pancake, mainly because it takes us back into Doctor-as-clueless-idiot territory, which after the greatly improved characterisation of 'The Time of Angels'/'Flesh and Stone' is a terrible shame. The idea that the Doctor might think it necessary to burst out of a cake rather than simply walk into the pub (having apparently done so at least once before at the *wrong* stag party), and moreover consider it appropriate to broadcast Amy's intended infidelity to everyone present, makes a total mockery of the character, and frankly causes one to regret even more the passing of the David Tennant era, when the inclusion of a scene such as this would have been absolutely unthinkable.

The Doctor's regenerations have always brought about changes in personality, but never before have they resulted in him losing great swathes of knowledge; and yet now he seems to be suddenly lacking in any understanding of the subtleties of human relationships. Would the third Doctor ever have been so crass as to go into his companion Jo Grant's engagement party in 'The Green Death' (1973) and tell her fiancé, 'She's only marrying you because she sees you as a younger version of me'? I really don't think so.

Fortunately, after the titles, things pick up with a much better TARDIS interior scene where the Doctor explains to Amy and a stony-faced Rory that seeing the wonders of the universe can turn a girl's head, and that consequently he wants to send them on a date together in a romantic historical setting. This improvement is short-lived, though, as there immediately follows a very jarring sequence where the TARDIS materialises right in the middle of a bustling waterfront marketplace in the Venice of 1580 and none of the locals so much as bats an eyelid! Even leaving aside the fact that a large blue police box appearing out of thin air should surely be seen to excite some interest if the scene is to be remotely believable, the whole point of the TARDIS looking like this is, of course, that its chameleon circuit is broken, so that it no longer blends in with its surroundings wherever it lands, and sticks out like a sore thumb in anywhere other than early- to mid-20th Century England. For this core idea of the show to be disregarded, as it is here, is an astonishing error of judgement. One half expects the Doctor to say that he has rigged up a temporary perception filter around the ship (similar to the way he adapted the TARDIS keys in 'The Sound of Drums' in Series Three), but sadly no such explanation is forthcoming.

On the plus side, the choice of 16th Century Venice as a backdrop to the action is excellent, and the setting is extremely well-realised with some superb location recording in Croatia, supplemented by some fine CGI embellishments by the Mill, giving these scenes a very attractive and high-budget look. In fact, save for some rather less convincing CGI work in the climactic scene where the Doctor scales the bell tower, the whole production is visually stunning. In addition to the impressive location work, not only in Croatia but also in Wales for the interiors, the creepy vampire girls are a definite highlight; and Signora Rosanna Calvierri's costume is particularly sumptuous and well-designed, its spiked collar ingeniously hinting at her true Saturnyne appearance.

It was a clever move on Whithouse's part to draw a parallel between Signora Calvierri and the Doctor; both survivors of near-extinct races from destroyed worlds. This offers a lot of dramatic potential, which is well exploited when the Saturnyne offers the Time Lord a partnership, and later when she asks him, 'Tell me Doctor, can your conscience carry the weight of another dead race?' However, the unexpected plot development of the Saturnynes turning out to be not really vampires at all but amphibious fish-like creatures – the realisation of which no doubt added considerably to the story's CGI expenditure – is totally superfluous. In fact, worse than that, it is actually detrimental, as it complicates things unnecessarily and dilutes the strong central idea encapsulated in the story's title. Given that it was established in the classic-era adventure 'State of Decay' (1980) that vampires are the Time Lords' ancient enemies, and themselves close to extinction, it would have worked far better, and reinforced the parallel between the two races, if Whithouse had simply stuck to that basic premise. Scarcely can there have been a better time to have presented a genuine vampire story in *Doctor Who*, given the incredible preoccupation with these creatures in popular culture at present, as manifested for instance in the *Twilight* novels and film franchise and in the TV series *True Blood* (HBO, 2008-).

The fact that the Saturnynes are not what they appear to be brings in the added contrivance of them needing to use perception filters (making it doubly regrettable that the TARDIS's seeming invisibility on arriving in Venice was not rationalised in such a way, as this would have strengthened further the Saturnyne/Time Lord parallel). This necessitates the inclusion of some rather convoluted explanations as to why their reflections can't be seen in mirrors and why their fangs are still visible. It also results in the unfortunate awkwardness of Signora Calvierri inexplicably stripping off her opulent robes, revealing one of the vampire girls' white smocks beneath, before jumping into the canal at the end, despite all her clothes being mere illusions. Director Jonny Campbell seemingly tries to fudge this a bit by having her fiddle with her damaged perception filter control box beforehand; or is this simply to demonstrate that she is unable to revert to her natural fish form, which would save her from being devoured by the male offspring in the canal? Either way, it doesn't really work as an explanation

Also unconvincing is the depiction of the vampires' sensitivity to light, which is highly inconsistent. While in some scenes the girls are seen sheltering under veils and parasols as they process through the streets – a really rather beautiful image – in others, such as when a group of them break into Guido's house through an upper floor window (strangely, given that there is no other indication in the story that the Saturnynes can fly), they are completely unprotected from the sun and yet appear to suffer no ill effects – until, that is, the Doctor waves his ultraviolet lamp at them, despite this being less bright than the real daylight to which they are already exposed! Even within the Calvierri school, in certain scenes the Saturnynes and their converts appear to be taking care to keep to the shadows, while in others they linger in an open courtyard during the daytime with total disregard of the sunlight streaming in. Guido's daughter Isabella fails to escape from the school because she is unable to stand the light of the newly-risen sun outside, which makes her shriek and recoil in pain, and yet in the very next scene she is stood by the edge of the canal, prior to being forced into the water, and the sunlight seems to be causing her hardly any discomfort at all. This lack of consistency seriously damages the story's credibility.

There are numerous other lapses in the scripting. Amy and Rory change into Venetian clothing in order to infiltrate the Calvierri school, and yet one has to wonder why they feel the need to bother, as their highly anachronistic 20th Century attire has attracted no attention whatsoever prior to this point. What with this and the lack of interest in the TARDIS's sudden arrival, it seems that the Venetians are so blasé about blatant incongruities appearing in their city that the Saturnynes could almost have got away without using perception filters at all!

Francesco warns his mother not to get too close to the canal without reverting to her natural form, or his brothers below the surface will mistake her for fish food like the executed Isabella; but later on he dives into the water himself while still in his human guise, and emerges unscathed.

Having received an electric shock that knocks him unconscious while escaping from the school, the Doctor is next seen back inside the building, none the worse for wear, seated in Signora Calvierri's throne – an incredible *non sequitur*! He then confronts the Saturnyne matriarch, warning her that he will 'tear down the House of Calvierri stone by stone' (paraphrasing a line from the 1931 movie *Dracula*), and yet despite this, unfathomably, she just lets him go – in fact, even has him escorted to the exit by her steward – only to send the vampire girls out to kill him straight afterwards! A completely baffling sequence of events, which actually makes one wonder if some important linking scenes have been cut out during editing.

A minor earthquake occurs, which the Doctor says will result in a tidal wave, and yet no tidal wave actually arrives. And how do the Saturnynes expect to cause an earthquake in the first place simply by creating a severe artificial storm? 'Manipulate the elements, you can trigger earthquakes,' says the Doctor; but if so, the scientific principles underlying earthquakes must be very different in the *Doctor Who* universe than in ours!

The incident where Amy kills the Saturnyne previously disguised as Francesco by reflecting a ray of bright sunlight onto it with a mirror is more mystifying than thrilling, as it has only just been established that the sky is covered by dark storm clouds. Amy's subsequent comment, 'That was lucky', seems to be a shameless acknowledgement of this implausibility, but hardly excuses it.

At the opposite extreme to their earlier blasé reaction to the TARDIS, the Venetian citizens fly into a blind panic when the strange storm clouds appear overhead and it starts to rain, and then actually give a round of applause when the Doctor causes the storm to dissipate, even though it is hard to see how they can know that he is responsible.

This is the story's biggest problem in a nutshell: far too little care seems to have been taken to maintain a sense of believability. The ending is a huge anticlimax, too, as although Whithouse attempts to disguise it by having the Doctor make a dangerous ascent of the bell tower – a sequence recalling his previous incarnation's similar pylon-scaling feats in both 'The Idiot's Lantern' in Series Two and 'Evolution of the Daleks' in Series Three – it basically comes down to him merely flicking a switch into the 'off' position.

One of the main ways in which Steven Moffat differs from Russell T Davies in his approach as *Doctor Who*'s showrunner is that he is, by all accounts, far less inclined to rewrite others' scripts. This has its advantages, in that it allows contributing writers' distinctive voices to come through more in the finished productions, but it has its disadvantages too; and in the case of 'The Vampires of Venice', it is difficult not to conclude that the script would have benefited greatly from a Davies-style polish. Admittedly, Davies's own plotting was not always watertight, and he himself was not above resorting to over-simplistic, flicking-a-switch type resolutions in a few stories toward the end of his tenure; most notably 'Partners in Crime', 'The Fires of Pompeii' and 'Journey's End'. However, it is hard to believe that he wouldn't have ironed out at least some of the implausibilities, confusions and loose ends in this latest script from Toby Whithouse.

What makes this all the more frustrating is that there is actually a great deal in the episode to admire and enjoy, and if its flaws had been rectified during production it could easily have been a real triumph. As already mentioned, it is a visual treat, convincingly transporting the viewer to the picturesque setting of 16th Century Venice. The dialogue is sharp and often very funny. There are some good performances too from the relatively small guest cast, with Helen McRory being particularly outstanding as Signora Calvierri and Lucian Msamati giving a nicely sympathetic portrayal of the luckless but ultimately heroic Guido. The scene where the Doctor first encounters the vampire girls, and tries to hold them back with what turns out to be an old library card (bearing a photo of his first incarnation!) rather than his psychic paper, is a fantastic set piece. So too is the surprisingly horrific sequence where Amy is strapped to a chair inside a sickly-green-lit room inside the school and an IV bag hung on a metal hook above her head before Signora Calvierri bites into her neck, leaving the vampire's characteristic twin puncture marks. Another stand-out is the comical fight sequence where a brave but inept Rory tries to fend off the sword-wielding Francesco with a broom.

There are again a number of references made to the ongoing story arc. As in 'Flesh and Stone', these seem a little inconsistent with what has gone before – the Saturnynes' home planet is said to have disappeared into one of the cracks in the universe, but clearly it was not erased from existence, as they still remember it – but nevertheless this steady drip-feed of tantalising hints succeeds in keeping the viewer keen to see how the series-spanning story will unfold.

One of the greatest strengths of 'The Vampires of Venice', though, is Whithouse's excellent characterisation of Amy and Rory. While the former shares the Doctor's gleeful excitement at the situation they encounter and follows him recklessly into danger, the latter is a distinctly reluctant adventurer whose main concern is simply to ensure his fiancée's, and his own, safety. This is addressed head-on in the tremendous scene where Rory angrily tells the Doctor: 'You know what's dangerous about you? It's not that you make people take risks, it's that you make them want to impress you. You make it so they don't want to let you down. You have no idea how dangerous you make people to themselves when you're around!' Although this perhaps suggests a rather deeper insight on Rory's part than is justified by the relatively short time he has spent around the Doctor, first in 'The Eleventh Hour' and now in this story, it presents a shrewd view of the Doctor-companion relationship that has not really been fully articulated prior to this point.

The idea that Rory now sees himself as having to compete with the Doctor for Amy's affections is astutely conceived and amusingly depicted, with the three characters being placed in a kind of twisted 'love triangle'. The Doctor's 'Let's not go there' comment when Rory says, in reference to their respective torches, 'Yours is bigger than mine' neatly sums up the dynamic between them – although the knowingness it implies on the Doctor's part sits uneasily with the naivety he demonstrated in the stag party scene – while Amy's tendency toward self-centredness again comes to the fore as she effectively plays the two off against each other. By the time they depart in the TARDIS at the end, the Doctor and Rory have little choice but to accept that they are 'her boys'.

Overall, despite its numerous shortcomings, 'The Vampires of Venice' still makes for a diverting interlude; and with Rory now coming on board the TARDIS as a second companion – recalling how Rose's boyfriend Mickey joined her on her travels with the Doctor part-way through Series Two – the stage is set for further intriguing developments ahead.

# 5.07 – AMY'S CHOICE

Writer: Simon Nye
Director: Catherine Morshead

DEBUT TRANSMISSION DETAILS

BBC One/BBC HD
Date: 15 May 2010. Scheduled time: 6.25 pm. Actual time: 6.24 pm.

Duration: 44' 13"

ADDITIONAL CREDITED CAST

Toby Jones (Dream Lord), Nick Hobbs (Mr Nainby), Joan Linder (Mrs Hamill), Audrey Ardington (Mrs Poggit).

PLOT

The TARDIS apparently arrives in Upper Leadworth, where the Doctor finds a heavily-pregnant Amy living with a ponytailed Rory five years after he last saw them. Suddenly, however, all three find themselves back in the TARDIS in the present time, as the ship's power abruptly fails. They are soon confronted by the mysterious Dream Lord, who tells them that of the two scenarios they are alternately experiencing – the first in Upper Leadworth, the second in the TARDIS – only one is real and the other is a dream. They must decide which is which, because they have a danger to face in each, and if they die in the dream they will wake up, but if they die in reality they will, of course, be dead. The Doctor eventually realises that *both* scenarios are dreams. The Dream Lord is a distillation of everything dark in his own persona, conjured into existence by some psychic pollen that has got stuck in the TARDIS's time rotor. He ejects the pollen from the ship, and things return to normal.

QUOTE, UNQUOTE

- **Doctor:** 'Blimey. Never dropped off like that before. Well, never, really. I'm getting on a bit, you see. Don't let the cool gear fool you.'
- **Amy:** 'You threw the manual in a supernova? Why?'
  **Doctor:** 'Because I disagreed with it!'
- **Doctor:** 'Now, we all know there's an elephant in the room.'
  **Amy:** 'I have to be this size – I'm having a baby.'
  **Doctor:** 'No, no. The hormones seem real, but no. Is nobody going to mention Rory's ponytail? You hold him down, I'll cut it off?'
  **Rory:** 'This from the man in the bow tie?'
  **Doctor:** 'Bow ties are cool.'

- **Rory:** 'Oh, a poncho. The biggest crime against fashion since lederhosen.'
  **Amy:** Here we go. Oh, my boys, my poncho boys, if we're going to die, let's die looking like a Peruvian folk band.'

## CONTINUITY POINTS

- The Doctor initially theorises that the TARDIS may have 'jumped a time track'. This is what happened at the start of 'The Space Museum' (1965).
- The Doctor says that he threw the TARDIS manual into a supernova because he disagreed with it. The manual was last seen in 'Vengeance on Varos' (1985).
- The Dream Lord's mention of the possibility of the Doctor having a 'little purple space dog' may be an allusion to K-9. Similarly, when he tells the Doctor, 'You're probably a vegetarian, aren't you, you big, flop-haired wuss', this may be a reference to the sixth Doctor's conversion to vegetarianism after the events of 'The Two Doctors' (1985). (Some of the subsequent Doctors have been seen to eat meat and fish, including the eleventh Doctor's own 'fish custard'.)
- The Dream Lord says to Amy, 'Loves a redhead, our naughty Doctor. Has he told you about Elizabeth the First? Well, she *thought* she was the first.' This alludes to the Doctor's sexual encounter with Queen Elizabeth, as first revealed in 'The End of Time' and also referred to in 'The Beast Below'.
- Amy says she has never told Rory that she loves him.
- The Doctor states that the psychic pollen comes from the Candle Meadows of the planet Karass Don Slava.

## PRODUCTION NOTES

- This episode was recorded with 'The Lodger' as Block Seven of Series Five's production schedule.
- The working title of the episode was 'The Dream Lord'. It acquired its final title only at the video editing stage.
- Recording on this episode began with some of the TARDIS interior scenes, from 18 to 22 February 2010 at the usual Upper Boat venue. From 23 to 25 February the crew were in Skenfirth, Monmouthshire, taping Upper Leadworth scenes in the village roads and in the ruins of Skenfirth Castle. On 26 February and 1 and 2 March, Keeper's Cottage in the village of St Mary Church near Cowbridge in the Vale of Glamorgan was used for the scenes in and around the Upper Leadworth home of Amy and Rory. On 3 March, taping took place in the nearby Llantwit Major, in both College Street and Church Street, the latter being the location of the butcher's shop, Alan Young Butcher's. On 6 March, Lanelay Hall in Pontyclun, Llantrisant was used for the interiors of the old people's home. Further studio work was undertaken on 9 March and 19 to 20 March. 19 March was also the last day of location work for the story, with shots being taped on the road outside the Church of St Ilan in Eglwysilan Road, Eglwysilan, Abertridwr, Caerphilly.
- This episode has an even longer pre-opening-titles section than 'The Time of Angels', running to 5' 49".
- Following the departure of Edward Thomas, who had been *Doctor Who*'s

production designer since its return to TV in 2005, this episode saw that role being taken instead by Tristan Peatfield. However, no new sets were required to be constructed; the TARDIS interior was the only one used at Upper Boat.

- The incidental music in 'Amy's Choice' consists of cues re-used from other episodes, embellished by some new pieces played by composer Murray Gold with no other musicians involved.

OOPS!

- At one point, at 6' 40" into the episode, the studio interior can be briefly glimpsed beyond the right-hand edge of the TARDIS set.

PRESS REACTION

- 'At its best, "Amy's Choice" is a fascinating study of the relationship between the Doctor, Amy and Rory. The three interact in a wholly believable way. Rory's inferiority to the Doctor and the Time Lord's natural tendency to show off cause a friction that is only partially abated by unconvincing reassurances from Amy. The central puzzle is engaging and pleasingly resolved, while the overall tone carries an unusual sensibility. It's tempting to compare it to a 1960s style of story (there's a fan-pleasing reference to "The Space Museum" early on), and in fact it has the curious off-kilter feel of a story from one of the 1960s annuals. There simply hasn't been another story like this since *Doctor Who* was reborn in 2005.' Jonathan Wilkins, Total Sci-Fi Online website, 14 May 2010.
- 'The laughs come thick and fast, including a satisfying running gag about Amy's ample belly, but moments of despair – such as Rory's "death" – or abject horror – such as a playpark full of vaporised kiddies – never shock in the way you might expect. The camera work, too, is a little flat. The transitions between dream worlds are handled nicely, but the largely static lens, with the odd crazy angle chucked in for good measure, fails to instil a sense of the strange a story set in the mind should. Not that there isn't a lot to like here. It's a great concept which, presuming you don't guess the ending five minutes in, will have you in two minds from start to finish. The use of birdsong as a warning before we jump between dreams is inspired – finding the terrifying in the everyday in much the same way "Blink" did for stone statues.' Jordan Farley, *SFX* website, 17 May 2010.
- 'Whether it was the Doctor being forced to wear tacky knitwear or Rory's ridiculous [ponytail], there was plenty of light entertainment in this episode. And again, just like last week's "The Vampires of Venice", there was plenty of time for character development. It must be said, Toby Jones is brilliant as the impish Dream Lord, taunting and teasing the Doctor and his companions at every turn. Of course, the main thrust of the episode was on the emerging decision Amy would have to make. I loved how the two realities were polarised between deep space and Leadworth – surely each one being a representation of the Doctor and Rory respectively? Certainly, that's how it felt as the episode progressed.' Gerard McGarry, Unreality Shout website, 16 May 2010.

CRACKS IN TIME

ANALYSIS

One always feels a slight sense of apprehension approaching the debut episode of a writer new to *Doctor Who* – and particularly one not known to be a dedicated fan who could be expected to come to it with an inherent understanding of its format and requirements. Will this newcomer be able to hit the target with his or her first shot – as, for instance, Keith Temple managed with the excellent 'Planet of the Ood' in Series Four – or fire well wide of the mark – as Matthew Graham did with the terrible 'Fear Her' in Series Two? Thankfully, Simon Nye, best known as the creator and writer of the irksome but strangely popular laddish sitcom *Men Behaving Badly* (1992-1998), falls very much in the former category: 'Amy's Choice' turns out to be a fantastic episode, and one of the undoubted highlights of Series Five.

The basic premise of the story is very well conceived. The previous six episodes having established that Amy is torn between her childhood fantasy of going off on adventures with the Doctor and her adult intention of settling down with Rory – which, as highlighted initially in 'The Vampires of Venice', puts the Doctor and Rory effectively in competition with each other for her affections – Nye now presents her with the dilemma of having to choose between the two. The way he sets this up, by placing the time travellers in two alternative dangers – one in the TARDIS, one in Upper Leadworth – and forcing them to decide which is real and which an illusion, is inspired; a kind of *Doctor Who* version of the famous Schrödinger's cat thought-experiment of quantum physics. It is also to some extent reminiscent of stories such as 'The Celestial Toymaker' (1966) and 'The Mind Robber' (1968), which similarly involved an adversary trapping the Doctor and his companions in a fantasy domain from which they had to try to escape.

The TARDIS interior scenes are pleasingly eerie, and the set actually looks a lot better than usual. This is partly because some very inventive camera angles are used, taking full advantage of the set's multiple levels, but mainly because, with the lights dimmed after the ship loses power, and later with a thick layer of frost covering its surfaces, its shortcomings are simply less visible! The danger presented here, of the TARDIS falling into a 'cold star', is relatively simple, but serves its purpose well enough. More fully-developed is the Upper Leadworth scenario of a group of old age pensioners harbouring parasitic Eknodine creatures, the single eyeballs of which are shown protruding from their mouths in a rather disturbing way courtesy of some fairly basic but well-realised CGI work, credited on this occasion to BBC Wales Graphics rather than the show's usual freelance contributors the Mill. The sight of the pensioners slowly advancing to attack their fellow villagers and the time travellers, some of them aided by Zimmer frames and walking sticks, is darkly comical, and well suited to *Doctor Who*, which is often at its best when transforming the mundane into the threatening. The frequent transitions between the two dream states, as signalled by the seemingly innocuous sound of birdsong, are also well achieved, with the Doctor and his companions repeatedly falling asleep in one place and then waking up in the other, unable to discern which of the two is real.

First and foremost, though, 'Amy's Choice' is a character piece. Having been kept mainly in the background in the previous episodes, the unresolved tension in the triangle of relationships between the Doctor, Amy and Rory is brought very much to the fore this time, and Nye's treatment of the three regulars is excellent.

138

The icing on the cake is the creation of the Dream Lord, who as a distillation of 'everything dark' in the Doctor's persona makes for a very unusual and effective antagonist. The only minor note of regret is that Steven Moffat missed the opportunity to give a nice nod to the past by slipping in a line of dialogue equating, or at least likening, this character to the Valeyard from 'The Trial of a Time Lord' (1986), who was similarly said to be a potential dark version of the Doctor – albeit in that case a more corporeal one, intermediate between his twelfth and final incarnations, rather than an illusory manifestation of part of his own psyche. (Of course, this does not prevent fans indulging in their own speculation that the two are somehow linked!)

To the Doctor, the dream of Amy's and Rory's life in Upper Leadworth is so dull as to be 'a nightmare', whereas to Rory it is an idyllic vision of the future. 'Did I say nightmare?' backtracks the Doctor. 'No. More of a really good … mare.' Amy is still undecided at this point, but seems more drawn toward life in the TARDIS:

> **Rory:** 'I want the other life. You know, where we're happy and settled and about to have a baby.'
> **Amy:** 'But don't you wonder, if that life is real, then why would we give up all this? Why would anyone?'
> **Rory:** 'Because we're going to freeze to death?'
> **Amy:** 'The Doctor'll fix it.'
> **Rory:** 'Okay. Because we're going to get married?'
> **Amy:** 'But we can still get married. Some day.'
> **Rory:** 'You don't want to any more? I thought you'd chosen me, not him.'
> **Amy:** 'You are always so insecure.'
> **Rory:** 'You ran off with another man.'
> **Amy:** 'Not in that way.'
> **Rory:** 'It was the night before our wedding.'
> **Amy:** 'We're in a time machine. It can be the night before our wedding for as long as we want.'
> **Rory:** 'We have to grow up eventually.'
> **Amy:** 'Says who?'

Once more, this equates travelling in the TARDIS with remaining in a child-like state; an idea that clearly resonates with Steven Moffat's oft-expressed belief that *Doctor Who*'s appeal is to the child in all its viewers, regardless of age. This again recalls storybook tales of characters such as Peter Pan and Mary Poppins, in which only children get to participate in magical adventures. Later, the Dream Lord puts a rather more negative slant on this, accusing the Doctor of abandoning his companions when they age: 'Your friends never see you again once they've grown up. The old man prefers the company of the young, does he not?' There is a hint of sexual innuendo here too; and as much as the Doctor might like to pretend that his feelings toward Amy are purely platonic, this is clearly not the case, as revealed when the Dream Lord refers to Rory as 'the gooseberry', says that the Doctor 'likes a redhead' and, even more so, gets Amy alone in the TARDIS and, reclining in a half-open robe with a gold medallion around his neck like a sleazy lothario, suggestively tells her, 'And now he's left you with me. Spooky old not-to-be-trusted me. Anything could happen.'

The dialogue throughout this episode is absolutely fantastic – arguably, some of the best that has ever featured in *Doctor Who* – and another of its great strengths. As might be expected from a writer known primarily for his sitcom work, much of it is humorous; but, again, the humour is very dark in tone. This is particularly so in the case of the scathing barbs aimed at the Doctor by the Dream Lord, which seem darker still once the viewer learns the secret of the latter's identity. 'If you had any more tawdry quirks,' the Dream Lord mocks, 'you could open up a tawdry quirk shop. The madcap vehicle, the cockamamie hair, the clothes designed by a first-year fashion student … I'm surprised you haven't got a little purple space dog, just to ram home what an intergalactic wag you are.'

For the show to present what amounts to a cynical deconstruction of its own central character is a wonderfully bold thing to do. The impression one is left with is that the eleventh Doctor's familiar idiosyncrasies are to some extent conscious affectations; and, moreover, that there is a part of him that despises himself for this. 'There's only one person in the universe who hates me as much as you do,' he tells his taunting alter ego. This is not so much dark as pitch black, and definitely breaks new ground for the show: never before has it been suggested that the Doctor has such a degree of self-loathing within him. Is this something particular to the eleventh Doctor – an after-effect, perhaps, of the 'Time Lord Victorious' phase he went through at the end of his previous incarnation – or has it always been there, lurking beneath the surface? At the end, Amy asks him, 'But those things he said about you; you don't think any of that's true?' But he avoids answering; and when he glances down at the TARDIS console, he briefly sees the Dream Lord's image reflected back at him from one of its panels, suggesting that this aspect of his nature has yet to be exorcised.

This is admirably sophisticated storytelling; and it almost makes one wonder if Simon Nye, despite his denial of being a devoted fan, was actually a closet reader of the New Adventures range of *Doctor Who* novels published by Virgin in the 1990s, noted amongst other things for their extended exploration of the 'dark Doctor' idea.

As well-written as Nye's script is, for the episode to be fully successful it needs to be complemented by a good performance from the actor cast as the Dream Lord. Fortunately, it gets this in spades: Toby Jones is brilliant in the role. It would have been so easy for this part to have been hammed up, but Jones pitches it at exactly the right level, his deceptively mild delivery perfectly counterpointing the maliciousness of what he is actually saying.

As expected by now, Matt Smith is also excellent as the Doctor. Karen Gillan and Arthur Darvill, on the other hand, continue to be somewhat underwhelming as Amy and Rory. The characters both come across as rather dour and lacking in charisma. Darvill also tends slightly to overplay Rory's comic ineptitude, making him seem such a hopeless sap that the viewer finds it hard to fathom what Amy sees in him, and how she could possibly choose him over the Doctor. Gillan, meanwhile, still fails to bring much warmth to her portrayal of Amy. The Upper Leadworth scene where Rory is apparently turned to dust by one of the Eknodines is a pivotal moment for her character, as she finally realises that it is her fiancé she wants and not the Doctor. When the Doctor tells her that he is unable to save Rory, she angrily asks him, 'Then what is the point of you?' – surely an intentional echo of a near-verbatim question posed by Gwen Cooper to Captain Jack Harkness when he apparently fails to save her own fiancé Rhys Williams in the *Torchwood* episode 'End of Days' (2007), those three characters having previously been in a very similar 'love triangle' situation. However, one never gets the impression that Amy is as distraught as she really ought to be at this point – certainly nowhere near as distraught as Gwen was in that *Torchwood* episode – and it is hard to feel emotionally invested in her plight.

If the story has one other minor weakness, it lies in its resolution. Some fan commentators have argued that the whole crisis being attributed to a handful of 'psychic pollen' is disappointingly simplistic, but this isn't really the issue: the important thing is not how the Dream Lord comes into being, but how the time travellers deal with him and the challenges he poses. The real problem lies in the fact that *both* scenarios – the one in the TARDIS *and* the one in Upper Leadworth – are ultimately revealed to be dreams. This rather undermines the drama of what has gone before, by implying that the Doctor, Amy and Rory were never in any real danger at all in either location. Admittedly they still face the risk of being unwittingly trapped in an ongoing dream life in the TARDIS; but, given that the fate of falling into the 'cold star' has already been averted by the time the Doctor realises this and causes the ersatz ship to explode, the reality he and his companions find themselves in afterwards seems little different from the dream they have just escaped from. Perhaps the intended implication here is that Amy's choice was, in the end, an artificial one, made under duress, and that in real life things are never that simple. Has her inner conflict between the Doctor and Rory really been resolved here, or will it resurface later on? Only time, and further episodes, will tell.

For now, it is enough to sit back and enjoy this hugely impressive debut offering from Simon Nye – brought very effectively to the screen by another newcomer in the person of director Catherine Morshead – and hope that, contrary to his comments in interviews to the effect that it is probably a one-off, he may one day be tempted back to contribute again to *Doctor Who*.

# 5.08 – THE HUNGRY EARTH

Writer: Chris Chibnall
Director: Ashley Way

DEBUT TRANSMISSION DETAILS

BBC One/BBC HD
Date: 22 May 2010. Scheduled time: 6.15 pm. Actual time: 6.18 pm.

Duration: 43' 21"

ADDITIONAL CREDITED CAST

Neve McIntosh (Alaya), Meera Syal (Nasreen Chaudry), Robert Pugh (Tony Mack), Nia Roberts (Ambrose[37]), Alun Raglan (Mo), Samuel Davies (Elliot).

PLOT

Instead of their intended destination of Rio, the Doctor, Amy and Rory arrive in the Welsh village of Cwmtaff in the year 2020. There, a geological research project drilling deep into the Earth's crust has run into problems, one of its team, Mo, having been mysteriously dragged down into the ground. It transpires that this is the work of a group of Silurians – the original rulers of Earth before the rise of mankind – who have been woken from hibernation by the drilling. The Silurians also abduct Amy and a young boy named Elliot – Mo's son – to serve as further hostages, believing the drilling to be a deliberate attack on them. The Doctor manages to capture one of the Silurians, the warrior Alaya, and plans to negotiate an exchange of prisoners. He returns to the TARDIS with Nasreen Chaudry, the head of the drilling project, just before the ship is also dragged down into the ground. On emerging, they discover that buried deep underground is a huge Silurian city.

QUOTE, UNQUOTE

- **Doctor:** 'No! No weapons. It's not the way I do things.'
  **Ambrose:** 'You said we're supposed to defend ourselves.'
  **Doctor:** 'Oh, Ambrose, you're better than this. I'm asking nicely. Put them away.'
- **Elliot:** 'I want to live in a city one day. Soon as I'm old enough, I'll be off.'
  **Doctor:** 'I was the same, where I grew up.'
  **Elliot:** 'Did you get away?'
  **Doctor:** 'Yeah.'

---

[37] Surname given in dialogue as 'Northover'. This is presumably also the surname of her husband Mo and son Elliot.

**Elliot:** 'Do you ever miss it?'
**Doctor:** 'So much.'
**Elliot:** 'Is it monsters coming? Have you met monsters before?'
**Doctor:** 'Yeah.'
**Elliot:** 'You scared of them?'
**Doctor:** 'No, they're scared of me.'
• **Rory:** 'Can't you sonic it?
**Doctor:** 'It doesn't do wood.'
**Rory:** 'That is rubbish.'
**Doctor:** 'Oi! Don't diss the sonic!'
• **Alaya:** 'I'm the last of my species.'
**Doctor:** 'No, you're really not. Because I'm the last of my species, and I know how it sits in a heart. So don't insult me. Let's start again. Tell me your name.'

CONTINUITY POINTS

• On arriving in the TARDIS, the Doctor, Amy and Rory see the future Amy and Rory of 2020 waving to them from the other side of the valley. 'Come to relive past glories, I'd imagine,' speculates the Doctor.
• The Doctor deduces that the ground below the drilling project was bio-programmed to attack in the event that it was disturbed. This technology uses bio-signals to resonate the internal molecular structure of natural objects, and should not exist on the Earth of 2020.
• Nasreen explains that Cwmtaff was chosen as the site for the drilling because the patches of blue grass found in the area contain trace minerals unseen in Wales for 20 million years.
• The Doctor says that the Silurians' venom glands take at least 24 hours to recharge after they have delivered a sting with their tongue.
• The Doctor implies that the Silurians have been hibernating beneath the Earth's surface for 300 million years; 'Once known as the Silurian race, or some would argue Eocenes, or *homo reptilia*.' It was the Doctor who was first heard to refer to the creatures as Silurians in 'Doctor Who and the Silurians' (1970), although he stated in 'The Sea Devils' (1972) that their being dated to that period was an error by the man who discovered them and that they should really be called Eocenes. (The term *homo reptilia* was first coined in the *Doctor Who* tie-in novels, which also refer to the creatures as 'Earth reptiles'.) In our universe, the Silurian period extended from about 445 million years ago to about 415 million years ago, when animal life was starting to evolve in the oceans but rudimentary plant life was all that existed on land. Dinosaurs were the dominant terrestrial vertebrates from about 230 million years ago – the late Triassic period – to about 65 million years ago – the end of the Cretaceous period. The Eocence period lasted from about 56 million years ago to about 34 million years ago, and was when mammals first appeared on land. If the Silurians did indeed rule Earth 300 million years ago, and at that time encountered apes whom they regarded as 'vermin' (and also, according to 'Doctor Who and the Silurians', kept captive dinosaurs), it would seem that in the *Doctor Who* universe, the Earth has a very different geological history.

PRODUCTION NOTES

- This episode was made with 'Cold Blood' as Block Four of Series Five's production schedule. It had the working title 'The Ground Beneath their Feet'.
- St Gwynno's Church in Llanwonno in the Rhondda Valley was used for recording of the church exterior and main interior scenes for both episodes of this story, from 20 to 24 October 2009. Bedwellty Pits in Tredegar, Blaenau Gwent, was the location chosen for scenes in and around the village, taped on 26 October. The following day saw recording take place at Tower Colliery, Hirwaun, Glamorgan, for the scenes in and around the drilling project. Mir Steelworks on Corporation Road, Newport, were used for the project's storage shed, taping being done there from 28 to 30 October. Hensol Castle in Hensol, the Vale of Glamorgan, was the location used for the church crypt, on 2 and 3 November. Studio recording took place at Upper Boat from 4 to 7 November for some of the Silurian city scenes and the TARDIS interiors.
- Around 15 minutes' worth of recorded material had to be deleted from this episode during editing, to bring it down to the correct running time. One of the deleted scenes, about 40 seconds long, was shown in the accompanying edition of *Doctor Who Confidential*, but the rest remain unseen by the viewing public.
- Chris Chibnall at one stage considered including the Sea Devils in this story as well as the Silurians, but decided against it as he felt it would overcomplicate matters. He did however propose introducing a different type of reptilian creature, to carry out the kidnapping of the human hostages on the Silurians' behalf. This idea was dropped mainly for budgetary reasons.

OOPS!

- Amy's nail varnish is purple in the scenes up to when she is pulled beneath the ground, but red in the ones where she is held captive in the Silurian base.

PRESS REACTION

- 'After the format-stretching antics of "Amy's Choice", "The Hungry Earth" presents a much more traditional *Doctor Who* adventure than we've seen for a long time – perhaps not since the end of the classic series in 1989, in fact. It starts with the Doctor and his companions landing somewhere much less exotic that they had expected – a running joke in the '70s and '80s – before getting split up and separately embroiled in a local mystery. Being the first of two parts, the story is revealed at a gentle pace far removed from the usual 45-minute rollercoaster, and the threat is tightly focused on a small cast that stands in for all humanity.' Paul Collins, Total Sci-Fi Online website, 20 May 2010.
- 'The return of the Silurians is a logical choice for this current series of *Doctor Who*. For we're in a run of the show where enemies have proper reasons for their actions, and given how comparably untapped the Silurians have been since the days of Jon Pertwee, they're an interesting choice to bring back. They've never been, and I say this as a fan of classic *Who*, the most sinister of

monsters. But they've got a solid backstory, in that they were the residents of the Earth long before human beings came along ("They're Earth-liens"). "The Hungry Earth" is respectful of that, and in bringing them to the fore of this episode, we get the first proper full-on person-in-a-suit monster of the series.' Simon Brew, Den of Geek website, 22 May 2010.

- 'Perhaps the key scene in the episode for most viewers was Matt Smith's Doctor trying to broker peace with the captured Silurian, Alaya. When he takes her mask off, he coos at her like a museum curator discovering some long-lost artefact, but he becomes insulted and stern whenever she tries to claim she's the last of her species. This is perhaps the first time we've seen Smith's Doctor tackling big, diplomatic issues, trying to secure peace or at the very least, avoid a full-scale war. Hilarious that the Silurians mistook the drilling project as a threat to their civilisation.' Gerard McGarry, Unreality Shout website, 23 May 2010.

ANALYSIS

Writer Chris Chibnall's previous *Doctor Who* episode, Series Three's '42', owed a lot of inspiration to 'Planet of Evil' (1975) from the fourth Doctor's era. This time, he delves even further back, to the third Doctor's era, to draw ideas from a number of stories, most notably 'Doctor Who and the Silurians' (1970), 'Inferno' (1970) and 'The Daemons' (1971). From the first of these, at the behest of showrunner Steven Moffat, he takes the concept of the Silurians themselves, as devised by Malcolm Hulke (who, unlike other creators of classic-era monsters revived in modern-day *Doctor Who*, deplorably receives no name-check in the closing credits). From the second, he reuses the idea of a drilling project penetrating deeper than ever before into the Earth's crust. From the third, he borrows the notion of a dome-shaped barrier isolating the local area – including its church – from outside interference. The idea of a drilling project in the Welsh countryside disturbing an underground threat also evokes memories of another story of the same era, 'The Green Death' (1973), set in and around a disused coal mine.

One interesting side-effect of this homage to the past is to illuminate some of the differences in storytelling approach between the current era of *Doctor Who* and that of the early 1970s (a period that also influenced a number of episodes scripted by Russell T Davies during his time as showrunner). In 'Doctor Who and the Silurians', the Silurians were realised by the traditional *Doctor Who* method of having the actors wear latex masks, giving them a very alien look, whereas in 'The Hungry Earth'/'Cold Blood', those whose faces are fully revealed (as opposed to being partially covered by metallic visors) are made up with much lighter prosthetics, retaining most of the actors' human features, in a manner more typical of *Star Trek* aliens. Similarly, while the body-suits of the 1970 versions were suitably reptilian in appearance, the 2010 versions have more fitted costumes, with guest star Neve McIntosh's emphasising her distinctly un-reptilian bust. The new Silurians' voices also lack the electronic treatment given to the originals, relying purely on the actors' own, unmistakably human vocal tones (in McIntosh's case, with a hint of a Scottish accent!) In 'Inferno', the drilling project was at the heart of a major industrial complex staffed by a team of lab-coated scientists and boiler-suited engineers, with its own nuclear reactor to supply the power and UNIT on hand to provide security. The equivalent endeavour in 'The Hungry Earth'/'Cold Blood', on the other hand, is being run from what appears to be a ramshackle converted mine works in a remote village, with only a handful of people employed there. (Small wonder perhaps that, despite believing that the 21 km depth they have reached is record-setting, they have actually managed to drill less far into the Earth's crust than the attempt in 'Inferno', not to mention Professor Zaroff's crazy scheme in 'The Underwater Menace' (1967), the laser-cut shaft to the Earth's core in 'The Runaway Bride' (2006) and the Osterhagen Project warheads placed beneath the Earth's crust in 'Journey's End' (2008), all of which must presumably have been kept secret – or else fallen into cracks in time!) And while the advent of the heat barrier in 'The Daemons' brought UNIT troops descending on the area, with plans to get the RAF to try to break through by firing missiles from above, the sudden appearance of the barrier in 'The Hungry Earth' seems to attract no outside attention at all, and one is left to wonder why the Silurians felt the need to bother with it.

In short, the production team of the early 1970s clearly aimed for a far higher degree of verisimilitude in their conception of how bipedal reptilian creatures might look and sound, of how a major drilling project might be set up and operated, and of how the authorities might actually react to a rural community being cut off by the sudden appearance of an invisible barrier. The production team of 2010, for their part, have taken a much less realistic approach to the presentation of what are, in essence, the same story elements; less science fiction, more storybook fantasy – an impression reinforced by the character Mo reading the famous children's book *The Gruffalo* to his son Elliot at the very start of 'The Hungry Earth'. The phrase 'gritty realism' has been used so often to describe the style of the early part of the third Doctor's era that it is now seen as something of a tired cliché. Possibly the same will one day be said of the 'dark fairytale' description applied to the early stories of Steven Moffat's tenure as showrunner. Nevertheless, the two phrases do delineate very well the highly contrasting approaches of these different eras, separated by some 40 years of television history.

Which of the two approaches one prefers is, of course, a matter of personal taste. That said, it is hard to defend the radical change in the depiction of the Silurians. While it is admittedly justified in narrative terms by the Doctor's comment that the new ones are 'a different branch of the species' from those he met before – just as the titular characters of 'The Sea Devils' (1972) were envisaged as amphibious 'cousins' of the Silurians – it has two significant drawbacks. First, it dilutes the underlying message that Malcolm Hulke was trying to put across with the Silurians, that although they may seem like monsters to us, they are an intelligent race with their own civilisation, and so deserve equal respect. The fact that the new versions seen in 'The Hungry Earth'/'Cold Blood' are far less monstrous than the originals – actually, quite aesthetically pleasing – rather undermines that basic warning against an unthinking dislike of the unlike. Secondly, and more prosaically, these new, humanised versions are simply nowhere near as visually impressive as the originals. Aliens created by applying scaly prosthetics to actors' faces are really ten-a-penny in TV science fiction shows, particularly American ones, whereas the original Silurian masks, superbly designed by Jim Ward of the BBC's Visual Effects Department, were quintessential *Doctor Who* creations, both strikingly distinctive and highly memorable.

What makes this all the more galling is that in the edition of *Doctor Who Confidential* accompanying 'The Hungry Earth', there is a brief shot of a workbench at Millennium FX on which stands a sculpt of their initial proposal for the new Silurians' look, which is very similar to the iconic Jim Ward design, complete with a third eye on the forehead – an iconic feature that, in the end, was omitted altogether. When this behind-the-scenes image was first transmitted, one could almost imagine thousands of fans up and down the UK simultaneously shouting at their TV sets, 'For heaven's sake, why didn't they use *that* design?' Two explanations have been offered for the rejection of that initial, far superior idea. The first is simply that the cost of making the masks would have been too high for the available budget. If that is really the case – and it would certainly seem likely, as the metallic visors worn by most of the Silurians are clearly another budget-saving measure, to avoid them all having to be given the full prosthetics – it makes one begrudge even more the money wasted on the construction of the awful new paradigm Daleks earlier in the series, which would have been far better spent here. But the second, and it seems principal, explanation put forward is that the actors' own expressions need to be visible if they are to be able to give effective performances. This is not the first time that such a view has been expressed in relation to *Doctor Who* monsters, but it is, to be frank, utter nonsense. One need only consider such notable precedents as Bernard Bresslaw's Varga in 'The Ice Warriors' (1967), Michael Wisher's Davros in 'Genesis of the Daleks' (1975) and Gabriel Woolf's Sutekh in 'Pyramids of Mars' (1975) to realise that a fine actor can give a wonderful portrayal of a monster despite having a full head-mask on, by using just his or her voice and posture. That members of the current *Doctor Who* production team should betray such a lack of confidence in what has traditionally been one of the show's characteristic strengths – the effective realisation of monsters through well-designed masks and body suits – is really rather disconcerting; and, it must be said, not something of which Russell T Davies and his team could ever have been accused.

However, unlike with the Fatleks, this design misstep is thankfully not so horrendous that it necessarily ruins the whole story. The basic idea of reviving the Silurians was an excellent one, as their history – of being the original rulers of Earth before the rise of mankind – offers a lot of untapped potential for dramatic storytelling. That potential has been recognised before by their inclusion in a number of the *Doctor Who* novels, audio dramas and comic strips, but it is very good to have them back in the TV show itself, particularly as their last appearance, alongside the Sea Devils in 'Warriors of the Deep' (1984), certainly did not do them full justice. The idea that this sub-species of Silurians have long tongues that they can lash out to inject venom into their prey is an appealing innovation, as is that of them taking hostages by dragging them down into the ground – recalling a similar device from another classic-era story, 'Frontios' (1984), the dialogue of which actually features the phrase 'The earth is hungry' a couple of times. The sequence where Amy is pulled down beneath the surface, despite the Doctor's best efforts to cling on to her, is particularly well-realised. Amy's fear and desperation, both here and later on when she is held captive inside the Silurians' medical bay, are excellently portrayed by Karen Gillan, who gives easily her strongest performance to date in this episode.

There is a nice gothic horror quality to the scenes where Silurians are glimpsed darting between the tombstones in the darkened graveyard and then snatching Elliot away just before he can reach the sanctuary of the church. The inclusion of a number of point-of-view shots here, showing the action from the Silurians' own perspective, works very well, and strongly recalls the use of a similar technique in 'Doctor Who and the Silurians'. The moment when the Doctor has to admit to Elliot's mother Ambrose that he is the one who inadvertently exposed the boy to danger, by carelessly allowing him to leave the church to fetch his headphones, is also memorably dramatic – and well-judged too, in that it reminds the viewer that the Doctor's alien thought-processes put him on a slightly different wavelength from the humans, who would never have let a child go off alone in such circumstances, but stops short of making him seem completely clueless; a problem that bedevilled some of the earlier episodes of this series.

Director Ashley Way – who makes his full *Doctor Who* debut on this story, although he previously handled the interactive game 'Attack of the Graske' (2005) and the Series Two 'Tardisodes' (2006) for the show's official website, plus some instalments of *Torchwood* – does an excellent job throughout. He succeeds in bringing an atmosphere of bleak isolation to the proceedings, and builds up a palpable sense of tension as the conflict between humans and Silurians starts to escalate. Another stand-out scene is the one where the Doctor talks to Alaya in the church basement after she is captured and tied up there. Matt Smith and Neve McIntosh are both excellent in this confrontation, as the Silurian at first tries unsuccessfully to convince the Time Lord that she is the sole survivor of her race – a situation with which he is all too familiar – and then admits that her 'warrior class' was revived in order to wipe out the human 'vermin' in response to their drilling, which was perceived as an attack.

There are, it must be said, a few credulity-stretching aspects to Chris Chibnall's script. One is the early incident outside the TARDIS where Rory gets Amy to take off her engagement ring and leave it behind because he is worried she might lose it – surely something that no man has ever said to his fiancée in reality! Another is the rather clumsy contrivance of the church door having a tendency to stick, which – predictably – turns out to be the obstacle that prevents Elliot from getting back inside when he is being stalked by the Silurians. Another is the suggestion that the Doctor's party manage to rig up a network of cameras, burglar alarms and other such devices all around the village in the space of just five minutes or so, which is almost as unbelievable as Bracewell taking his Spitfires-in-gravity-bubbles scheme from drawing-board to fruition in a similar space of time in 'Victory of the Daleks'!

These, however, are fairly minor shortcomings in what is, overall, a well-written and pleasingly-executed episode. One does get the impression, though, that its main purpose is simply to serve as a scene-setter for what promises to be an even more dramatic and exciting second part – an impression that is reinforced when, in a thrilling cliffhanger ending, the Doctor and his new friend Nasreen Chaudry discover that the Silurian dwelling, buried deep beneath the drilling project, is not just a small base like the one seen in 'Doctor Who and the Silurians', but an entire city! It seems that 'Cold Blood' will be taking the action to a new level in more ways than one.

# 5.09 – COLD BLOOD

Writer: Chris Chibnall
Director: Ashley Way

## DEBUT TRANSMISSION DETAILS

BBC One/BBC HD
Date: 29 May 2010. Scheduled time: 7.00 pm. Actual time: 7.02 pm.

Duration: 45' 40"

## ADDITIONAL CREDITED CAST

Neve McIntosh (Alaya/Restac), Meera Syal (Nasreen Chaudry), Robert Pugh (Tony Mack), Nia Roberts (Ambrose), Richard Hope (Malohkeh), Stephen Moore (Eldane), Alun Raglan (Mo), Samuel Davies (Elliot)

## PLOT

The Doctor tries to get the Silurians to make peace with the humans. He is opposed by Alaya's sister, the aggressive military commander Restac, but receives support from the Silurians' leader, Eldane. Nasreen and Amy are given the task of negotiating with Eldane on behalf of the human race, but progress is halted after the Silurians learn that Elliot's mother Ambrose has killed Alaya. Eldane helps the Doctor and the humans to escape by releasing a fumigation gas into the city, forcing Restac's warriors to return to hibernation. Nasreen remains behind with Ambrose's father Tony, who needs to undergo treatment for a venomous bite that Alaya inflicted on him before her demise. Eldane, Nasreen and Tony will then enter hibernation also. Restac, however, has remained at large, and before she falls victim to the fumigation gas she shoots Rory dead. Rory is then engulfed by energy from one of the cracks in time, which has appeared in the city, and is erased from existence, being forgotten by everyone but the Doctor. The Doctor's party return to the surface in the TARDIS just before the drill explodes, sealing the Silurians in their city. They are due to revive again in a thousand years' time …

## QUOTE, UNQUOTE

- **Rory:** 'I promise you, Ambrose, I trust the Doctor with my life. We stick to his plan. Keep that creature safe.'
- **Amy:** 'Okay, sorry. As rescues go, it didn't live up to its potential.'
  **Doctor:** 'I'm glad you're okay.'
  **Amy:** 'Me too. Lizard men, though.'
  **Doctor:** '*Homo reptilia*. They occupied the planet before humans. Now they

want it back.'

**Nasreen:** 'After they've wiped out the human race.'

**Amy:** 'Right. Preferred it when I didn't know, to be honest.'

- **Doctor:** 'So, here's the deal. Everybody listening. Eldane, you activate shutdown. I'll amend the system, set your alarm for a thousand years time. A thousand years to sort the planet out. To be ready. Pass it on, as legend or prophecy or religion, but somehow make it known: this planet is to be shared.'

CONTINUITY POINTS

- The Doctor tells the Silurian scientist Malohkeh, who is preparing to 'decontaminate' him, 'Remove all human germs and you remove half the things keeping me alive'. This indicates that bacteria carried by but not essential to humans are vital to the Doctor. When Malohkeh halts the process, the Doctor says, 'That's much better, thanks. Not got any celery, have you?' It was established in the fifth Doctor's era that celery has a restorative effect on the Time Lord.

- The Doctor says that the Silurians originally went into hibernation because their astronomers predicted that an approaching planet would crash into the Earth. What actually happened was that the planet went into orbit and became the Moon. This restates the backstory originally established in 'Doctor Who and the Silurians' (1970). The Doctor recalls that – as seen in the latter story – the first Silurian tribe he encountered were attacked and killed by the humans. However, he omits to mention that the Silurians also attacked the humans.

- The Doctor tells Nasreen: 'There are fixed points through time, where things must always stay the way they are. This is not one of them. This is an opportunity; a temporal tipping point. Whatever happens today will change future events, create its own timeline, its own reality. The future pivots around you, here, now.' This restates and elaborates on the distinction between fixed and non-fixed points in time established in previous stories, most notably 'The Fires of Pompeii' (2008).

- The Doctor sets the Silurians' system to revive them in a thousand years' time. This would be in the 31st Century. He no doubt has it in mind that this coincides with the time when the human population of Earth temporarily leaves due to solar flare activity, as seen in 'The Beast Below'. Presumably the hotter climate resulting from the solar flares would suit the Silurians, and they would have a chance to establish themselves before the humans returned, improving the prospects of a successful negotiation over the planet's future.

- On seeing the crack in time in the Silurian city, the Doctor says, 'All through the universe, rips in the continuum … Some sort of space-time cataclysm. An explosion, maybe. Big enough to put cracks in the universe. But what …? The Angels laughed when I didn't know. Prisoner Zero knew. Everyone knows except me. But where there's an explosion, there's shrapnel.' He reaches into the crack with his arm and pulls out an object, which he keeps wrapped in a handkerchief. When he later looks at it, he discovers that it is a part of the sign from the TARDIS door.

- When Rory is erased from existence by the energy from the crack in time, this causes everyone – except the Doctor – to forget about him, but does not erase the things he did while he was alive, such as buying Amy's engagement ring, which remains in its box in the TARDIS. This is in line with how the time energy worked when the Church clerics and the Weeping Angels fell into the crack in 'Flesh and Stone'.

- Although Amy, by virtue of being a time traveller, remembered the things that were erased from time in 'Flesh and Stone', she does not remember Rory. The Doctor explains that this is because, unlike those other things, he was part of her world; this time, her own history has changed.

## PRODUCTION NOTES

- This episode was made with 'The Hungry Earth' as Block Four of Series Five's production schedule.
- See 'The Hungry Earth' for some of this episode's production dates. In addition, recording took place from 9 to 12 November 2009 at the Temple of Peace in Cardiff for certain Silurian city scenes, including those in the senate chamber, and on 13 November at the Plantasia, Parc Tawe, Swansea for other Silurian city scenes. Further studio work was done at Upper Boat from 16-18 November, again for Silurian city interiors. Some studio pick-up shots were completed on 13 and 29 January 2010.
- Unusually, the cliffhanger ending of the first part of this story is not included in the reprise at the start of the second.
- Like 'The Hungry Earth', 'Cold Blood' underwent significant changes at the video editing stage, with some sequences being dropped and others being rearranged into a different order.

## OOPS!

- When the Doctor and Nasreen are shown entering the Silurian city after the opening title sequence, the Doctor is on Nasreen's right in the first shot, but on her left in the next.
- In the TARDIS scene where Amy is struggling to hold on to her memories of Rory, the flashback clip of him being shot by Restac is missing the CGI effect of the beam from her gun.
- As they haven't travelled back in time, why do the Doctor and Amy again see the future Amy waving to them from across the valley, before they depart in the TARDIS? Given that they first saw her (with the now-vanished Rory) when they arrived hours earlier, wouldn't she have left by now ...?

## PRESS REACTION

- 'How about the fact that *Doctor Who* did what it's been reluctant to do ever since it returned: kill off a major character? Granted, Rory is hardly assistant rank in the TARDIS, but he's not far off. And when you consider how dramatically Russell T Davies pulled back from even giving one of the assorted characters a scratch in "Journey's End" after threatening to bump at least one of them off, then this is radical stuff ... Because this is, after all, a

Saturday teatime show … Now, granted, it wasn't the most convincing way to go (there was a bit of a *Die Hard* ending about Restac crawling through rubble and firing off a shot), but nonetheless, Rory was shot, and Rory went down. Furthermore, the light coming through the crack got him, which most of us, we'd wager, suspect is the way that he will come back to life. Truthfully, we'd be shocked if he didn't … But for now, that's a genuinely shocking conclusion.' Simon Brew, Den of Geek website, 29 May 2010.

- 'The Doctor seems to get on his high horse a little too often here with the humans, blaming them for much of what has happened when in fact Malohkeh and Alaya had actually taken it upon themselves to attack the humans. He's quite happy tearing strips off Ambrose for what she's done, looking down his nose at her and the others for not being the shining exemplars he pompously expected them to be, but he's hardly been a reliable moral compass in this story. Eldane isn't exactly leadership material either and seems a rather pallid and ineffectual creature in the face of the military might of Restac. And just why was there a vast army of Silurians hidden away underground? When did their culture become so militarised?' Frank Collins, Cathode Ray Tube website, 31 May 2010.
- '[In] "Cold Blood", a complex and thoughtful script is beautifully realised by the talent at BBC Wales. Although it is obviously done on a limited budget (hence the Silurian city is deserted, except for the few who have been awakened) the creation of an underground civilisation is convincingly done (and much better than the cave complex and cages that appeared in the 1970s Silurian serial). It all looks, feels and sounds much more like classic *Doctor Who* than most of the episodes since the return of the series, and that's not a bad thing at all.' Brian J Robb, Total Sci-Fi Online website, 26 May 2010.

ANALYSIS

Taking a leaf out of Steven Moffat's book, Chris Chibnall gives the second half of this two-part story a very different feel from the first, and has most of it take place in a very different setting. Whereas 'The Hungry Earth' was all about the gradual build-up of atmosphere and suspense in the isolated Welsh village, 'Cold Blood' is a more epic and action-packed piece, located mainly in the impressively-realised Silurian city. This change of tack gives the story a real boost, and 'Cold Blood' turns out to be easily the more enjoyable of the two episodes.

The Silurians are seen *en masse* here for the first time. The idea of them having a whole civilisation lying dormant deep underground, their city bordered by magma from the Earth's core yet still somehow kept cool enough to inhabit, is a logical and fitting extension of Malcolm Hulke's original concept. It recalls 'hollow Earth' myths and similar notions in classic stories such as Jules Verne's *A Journey to the Centre of the Earth* and Sir Arthur Conan Doyle's *The Lost World*; and in fact it is rather a pity that this parallel isn't developed further by having the Doctor and his friends encounter a few ferocious dinosaurs, or at least see one or two pterodactyls wheeling overhead (it having been established in 'Doctor Who and the Silurians' (1970) that the Silurians do keep pet dinosaurs). But no doubt that would have over-stretched the production's CGI budget.

Leaving aside the oddity of reptiles having breasts, it was an interesting idea to make the Silurians' warrior class exclusively female. Also a smart move was to have their commander, Restac, be the sister of Alaya, and portrayed by the same actress (another money-saving wheeze, perhaps ...?) Neve McIntosh skilfully distinguishes between the two characters through the nuances of her performance, aided by the different facial prosthetics used for Restac, featuring red detailing and a scar; the most visually striking make-up afforded to any of the Silurians in this story.

A nice touch is that the Silurians' guns have disc-shaped muzzles, intentionally resembling the Sea Devils' weapons in 'The Sea Devils' (1972) and 'Warriors of the Deep' (1984), just as the webbing on their body-suits recalls the fishing-net costumes seen in the former story. It does make one wonder, though, why the design team did not go the whole hog and make them *identical* to the Sea Devils' weapons, which were more imaginative and original in appearance than the standard machine-gun-like ones used here. In fact, throughout 'The Hungry Earth'/'Cold Blood' there are quite a few opportunities missed for giving additional nods to the classic-era Silurian and Sea Devil stories by reusing appropriate prop designs, sound effects and so on – something of a pity, as surely part of the point of reviving classic-era monsters is to take advantage of some of the trappings that made them distinctive and memorable in the first place.

Although 'Cold Blood' is more action-orientated than 'The Hungry Earth', Chibnall thankfully does not lose sight of his characters, and this is one of the story's great strengths. Particularly notable is the way he brings an added dimension to their interactions by giving them familial relationships. While on the Silurian side there is the sisterly bond between Alaya and Restac, on the human side there is Ambrose's family: her father Tony Mack, her husband Mo and her son Elliot. While Nasreen seems at first to be the only outsider to this group, she is effectively brought within it as the story unfolds, through her burgeoning romantic relationship with Tony. In this way, Chibnall is able to escalate the drama to a level that would have been difficult to achieve if the drilling team had been just a gathering of unrelated individuals. Ambrose is a particularly well-drawn character, and very well portrayed by Nia Roberts. The fact that her killing of Alaya is done out of a desperate desire to protect her father, husband and son makes her seem rather more sympathetic than if she had been driven purely by xenophobia. The cost of her rash action is that she loses her father for good, along with Nasreen, who chooses to remain with him in the Silurians' base when it is sealed off. She is, though, given a chance of partial redemption at the end, when the Doctor tells her: 'An eye for an eye; it's never the way. Now you show your son how wrong you were. How there's another way. You make him the best of humanity ... in the way you couldn't be.'

Chibnall also astutely ensures that each of his principal Silurians has a different personality and motivation, just as in 'Doctor Who and the Silurians', effectively mirroring the distinct characters within the humans' group and reinforcing the idea that, although the two races may look very different, they actually have much in common. Another noteworthy performance comes from Stephen Moore as the Silurian leader Eldane, to whom Chibnall gives the unusual device of a topping-and-tailing narration, delivered from the vantage point of a thousand years in the future when the Silurians are due to emerge once again from hibernation.

As for the regulars, Arthur Darvill's Rory is still failing to make much of an impression at this point in the series, despite 'dying' for the second time in the space of two stories; on this occasion seemingly more permanently as, after being fatally shot by Restac, he is also erased from existence by the energy emanating from one of the cracks in time. On the other hand, as in 'The Hungry Earth', Karen Gillan turns in an exceptionally strong performance. She is particularly good in the TARDIS interior scene after Rory's demise, when she really makes the viewer feel for Amy's plight as she struggles, and ultimately fails, to hold on to her memories of her fiancé – existence again being equated here with being remembered, as in 'Flesh and Stone'.

That said, Amy is still at times a difficult character to like. When Rory, given a chance to talk to her in the Silurian base via a monitor, admits that he thought he had lost her, she delivers the withering put-down: 'What, 'cause I was sucked into the ground? You're so clingy!' One can only hope that she is being drily humorous here, as a kind of defence mechanism to mask her true emotions. In 'The Time of Angels', she also asked the Doctor 'Do I look that clingy?', so it would seem that she views 'clinginess' as a typical but undesirable feature of relationships – which may go some way to explaining her apparent reluctance to expose her feelings toward Rory. It may be that, having been left waiting by the Doctor as a child, she now has a fear of abandonment, and deals with this by trying to avoid any appearance of commitment. Perhaps significantly, when talking to Rory about her engagement ring in 'The Hungry Earth', she says 'I thought you liked me wearing it,' but gives no indication that she actually likes wearing it herself.

Commitment issues aside, though, Amy's default demeanour seems to be wilful and petulant, and she remains unattractively self-centred. This is perhaps most starkly illustrated when, after the Doctor gives her and Nasreen the momentous task of negotiating a settlement with the Silurians on behalf of the entire human race, she is seen just a short while later resting her head on her arms on the conference table in apparent boredom! Admittedly, this scene is another credulity-straining aspect of Chris Chibnall's story – again, more fantastical storybook idea than realistic science fiction – as there seems no chance at all that the Earth authorities would actually be prepared to honour any agreement the two women might make with the reptiles. However, one would certainly expect Amy to take this weighty responsibility a bit more seriously. Perhaps some might argue that the Doctor's companions do not actually *have* to be characters that the viewer likes and admires; but then, one would have to start questioning his judgment in choosing them to travel with him, and the overall appeal of the show would surely be diminished ...

That said, possibly Amy is simply becoming exasperated with Nasreen, who patently fails to live up to the Doctor's high expectations when, in response to the suggestion that the Silurians could inhabit the areas of Earth with climates unfavourable to humankind, she says: 'Yes, fine, but what happens when their population grows and breeds and spreads?' And this in earshot of Eldane! One is uncomfortably reminded here of the racist views sometimes expressed on issues such as immigration and real-world territorial disputes like that between the Israelis and the Palestinians – the kind of intolerance that was of concern to Malcolm Hulke when he originally created the Silurians.

Matt Smith, meanwhile, continues to shine as the Doctor, whose faith in 'the best of humanity' is inspiring but – in light of Ambrose's murderous actions and

Nasreen's questionable comments (mercifully, not in his presence) – seems increasingly like a triumph of optimism over experience. The only significant oddity in Chibnall's characterisation of the Time Lord is that he unaccountably has him express fulsome admiration for the Silurian scientist Malohkeh – 'Malohkeh, I rather love you' – despite the fact that the latter has just admitted that he has been abducting and carrying out tests on human children for hundreds of years, and has earlier been revealed to have performed vivisection on Mo, with the intention of doing the same to Amy! It may well have been he, too, who stole the bodies missing from the local graveyard for use in his work (an aspect of the plot that is otherwise unexplained) …

In a final homage to 'Doctor Who and the Silurians', and to the third Doctor's era more generally, the crisis is resolved with a huge explosion, as the drilling project is blown to smithereens. The Doctor and Amy then make their way back to the TARDIS, with only the former realising that one member of their party is now missing … Even at the time of transmission, many viewers probably guessed that this would not be the last that would be seen of Rory – and certainly fans who had been following reports of the location recording of later episodes knew that he would soon be back. For others though, and particularly for many children in the audience, his apparent death would doubtless have come as quite a shock. Long-time viewers may have recalled their reaction to the demise of Adric in 'Earthshock' (1982), and *very* long-time viewers may even have cast their minds back to the sad losses of Katarina and Sara in 'The Daleks' Master Plan' (1965/66). This, though, is the first such fate to befall a regular character in 21st Century *Doctor Who*. It consequently stands as perhaps the most memorable aspect of what is, all in all, an enjoyable if not absolutely outstanding story.

# 5.10 – VINCENT AND THE DOCTOR

Writer: Richard Curtis
Director: Jonny Campbell

DEBUT TRANSMISSION DETAILS

BBC One/BBC HD
Date: 5 June 2010. Scheduled time: 6.40 pm. Actual time: 6.41 pm.

Duration: 46' 41"

ADDITIONAL CREDITED CAST

Tony Curran (Vincent), Nik Howden (Maurice), Chrissie Cotterill (Mother), Sarah Counsell (Waitress), Morgan Overton, Andrew Byrne (School Children)

UNCREDITED GUEST STAR

Bill Nighy (Dr Black)

PLOT

On a visit to the Musée d'Orsay in Paris in 2010 to view an exhibition of the work of Vincent van Gogh, the Doctor spots that the artist has incorporated a small image of a fierce-looking alien creature in his painting *The Church at Auvers*. He takes Amy back in time and they meet van Gogh. The artist, a sufferer of depression, is able to see the alien creature, a Krafayis, which to everyone else is invisible. The Krafayis is blind and has been abandoned on Earth by its own kind. It is eventually killed by being impaled on Vincent's easel when the artist and the time travellers try to defend themselves against its attack. The Doctor takes Vincent to the 2010 exhibition of his work to show him how lauded he will one day become. However, this does not prevent him from committing suicide after he is returned to his own time.

QUOTE, UNQUOTE

• **Vincent:** 'It's colour. Colour that holds the key. I can hear the colours. Listen to them. Every time I step outside, I feel nature is shouting at me: "Come on. Come and get me. Come on. Come on! Capture my mystery!"'
• **Doctor:** 'What's the worst that can happen?'
  **Amy:** 'You could get torn into pieces by a monster you can't see.'
  **Doctor:** 'Oh, right, yes. That.'
• **Doctor:** 'Is this how time normally passes? Really slowly. In the right order.'

- **Vincent:** 'Doctor, my friend. We have fought monsters together, and we have won. On my own, I fear I may not do as well.'
- **Dr Black:** 'Certainly the most popular great painter of all time; the most beloved. His command of colour, the most magnificent. He transformed the pain of his tormented life into ecstatic beauty. Pain is easy to portray, but to use your passion and pain to portray the ecstasy and joy and magnificence of our world ... No-one had ever done it before. Perhaps no-one ever will again. To my mind, that strange, wild man who roamed the fields of Provence was not only the world's greatest artist, but also one of the greatest men who ever lived.'

## CONTINUITY POINTS

- Unseen by viewers, the Doctor has recently taken Amy on visits to Arcadia and to the Trojan Gardens. It is implied that he is being particularly nice to her because of her recent loss of Rory, even though she does not remember her fiancé – as emphasised when, toward the end of the episode, she tells Vincent van Gogh 'I'm not really the marrying kind'.
- The Doctor retrieves from a trunk in the TARDIS an electronic device incorporating a mirror, similar to a car's wing mirror, which he uses to observe and identify the Krafayis. He says that he was given this device as 'an embarrassing present from a dull godmother with two heads and bad breath'. When he connects the device to the TARDIS console and looks into the mirror, it correctly identifies him as the Doctor from the planet Gallifrey, and displays images of his first two incarnations.
- The Doctor says of the Krafayis: 'They travel in space. They travel as a pack. Scavenging across the universe. Sometimes one of them gets left behind and, because they are a brutal race, the others never come back. So, dotted all around the universe are individual, utterly merciless, utterly abandoned Krafayis. And what they do is ... well, kill. Until they're killed. Which they usually aren't, because other creatures can't see them.'
- The Doctor states that he has watched Michelangelo painting the Sistine Chapel, and that he has met Picasso.

## PRODUCTION NOTES

- This episode and 'The Vampires of Venice' were made as Block Five of 'Series Five's production schedule.
- 'Eyes that See the Darkness' was an early working title for the episode.
- Llandaff Cathedral in Llandaff, Cardiff was used as the exterior of the Church at Auvers, recording taking place there on 24 November 2009. Two days later, the crew taped the Musée D'Orsay interior scenes at the National Museum of Wales in Cardiff. The scenes not in France were committed to tape (along with location work for 'The Vampires of Venice') in and around the Croatian villages of Trogir and Vrsine between 30 November and 13 December. On the crew's return to Wales, Sutton Farm on Sutton Road, Llandow became the interior of Vincent's house on 14 and 15 December. The scenes of the Doctor,

Amy and Vincent battling the Krafayis in the church crypt were recorded in Neath Abbey in Swansea on 5 January 2010. The shots of the TARDIS materialising outside the Musée d'Orsay were taped in Roald Dahl Plass, Cardiff, the following day. 7 and 8 January saw recording take place at Llancaiach Fawr on Gelligaer Road, Nelson, Treharis for some pick-up shots for the Church at Auvers exterior scene and for the confessional box interior. A small amount of studio recording was done at Upper Boat, on 25 November 2009 and 4 and 6 January and 13 and 19 March 2010.

- Distinguished actor Bill Nighy agreed to play the part of museum guide Dr Black due to his long association with writer Richard Curtis, but asked not to be credited either on the episode itself or in associated cast listings.
- As with a number of other Series Five episodes, quite a lot of material had to be cut from the episode at the editing stage to bring it down to the required length.
- Over the end credits of the episode on its first transmission, a BBC continuity announcer gave details of a website and helpline number from which viewers could seek support if they had been affected by the issues raised in the programme (which deals with van Gogh's mental illness). This is the only time to date that such an announcement has been made in connection with a *Doctor Who* episode.
- Emma Freud, credited as an additional script editor on this episode, is the partner of writer Richard Curtis and regularly helps him in finalising his scripts. Her niece Martha Freud, Curtis's personal assistant, also received a thanks credit on the episode.

## OOPS!

- In the scene where the Doctor first spots the Krafayis depicted in van Gogh's *The Church at Auvers* in the Musée d'Orsay, he ruffles his own hair – but with his right hand when seen from behind, and with his left hand when the picture cuts to a front view.
- Amy is wearing dark-coloured tights throughout the story, except in the scenes where she, the Doctor and Vincent are at the church, where she appears to be barelegged. (Possibly, unseen by the viewer, she takes her tights off just prior to this, and puts them back on again later?)
- At about 29' 30" into the episode, the Doctor is knocked down by the Krafayis, and his sonic screwdriver falls to the ground. However, he then produces the sonic screwdriver from inside his jacket. (Possibly he carries more than one now?)

## PRESS REACTION

- 'The most wondrous thing about it was the direction by Jonny Campbell. My god, that was a beautiful piece of work. You could probably flag up a few movies that have tried to be that beautiful and bring art to life (*The Girl with a Pearl Earring*, *Prospero's Book*), but this is first time that I've seen a sci-fi drama try to do it and succeed ... Normally, CGI is a thing to be irritated by, but the recreation of *Starry Night* to the narration of Tony Curran's van Gogh was a thing of awe. Add on the sunflowers and the fields of corn, and you have some true moments of TV joy.' Rob Buckley, The Medium is Not Enough website, 7 June 2010.

- 'Van Gogh was something of a revelation. Completely brilliantly played by Tony Curran, he was totally believable. From the moment he first appeared, looking exactly like the Dutch artist, he held the screen. I loved his interactions with Amy and the Doctor, sympathised for his depression, and cheered him on in the gallery at the end. Curran nailed it completely. I even loved his question to Amy, asking if she came from Holland too, as she had the same accent as him! Obviously the TARDIS translation circuits are a little fritzed, making Dutch sound like Scottish in translation. The flow of the story was gentle, but nicely paced, and the whole invisible chicken thing was a bit of a red herring really ... The meat of the episode was the final ten minutes which had me crying both times I watched it ... moving and respectful, brilliantly acted, superbly paced and played ... it's testament to what *Doctor Who* can do given the right material.' David J Howe, Howe's Who blog, 11 June 2010.
- '[Richard] Curtis's "Vincent and the Doctor" shows that the man knows how to write top quality *Doctor Who*. It may include some of the more recognisable Curtis hallmarks such as an unsubtle schmaltz-fest near the end of the episode and also Bill Nighy, but even detractors of these two familiar elements may grudgingly agree that the story works like a charm.' John Bensahlia, Shadowlocked website, 16 November 2011.
- 'What would Vincent van Gogh make of the fact that, though he died penniless and unrecognised, he's now regarded as one of the world's greatest artists? That sounds like the starting point for some kind of earnest talking heads discussion, but no, this was *Doctor Who* time travelling into surprising territory. Taking us into an impressive imagining of van Gogh's world and his starry, starry night, Richard Curtis's story mixed arch jokes ("Sunflowers? They're not my favourite flower") with a dark voyage into a tortured life that gambled on a feel-good twist and, against the odds, pulled it off.' Keith Watson, *Metro*, 6 June 2010.
- 'Richard Curtis is back with a bullet, his mojo apparently restored by one of our great small-screen institutions, and if you haven't yet seen it, then settle down to his terrifically clever, funny, likeable wildly surreal episode of *Doctor Who*.' Peter Bradshaw, *Guardian* website, 8 June 2010.

ANALYSIS

Another writer new to *Doctor Who* makes his debut on this episode, and he is without doubt the most distinguished ever to have contributed to the show. Richard Curtis has a hugely impressive list of TV and film credits to his name, as a writer, director, producer and even actor, as well as being the founder of the Comic Relief charity; and amongst his many other accolades, he was given the special BAFTA Fellowship award in 2007 in recognition of his achievements. Furthermore, just as with Simon Nye on 'Amy's Choice', any concerns that he might be unsuited to writing *Doctor Who* are quickly dispelled, as 'Vincent and the Doctor' proves to be an absolute gem of an episode.

Previous 'celebrity historical' stories have featured a famous novelist (Charles

Dickens), a famous monarch (Queen Victoria), a famous playwright (Shakespeare), a famous crime writer (Agatha Christie) and even, earlier in Series Five, a famous politician (Winston Churchill). This time, it is the turn of a famous artist, in the person of Vincent van Gogh.

Some fan commentators have criticised the story for a lack of historical accuracy, and there is a degree of validity to this. The café where the Doctor and Amy first meet van Gogh is designed to match the one that he painted in Arles in 1888, and similarly his home is clearly intended to be the Yellow House in Arles where he lived at that time. On the other hand, the painting known as *The Church at Auvers*, which features significantly in the plot, was done in 1890 in Auvers, as was *Wheatfield with Crows*, seen being worked on at the start of the episode, and also *Portrait of Dr Gachet*, shown hanging on the artist's wall. In the story, it is implied that van Gogh starts painting sunflowers at Amy's suggestion, yet his first sunflower paintings were actually completed around 1887, and the one he dedicates to her, *Vase with 12 Sunflowers*, was done in 1888. In addition, the artist cut off the lower part of his left ear lobe in December 1888, but there is no sign of this injury on screen. So, is the story set in 1887, or in 1888 or – as seems to have been the intention, given that the Doctor goes to the trouble of obtaining the date from the museum guide, Dr Black – in 1890? And does it take place in Arles or in Auvers?[38] The biographical aspects are rather confused, to say the least. Arguably, however, to focus on such details is rather to miss the point. What Richard Curtis has clearly aimed to achieve here is to present (appropriately enough) an impressionistic portrait of the artist, which is truthful to the essence of the man even though it is not strictly chronological; and in this, he has succeeded admirably.

The most notable aspect of Curtis's excellent characterisation of van Gogh is that, commendably, he does not shy away from depicting the artist's battle with depression. On the contrary, he makes it the central focus of the narrative. Of course, he gives it a *Doctor Who* twist, using the Krafayis as a metaphor for the 'invisible monster' stalking the man – a sensible move ensuring that, as always when the show is at its most effective, the story works on more than one level, and can be appreciated as a simple 'Doctor-versus-alien-threat' tale if one prefers. However, the writer's intent is clear, and the end result is a remarkably sensitive and insightful depiction of the troubled artist. This contrasts starkly with the caricatured portrayal of Churchill – another sufferer of depression – only a few stories earlier, emphasising just what a superior a piece of work Curtis's script is.

One of the key scenes of the episode comes at the very end in the museum, when Amy is upset to realise that, despite having been shown how highly-regarded his art will ultimately become, van Gogh has still committed suicide shortly after being returned home in the TARDIS. The implication here is that the real-life demon of depression is not as simple to overcome as a fantastical creature such as the Krafayis; unusually serious and thought-provoking fare for *Doctor Who* to be placing before its early Saturday evening audience. Far from leaving things on a downbeat note, however, the story's conclusion is essentially an optimistic

---

[38] In one of the videos for the 'Amy's Treasure Hunt' game, released on the official *Doctor Who* website two months later (see Chapter Three for further details), Amy says that she and the Doctor met van Gogh in Arles.

one, as the Doctor tells Amy: 'The way I see it, every life is a pile of good things and bad things ... The good things don't always soften the bad things, but *vice versa* the bad things don't necessarily spoil the good things or make them unimportant. And we definitely added to [Vincent's] pile of good things.'

There are, indeed, many 'good things' to be found in 'Vincent and the Doctor'. A prime example is the rather sweet bond that develops between Amy and Vincent, stemming initially from the simple fact that they both have red hair and the same accent – courtesy, it seems, of the TARDIS translation circuits equating Scottish with Dutch! – and then being reinforced by her admiration of his art and his appreciation of her beauty and spirit. Vincent's exceptional insight allows him not only to see the Krafayis, but also to sense that Amy has recently suffered a loss – the death of Rory – of which she herself no longer has any conscious memory, as poignantly shown in the scene where he questions her over the fact that she is unknowingly crying. An even more touching demonstration of their mutual affection is that she inspires him to paint sunflowers, and he then dedicates one of his greatest pictures of them to her, as she sees in the emotional museum scene at the end.

The interactions between the Doctor and Vincent are also very well depicted. A stand-out scene is the one where the former tries rather awkwardly to console the latter by telling him, 'My experience is that there is, you know, surprisingly, always hope' – to which the distraught artist replies, 'Then your experience is incomplete. I know how it will end, and it will not end well.' The only arguable lapse in the episode's dialogue comes when Curtis resorts to the unnecessary hyperbole of having the Doctor refer to van Gogh as 'the greatest artist who ever lived' – just as he rather ludicrously described Shakespeare as 'the most human human there's ever been' in 'The Shakespeare Code' (2007) and Agatha Christie as the world's 'best' crime writer in 'The Unicorn and the Wasp' (2008). It is all very well to have Dr Black, an obvious fan of the artist's work, speak of him in such terms, but surely the Doctor should show a bit more perspective. The line actually seems even more out of place in light of an earlier comment he makes to the effect that impressionists like van Gogh 'are not accurate enough' by comparison with 'Gainsborough or one of those proper painters'. In fact, there are a couple of points in the episode where, rather surprisingly (and at odds with previous indications in stories such as 'City of Death' (1979)), the Doctor is portrayed as a bit of a philistine when it comes to art. This is best illustrated in the very amusing sequence where he tells van Gogh: 'I remember watching Michelangelo painting the Sistine Chapel. Wow! What a whinge. I kept saying to him, "Look, if you're scared of heights, you shouldn't have taken the job, mate" ... And Picasso. What a ghastly old goat. I kept telling him, "Concentrate, Pablo. It's one eye, either side of the face."' Possibly, though, the Doctor is simply joking here, to try to relieve the tension of the situation.

There is actually quite a bit of humour in Curtis's dialogue throughout the episode, and even the occasional sequence of broader comedy, such as when the Doctor tries to repel the attacking Krafayis with a stick but fails miserably due to his inability to see it. This lightness of touch is very welcome, as it avoids any risk of things becoming too downbeat, given the underlying seriousness of the subject matter of van Gogh's affliction.

Another distinctive aspect of the episode is its pacing, which is markedly less frenetic than that of most 21st Century *Doctor Who*. This serves Curtis's story well, giving the growing friendship between the time travellers and Vincent a chance to breathe and allowing for the inclusion of some relatively inconsequential but nonetheless affecting scenes such as the one where they pause respectfully at the roadside as a small procession of local villagers passes by carrying the sunflower-adorned coffin of a young woman killed by the Krafayis. A particular highlight comes when, after the Krafayis itself has been killed, the three friends lie down in a field together and look up at the night sky, while Vincent tries to explain how he sees the world: 'Look at the sky. It's not dark and black and without character. The black is in fact deep blue. And over there, lighter blue. And blowing through the blueness and the blackness, the wind swirling through the air and then, shining, burning, bursting through – the stars!' As this dialogue is delivered, the image of the sky is transformed via some superb CGI work into one resembling van Gogh's famous painting *The Starry Night* – a truly breathtaking sequence, unlike any other ever seen in *Doctor Who*.

Perhaps the most memorable scene of the whole episode, though, is the very moving one where the Doctor and Amy take Vincent in the TARDIS to the exhibition of his work at the Musée d'Orsay in the Paris of 2010 – exactly the kind of thing one might be tempted to do if one really had a time machine. With the rock group Athlete's song 'Chances' pointing up the action on the soundtrack – another striking innovation for *Doctor Who* (although something similar has been done a couple of times before in *Torchwood*) – Vincent is moved to tears as he hears the learned Dr Black speak glowingly of his work and describe him as 'not only the world's greatest artist, but also one of the greatest men who ever lived'. Some reviewers have criticised this as being overly sentimental – one even going so far as to describe it as 'self-indulgently mawkish' – but to view it in that way is very mean-spirited. Besides, this type of scene is absolutely emblematic of Richard Curtis's work, particularly in feature films; and surely if a writer of Curtis's calibre and reputation is persuaded to contribute an episode to the show, then one wants it to be written recognisably in his signature style.

The quality of Curtis's script is thankfully matched by that of its realisation. Director Jonny Campbell's work on this production is much better than on 'The Vampires of Venice' – rather curiously, given that the two episodes were made concurrently – and the location recording done in Croatia looks fantastic, capturing the feel of 19th Century rural France even better than it did that of 16th Century Venice. There are some beautifully-composed shots presented here, such as the one where Vincent opens his window to see Amy surrounded by sunflowers outside his house. Tony Curran's performance as van Gogh is absolutely stellar, aided by the fact that he bears an uncanny resemblance to the famous artist; and Bill Nighy – at one point the bookmakers' favourite to be cast as the ninth Doctor back in 2004 – turns in a pleasing uncredited cameo as Dr Black, who whether by accident or design wears glasses that make him look strikingly similar to the BBC's arts editor Will Gompertz, often seen reporting on prestigious exhibitions. Regulars Matt Smith and Karen Gillan are also excellent in their respective roles, the latter having really grown into the part of Amy by this point in the series' production.

Some fans have slated the CGI design of the Krafayis on the grounds that it resembles a giant, ferocious chicken, which is actually not far wide of the mark, but it is unclear why they consider this problematic. It is supposed to be a fierce but relatively unintelligent alien animal, lashing out instinctively rather than through

# 5.10 – VINCENT AND THE DOCTOR

any malicious intent, and there seems nothing at all incongruous about its appearance. It is, in any case, invisible for much of the time – doubtless a useful budget-saving measure – and, as previously mentioned, it serves mainly as a metaphor for Vincent's depression, which he symbolically tries to fend off with his easel. There is a nice symmetry, too, in the fact that the Krafayis can neither be seen (save by Vincent) nor see, owing to its blindness.

In the end, of all the many fine aspects of this episode, it is the compassionate depiction of van Gogh's depression that will linger longest in the viewer's memory. This may not be quite what *Doctor Who*'s creators pictured back in 1963 when they envisaged the show having a semi-educational role – certainly the imprecision over the biographical details of van Gogh's life will have tried the patience of any historians in the audience! – but it still arguably fulfils that remit, by helping to raise awareness of one aspect of the very important but often sidelined issue of mental illness. While the show would not work if every story was in this vein, the fact that it is flexible and confident enough to incorporate an exceptional entry like 'Vincent and the Doctor' presents *Doctor Who* at its very best.

# 5.11 – THE LODGER

Writer: Gareth Roberts
Director: Catherine Morshead

DEBUT TRANSMISSION DETAILS

BBC One/BBC HD
Date: 12 June 2010. Scheduled time: 6.45 pm. Actual time: 6.47 pm.

Duration: 42′ 31″

ADDITIONAL CREDITED CAST

James Corden (Craig [39]), Daisy Haggard (Sophie), Owen Donovan (Steven), Babatunde Aleshe (Sean), Jem Wall (Michael), Karen Seacombe (Sandra), Kamara Baccus (Clubber).

PLOT

The TARDIS materialises in the 21st Century in the town of Colchester and ejects the Doctor before dematerialising again with Amy still inside. This rapid departure has been caused by a powerful presence apparently inhabiting the flat above the one where a man named Craig Owens lives. The Doctor becomes Craig's lodger and eventually discovers that there is actually an alien ship above his flat. The false impression of there being another storey was created by its perception filter. The ship crashed-landed some time ago, and its occupants were killed. The emergency crash program is now causing it to ensnare innocent passers-by in the hope they will take over as its pilot, but their human brains are not strong enough and are being burnt out in the process. The ship now wants the Doctor to become its pilot, but his brain is too strong, and this would result in the destruction of the whole solar system. Craig and his friend Sophie are able to deactivate the ship's engine by admitting their previously-undeclared love for each other; the ship needs to draw on the energy of people who want to leave, not those who are happy to stay where they are. The ship implodes and is destroyed, after which the TARDIS is able to rematerialise, reuniting the Doctor and Amy.

QUOTE, UNQUOTE

* **Doctor:** 'So who's the girl [in the photograph] on the fridge?'
  **Craig:** 'That's my friend, Sophie. Girlfriend. Friend who's a girl. There's nothing going on.'

---

[39] Surname given in dialogue as 'Owens'.

**Doctor:** 'That's completely normal. Works for me.'
- **Craig:** 'Why am I telling you this? I don't even know you.'
**Doctor:** 'Well, I've got one of those faces. People never stop blurting out their plans while I'm around.'
- **Craig:** 'Has anyone ever told you that you're a bit weird?'
**Doctor:** 'They never really stop. Ever been to Paris, Craig?'
**Craig:** 'Nah, I can't see the point of Paris. I'm not much of a traveller.'
**Doctor:** 'I can tell from your sofa.'
**Craig:** 'My sofa?'
**Doctor:** 'You're starting to look like it.'
- **Doctor:** 'All I've got to do is pass as an ordinary human being. Simple. What could possibly go wrong?'
**Amy:** 'Have you *seen* you?'

CONTINUITY POINTS

- The Doctor says that he likes sweets. He also says that he doesn't know why people call him 'Doctor', or why he calls himself that.
- It is implied that the Doctor will later arrange for there to have been a vacant room waiting for him in the flat by going back in time and ensuring that the owner, Mark, moved out when, as Craig says, 'this uncle he'd never even heard of died and left a load of money in the will'. Similarly, he will later go back in time and put a note written by Amy in the local newsagents' window, drawing his attention to the advert that Craig has placed there seeking a lodger. These are examples of what is sometimes referred to as a 'predestination paradox'.
- The alien ship above Craig's flat causes the TARDIS to go into a 'materialisation loop', whereby it repeatedly attempts to materialise nearby but is unable to do so. It also causes temporary localised time loops and time distortion. There is a risk that the TARDIS could be flung off into the time vortex with Amy inside it, lost forever. The Doctor deduces that the effect is 'almost unbelievably powerful and dangerous'. He builds a scanner device to try to find out more, using 'non-technological technology of Lammasteen'. When he eventually gets to see inside the ship, he describes it as a 'time engine' and 'someone's attempt to build a TARDIS'. It has disguised itself as the (non-existent) second storey of Craig's building by way of a perception filter, which he says works by tricking the memory. The origins of the ship remain a mystery.
- Craig has a fridge magnet of a Vincent van Gogh self-portrait, of which the Doctor and Amy have recently seen the original in the artist's own possession.
- The Doctor is able to convey information directly into Craig's mind by head-butting him. He confirms that his current face is his eleventh.
- At the end of the episode, one of the cracks in time appears behind the fridge in Craig's kitchen. Meanwhile, in the TARDIS, Amy looks in the Doctor's pocket for a pen and instead finds a boxed engagement ring. This is the ring that Rory previously gave her; something she has forgotten about since his existence was erased by another of the cracks in time.

## PRODUCTION NOTES

- This episode was recorded with 'Amy's Choice' as Block Seven of Series Five's production schedule.
- The location used for the exterior of Craig's house was in Westville Road, Cardiff, where recording took place on 3 and 4 March 2010. On the same day, the opening scene of the TARDIS attempting to materialise and ejecting the Doctor was taped in Mill Gardens, Cardiff. On 5 March, the football match was staged in Victoria Park, Cardiff. The interiors of Craig's workplace were recorded on 6 March at Lanelay Hall, Pontyclun. The interiors of Craig's flat were taped in studio, as usual at Upper Boat, between 9 and 20 March.
- At one point early in the story's development, writer Gareth Roberts considered having the alien ship belong to Meglos, the xerophyte villain from the classic-era story 'Meglos' (1980).
- In the scene where the Doctor imparts information about himself to Craig, a montage of clips is shown featuring (in this order) the ninth, tenth, eighth, fourth, third, second and first Doctors, plus the eleventh Doctor and Amy from the beginning of 'The Beast Below'. This is the latest of a number of references back to past Doctors in Series Five. The first Doctor appears the most, on four separate occasions: first in the montage of all the past Doctors in 'The Eleventh Hour'; secondly on the Doctor's library card in 'The Vampires of Venice'; thirdly in the output from his scanner device in 'Vincent and the Doctor'; and fourthly here.

## PRESS REACTION

- '"The Lodger" moves in with what feels like remarkable timing, scheduled as it is on the second day of the World Cup and ending almost to the second before England and the USA kick off in South Africa. Not only is it the blokey-est *Doctor Who* episode to date, it contains a whopping great scene in which the Time Lord proves himself beyond a natural at the glorious game – wearing a number 11 shirt, of course! If you're both a footie fan and a *Who* nut – and there must be a fair few in that Venn diagram – this seems like spectacularly adept planning, with "The Lodger" serving as the perfect pre-match warm-up.' Patrick Mulkern, *Radio Times* website, 12 June 2010.
- 'There was much to like about "The Lodger" and its domestic take on the Doctor, with some genuinely funny moments and a central conceit that delivered a welcome bit of feel-good fuzz. In terms of monster-of-the-week thrills, though, it simply couldn't deliver the much needed atmosphere, and the whole thing threatened to unravel as it reached its poorly-delivered, undercooked conclusion.' Matt Wales, IGN website, 14 June 2010.
- 'There's a danger, arguably, that Matt Smith's Doctor is becoming an out and out comic figure in a way perhaps only formerly true of Tom Baker, predominately during Season 17. For a lot of people that won't be a bad precedent, but given that the whole series was pitched at a more blatantly comic register it does give rise to the question of how appropriate it is to the 'dark fairytale' stylings of the Moffat administration ... The Doctor's eccentricity may be exaggerated (the air-kisses), but Smith is in the enviable

position of making it seem perfectly natural, and in fact delivers what may prove to be one of his definitive performances as the character. Also, whereas the fourth Doctor would probably be too aloof and alien for such a domestic arrangement, the eleventh's enjoyment of the situation is what brings this rather glorious concept alive.' Neil Clarke, Kasterborous website, 13 June 2010.

ANALYSIS

Like his Series Two contribution 'The Shakespeare Code', writer Gareth Roberts' latest episode owes a debt of inspiration to one of his earlier *Doctor Who Magazine* comic strip stories – in this case, quite a large debt. That story, also called *The Lodger*, appeared in Issue 368 in April 2006 and saw the tenth Doctor dropping in to stay at the flat of Mickey Smith while waiting for Rose Tyler to catch up with him in the TARDIS. This time, it is the eleventh Doctor who descends upon the home of a new character, Craig Owens, while Amy is the companion stuck inside the TARDIS. Other elements carried over from the comic strip original include the Doctor making an amazing omelette; the sonic screwdriver being mistaken for a toothbrush; the Doctor impressing Mickey's friends with his skills in a local football match; and the Doctor interrupting a romantic interlude between Mickey and a potential girlfriend, Gina, who then invites him to join them for a drink and realises through his prompting that she is wasting her life in her current mundane job when there is a whole world of opportunity available to her. In the TV telling, Gina is replaced by Sophie, and Craig is secretly in love with her, whereas in the comic strip version Mickey's real affections lie with Rose.

This is not the first time that the Doctor has been seen to have essentially the same adventure twice, in two different incarnations and in two different media. The first major examples of this came in Series Three, when 'Human Nature'/'The Family of Blood' adapted the 1995 New Adventures novel *Human Nature*, and 'Blink' reworked the *Doctor Who Annual 2006* story *'What I Did On My Christmas Holidays' by Sally Sparrow*. This effectively put the last nail in the coffin of the idea that it might be possible to reconcile every officially-sanctioned *Doctor Who* story from every medium – TV shows, novels, short stories, audio dramas, comic strips and so on – into a single coherent continuity. We are now arguably in a 'post canon' era, where really anything goes, continuity-wise. While this may still offend the sensibilities of some fans, there are ways to explain it within the fiction of the show itself, including the possibility that stories in different media take place in different parallel universes, and the notion that any anomalies are due to the lingering after-effects of the last great Time War. Series Five even presents us with a new potential get-out in the form of the cracks in time, erasing great swathes of existence from people's memories.

For non-fans, of course, this is basically a non-issue. Of the millions of people who regularly watch the TV show, only a tiny minority will be aware of the tie-ins in other media; and even some fans prefer to focus solely on the TV stories, regarding everything else as apocryphal. As far as 'The Lodger' is concerned, there are at any rate two new plot strands that help to distinguish it from its comic strip antecedent. One of these is the burgeoning romance between Craig and Sophie, to whom the Doctor effectively acts as matchmaker, and the other is the mystery of what exactly is going on in the flat above Craig's.

# CRACKS IN TIME

Craig and Sophie are nicely-observed characters of a kind rarely featured prominently in *Doctor Who*: ordinary, down-to-earth people doing ordinary, down-to-earth jobs. This really provides the starting-point for the story: how will the Doctor cope with having to live alongside regular people like this and pass himself off as human? The way this situation plays out is highly amusing, as the Time Lord befuddles Craig with his strange and unconventional behaviour: greeting him with theatrical air-kisses; proffering a carrier bag full of cash by way of rent; apparently talking gibberish to himself in his room as he communicates with Amy via a scrambler device; proving to be unfeasibly skilled at football; misconstruing colloquialisms (particularly when one of Craig's footballing friends vows to 'annihilate' a rival pub team); charming the boss and other staff at the call centre; building a bizarre device out of an array of everyday items stacked on his bed, which he tries to pass off as a work of art when Craig sees it; and even psychically conversing with the cat!

This is all great fun. There is, though, a slight problem with it, in that it seems out of kilter with how the new Doctor is characterised throughout most of the rest of Series Five. His quirky, mad-professorish traits are usually offset by a more serious demeanour at other times, but here they seem to have taken over completely. Thankfully he does not at any point sink to the level of inanity seen in the terrible stag party scene at the start of 'The Vampires of Venice', but it is nevertheless hard to believe that he is not more *au fait* with everyday life in 21st Century England than he appears to be here. He has, after all, spent a great deal of time in or close to this era in previous incarnations, albeit usually in less domestic environments such as UNIT HQ. Has he really lost a lot of that knowledge and experience in his most recent regeneration – even to the extent of not realising that an ordinary screwdriver, unlike a sonic one, has no on switch? Certainly the tenth Doctor seemed to know what football was, and to have a good grasp of colloquialisms, when he saw a group of students exercising outside the Rattigan Academy in 'The Sontaran Stratagem' (2008) and told Luke Rattigan 'I wouldn't mind a kick-around; I've got me daps on' ('daps' being a fairly obscure slang term for trainers); and yet here, when Amy first mentions football, the eleventh Doctor seems to mistake it for hockey, asking 'Now, football's the one with the sticks, isn't it?' It is hard to shake the feeling that the credibility of the character is being somewhat undermined here simply for the sake of a few laughs.

The other awkwardness about this is that if the Doctor is really such a fish out of water when placed in an ordinary domestic setting, how is it possible that he is immediately able to spot the mutual romantic attraction between Craig and Sophie, when even they themselves are unaware of each other's feelings? This suggests an awareness of the subtleties of human relationships that, while it accords with what we have seen of him in his previous incarnations, isn't really consistent with the unworldliness he shows at other times in 'The Lodger'.

There are a few other problems with the story, too. For one thing, if one thinks about it for any length of time, it becomes apparent that there are a number of plot glitches and loose ends left hanging. Why does the Doctor interrupt working on his scanner device to go off and play football and then fill in for Craig at his job? Admittedly he is not to know that, while he is messing about like this, luckless passers-by are being lured into the upstairs flat and killed – this is something he discovers only after talking to the cat! – but there seems no good reason why he should put off attending to the main problem at hand, particularly when Amy is still in danger trapped inside the TARDIS. What exactly is the mould-like stain that spreads across one corner of the ceiling in Craig's flat and is poisonous to the touch? The Doctor says that it is caused by the killing of the people in the flat above, but it is unclear in what way, and – unless, unseen by the viewer, Craig paints over it – the stain simply vanishes at the end of the episode. Who were the original owners of the alien ship, and what caused it to crash-land above Craig's flat, apparently killing all on board in the process? Are these points that will be returned to later on, perhaps as part of the ongoing story arc, or are viewers simply expected to take them at face value, without further explanation?

There are also, sadly, some serious shortcomings in the way the set-up with the alien ship is depicted on screen. When the viewer finally gets to see it from the outside, it doesn't look like a crash site at all; the ship is simply standing on the roof of the building below, and both are seemingly completely intact. Its design, with four spider-like legs, was apparently intended as a homage to that of the Jagaroth vessel in 'City of Death' (1979), but it doesn't really fit the story, as it makes it even more difficult to see how any residue from the killings could have seeped down to stain the ceiling of Craig's flat, and really impossible to understand how the unfortunate victims could have got on board in the first place – surely the perception filter disguising the ship could not have conjured up a non-existent set of stairs for them to ascend, and a non-existent hole in the roof for them to pass through on the way? Moreover, the house chosen as the location for Craig's flat is really the wrong type of building. It is very unlikely that anyone would ever build a one-storey extension jutting out at the end of a row of two-storey terraced houses – architecturally, it just looks completely incongruous – and this makes it far too obvious that the upper story of the real house on location has simply been painted out in post-production. The internal layout of Craig's flat, with its adjoining hall, is also all wrong for what is supposed to be, in truth, a one-storey building; and there is even a prominently-featured two-button intercom buzzer fixed outside the front door, which can still be seen there even after the alien ship has been destroyed.

However, easily the most regrettable aspect of the episode comes when, unbelievably, the Doctor actually head-butts Craig – not once, but twice! – in order to quickly impart some information to him. The inclusion of this scene is a jaw-dropping and unforgivable lapse of judgment by the programme-makers, and it is really surprising that it did not draw more complaints from viewers. After the episode's debut transmission, there were at least a couple of reports on the online fan forums of children badly hurting themselves, and others, by copying the Doctor's actions here. Admittedly that is only anecdotal evidence of harm being caused, but surely it should have been obvious to anyone involved in the production that this was the type of thing that was liable to be imitated by impressionable youngsters, with potentially injurious consequences. Even given the urgency of the situation, it is impossible to imagine any of the previous Doctors having resorted to such a measure, and one would like to think that if he had been longer-established in the role, and felt more confident to assert himself, Matt Smith would actually have refused to play this scene as scripted. (One can only imagine the kind of apoplectic reaction the production team of the day would have got from Tom Baker if they had dared to present him with something like this!) It can only be hoped that this bizarrely violent Time Lord information-sharing technique is not one that will ever be seen again in the show.

But to focus on the negative aspects of the episode seems churlish when there are so many positive ones. There is some fantastic dialogue throughout, and Gareth Roberts makes a great job of depicting the relationship between Craig and Sophie. Particularly pleasing is the way he manages to tie this in very neatly with the other aspect of the plot involving the alien ship, when at the end of the episode it is the couple's previously-undeclared love for each other that saves the day. Adding considerably to the effectiveness of the episode are the superb contributions of guest stars James Corden – best known for his comedy work, including on his co-written BBC success *Gavin & Stacey* – and Daisy Haggard, who hit exactly the right note with their performances. In fact, given that they effectively serve as stand-in companions here, one cannot help but think that they make a rather more engaging and well-portrayed couple than Amy and Rory … Karen Gillan herself puts in only a few brief appearances this time around – whereas previous series have featured 'Doctor-lite' episodes, here we get a 'companion-lite' one – and it may actually have been to the story's benefit if these had been cut down even more, as they tend to become rather repetitive after a time, being mostly just variations on the theme of Amy being buffeted around in the errant TARDIS while communicating with the Doctor via his earpiece device.

There is one slight oddity in Catherine Morshead's direction of the episode. In a scene where Craig and Sophie have a conversation in the hallway by the front door, she seems for no apparent reason to guide the viewer's attention to the wall between them, on which hangs a rather spooky, oval-shaped framed portrait seemingly depicting the 19th Century music hall star Dan Leno! (Surely this particular mystery couldn't have anything to do with the ongoing story arc, could it …?) Other than that, however, her work here is equally as polished as on 'Amy's Choice', and she gets maximum value out of both the humour in Roberts' script and the suitably scary bits where passing strangers get lured into the upstairs flat by disembodied voices emanating eerily from the intercom outside. The dramatic reveal of the large, curiously TARDIS-like interior of the alien ship – a nicely-designed set, albeit again showing no signs of any crash having occurred – is also well achieved.

It seems that, like a number of the other episodes of Series Five, 'The Lodger' would just have benefited from going through one or two more script drafts before entering production, in order to iron out some of the problems discussed above. It is about 80% of the way there to being an absolute classic; it is just the other 20% that lets it down a bit.

# 5.12 – THE PANDORICA OPENS

Writer: Steven Moffat
Director: Toby Haynes

## DEBUT TRANSMISSION DETAILS

BBC One/ BBC HD
Date: 19 June 2010. Scheduled time: 6.40 pm. Actual time: 6.39 pm.

Duration: 48′ 42″

## ADDITIONAL CREDITED CAST

Tony Curran (Vincent), Bill Paterson (Bracewell), Ian McNeice (Winston Churchill), Sophie Okonedo (Liz Ten), Marcus O'Donovan (Claudio), Clive Wood (Commander), Christopher Ryan (Commander Stark), Ruari Mears (Cyber Leader), Paul Kasey (Judoon), Howard Lee (Doctor Gachet), Barnaby Edwards (Dalek), Simon Fisher-Becker (Dorium), Joe Jacobs (Guard), Chrissie Cotterill (Madame Vernet), David Flynn (Marcellus).

## PLOT

A previously-unknown van Gogh painting showing the TARDIS exploding is passed down via Churchill and Bracewell to Liz Ten and then to River Song, who travels back in time using a vortex manipulator and poses as Queen Cleopatra in order to set up a rendezvous with the Doctor and Amy in the Roman-occupied Britain of 102 AD. Together, the three friends discover that in an underground chamber beneath the nearby Stonehenge is the Pandorica, a large sealed cube designed as a highly secure prison cell. The Pandorica starts to open and broadcasts a signal summoning a huge fleet of spaceships carrying Daleks, Cybermen, Sontarans and many others. These races have allied themselves against the Doctor and built the Pandorica as a trap for him. They believe that he will one day be responsible for the cracks in time, which are caused a future explosion of the TARDIS, and wish to save the universe from destruction by preventing this from happening. Ignoring his protests, they seal him within the Pandorica. Amy has meanwhile been reunited with an apparently resurrected Rory, but this is really an Auton duplicate – the Nestenes are part of the alliance – and he shoots her with his hand-weapon. River is trapped inside the TARDIS after returning there to fetch it for the Doctor, and is unable to prevent it from exploding on the fateful date of 26 June 2010, after a mysterious voice intones 'Silence will fall'. All the stars at every point in history turn supernova and burn out, leaving the Earth hanging in empty space.

QUOTE, UNQUOTE

- **Doctor:** 'There was a goblin, or a trickster, or a warrior. A nameless, terrible thing, soaked in the blood of a billion galaxies. The most feared being in all the cosmos. And nothing could stop it, or hold it, or reason with it. One day it would just drop out of the sky and tear down your world.'
- **Doctor:** 'Yes. Okay, okay, okay, okay. Dalek fleet. Minimum 12,000 battleships, armed to the teeth. Aaargh! But we've got surprise on our side! They'll never expect three people to attack 12,000 Dalek battleships. 'Cause we'd be killed instantly. So it would be a fairly short surprise. Forget surprise.'
- **Doctor:** 'Hello, Stonehenge! Who takes the Pandorica, takes the universe! But bad news, everyone. 'Cause guess who? Hah! Listen, you lot, you're all whizzing about, it's really very distracting. Could you all just stay still a minute? Because I – am – talking! Now, the question of the hour is, who's got the Pandorica? Answer: I do. Next question, who's coming to take it from me? Come on! Look at me. No plan, no back-up, no weapons worth a damn. Oh, and something else. I don't have anything – to – lose! So if you're sitting up there in your silly little spaceship, with all your silly little guns, and you've got any plans on taking the Pandorica tonight, just remember who's standing in your way. Remember every black day I ever stopped you. And then, *and then*, do the smart thing. Let somebody else try first.'

CONTINUITY POINTS

- Stonehenge was built above the chamber containing the Pandorica, both to mark its location and to act as a transmitter. The transmitter broadcasts a signal to 'everyone, everywhere, to every time zone', alerting the monster alliance to the Doctor's arrival there in 102 AD. This signal is also picked up psychically by van Gogh and causes him to paint *The Pandorica Opens*, a picture of the TARDIS exploding, which incorporates the time and place co-ordinates of Stonehenge in 102 AD.
- Van Gogh's painting is later found behind the wall of an attic in France and passed to British Prime Minister Winston Churchill in the Cabinet War Rooms in 1941. This must be shortly after the events of 'Victory of the Daleks', as the Bracewell android is also present and has a black-gloved left hand; the replacement for the one that was shot off by a Dalek. It is not explained why Bracewell has returned here, having previously expressed his intention to leave and find the girl named Dorabella.[40]
- Churchill phones the Doctor to tell him about van Gogh's painting, but he does not answer and the TARDIS instead reroutes the call via the time vortex to River Song, who is in a cell in the Stormcage Containment Facility in the

---

[40] In one of a series of fictitious Churchill diary entries that Mark Gatiss later contributed to *Doctor Who – The Brilliant Book 2011* (see Appendix G for further details), he indicated that the Prime Minister decided to track Bracewell down and put him to work with other 'boffins' as he was concerned that the 'mechanical man' was still at large and might be susceptible to falling under Dalek influence again.

year 5145. This is at a point in her life before the events of 'The Time of Angels'/'Flesh and Stone', when she was said to be held in the Facility in the earlier time period of the 51st Century. This implies that she will at some stage travel back in time to the 51st Century, and that the authorities of that era will return her to the Facility because they are somehow aware of her being sentenced to imprisonment there in the future. She must however be released at some point because, also in the 51st Century, she is seen working as an archaeologist in 'Silence in the Library'/'Forest of the Dead' (2008).

- River Song escapes from her cell and finds van Gogh's painting in the Royal Collection, it having presumably been there since Churchill's time. Liz Ten catches her stealing the painting, but allows her to leave with it when she sees what it depicts. It is unclear if this occurs on Starship UK, on Earth or elsewhere. 'The Beast Below' was set around the 32nd Century, when Liz Ten was already some 300 years old, but it was established in that story that her body ages at a very slow rate. By the 52nd Century, she must have been 'the bloody Queen', as she puts it, for over 2,000 years.

- River Song visits a bar or nightclub called the Maldovarium, still in the year 5145, and obtains from a man named Dorium a time agent's vortex manipulator of the same kind seen previously on the wrist of Captain Jack Harkness, who was a time agent in the 51st Century. She uses this vortex manipulator to travel back in time to Planet One, the oldest planet in the universe, where she etches a message in 50-feet-high letters on a diamond cliff-face for the Doctor to see, reading 'Hello Sweetie' and giving the co-ordinates recorded in van Gogh's painting. She then travels to Salisbury Plain in 102 AD and waits for the Doctor to arrive there.

- A Calisto Pulse is a device that can disarm micro-explosives from up to 20 feet. River Song has one contained in an earring, which she gives to Dorium in exchange for the vortex manipulator, so that he can disarm the micro-explosives she has placed in his wine.

- The Roman occupation of Britain was Amy's favourite topic at school. She wrote an essay called *Invasion of the Hot Italians*, but was marked down for the title. She also had a children's picture book depicting Roman soldiers, but her favourite book was *Pandora's Box*, about a box 'with all the worst things in the world in it' (in fact, a story from Greek mythology). When the TARDIS takes River Song to Amy's deserted house in Leadworth, she finds burn marks on the grass outside, implying that one of the alliance members must have landed there previously in a space shuttle. The Doctor says: 'If they've been to her house, they could have used her psychic residue. Structures can hold memories; that's why houses have ghosts. They could've taken a snapshot of Amy's memories. But why?' It transpires that the alliance have used Amy's memories to construct their trap for the Doctor. The Pandorica resembles the picture of Pandora's Box on the cover of Amy's favourite book, and similarly the Roman soldiers camped near Stonehenge are Auton duplicates based on those depicted in her other book. The Centurian Rory is based on a snapshot of Rory in a Roman fancy dress costume, standing beside Amy in her policewoman kissogram outfit. As River says to the Doctor, 'They used Amy to construct a scenario you'd believe, to get close to you.'

- It was established in their first TV appearance in 'Spearhead from Space'

(1970) that there are different types of Autons, all made of plastic and animated by the Nestene Consciousness. Some are fairly crude mannequins, resembling shop window dummies, while others are more sophisticated facsimiles of real people. In 'Spearhead from Space', the people on whom the facsimiles were based were kept alive, implying that their memories and personalities were needed in order to maintain the facsimiles. The same was true of the Auton Mickey Smith seen in 'Rose' (2005). Apart from Rory's, the duplicates in 'The Pandorica Opens' seem to be intermediate between the two types seen in 'Spearhead from Space'. They have convincing human features, but are not based on real individuals. Until activated by a signal, they do not even realise that they are Autons, but believe themselves to be real Roman soldiers (which is why, improbably, River's hallucinogenic lipstick works on them). The Rory duplicate is also initially unaware of his true nature, but seems more akin to one of the facsimiles first seen in 'Spearhead from Space', in that he is based on a real person – although in this instance, as that person is dead, his memories and personality are presumably drawn from Amy's subconscious mind instead. However, he also remembers his life as a Roman – he says he found himself here with his head 'full of Roman stuff', as if he had woken from a dream of being Rory.

- River describes the Pandorica as, 'A box. A cage. A prison. It was built to contain the most feared thing in all the universe.' On scanning it, she finds that it is protected with 'every' kind of security, including 'deadlocks, time-stops, matter-lines'. At least one Cyberman was left on sentry duty after the Pandorica was buried in the Underhenge, but it is now severely damaged, and its organic components are long-dead. The Doctor speculates that this damage was inflicted by the local Celts.
- River detects that hovering above Stonehenge are not only Dalek, Cyberman and Sontaran ships but also: 'Terileptil, Slitheen, Chelonian, Nestene, Drahvin, Sycorax, Haemogoth, Zygon, Atraxi, Draconian'. A number of these races have not yet featured in 21st Century *Doctor Who* on TV. The Chelonians are militaristic, turtle-like creatures that have made a number of appearances in the original *Doctor Who* novels and other tie-in media, beginning with Gareth Roberts' novel *The Highest Science* in 1993, but not so far in the TV show itself (although they were at one point considered for inclusion in the 2009 Easter special 'Planet of the Dead'). The Doctor encountered the Drahvins in 'Galaxy 4' (1965), the Zygons in 'Terror of the Zygons' (1975) and the Draconians (with whom he had previously had some off-screen dealings) in 'Frontier in Space' (1973). The Haemogoths featured in the novel *The Forgotten Army* by Brian Minchin, published the month before 'The Pandorica Opens' was transmitted.
- In addition to the Autons, the monster races of which members are actually seen on screen are: Dalek, Cyberman, Judoon, Sontaran, Silurian, Roboform, Hoix, Sycorax and, fleetingly, Blowfish (from *Torchwood*), Uvodni (*The Sarah Jane Adventures*) and Weevil (*Torchwood*). An Atraxi ship is also seen amongst those gathered above Stonehenge.
- The Cyber Leader says, with reference to the cracks in time, 'All universes will be deleted.' This, along with their appearance and the 'C' logos on their chests, suggests that the Cybermen featured here are Cybus-originated ones from the parallel universe first seen in 'Rise of the Cybermen'/'The Age of Steel' (2006).

The head of the damaged Cyberman contains within it a complete human skull rather than just a brain.

- The Doctor appears to confirm indications given in earlier episodes that when people are erased from existence by the energy from the cracks in time, they still leave behind all the effects and consequences of their lives before they were erased. They are simply forgotten by everyone who knew them; and even then, not completely forgotten. He says: 'People fall out of the world sometimes, but they, they always leave traces. Little things we can't quite account for: faces in photographs, luggage, half-eaten meals … rings. Nothing is ever forgotten, not completely. And, if something can be remembered, it can come back.' He adds that he initially took Amy with him on his travels because of her house: 'It was too big, too many empty rooms. Does it ever bother you, Amy, that your life doesn't make any sense?' This suggests that the members of Amy's family who at one time lived with her in her house have also fallen victim to the cracks in time and been forgotten.

- Just as Amy did not recall the Daleks in 'Victory of the Daleks', she does not know what Cybermen are either, despite having presumably seen them during the events depicted in 'Army of Ghosts' (2006).

- The Doctor says: 'There are cracks. Cracks in time. There's going to be a huge explosion in the future, on one particular day. And every other moment in history is cracking around it.' The day in question is 26 June 2010, as previously revealed in 'Flesh and Stone', and it is the TARDIS that explodes, as implied when the Doctor found a fragment of its door sign in one of the cracks at the end of 'Cold Blood'. (Clips from both episodes are included in 'The Pandorica Opens' to remind the viewer of these points.) Inside the TARDIS, a mysterious voice is heard saying 'Silence will fall' a total of three times before the ship explodes, but the significance of this is unclear. The phrase 'Silence will fall' was previously spoken by Prizoner Zero in 'The Eleventh Hour', suggesting that it had foreknowledge of the event. Possibly it gained that foreknowledge from its Atraxi captors, given that they are revealed here to be members of the monster alliance; although, on the other hand, the alliance themselves seem to be unaware of the exact circumstances of the TARDIS's explosion. It remains unclear what causes the explosion, although River says that the TARDIS is being flown by 'an external force' and that she has 'lost control'. The Doctor tells her to leave the ship, and that 'if there's no-one inside, the TARDIS engines shut down automatically' – which seems to be at odds with a number of previous indications that the TARDIS can dematerialise and rematerialise despite there being no-one on board, such as in 'The Android Invasion' (1975) – but she is unable to do this, as when she finally manages to open the doors, she finds a solid wall on the other side.

- River says that the Doctor taught her how to fly the TARDIS, which suggests that she was joking when in 'The Time of Angels' she implied that that was not the case. The Daleks believe, wrongly, that only the Doctor can pilot the ship.

## PRODUCTION NOTES

- This episode and 'The Big Bang' were made as Block Six of Series Five's production schedule.

CRACKS IN TIME

- The scene in Churchill's office was shot at the West Cross Anti-Aircraft Operations Room in Swansea on 26 August 2009, and the shots of the adjoining corridor at Brackla Bunker, Brackla, Bridgend on 31 August, during production of 'Victory of the Daleks'. Similarly, the scene featuring Liz Ten was shot during the location work for 'The Beast Below', on 22 September at the Orangery, Margam Country Park, Port Talbot; and the one at van Gogh's house was done during recording for 'Vincent and the Doctor', the establishing shot of the exterior on 3 December in Vrsine, Croatia, and the interiors on 15 December at Sutton Farm, Sutton Road, Llandow. Both taped on 25 January 2010 were the scene of River Song breaking out of her Stormcage cell, in fact part of the car park of the Millennium Stadium in Cardiff, and the one of her acquiring the vortex manipulator in Dorium's Maldovarium, the interior of which was actually the Crystal nightclub in Cardiff. The Vicarage in Rhymney, Gwent was as usual the location used for Amy's home in Leadworth, recording taking place there from 27 to 29 January. The scene of the Roman camp where the TARDIS materialises was recorded back at Margam Country Park on 2 February. The location scenes of Stonehenge in Wiltshire were taped on 2 and 3 February, while the shots of the Doctor, Amy and River riding on horseback toward the monument were captured on Gelligaer Common, Fochriiw, Merthyr. Further recording at Margam Park took place on 5 February. Studio work for this episode and 'The Big Bang', including for certain Stonehenge scenes that could not be done on location, took place at Upper Boat between 6 February and 3 March. A couple of final insert shots were taped on location on 4 and 18 March during work on 'The Lodger'.
- This episode features a 7' 18" pre-opening-titles section – the longest yet.
- A clip from the opening title sequence is used to depict the TARDIS travelling through the time vortex.
- There is no 'Next Time' teaser at the end of this episode, only a 'To Be Continued' caption.

OOPS!

- In 102 AD, Stonehenge was actually far more intact than it is seen to be in this episode – so Amy's question 'How come it's not new?' is understandable!
- There are a considerable number of reversed shots used in the episode, some of which are particularly obvious as the Doctor appears with his floppy fringe over the wrong side of his face.

PRESS REACTION

- 'The *Doctor Who* production team have said lots this year about their desire to make the show more fairytale-ish, and never has that been more apparent than in this finale. The legend of the Pandorica and its contents has a real book-at-bedtime feel (especially when you realise its Pandora's Box origins), and of course, it makes perfect sense that the "most deadly being in the universe" should be the Doctor – for Daleks, Cybermen and lesser villains, he *is* the Big Bad Wolf. Now we're left to wonder whether this particular story will have a suitably happy ending, or whether it'll go somewhere altogether more grim. Next Saturday can't come soon enough.' Richard Edwards, *SFX* website, 19 June 2010.

- 'Some clues, finally, about who, or what, or indeed when, impossible Amy Pond actually is. Here is a world created out of the imagination of that young girl. The Roman gladiators [sic] coming to rescue her, animated from her short story "Invasion of the Hot Italians". Rory apparently remembered back into existence by her confusion at finding the engagement ring. And the most obvious one of all, the Pandorica itself, a prison box constructed out of her favourite story as a little girl, Pandora's Box. A story, remember, about all the evils of the universe being released when a box belonging to a girl is opened. Amelia really must have been one disturbed little girl – and we know who surely contributed to that, don't we?' Dan Martin, *Guardian* website, 19 June 2010.

- 'Sensational. What this year's series had arguably lacked had been the epic, cinematic tale to stick in the memory. But here Steven Moffat remedied this with a taut episode that, despite its rather self-referential opening, propelled the viewer on a gripping adventure with plenty of shocks and surprises, leavened with more emotional and humorous material for a heady mix.' Gavin Fuller, *Telegraph* website, 18 June 2010.

- '"The Pandorica Opens" was classic fairytale, and aimed, as always, at a family audience. Every available monster from *Who* was released from the cupboard for this one, not least my favourite "Dulux" Daleks, who were as threatening as ever. I daren't hide behind the sofa for fear of what I might find there, but these monsters still have the power to unsettle. Coming face-to-face with a Cyberman, even the arm of one as happened last night, is particularly unpleasant. However, I'm not quite clear as to how you embed a knife in a Cyberman when they're able to repel bullets. A mere detail. Matt Smith and Karen Gillan now seem so complete in their respective roles. Remember David Tennant, Billie Piper? It seems aeons away. Are Smith and Gillan the best Doctor and assistant in history? Not yet, but their following is definitely growing, as is their confidence. There may, however, be issues with the budget. After the marvellous exteriors at Stonehenge, we plunged into a dungeon that made me think of the clunky series from the '70s. "Watch out for that scenery!" Don't cut the budget now, BBC ... [*Doctor Who*] is one of the crown jewels and should be protected.' Uncredited reviewer, *Daily Express* website, 20 June 2010.

ANALYSIS

Following the pattern established during Russell T Davies's time as showrunner, Steven Moffat ends his first year in charge of *Doctor Who* with a thrilling two-part finale. In fact, 'The Pandorica Opens' has something of the feel of a 'Series Five's Greatest Hits' package to it, as it reprises some of the most memorable aspects of the previous 11 episodes and starts to draw together the threads of the ongoing story arc.

The action opens with a quick-fire succession of imaginatively-interlinked scenes in which some of this series' most prominent guest characters – van Gogh,

Churchill, Bracewell and Liz Ten – make brief return appearances. This is quite unlike anything ever seen before in the show – something not easy to achieve after the best part of 50 years – and gets things off to a really cracking start. River Song is also involved again, and the idea of her summoning the Doctor with a message left in a place where he is bound to find it one day – in this case, etched on a diamond cliff-face on the universe's oldest planet – is essentially a repeat of the trick she pulled with the *Byzantium*'s home box in 'The Time of Angels'. Similarly, the notion of van Gogh painting a picture incorporating the coordinates of the opening of the Pandorica, which indirectly triggers that very event and thus causes him to receive the coordinates in the first place, is another of the predestination paradoxes seemingly beloved of Steven Moffat, as seen most recently in the way the Doctor secured a vacant room for himself in Craig Owens' flat in 'The Lodger'. The luckless Rory is back too – albeit, as it turns out, in Auton duplicate form – and at one point we are shown a photo of him with Amy in her iconic policewoman's outfit from 'The Eleventh Hour'. We even get to pay a return visit to Amy's eerily deserted house in Leadworth, as she left it on the night before her wedding, when she first joined the Doctor on his travels. Then, at the climax, we are presented with a whole host of returning monsters, not only from Series Five but also from earlier eras, and even a few from the spin-off shows *Torchwood* and *The Sarah Jane Adventures*. This all makes for a heady mix of exciting elements, giving the episode a real blockbuster impact.

It is fantastic to have Alex Kingston back again as River Song. She is by this point well on her way to establishing herself as one of *Doctor Who*'s greatest semi-regular characters, and each time she reappears she gives the story a real boost. 'The Pandorica Opens' is full of superb scenes for her, too, including the one where she obtains the vortex manipulator from Dorium – a nice cameo part for Simon Fisher-Becker as a blue-skinned character somewhat in the mould of Sydney Greenstreet's nightclub owner from the famous wartime movie *Casablanca* (1942) – and the one where she is first seen in Roman Britain amusingly posing as Cleopatra, who actually died some 130 years earlier. She works wonderfully well alongside Matt Smith's Doctor, and is equally good in the scenes toward the end where she is trapped alone inside the malfunctioning TARDIS. A superlative performance from Kingston.

The reappearance of Rory is also welcome, and given an unexpected twist with the revelation that this is actually an Auton replica of the original, created from Amy's memories. Again this brings to the fore the key Series Five idea that existence is dependent upon, or even equivalent to, being remembered. One of the undoubted highlights of 'The Pandorica Opens' is the heart-wrenching scene where, at Rory's urging, a tearful Amy starts to regain her memories of him, only for his Auton nature to kick in and compel him to shoot her with the weapon concealed within his hand. Karen Gillan is excellent here, in what is altogether another strong episode for her; and Arthur Darvill gives arguably his best performance in the show to date. The only slight irritation is that, for some unknown reason, the sound effect used for the firing of the Auton weapon is not the same, and nowhere near as good or memorable, as that heard in all their previous appearances. This may seem a minor slip, but coming not long after the awful redesign of the Daleks and the disappointing reimagining of the Silurians, it does give the impression that under Steven Moffat's stewardship there is rather less respect being paid to the show's classic monsters than was the case under Russell T Davies's.

Another particularly impressive performance in this episode comes from Matt Smith, who is superb throughout. However, one cannot help but be struck once more by the inconsistency in the way the Doctor has been written in this series. The multi-faceted character depicted in 'The Pandorica Opens' is not without his eccentricity or humour, but is for the most part essentially serious, and displays a range of credible emotions including concern, resolve, fascination, defiance, apprehension and even occasionally anger. This, to be fair, accords with how he is portrayed in most of the other episodes; but it is really quite far removed from the simpler, more comedic version seen in the immediately-preceding 'The Lodger'. Some might perhaps argue that a less serious story demanded a less serious Doctor, but such discrepancies between episodes surely risk compromising the believability of the character; and, in any event, the way he is depicted in 'The Pandorica Opens' is far more dramatically satisfying and effective.

A particular highlight is the scene where the Doctor stands atop one of Stonehenge's fallen stones and, amplifying his voice through River Song's communicator device, addresses the huge gathering of spaceships above, reminding his monstrous adversaries of all the times he has defeated them and effectively daring them to attack. While at first this seems to be simply a more bombastic repeat of the type of warning he issued to the Atraxi at the end of 'The Eleventh Hour', delivered almost in the manner of an evangelical preacher or perhaps a sporting event announcer, later on it is cleverly undercut with the revelation that the Doctor has actually completely misjudged the situation. The assembled monster races have not, in fact, been given pause for thought by his rhetoric, but are simply holding off until he steps into their carefully-laid trap. In other words, he is behaving just as they predicted he would, and has been undone by his own hubris. It is notable that at one point during his address to the alliance he shouts 'I – am – talking!' in exactly the same way as the obnoxious Eddie Connolly boorishly demanded his son Tommy's attention in the Series Two episode 'The Idiot's Lantern'. As the old saying goes, pride comes before a fall, and the Doctor's fall results in him being sealed within the Pandorica.

It was characteristically astute of Steven Moffat to hit upon the realisation that, far from needing the Doctor to remind them of his reputation, his enemies already regard him as a merciless 'goblin' who brings death and destruction to their races. This was, in a way, foreshadowed in 'The Hungry Earth', when young Elliot asked the Doctor if he was scared of monsters, and he replied, 'No, they're scared of me'. It also recalls the fact that, as mentioned in 'The Lodger', some of his adversaries refer to him as 'the Oncoming Storm' (a term originating from the New Adventures novels of the 1990s.) However, 'The Pandorica Opens' gives this notion easily its fullest expression to date; and, typically, Moffat has the Doctor recount the legend of the creature imprisoned in the Pandorica – which, ironically, turns out to be his own legend – by quoting a passage from a fairytale (making this the third episode of Series Five to actually feature the word 'fairytale' in its dialogue).

The mythic quality of the story is enhanced by the inspired choice of Stonehenge as a setting, and by the excellent idea of having the Doctor, River and Amy ride up to it on horseback, which makes for a much more stirring sequence than if they had simply taken the TARDIS. This is not the first time that Stonehenge has been used in a *Doctor Who* story. Most notably, it featured in two of the original novels, *No Future* (1994) and *Rags* (2001); and in the TV serial 'The Time Meddler' (1965), the Meddling Monk claimed to have helped build it using anti-gravity lifts. This, though, is its first on-screen appearance in the show, and it makes for a brilliant location: very striking and atmospheric, and instantly recognisable (perhaps the reason why no attempt was made to depict it as it really looked in 102 AD, with almost all the stones standing?)

As specified in the script, there is a definite *Indiana Jones* vibe to the scenes where the Doctor, River and Amy venture down to explore the Underhenge with flaming torches held aloft. Apparently director Toby Haynes even had some of John Williams' *Indiana Jones* soundtrack music played into the studio during recording to help set the mood. The negotiation between River Song and Dorium at the start of the episode also bears certain similarities to the opening nightclub scene of *Indiana Jones and the Temple of Doom* (1984) (as well as to the famous cantina scene in *Star Wars* (1977)), so it seems that Moffat must have had that movie franchise very much in mind when writing this episode.

Another stand-out action sequence comes when the Doctor and Amy are assailed by the damaged Cyberman. The notion that the Cyberman remains dangerous even though decapitated, with one arm missing and with its organic components long-dead, and moreover that its head and arm can still launch attacks even though separated from its body, is absolutely inspired. The sequence is brilliantly realised, too, and boasts some outstanding effects work. Particularly memorable are the shots of Amy wrestling with the severed head as the writhing cables protruding from its neck attempt to ensnare her. In fact, all in all, this is probably the most thrilling Cyberman appearance since *Doctor Who* returned to TV in 2005. Fantastic stuff!

One of the most notable things about 'The Pandorica Opens' is its pacing. The action for the most part fairly rattles along, and the overall effect is quite exhilarating, although Moffat still skilfully manages to work in some quieter, more intense scenes such as the aforementioned one culminating in Amy being shot by Auton Rory. The showrunner also starts to give up some long-awaited answers to the questions at the heart of the ongoing story arc; and the confirmation that the cracks in time have been caused by the destruction of the TARDIS in a universe-shattering explosion is suitably shocking and dramatic, leading on to an apocalyptic cliffhanger ending.

All things considered, this is probably the strongest of Moffat's own script contributions to Series Five. However, it must be noted that, as with so many other episodes in this run, there are a number of plot points left unexplained. Some of these are relatively minor. For instance, if all the elements of the Pandorica trap are based on Amy's memories as collected from her house – presumably by one of the alliance members – immediately after she left it at the end of 'The Eleventh Hour', how is it that Rory's Auton duplicate recalls his death in the later events of 'Cold Blood'? And if the monster alliance had no way of telling when the Doctor would find the Pandorica – hence the need for them to be alerted to his arrival there by way of a signal broadcast via Stonehenge – how did they know to have a force of Autons stationed nearby in 102 AD, conditioned to act as Roman soldiers modelled on those in Amy's childhood book? A more major omission is that the circumstances surrounding the setting up of the alliance's trap for the Doctor are left a complete mystery. How was the alliance formed in the first place? How did they agree on the objective of imprisoning the Doctor rather than, as would seem more sensible from their point of view, simply killing him? How are all the members of the alliance, along with their spaceships, able to gather together in 102 AD when some of them, including the Cybermen and the Silurians, do not really belong in this time period and should not yet have encountered the Doctor? And why does the alliance include such apparently incongruous members as Roboforms, which are androids rather than living beings, and Weevils, which as established in *Torchwood* are relatively unintelligent creatures acting on instinct?

The real reason for the latter oddity is that the design teams simply reused whatever monster costumes and make-ups they could pull together from existing stock, regardless whether or not they were appropriate in terms of the characters. Unfortunately, this is rather too obvious, giving the impression that some budgetary corners have been cut here. As for the other unexplained points, the viewer can of course speculate as to the answers. Perhaps (as discussed in 'Continuity Points' above) the memories that drive Rory's Auton duplicate come not from what the alliance gleaned from the house in Leadworth, but from Amy's own subconscious mind. Possibly it was the Judoon who insisted that the Doctor be imprisoned rather than killed, given their status as interplanetary police-for-hire who rigidly enforce law and order. And maybe it was the Daleks who brought all the other alliance members to 102 AD from various different points in history using their time travel technology. However, it does seem unsatisfactory that such significant points are not addressed in the narrative itself.

The scenario of a host of different monster races allying themselves against the Doctor is one that has doubtless featured in a lot of young fans' playground games and exercise-book fiction, and – in keeping with Steven Moffat's general approach to the show – seems designed to appeal to the child in all its viewers. In this respect, it can perhaps be likened to the Daleks -v- Cybermen face-off in the Series Two finale 'Army of Ghosts'/'Doomsday'. It also recalls the alliance of galactic delegates put together by the Daleks in 'Mission to the Unknown' (1965) and seen again in 'The Daleks' Master Plan' (1965/66). That said, however, it would really have been better if Moffat had restricted himself to just three or four of the most popular races – Daleks, Cybermen, Sontarans and Judoon perhaps – to make the idea of the alliance more plausible and avoid over-stretching the show's resources. The other monsters are in any case used only to make up the numbers as briefly-glimpsed and non-speaking crowd members, which really does them something of a disservice, so all in all it would definitely have been preferable for them to have been omitted.

There is also a problem with having the Daleks involved, which is that it inevitably means the return of the terrible new versions from 'Victory of the Daleks'. Yes, *Doctor Who*'s very own Fatback Band are back; and it isn't good to see them. Thankfully, though, the two most horribly garish ones – the blue and the orange – are absent this time around, and the white one is kept to the front, with the red one and the yellow one more in the background. Toby Haynes also does his best to frame his shots of them in a sympathetic way, such that their big rear-end bulges are never fully exposed to view.

Haynes is another director gaining his first *Doctor Who* credit here. In fact, none of the six directors engaged to handle the episodes of Series Five had worked on the show previously (although some had an indirect connection, most notably Ashley Way's engagement on *Torchwood*). This may perhaps indicate a desire on the part of Steven Moffat's team to put their own stamp on the show – somewhat akin to the way John Nathan-Turner did when he took over as producer back at the start of the 1980s – or at least to give it an infusion of new blood behind the scenes. To bring in so many new directors to work on a single series was arguably a risky move, but fortunately it largely paid off, with only Andrew Gunn seeming not really cut out for the task on 'The Beast Below' and 'Victory of the Daleks'. Certainly in Haynes' case the choice was an excellent one, as he does an absolutely outstanding job on this episode and the next, displaying a real feel for the show and its requirements. It comes as no surprise to learn that, like so many other successful contributors to 21st Century *Doctor Who*, he is a long-time fan. Aided by his chosen director of photography, Stephan Pehrsson, he gives the production a rich, cinematic quality, full of beautifully-composed images. His use of slow motion for the momentous events leading up to the cliffhanger is particularly inspired. A really top-class debut.

A word of praise, too, for incidental music composer Murray Gold, whose contribution to modern-day *Doctor Who* is often undervalued. His score for this episode is especially strong, and enhances the drama enormously.

In fact, 'The Pandorica Opens' is an excellent episode all round, and builds to an exciting climax that leaves the viewer on tenterhooks to discover what will happen in the closing instalment of the story, and of the series as a whole.

# 5.13 – THE BIG BANG

Writer: Steven Moffat
Director: Toby Haynes

DEBUT TRANSMISSION DETAILS

BBC One/BBC HD
Date: 26 June 2010. Scheduled time: 6.05 pm. Actual time: 6.06 pm.

Duration: 53' 44"

ADDITIONAL CREDITED CAST

Caitlin Blackwood (Amelia), Susan Vidler (Aunt Sharon), Frances Ashman (Christine), Barnaby Edwards (Stone Dalek), William Pretsell (Dave[41]), Halcro Johnston (Mr Pond[42]), Karen Westwood (Tabetha[43]), Nicholas Briggs (Dalek Voices)

Daleks Created by Terry Nation

PLOT

The exploding TARDIS is causing a gradual collapse of time and space, with the Earth the last planet to survive. In 1996, following a trail of clues left for her, young Amelia Pond visits the National Museum, where the Pandorica is on display. She touches it and it opens, revealing her older self, Amy, inside. The Doctor has swapped places with the dead Amy in 102 AD after getting Auton Rory to use the sonic screwdriver to release him, then using River's discarded vortex manipulator to travel back in time and lend Auton Rory the sonic screwdriver to enable him to do this. Amy has been kept in stasis inside the Pandorica for almost 2,000 years until being resurrected by its restoration field using Amelia's identical DNA. All that time, Auton Rory has kept guard nearby, giving rise to the legend of the Lone Centurion. Having also used the vortex manipulator to leave the trail of clues for Amelia and to rescue River from the exploding TARDIS, the Doctor then wires the device into the Pandorica. This enables him to crash the Pandorica into the explosion, the energy from which is sufficient for its restoration field to reboot the entire universe, extrapolating from the atoms of the original that are stored within it. The cracks in time close, but the Doctor is trapped behind them. However, as his timeline unravels, he is able to seed the sleeping Amelia's subconscious mind with words that will eventually cause her to remember him at her wedding reception in

---

[41] The best man at the wedding of Amy and Rory, unnamed in dialogue.
[42] First name given in dialogue as 'Augustus'.
[43] Amy's mother.

2010, through the traditional phrase 'Something old, something new, something borrowed, something blue' – a description of the TARDIS. When she does so, the TARDIS is restored to existence, with him inside it. River departs using the vortex manipulator, and the Doctor and the now-married Amy and Rory head off in the TARDIS for further adventures.

- **Amy:** 'Okay, kid. This is where it gets complicated.'
- **Doctor:** 'You need to get me out of the Pandorica.'
  **Rory:** 'But you're not in the Pandorica.'
  **Doctor:** 'Yes, I am. Well, I'm not now, but I was back then. Well, back now from your point of view, which is back then from my point of view. Time travel, you can't keep it straight in your head.'
- **River:** 'Amy! And the plastic Centurion?'
  **Doctor:** 'It's okay, he's on our side.'
  **River:** 'Really? I dated a Nestene duplicate once … swappable head. It did keep things fresh. Right then, I have questions. But number one is this: what in the name of sanity have you got on your head?'
  **Doctor:** 'It's a fez. I wear a fez now. Fezzes are cool.'
- **Doctor:** 'It's funny. I thought if you could hear me, I could hang on somehow. Silly me. Silly old Doctor. When you wake up, you'll have a mum and dad … and you won't even remember me. Well, you'll remember me a little. I'll be a story in your head. But that's okay. We're all stories in the end. Just make it a good one, eh? 'Cause it was, you know. It was the best. A daft old man who stole a magic box and ran away. Did I ever tell you that I stole it? Well, I borrowed it; I was always going to take it back. Oh, that box. Amy, you'll dream about that box. It'll never leave you. Big and little at the same time. Brand new and ancient. And the bluest blue ever. And the times we had, eh? Would've had … Never had. In your dreams, they'll still be there. The Doctor and Amy Pond. And the days that never came.'

- The explosion of the TARDIS, apparently at the instigation of the mysterious Silence, results in cracks in time appearing throughout history and triggers the gradual collapse of the universe, with Earth – the proverbial eye at the centre of the storm – the last planet to succumb. The Pandorica's restoration field reboots the universe to the state it was in before the explosion occurred and also causes the cracks to close. The Doctor says: 'The perfect prison. Inside it, perfectly preserved, a few billion atoms of the universe as it was. In theory, you could extrapolate the whole universe from a single one of them, like cloning a body from a single cell. And we've got the bumper family pack.' However, it would seem that this does not bring back any of the things that have previously fallen into the cracks; those things are permanently lost to existence unless someone remembers them, as when Amy remembers her parents, Rory and finally the Doctor.
- When Rory releases him from the Pandorica using the sonic screwdriver, the

Doctor touches his own sonic screwdriver against it, causing a spark of energy to be discharged – showing that it is the same object at two different points in its own timestream. This phenomenon is consistent with what has been established in previous stories, most notably 'Mawdryn Undead' (1983). There is no similar release of energy when, later, the Doctor touches his own future self, but this is also consistent with what has been seen previously, particularly in multi-Doctor stories such as 'The Three Doctors' (1972/73), and may be accounted for by his Time Lord nature. There is no release of energy when Amy touches Amelia either, but this may be due to the fact that, although they have identical DNA, they have grown up in radically different versions of the universe, and so are from two different timestreams.

- On seeing petrified Daleks, Cybermen and Auton Romans outside the Pandorica, the Doctor explains: 'History has collapsed. Whole races have been deleted from existence. These are just like after-images. Echoes, fossils in time. The footprints of the never-were.'
- As recorded in a wall display at the Museum, the partial history of the Pandorica after 102 AD is: Taken Back to Rome Under Armed Guard (118 AD); Raided by the Franks (420 AD); Prized Possession of the Knights Templar (1120); Donated to the Vatican (1231); Sold by Marco Polo (date obscured). According to an audio guide, the legendary Lone Centurion was seen dragging it from a burning storage warehouse during the London Blitz of 1941.
- When Amy expresses surprise that the Doctor has deceived them about his future self having been killed by the stone Dalek, so that they can create a diversion, River tells her: 'Rule one: the Doctor lies'.
- When Amy asks River what will happen after 'Big Bang Two', she replies: 'We all wake up where we ought to be. None of this ever happens and we don't remember it.' This indicates that the dying version of the universe seen in this episode will not be remembered even by the Doctor and his companions. Presumably they will recall only the events of 'The Pandorica Opens' and then the universe's new timeline.
- Three weeks before the events of 'The Pandorica Opens'/'The Big Bang', the Doctor and Amy went on a trip in the TARDIS to 'Space Florida'. This may have been one of the treats referred to in 'Vincent and the Doctor' that the Doctor gave Amy after Rory was killed and erased from her memory at the end of 'Cold Blood'.

PRODUCTION NOTES

- This episode and 'The Pandorica Opens' were made as Block Six of Series Five's production schedule.
- According to Steven Moffat in later interviews, the title 'The Big Bang' has an in joke double meaning: it refers not only to the rebooting of the universe but also to the fact that, after leaving in the TARDIS on their wedding night at the end of the story, Amy and Rory conceive their daughter (unseen by the viewer, naturally!)
- See 'The Pandorica Opens' for some of this episode's production dates. In addition, recording took place from 18 to 23 January 2010 at Brangwyn Hall,

CRACKS IN TIME

Guildhall, Swansea for the National Museum interiors; on 25 January 2010 outside the National Museum of Wales, Cathays Park, Cardiff for the National Museum exteriors; and on 26 and 27 January at Miskin Manor, Miskin, Pontyclun for the wedding reception scenes.

- The tannoy announcement in the Museum and the recorded account of the legend of the Lone Centurion are both spoken, uncredited, by Dalek voice artist Nicholas Briggs.
- The episode closes with a caption reading: '*Doctor Who* Will Return Christmas 2010'.

OOPS!

- In the scene where, after emerging from the Pandorica, Amy places her hand on Amelia's head to judge her height and thereby work out what year it is, a member of the production crew briefly encroaches on the right hand side of the picture, then steps back out of shot.
- The TARDIS is at the heart of a huge explosion that acts as a substitute sun for the Earth, so why does River see only a rock wall outside when she opens the doors? (Possibly this is part of the TARDIS's attempt to protect her from the explosion; the Doctor does say: 'The TARDIS has sealed off the control room and put her into a time loop to save her.')

PRESS REACTION

- 'From the off, the show tossed a curve-ball, starting exactly where the season began with young Amelia Pond, albeit in a universe suffering the effects of a total collapse of time and space. From there on in, "The Big Bang" practically danced a jig on the carcass of expectation, confounding with a complete shift in time and a pre-credit cliffhanger that set the tone for a thoroughly breathless 55-minute time-hopping ride. We said "The Pandorica Opens" was audacious in scope but it paled in comparison to "The Big Bang", which gave us disappearing stars, two Amys, a stone Dalek, Rory's 2000-year pledge, an increasingly ruthless River Song, a mind-boggling amount of wibbly-wobbly, timey-wimey cleverness, plenty of pay-off, even more set-up, an exploding fez and some genuinely emotional moments that ranged from fist-pumping to heart-breaking. Yet somehow the episode hopped nimbly through a narrative that – just about – made total sense.' Matt Wales, IGN website, 28 June 2010.
- 'What *The Big Bang* does that's so different from any of the series finales we've seen before, is it ignores the magnitude of the peril we encounter at the previous episode's cliffhanger and presents us with a small, intimate and as light-on-its-feet as you please chamber episode instead. Gone are the Cybermen, Sontarans and Silurians ... and in their place we have a delightful and witty little runaround (inside a night at a museum) with a stone Dalek. There's a fez, a mop, and a momentarily-dead fop, and its displacing qualities are breathtaking. We ought to have been expecting the Monster Alliance Retribution; nobody was expecting *this*.' J R Southall, *Starburst* website, 24 August 2011.
- 'This was one of the most high-concept *Doctor Who* episodes ever. At one

186

stage Rory expressed his difficulty understanding what was going on, and he might be speaking for much of the audience. Moffat's love of playing with the potentialities of time, evident in several of his [earlier] episodes, was evident throughout. Unfortunately, this made the escape for the Doctor somewhat too easy, and rather paradoxical in nature – he only escapes as Rory lets him out once given the means to do so by the Doctor travelling back in time once he's escaped. Also we had the blight of the climactic episodes of the Russell T Davies era, in the *deus ex machina* that solves everything. Here it was the Pandorica itself in its ability to bring people back to life, thus saving Amy, Rory *et al* far too easily in the end, even if the Doctor using it was something of a refreshing change from previous years, when he's tended to watch others magically save the day.' Gavin Fuller, *Telegraph* website, 26 June 2010.

- 'Viewers tuned into BBC One to see "The Big Bang", a thrilling climax to the series that captivated and confused in equal measure. Fans were treated to an army of villains, the Doctor dancing, the recreation of the universe, the wedding of Amy and Rory, and even something that may have been a proposal from the Doctor to River Song. Afterwards viewers took to Twitter to express their delight at what they had just seen. TabithaBurch summed up the general mood, when she tweeted: "Dr Who made me cry, but it was so good!"' *Metro* website, 28 June 2010.

## ANALYSIS

When it comes to the second instalment of a Steven Moffat-scripted two-parter, it is always as well to expect the unexpected; and that has never been more true than in the case of 'The Big Bang'. The cliffhanger ending to 'The Pandorica Opens' was arguably the most mind-boggling in the show's entire history: Amy is killed by Auton Rory; the Doctor is sealed within the Pandorica; the TARDIS, with River trapped inside it, is destroyed in a huge explosion; and all the stars at every point in history turn supernova and burn out! The viewer can only wonder: how in heaven's name is Moffat going to write himself out of *that* one?

In one respect, as it turns out, he does so quite easily. In the long tradition of 'with one bound he was free'-type get-outs to seemingly inescapable predicaments, the Doctor simply releases himself from the Pandorica, or rather gets Auton Rory to do so, by using River's vortex manipulator to travel back in time from a slightly later point in his own timestream and lend Auton Rory the sonic screwdriver; another of the predestination paradoxes that are by this point becoming something of a Moffat trademark. Once the Doctor is free, he can then start to put everything else to rights; and in doing so, he creates several more predestination paradoxes along the way.

Some commentators have argued that this is a cheat or a cop-out; but really it is no more so than when one of these paradoxes formed the basis of the universally-lauded 'Blink' back in Series Three. It is just that here Moffat has the Doctor use the same trick rather more blatantly, and repeatedly. It's a case of 'wibbly-wobbly, timey-wimey' taken to the max. Of course, this is not the sort of thing the Doctor would have done back in the days of the classic series; but perhaps now that his fellow Time Lords are no longer around to keep an eye on things, the laws of time are more susceptible to being bent or broken. Admittedly this does pose something of a problem in storytelling terms, in that it begs the question why the Doctor does not always resort to such flagrant temporal rule-breaking in order to extricate himself from tricky situations. However, the suggestion seems to be that he gets away with it in 'The Big Bang' only because of the parlous state the universe is in, and perhaps also because he is using the 'cheap and nasty' time travel method of the vortex manipulator. Desperate circumstances call for desperate measures, and it is difficult to imagine any circumstances more desperate than those he faces here.

Another expectation-defying aspect of 'The Big Bang' is that, whereas 'The Pandorica Opens' had an epic sweep to it, this follow-up episode is more closely-contained, with much of the action confined to the National Museum. It is more character-focused too, with a greater emotional content. The most emotional scenes of all are the Doctor's two apparent farewells: the first with adult Amy as he prepares to sacrifice himself to save the universe, the second with young Amelia as he sits beside her bed and talks to her while she sleeps. Matt Smith's performance in both these scenes is phenomenal – his strongest yet as the Doctor – and Karen Gillan is also superb in the former. It could perhaps be argued that the one with Amelia involves another cheat of sorts by Moffat, in that he misleadingly has the Doctor appear broken and defeated, as if he believes that this really is the end for him, when in fact he is deliberately seeding Amelia's subconscious mind with key words that will cause her to remember him on her wedding day – and, it later transpires, is so confident that she will do so that he even dresses up in top hat and tails for the occasion! However, this piece of misdirection can be excused on the grounds of dramatic licence – particularly as the Doctor's monologue is so beautifully written and heart-wrenchingly delivered.

Indeed, one thing that 'The Big Bang' has very much in common with 'The Pandorica Opens' is a superlative script by Steven Moffat, which is as wildly imaginative, brilliantly structured and replete with quotable dialogue as the viewer has come to anticipate from him. To have the opening recap immediately followed by a virtual reprise of the sequence at Amelia's house in Leadworth at the start of 'The Eleventh Hour' is a typically inspired idea, giving a kind of symmetry to the series-spanning story and continuing the 'Series Five's Greatest Hits' approach of this two-part finale. It also affords Moffat a very effective way of illustrating the impact of the universe's ongoing collapse, by showing how it changes young Amelia's life. This time, although no raggedy Doctor appears in her garden when she prays to Santa (instead she hears only a faint sound outside, as their meeting is erased from history), she still ends up having psychiatric treatment, because now she is fixated on the fanciful idea that there ought to be stars in the night sky … It is great to see Caitlin Blackwood back again as Amelia, and once more she gives an excellent performance in the role.

Further indications of the way this doomed universe differs from ours are seen in the amusing sequence where Amelia hurries through the Museum to the section called 'The Anomaly', with its exhibits including (according to the flyer) 'Dinosaurs in Ice' and 'Nile Penguins' – not to mention two stone Daleks. To have the Daleks depicted as petrified relics of the original timeline is another great move on Moffat's part, as it allows for the severe shortcomings of their 'Victory of the Daleks' redesign to be disguised as much as possible. Gone are the awful garish colours; and again director Toby Haynes manages to shoot them in such a way that their humped backs are for the most part concealed from view. This means that, when one of the Daleks starts to revive after the light from the Pandorica strikes it, it can actually serve as a more credible menace again. One of the most memorable scenes of the whole episode comes when River confronts the Dalek while its power is still depleted, makes it repeatedly beg for mercy, and then nevertheless – unseen on screen – destroys it with a shot from her gun. Even allowing for the fact that she is under the mistaken impression that the Dalek has just killed the Doctor, this reveals a startlingly ruthless aspect to her character that we have not really seen before, and makes it rather easier to believe that she might be a convicted murderer. Again, Alex Kingston deserves considerable praise for her fantastic performance here, and throughout the episode.

Other highlights include Auton Rory making a heroic reappearance in the guise of a Museum security guard, after almost 2,000 years spent watching over the Pandorica as the now-legendary Lone Centurion; the Doctor donning a fez and wielding a mop, in a sequence surely inspired by the one where his seventh incarnation did exactly the same thing, albeit more briefly, in 'Silver Nemesis' (1988); Amy and River later joining forces to blow up the fez (actually rather a pity, as for some strange reason it really seems to suit this Doctor, and would have made a nice addition to his regular outfit!); the Doctor popping back to the *Byzantium* during the events of 'Flesh and Stone' and urging Amy to remember what he told her when she was seven (a scene that in 'Flesh and Stone' itself was thought by many fans to contain a blooper, as this future Doctor is wearing his jacket, whereas the one of that time was in his shirtsleeves); and the superb wedding reception scenes at the end, where the guests are astonished to see the TARDIS materialise right before their eyes (something that Amy presumably has to try to explain away later – as part of a magician's act, perhaps …?)

There is a real celebratory air to these closing party scenes. Particularly amusing are the shots of the Doctor doing his strange dance moves – including one with his arms pointing straight up, apparently referred to during production as 'the drunken giraffe' – and then teaching them to a group of children. The only slightly sour note comes when Amy's selfish disregard for Rory's feelings re-emerges, as she tries to kiss the Doctor on the lips when he first arrives, and then chides him for preparing to leave before they have 'had a snog in the bushes'. When the hapless Rory protests, she dismissively retorts 'Shut up; it's my wedding!', to which he can only respond '*Our* wedding!' It seems that Steven Moffat intends this to be an enduring character trait of Amy's; but, while it would admittedly be pretty dull if the Doctor's companions always acted like saints, it still feels disconcerting to have one of them displaying such an unlikeable streak.

The only really significant flaw in this episode's script, though, is the way the Pandorica becomes a kind of miraculous cure-all for the dying universe. The problem lies not so much in the idea that its restoration field can reboot the universe by extrapolating from the few billion atoms of the original that are sealed within it – arguably a reasonably sound science fiction concept – but more in the fact that the monster alliance gave it a restoration field in the first place. It seems strange enough that they chose to imprison the Doctor rather than simply kill him outright, but stranger still that they should have gone to such lengths to ensure that he stayed alive throughout all the millennia they envisaged him remaining trapped. Some fans have speculated that they did this because they had all tried to kill the Doctor numerous times before and always failed, and so had come to regard it as effectively impossible. However, that explanation doesn't really hold water; they had, after all, tried to imprison him many times before as well, and always failed in that too. Maybe it is simply evidence that certain members of the alliance, such as the Daleks, have a highly vindictive streak? Also overly contrived is the fact that the Pandorica can be opened not only by a sonic screwdriver – something the alliance should surely have taken precautions against, in case one of the Doctor's friends had one – but even by being touched by the DNA of the person imprisoned within. Of course, the story wouldn't really work if the Pandorica couldn't be opened and didn't have a restoration field – the Doctor wouldn't even be able to bring Amy back to life, let alone reboot the universe – but it does all seem rather too convenient.

Then again, perhaps this reliance on an almost magical device is part and parcel of Steven Moffat's overall approach to the show. There has been much talk within *Doctor Who* fandom, and even some in the mainstream press, about the Series Five story arc being perplexingly complex; but that isn't really the case. The key to it is to grasp its fairytale-like central notion, signposted throughout the 13 episodes, that existence is akin to being remembered. When things are erased from existence by the cracks in time, this doesn't mean that all the effects of their existence are also expunged; it is just that no-one can remember any more what caused those effects. So although there are no ducks in Leadworth, this doesn't stop the Doctor finding a duck pond there in 'The Eleventh Hour'; when the Weeping Angels fall into one of the cracks in 'Flesh and Stone', this doesn't mean that the crash of the *Byzantium* never happened; when Rory is erased in 'Cold Blood', this doesn't cause Amy's engagement ring suddenly to disappear; and when the Doctor is trapped on the wrong side of the cracks after they close, this doesn't mean that all the alien invasions of Earth he has repelled in the past now succeed. The ducks, the Weeping Angels, Rory, the Doctor and everything else that has vanished into the cracks has simply been wiped from memory. Then, at the end of 'The Big Bang', after the Doctor reboots the universe by flying the Pandorica into the exploding TARDIS, we see that the reverse is also true. When Amy, the special girl who grew up with one of the cracks in her bedroom wall, defies their effect by remembering people she ought to have forgotten – her parents, Rory and ultimately the Doctor – those people are restored to existence, just as they were before they were erased (although in Rory's case, he seems somehow to have acquired some memory of his Auton duplicate too). Simple really.

Well, okay, maybe not *that* simple. For a start, there must surely be many *other* things that fell into the cracks in time and have *not* been brought back into existence, because Amy never even knew about them, let alone remembered them. Presumably those things have now been permanently erased from the universe. This, though, can actually be seen as a clever move on Moffat's part, as it means that he is now effectively free to pick and chose which elements of established *Doctor Who* lore he wants to use and which he prefers to ignore. It is not only the universe that has been rebooted here, but also *Doctor Who* continuity.

Another complication is that it is unclear to what extent the events of Series Five itself have been affected by the new Big Bang. At one point there is a sequence where, after he is cut off from the universe behind the closing cracks in time, the Doctor witnesses his own timestream 'rewinding … unravelling, erasing', right back to the night of his now-undone first meeting with Amelia. It may well be that this unravelling is reversed when he is brought back into existence – that is, when all the lost memories of him are restored – but does the disappearance of the cracks mean that Prisoner Zero never escaped; that the Saturnynes never came to Earth; that the Pandorica was never constructed; and so on? Certainly, given that her parents have also been remembered back into existence, it seems unlikely that seven-year-old Amelia would have been all alone in her house at night when the TARDIS crash-landed in her garden in this new version of the universe. So, are the adventures that the viewer has seen unfold over the course of these 13 episodes now preserved only in a defunct timeline remembered by no-one but Amy, Rory and the Doctor?

And then there is River. She too clearly remembers at least parts of the original timeline; but more than that, she remembers the Doctor even *before* Amy brings him back into existence. In fact, it is actually she who prompts Amy to do this, by giving her the police-box-design diary with all its pages rendered blank by the Doctor's absence. How is it possible that she remembers him? The short answer is: we don't know, because it is left unexplained.

The reason for this becomes clear as 'The Big Bang' approaches its conclusion: the ongoing story arc, which most viewers doubtless assumed – and many probably hoped – would be neatly wrapped up at the end of Series Five, is actually going to continue on into Series Six, and maybe even beyond. So, while the cracks in time element of it is effectively resolved here, there are a number of other aspects over which everyone is kept guessing.

The mystery surrounding River is certainly one of those aspects, as pointed up in the terrific scene where the Doctor talks to her outside the wedding reception and, without much success, fishes for clues as to whether or not, as previously hinted, she will one day be his wife – the very thing that many fans have also been wondering ever since she first appeared in 'Silence in the Library'/'Forest of the Dead'. 'River … who are you?' he asks her. 'You're going to find out very soon now,' she replies. 'And I'm sorry, but that's when everything changes.' We also have yet to discover the full story behind River getting locked up in the Stormcage Containment Facility – apparently in the 52nd Century initially and then later, curiously, in the 51st Century – for killing, in her words, 'The best man I've ever known'.

Something else that remains a puzzle is the meaning of the phrase 'Silence will fall', and how it relates to the destruction of the TARDIS. 'So,' says Amy, 'the TARDIS blew up and took the universe with it. Why would it do that? How?' 'Good question for another day,' responds the Doctor. Later, after the ship has been restored in what he describes as 'Big Bang Two', the Doctor comments: 'Space and time isn't safe yet. The TARDIS exploded for a reason. Something drew the TARDIS to this particular date, and blew it up.' But that is how the matter is left, and it remains to be seen exactly where this aspect of the overarching story is heading.

Other questions also remain unanswered, including how Prisoner Zero and its Atraxi captor were seemingly able to emerge from one of the cracks in time at will in 'The Eleventh Hour'; how Craig Owens came to have a crashed spaceship on top of his flat in 'The Lodger'; and what happens when, at the end of 'The Big Bang', the Doctor responds to an intriguing phone call about 'An Egyptian goddess loose on the *Orient Express* … in space'. But whether or not these points will ever be returned to is more uncertain.

For the time being, 'The Big Bang' rounds off a rather variable run of stories in fine style. The era of the eleventh Doctor is well and truly under way, but has to pause now for the customary six month break in transmission before the annual Christmas special.

# 6.00 – A CHRISTMAS CAROL

Writer: Steven Moffat
Director: Toby Haynes

<u>DEBUT TRANSMISSION DETAILS</u>

BBC One/BBC One HD
Date: 25 December 2010. Scheduled time: 6.00 pm. Actual time: 6.01 pm.

Duration: 61' 47"

<u>ADDITIONAL CREDITED CAST</u>

Michael Gambon (Kazran/Elliot Sardick), Katherine Jenkins (Abigail[44]), Laurence Belcher (Young Kazran), Danny Horn (Adult Kazran), Leo Bill (Pilot), Pooky Quesnel (Captain), Micah Balfour (Co-Pilot), Steve North (Old Benjamin), Bailey Pepper (Boy & Benjamin), Tim Plester (Servant), Nick Malinowski (Eric), Laura Rogers (Isabella), Meg Wynn-Owen (Old Isabella)

<u>PLOT</u>

On a Christmas Eve in the 44th Century, a starliner with 4,003 people on board, including Amy and Rory on their honeymoon, is caught in a dangerous storm of electrically-charged clouds over a human colony planet. The misanthropic Kazran Sardick, patriarch of Sardicktown, can control the clouds with a machine created by his late father Elliot, but he refuses to let the starliner land safely. The Doctor takes the TARDIS back in time to when Kazran was 12, to try to influence him to grow up a better person. They are attacked by a flying shark – the fish of this planet are able to swim through the fog – but the creature is pacified when a young woman named Abigail sings to it. Abigail has been released by young Kazran from the cryogenic storage tube in which she was being held as collateral against a loan made by Elliot to her impoverished family. After enjoying Christmas Eve with the Doctor and young Kazran, Amelia is refrozen. The three then reunite on several subsequent Christmas Eves, while Kazran grows into a man and falls in love with Abigail. Then one year Kazran abruptly halts these reunions. He has learned that Abigail was ill and had only eight days left to live when she was originally frozen; now she has only one. The elderly Kazran remains embittered and still refuses to help. However, the Doctor then revisits him as a young boy and brings him forward in time to see how his future self will turn out. This finally succeeds in transforming Kazran's disposition. Now, though, the isomorphic controls of his machine will not recognise him, so he still cannot save the starship. The Doctor

---

[44] Surname given in dialogue as 'Pettigrew'.

convinces him to release Abigail for her final day, Christmas Day, and the amplified sound of her singing tames the storm, allowing the starship to land.

QUOTE, UNQUOTE

- **Kazran Sardick:** 'On every world, wherever people are, in the deepest part of the winter, at the exact mid-point, everybody stops and turns and hugs as if to say, "Well done. Well done, everyone. We're half way out of the dark." Back on Earth, we called this Christmas or the Winter Solstice. On this world, the first settlers called it the Crystal Feast. You know what I call it? I call it expecting something for nothing!'
- **Doctor:** 'Big flashy-lighty things have got me written all over them. Not actually, but give me time, and a crayon.'
- **Amy:** 'Have you got a plan yet?'
  **Doctor:** 'Yes, I do.'
  **Amy:** 'Are you lying?'
  **Doctor:** 'Yes, I am.'
  **Amy:** 'Don't treat me like an idiot.'
  **Rory:** 'Was he lying?'
  **Amy:** 'No, no.'
- **Doctor:** 'Right, then. Your bedroom. Great! Let's see, you're 12 years old, so we'll stay away from under the bed. Cupboard! Big cupboard. I love a cupboard. Do you know, there's a thing called a face spider. It's just like a tiny baby's head with spider legs, and it's specifically evolved to scuttle up the backs of bedroom cupboards … which, yeah, I probably shouldn't have mentioned. Right, so, what are we going to do? Eat crisps and talk about girls? I've never actually done that, but I bet it's easy. Girls! Yeah?'

CONTINUITY POINTS

- The planet in this story is not named on screen, although it was subsequently identified in the online role-playing game *Doctor Who: Worlds in Time* (2012) as Ember.
- The starliner, also unnamed, is from Earth and is described as a 'galaxy class' ship. The Doctor is unable to land the TARDIS on board because it 'can't lock on', presumably due to the storm.
- The Doctor says he has always known Father Christmas as 'Jeff'. He shows Kazran a snapshot of the two of them together at Frank Sinatra's hunting lodge in 1952, along with Marilyn Monroe and Albert Einstein. Presumably Jeff is a man who has dressed up as Father Christmas, although this is not made clear in the story.
- Kazran says that his cloud-controlling machine has isomorphic controls that respond only to him – or more precisely, as the Doctor later says, to his brain waves. The Doctor is initially dismissive – 'Isomorphic! There's no such thing' – but then establishes that the man is telling the truth. In 'Pyramids of Mars' (1976), the fourth Doctor told the Osiran god Sutekh that the TARDIS's controls were isomorphic. However, given that various other people have been seen to operate the TARDIS over the years, it appears that was a deception – or

perhaps that the TARDIS's isomorphic function is unreliable.

- A portrait of Elliot Sardick on Kazran's study wall – later replaced by one of Abigail as the timeline changes – gives his date of birth as 4302 and his date of death as 4378. The Doctor estimates that when he arrives it is '20 years' later. This means that these scenes must take place at the very end of the 44th Century.
- The Doctor is inspired to try to change Kazran's timeline when he recalls the famous story *A Christmas Carol* by Charles Dickens. He met Dickens in the Series One episode 'The Unquiet Dead', and declared himself to be a big fan of the writer's work.
- The Doctor, claiming to be young Kazran's new babysitter, tells him 'I think you'll find I'm universally recognised as a mature and responsible adult'. He holds up the psychic paper to prove his credentials, but it shows, according to Kazran, 'just a lot of wavy lines'. The Doctor says: 'Yeah, it's shorted out. Finally a lie too big.' It is unclear if this problem is permanent or only temporary.
- The clouds above the planet have fish living in them. The fish can also swim in the fog at ground level, being supported by the electrically-charged ice crystals of which it is composed. The Doctor says that the reason the fish like people singing to them is that 'the notes resonate in the ice, creating a delta wave pattern in the fog'. He adds: 'That's how the machine controls the cloud belt. The clouds are ice crystals. If you vibrate them at the right frequency, you could align them.'
- The Sardick house is built on a fog lake, which is what Elliot has used to freeze people in cryogenic storage units.
- When the sonic screwdriver is bitten in two by the flying shark, one half continuously signals to the other as it tries to repair itself.
- The Doctor, Kazran and Abigail appear to share seven Christmas Eves together, as the counter on the front of Abigail's cryogenic storage unit ticks down from 8 to 1. Amongst the places they visit are the pyramids and Sphinx at Giza in Egypt, where the Doctor and young Kazran both wear fezzes; and an area with snow-covered mountains, where they both wear striped multicoloured scarves, somewhat similar to the one that was part of the fourth Doctor's regular attire. It seems the Christmas Eves are not consecutive ones, as between the counter decreasing from 4 to 3, Kazran appears to age by several years, growing from a child into a young man. On that Christmas Eve, the three friends remain in Sardicktown and visit Abigail's family. The following year, it appears that they visit New York, Australia and Paris, being photographed in front of various famous tourist attractions. Their final Christmas Eve trip in the TARDIS is to California in 1952, where the Doctor again spends time with Frank Sinatra and Marilyn Monroe – but on this occasion at a Hollywood mansion with a pool rather than at Sinatra's hunting lodge. The Doctor gets 'accidentally' engaged to Monroe, and then apparently marries her – although later, when she phones him in the TARDIS, he tells Amy and Rory 'That was never a real chapel!'
- When the elderly Kazran hugs himself as a young boy, there is no discharge of energy as would normally be expected when someone comes into contact with himself at a different point in his own timestream, as established in 'Mawdryn

Undead' (1983). This may be because Kazran's timestream is still in the process of changing at this point, so that (as when Amy touched Amelia in 'The Big Bang') they do not in fact have the same timestream.

## PRODUCTION NOTES

- 'A Christmas Carol' was the first episode to go before the cameras in the Series Six production schedule.
- Recording got under way at the Mir Steel works in Newport from 12 to 15 July 2010 for the Sardicktown exterior scenes. From 19 to 22 July, the Coal Exchange in Mount Stuart Square, Cardiff was used as the location for the youngest Kazran's bedroom and the adjacent roof area. 22 July also saw recording take place outside Wrinstone House, Wenvoe, Cardiff for the brief sequence by the pool of a Hollywood mansion in 1952. The Dupont Building on Cardiff's Mamhilad Park Industrial Estate was used from 3 to 6 August and on 9 August for the ice vault sequences. Studio recording, primarily for the scenes of the starliner bridge, Kazran's study and the TARDIS interior, took place at *Doctor Who*'s usual Upper Boat facilities on various dates between 16 July and 2 August.
- For the first time, Arthur Darvill's name is included in the opening titles, after Matt Smith's and Karen Gillan's.
- At the end of the closing titles there is a Coming Soon trailer for the rest of Series Six, running for approximately one minute. (This is included in the total duration noted above.)

## OOPS!

- When first seen in Kazran's house, the TARDIS is beyond a set of double doors. The Doctor goes through these doors and closes them behind him, then the TARDIS's dematerialisation noise is heard, indicating that it has departed. However, the light from the police box windows can still be seen through the crack between the double doors, even after it has supposedly gone.
- The flying shark is said to be dying after it ingests half the sonic screwdriver – 'I doubt they can survive long outside the cloud belt,' says the Doctor, 'just quick raiding trips on a foggy night' – but then for no apparent reason it suddenly revives and attacks the Doctor and the youngest Kazran in the ice vault.

## PRESS REACTION

- 'Steven Moffat was clearly ding dong merrily high on something when he came up with this beguiling Christmas whimsy. Eschewing the broad strokes, action-packed, *Die Hard With A TARDIS* approach of the [Russell T] Davies Christmas specials he instead gives us a festive fairytale – sweet, tender and shamelessly sentimental. It feels like the ultimate incarnation of the "dark fairytale" approach he's taken with his vision of *Who*. This is about as far from *Who*'s SF heartland as the show has ever strayed; you could argue it's total fantasy. Let's face it, most of the technobabble exposition could just as easily be replaced with [Harry] Potter-style "Singasongalarius" magical gubbins. And yet, ironically, in many ways it is also the most *adult* Christmas special we've yet been given, with some complex storytelling techniques, a plot driven by the characters and some quite mind-bending concepts.' Dave Golder, *SFX* website, 25 December 2010.

- 'Now how about that for packing plenty into one 60 minute episode? Taking the basics of Charles Dickens' *A Christmas Carol* as its basis, Steven Moffat skilfully wove the well-known and well-filmed tale into a intriguing and layered *Doctor Who* story. For a Christmas episode, too, it was relatively light on action, as instead, Moffat pooled together the ingredients for a real cracker of a story.' Simon Brew, Den of Geek website, 24 December 2010.
- 'The title gives you a clue as to what you're in for, but the *Doctor Who* team takes the classic set-up and adds an element of the fantastic. Time travel, flying fish, and Matt Smith jumping on the furniture – yes, this is definitely *Doctor Who*. That's the brilliance of the Christmas specials: they're a perfect fusion of a holiday story and a *Doctor Who* adventure, not simply another episode with a cursory holiday element or a narrative with the sci-fi elements squeezed into it. There's laughter, there's tears, and there's a plot that isn't going to bend your brain. It's just good, clean fun, which isn't necessarily easy to find anymore.' Brittany Frederick, Starpulse.com website, 25 December 2010.
- 'Steven Moffat's re-working of *A Christmas Carol* was gently demented. Highlights included Katherine Jenkins serenading a shark, fish that could swim in the fog, and the Doctor marrying Marilyn Monroe. It started like an episode of *Space: 1999* with 4,003 people trapped in the skies, controlled by Kazran Sardick, a cross between Scrooge and Citizen Kane. "How can I have new memories?" he groaned, as the Doctor invaded his past. Michael Gambon gave one of his greatest performances, bestowing dignity and emotion upon what was at times a bewildering piece of science fiction. By contrast, Matt Smith's mannered gabbling is becoming smug and rather grating. Amy Pond was – again – parked on the sidelines. But her legs were as great as ever.' Jim Shelley, *Daily Mirror*, 27 December 2010.

ANALYSIS

*Doctor Who*'s Christmas specials have generally been rather curious beasts, standing somewhat apart from the regular series in terms not only of their scheduling but also of their content. Aside from the sole and remarkable exception of 'The End of Time' Part One, they have always sought to make allowances for the fact that their Christmas Day audiences are unlikely to be in the mood for anything too heavy or challenging, and will probably include many people who are not regular viewers of the show. Consequently they have tended to be quite light on plot, big on spectacle and overtly Christmassy in tone, and to feature household-name guest actors – such as Catherine Tate in 'The Runaway Bride' and Kylie Minogue in 'Voyage of the Damned' – in place of the Doctor's regular companions.

'A Christmas Carol' continues this tradition, being explicitly inspired by Charles Dickens' festive favourite of the same title and guest starring both acclaimed classical singer Katherine Jenkins, making her drama debut here, and distinguished actor Sir Michael Gambon, probably best known these days for playing Dumbledore in most of the hugely successful *Harry Potter* films, the family audience demographic of which is very similar to *Doctor Who*'s. Amy and Rory do appear as well, but have only a relatively minor involvement, being for the most part stuck aboard the starliner, where they are amusingly disturbed while on honeymoon wearing their iconic policewoman and centurion outfits from Series Five ('It is just a bit of fun,' says an embarrassed Rory) – another demonstration of Steven Moffat's penchant for reprising popular aspects of his previous scripts.

Although the plot is driven by the plight of the starliner – the bridge of which is laid out to resemble that of *Star Trek*'s USS *Enterprise*, making it instantly recognisable for what it is – most of the action unfolds on the planet below. Here we are introduced to the elderly Kazran Sardick, obviously conceived as a Scrooge figure, who is following in his late father Elliot's footsteps by being generally mean and miserly toward the poor populace of his town, while also showing a heartless disregard for the lives of the 4,003 people on board the starliner by refusing to let it land safely. The Doctor consequently casts himself as the ghost of Christmas past and the ghost of Christmas future – with Amy filling in, in hologram form, as the ghost of Christmas present – as he pilots the TARDIS back and forth to various different points in Kazran's life, trying to influence his development so that by the time of the crisis he has become a better person.

In other words, this in essence is another 'cheating with time travel' type story, where the Doctor plays fast and loose with the timeline in a way that surely none of his previous incarnations would have contemplated. 'Time can be rewritten' says Amy – a phrase first used in 'Flesh and Stone' and then again in 'The Big Bang' – and this now seems to be becoming something of a mission statement for the eleventh Doctor's era. In some fans' eyes, this is a worrying development. Like the repeated use of predestination paradoxes in 'The Big Bang' – which arguably had a stronger justification in that the whole universe was on the point of collapse – the Doctor's cavalier rewriting of Kazran's history begs the awkward question why he does not always resort to such timey-wimey trickery in order to solve the problems he faces. There is clearly a risk here of the whole format of the show being undermined. On the other hand, though, it could be argued that, considering it boasts time travel as one of its key elements, *Doctor Who* has previously been too reluctant to explore the implications of this fascinating concept. In the main, the TARDIS has been used simply as a device to get the Doctor and his companions from one adventure to the next, and writers have shied away from exploiting the full potential of its capabilities as a time machine. Steven Moffat, though, has no such reservations; and in 'A Christmas Carol' he taps that potential to excellent effect.

In the process of the Doctor's flitting about through time we see Kazran not only as an elderly man, played by Michael Gambon, but also as a boy, played by Laurence Belcher, and as a young man, portrayed by Danny Horn; and all three actors are very good in their respective roles. As might perhaps be expected, Gambon is particularly impressive, not only as Kazran but also in his brief appearances as Elliot, subtly distinguishing the two generations of Sardick patriarch through the nuances of his performance.

An especially smart piece of writing by Moffat comes in the early scene where the elderly Kazran watches a video-recording that he made of himself as a boy, projected by the Doctor onto the wall of his study. As the recording continues to play, the Doctor departs in the TARDIS, only to reappear in the projected image and strike up a conversation with the boy, causing the elderly man's memories gradually to change as this newly-created childhood experience unfolds before his eyes. This neatly encapsulates the essential principle of what it is that the Doctor is trying to achieve, in a way that is relatively easy for the audience to grasp; something that is also aided by its similarity to Dickens' original idea, with which most would already be familiar.

We are next introduced to Katherine Jenkins' character, Abigail Pettigrew, as the Doctor and the boy Kazran release her from the cryogenic storage unit in which she is held, allowing her to enjoy a day of freedom with them on Christmas Eve. This is something that they then repeat on the same date on several subsequent occasions, as the Doctor returns again and again in the TARDIS, while Kazran gets a little older each time and eventually grows into a young man, who falls in love with Abigail. This is all superbly depicted on screen, in part by way of a collection of amusing snapshot photos perused by the elderly Kazran as he marvels over all these newly-formed memories. Jenkins' role is relatively undemanding, but she carries it off well, and her inexperience as an actress is certainly not apparent from her performance.

The notion of Elliot having put people into cold storage as collateral for loans is an excellent one, but perhaps not as fully developed as it might have been. Particularly strange is the fact that the Doctor is never heard to raise any objection to this callous practice – apart from telling young Kazran 'Hard man to love, your dad' – and seems quite content for Abigail to be refrozen after each of their Christmas Eve jaunts, even though at that stage he has no idea that she has only a few days left to live. The latter revelation is rather problematic in itself. For one thing, it raises the question how anyone could possibly have known in advance exactly how many days Abigail had remaining to her, as recorded on the counter on the front of her storage unit – and presumably the same applies to all the other frozen citizens as well, as they all appear to have similar counters. The elderly Kazran's comment 'I suppose the rest in the ice helped her' may perhaps account for the fact that she does not look or sound in the slightest bit ill. If so, though, it is a pretty flimsy explanation; and even if one accepts that her condition may originally have had more obvious symptoms, there must surely have been an element of doubt as to exactly how many days she would survive.

Another puzzle is, if Abigail had only a few days left to live in the first place, why did Elliot consider her suitable as collateral for a loan? One can only assume that the loan amount – '4,500 gideons' – was quite a small one by his standards. In addition, it is rather odd that we never learn the fate of all the other frozen citizens. It could perhaps be that the elderly Kazran is such a reformed character by the end of the story that he simply lets them all go, but it is a pity that this loose end is not tied up on screen, if only by way of a few extra lines of dialogue. It seems strange, too, that once again the Doctor is not heard to express any concern for their plight – rather ironically, given his earlier statement, 'I have never met anyone who wasn't important'.

Also curious is the fact that when, as a young man, Kazran first learns of Abigail's illness, he keeps it to himself and does not tell the Doctor. Even allowing for the fact that her condition must presumably be incurable on their own planet, wouldn't his first reaction be to hope that the Doctor could use the TARDIS to take her somewhere she could get effective treatment? Come to think of it, when the Doctor finally learns of her illness, why *doesn't* he do precisely that? Given the huge liberties he has already taken with Kazran's timeline, surely this would be a relatively modest additional intervention in the course of history? Perhaps this difference in attitude is due to the fact that, as a Time Lord, he has a unique perspective on such matters. As he tells Amy in the closing scene, 'Everything has to end sometime, otherwise nothing would ever get started.' Nevertheless it must be said that this whole aspect of the story concerning Abigail's illness does seem rather contrived and unconvincing.

Some fan commentators have also baulked at the scientifically dubious idea of alien fish, and more unlikely still a huge shark, being able to swim in an atmosphere seeded with a fog of tiny ice crystals – even leaving aside the lack of any obvious adverse effect of those crystals on the lungs of all the people who must presumably be inhaling them. In this case, though, one can forgive a little dramatic licence, as the Mill's brilliantly-realised CGI images of the fish swimming – or should that be flying? – through the air are really rather beautiful, and have a magic realism quality to them that seems perfectly in keeping with Steven Moffat's dark fairytale take on *Doctor Who*. The flying shark also makes for a suitably scary threat when it first appears in the boy Kazran's bedroom and swallows the Doctor's sonic screwdriver. Fittingly, the later sequence where the now-pacified shark tows the Doctor, Kazran and Abigail across the sky in a two-wheeled open carriage strongly recalls the familiar image of reindeer pulling Father Christmas through the air on his sleigh – a parallel nicely emphasised by the Doctor and Kazran wearing red Santa hats – not to mention the 2009 BBC One Christmas channel idents of reindeer towing David Tennant's Doctor along on top of his TARDIS!

In fact, the whole production has a magical feel to it that works really well in the context of a Christmas special. The Doctor at one point references the film of *Mary Poppins* (1964), which often seems to grace the Christmas TV schedules and likewise involves people improbably flying through the air; and the name Sardicktown recalls that of Pottersville in another Christmas Eve-set tale with fantasy elements, Frank Capra's *It's a Wonderful Life* (1946), which was itself inspired by Dickens' *A Christmas Carol* and also receives frequent seasonal screenings. We even get to hear people singing the actual Christmas carols 'Ding Dong Merrily on High', 'In the Bleak Midwinter' and 'Silent Night'. All in all, it would be fair to say that Steven Moffat has probably succeeded in his stated aim of making this *Doctor Who*'s most Christmassy Christmas special yet.

This is the third episode in a row (on transmission, though not in production) to be directed by Toby Haynes, and it confirms him to be the very best of the new crop of directors brought onto the show for Series Five. Again he does an outstanding job here, rising to the script's challenges with aplomb and giving the production a feature film look on a TV show budget.

Also worthy of considerable praise is the debut contribution to the show by its new regular production designer Michael Pickwood. It did seem from Series Five that his predecessor Edward Thomas was past the peak of his creative input – which covered the entirety of new-era *Doctor Who* up to that point – as evident in the ill-conceived and uninspired redesign of the TARDIS interior, so it is good to have someone new in charge of this department. Pickwood's designs for 'A

Christmas Carol' are highly imaginative and appealing. They combine elements of Dickensian Victoriana with a kind of nautical steampunk look, as seen for instance in the buildings having porthole-like windows, picking up on the flying fish aspect of the story. This same mix of styles is also apparent in the costumes, designed by another new addition to the team, the highly distinguished Barbara Kidd, who previously had a semi-regular stint on the show in the mid-1970s on stories such as 'Frontier in Space' (1973), 'Genesis of the Daleks' (1975) and 'Pyramids of Mars' (1976) and a further one-off credit on 'Kinda' (1982). The overall effect recalls that of the cult classic Jeunet and Caro movie *The City of Lost Children* (1995), and again is very well suited to the Steven Moffat version of *Doctor Who*.

If the story has a weakness, it is that its resolution is rather unsatisfying. Even leaving aside the niggle that we never find out what happens to all the frozen citizens, it is disappointing that the Doctor's rewriting of Kazran's timeline – the main element inspired by Dickens' original – turns out to have no direct bearing on the way the starliner and its occupants are saved from destruction. Instead, their rescue relies on the incidental discovery that the storm clouds can be 'tamed' by the amplified sound of Abigail's voice, on the Murray Gold-composed song 'Silence is All You Know' (the title and lyrics of which seem to refer obliquely to the ongoing story arc featuring the Silence). This seems rather too convenient, and perhaps a touch too whimsical as well; and it also leaves unanswered the question of how Sardicktown's longer-term problems will be addressed, particularly given that Kazran can no longer operate his cloud-controlling machine. It was just lucky that Abigail could hold a tune, really, and that there wasn't a different genre of music needed to resonate with the clouds, such as funk or heavy metal ... That said, while Katherine Jenkins' operatic style of singing sadly does nothing at all for this author, her rendition of Gold's song seems to have been well received by those who like that sort of thing – and certainly by the flying shark!

Minor reservations aside, 'A Christmas Carol' can be counted a great success, and one of the most enjoyable of the seasonal specials to date – possibly even the best. The icing on the Christmas cake is that, as in most previous years, it concludes with an exciting trailer for the forthcoming run of episodes, which whets the viewer's appetite very nicely. Roll on Series Six!

# OVERVIEW

As a lifelong fan of *Doctor Who*, going right back to the 1960s when I grew up with the William Hartnell (first) and Patrick Troughton (second) Doctors as my childhood heroes, I really dislike having to write negative things about the show; and certainly I would never want to upset or cause offence to any of the highly talented individuals who work on it. In the end, though, I can only offer an honest opinion, and I have to say that, for me, Series Five was overall a disappointment, and definitely the weakest since *Doctor Who* returned to TV in 2005.

Admittedly that is a very exacting standard by which to judge it. In previous books in this range, I have made no secret of the fact that, in my eyes, Russell T Davies's time as showrunner, and particularly Series One to Three, saw it rise to an unprecedented pinnacle of quality. Certainly it has never been more popular with the general viewing public, or more feted within the television industry, than it was during the period 2005 to 2009. But really, the comparison is unavoidable.

In some respects, in fact, Series Five seems almost to invite comparison with the previous era; most notably in the way that the dynamic between the Doctor, Amy and Rory comes over as a kind of dark reflection of that between the Doctor, Rose and Mickey back in Series One and Two. While this was a good idea in principle, neatly pointing up how new showrunner Steven Moffat's vision of *Doctor Who* differs from Davies's, it ultimately proves unfortunate, because Amy and Rory as characters are not as engaging or identifiable as Rose and Mickey; and Karen Gillan and Arthur Darvill, although they give progressively stronger performances as the series goes on, are no match for Billie Piper and Noel Clark in terms of either acting ability or sheer star quality. And given that I regard David Tennant as the best Doctor the show has ever had, it was always likely that I would find Matt Smith something of a comedown.

That said, however, Smith does do an excellent job in the part. It is one he could almost have been born to play, as his own manner and physicality are distinctly 'Doctorish' even before he starts to act. The 'mad man with a box' description from 'The Eleventh Hour' is actually an excellent encapsulation of his approach to the role. He gives his Doctor a mad professor quality that is hugely entertaining, capturing the essence of the character while at the same time bringing something new to it that makes it distinct from any of his predecessors' portrayals; no easy thing to achieve. His costume, the design of which the actor significantly influenced, is absolutely spot-on too, its old-fashioned, rather geeky look perfectly complementing his performance and helping to counteract any lingering concern the viewer might have that he is too young to play the part. This is by no means a one-dimensional interpretation of the Doctor either; there is light and shade to it, as seen in his more brooding and serious moments, and even in his occasional flashes of anger – such as when he discovers the secret behind Starship UK in 'The Beast Below', and when he is desperate to find a way of rescuing Amy from the forest of Weeping Angels in 'Flesh and Blood'. It must be noted, though, that Smith is not always helped by the way the character is scripted. At some points the writers go over the top in playing up his eccentricity; and at others, the characterisation is simply inconsistent, not only between episodes but even within the same episode. Possibly the most obvious example of this comes in 'The Lodger', when the Doctor seems largely clueless about everyday human social interaction, but nevertheless shows a better understanding of the relationship between Craig and Sophie than they do themselves.

It is interesting that Smith has often expressed his admiration for Patrick Troughton's portrayal of the Doctor. Of all the previous Doctors' costumes, it is certainly Troughton's to which Smith's bears the closest resemblance; and certain aspects of Smith's performance recall Troughton's as well. But, whether by design or by curious coincidence, the parallels go deeper than that. In his first few stories, Troughton's Doctor also suffered from inconsistent characterisation and a rather forced, over-exaggerated eccentricity. He even had the same penchant for different types of hats that Smith's Doctor displays; 'I would like a hat like that' almost qualified as an early catchphrase. The one-off inclusion of 'internal monologue' voice-overs for him and his companions at the start of his third story, 'The Underwater Menace', was the same kind of anomalous experimentation in the depiction of the characters as witnessed with the 'roaming eye' effect in Smith's debut outing, 'The Eleventh Hour'. Amy and Rory bear certain similarities to the second Doctor's original companions, Polly and Ben; and, at the risk of stretching the analogy too far, it is even possible to see an equivalence between River Song and Jamie, a character who was originally intended to appear in just a single story but who was ultimately kept on as an addition to the regular team and proved a rather better foil for the Doctor than the two who had been devised as companions in the first place. The encouraging thing is that, after those few early wobbles, the second Doctor's era quickly settled down to become one of the most consistently superb in the show's long history; so if the eleventh Doctor's era continues to mirror it, we are in for a real treat over the coming few years.

In order to achieve that full potential, though, Steven Moffat and his colleagues on the production team will need to address four issues. The first is to ensure that the unprecedentedly ambitious and complex story arc begun in Series Five is ultimately given a proper resolution, with all the loose threads tied up in a coherent and satisfactory way. The second is to give the scripts more of a polish so that upcoming stories are more fully thought-through and contain fewer implausibilities and loose ends. The third is to iron out the inconsistencies in characterisation of the regulars and bring a bit more likeability to the depiction of Amy and Rory. And the fourth is to ensure there is no recurrence of the design problems that plagued the early part of Series Five in particular, with the poorly-conceived updating of the TARDIS interior and the Silurians' appearance and, most vexing of all, the unforgivably atrocious remodelling of the Daleks.

Sad to say, the arrival of these Fatleks fatally undermined Series Five in my estimation. This might seem an overreaction, but to me it's like having a lovely picnic spread out before you, only to see a huge, slimy slug crawling across it. However appetising the picnic might otherwise have been, even the parts that the slug didn't touch are never going to seem as appealing after that. And in my eyes, the redesigned Daleks were the slug to Series Five's picnic. Consequently, they rather put me off the whole thing. After their introduction in 'Victory of the Daleks', it seemed horribly inevitable that they would reappear in a later story – as indeed proved to be the case – and this meant that instead of anticipating the rest of the series with optimism and excitement, as should have been the case, I approached it with a degree of trepidation. In the event, thanks partly to Toby Haynes' excellent direction and to Steven Moffat's valiant rescue attempt of presenting them mainly in the form of stone Daleks, their severe shortcomings were partly disguised in 'The Pandorica Opens'/'The Big Bang'. But by that point the damage had already been done. My confidence in the new production team had been severely dented.

However, in all fairness, I must add that having re-watched each of the episodes numerous times in the course of researching and writing this book, I have lately come to appreciate Series Five rather more than I did on its original transmission. Undeniably there is much in it to admire and enjoy. It may have more so-so stories than usual, but it also boasts some *bona fide* classics in 'Amy's Choice', 'Vincent and the Doctor' and 'The Pandorica Opens'/'The Big Bang', and several others that are very good indeed; particularly 'The Time of Angels'/'Flesh and Stone' and 'The Lodger'. Steven Moffat's approach to *Doctor Who* is highly imaginative and original, for all that in this series he reuses a number of ideas from his earlier stories, and his oft-cited dark fairytale vision for the show has given it a new and very appealing ambiance. The incorporation of an ongoing story arc far more involved than any of those previously attempted in the show – most notably in the Key to Time season in 1978/79 – was a bold innovation well worth trying. At its best, too, the production has a really sumptuous look to it, with some superb camerawork and effects. And in Toby Haynes, *Doctor Who* has surely found a new star director. Fingers crossed he will handle many more episodes in future.

Hopefully, with the benefit of a couple of years' hindsight, the less successful aspects of the eleventh Doctor's debut series will come to be seen as simply the teething problems of a new production team faced with the daunting task of taking over one of British TV's most popular and successful shows at a time of significant financial and other pressures. The excellent 'A Christmas Carol' certainly suggests that they are moving in the right direction. And if they have the good sense to learn from their mistakes and avoid reusing those horrible new Daleks, that at least will count strongly in their favour!

# PART FIVE
# APPENDICES

# APPENDIX A
# THE ADVENTURE GAMES

During the course of 2010, the official *Doctor Who* website made available to download free of charge in the UK a series of four computer games, for PC or Mac, under the umbrella title *The Adventure Games*.[45] The titles were 'City of the Daleks', 'Blood of the Cybermen', 'TARDIS' and 'Shadows of the Vashta Nerada'. These games were third-person and puzzle-based. International versions were also released commercially via the company Direct2Drive, although only for PC, not Mac. The games featured Matt Smith and Karen Gillan voicing their usual roles of the Doctor and Amy, with guest characters, in fully-animated scenes. If run through seamlessly without error, 'City of the Daleks' took about 40 minutes to complete, 'Blood of the Cybermen' about 55 minutes, 'TARDIS' about 25 minutes and 'Shadows of the Vashta Nerada' about 45 minutes. Versions of the usual *Doctor Who* opening and closing title sequences were used, as were stock sections of Murray Gold's incidental music. In announcing the games, *Doctor Who* executive producer Piers Wenger said: 'There aren't 13 episodes of *Doctor Who* this year. There are 17 – four of which are interactive. Everything you see and experience within the games is part of the *Doctor Who* universe.' The games were thus intended to be seen as part of the Series Five continuity. As the 'Victory of the Daleks'-style Daleks are featured, Amy has no prior knowledge of the Cybermen and Rory is not mentioned, it seems likely that they take place sometime after 'Cold Blood' and before 'The Pandorica Opens'.

CREDITS[46]

MAIN CAST

Matt Smith (The Doctor)
Karen Gillan (Amy Pond)

PRODUCTION TEAM

Voice Director: Gary Russell, Charles Cecil

---

[45] A second series was subsequently commissioned, intended for release in 2011, although in the event only one further game – 'The Gunpowder Plot' – saw the light of day, then the series was cancelled.
[46] In this listing, the games are numbered 1.01 to 1.04. Where a game number (or more than one) appears in brackets after a person's name in the listing, this means that they were credited only on the game (or games) indicated. Otherwise, the person concerned was credited on all games. Some production roles were credited only on certain games.

Sumo Digital
Programming Lead: James Sutherland
Programmer: Phil Woods, Carl Dixon, Dan Mallinson, Henry Durrant, Sean Davies, Tom Seddon
Design Lead: Will Tarratt
Design and Scripting: Nana Nielsen, Stuart Yarham, Mike Welsh, Sarah Cook
Concepts/Storyboards: Richard Jordan
Art Lead: Mick Hirst
Artist: Chris Pepper, Igloo Digital Arts, John Hackleton
Animation Lead: Ian Deary
Animator: Lee Taylor, Phil Hanks, Steve Thomas, Shruti Rao, Simon Wottge, Robin Butler, Simon Bradley
Graphic Design Lead: Chantal Beaumont
Sound and Music Editor: Pat Phelan
F9 VP of QA: Jack Brummet (all except 1.01)
F9 QA Manager: Bill Schneider (all except 1.01)
F9 QA Lead: Mark Bridges
F9 QA: Mark Freeman, Tom Barker, Nate Umipeg, Philip Palermo, Chase Lawhead (1.01), Jason Ausmus (all except 1.01), Nick Deakins (all except 1.01)
Additional Support: Mark Thackery, James Drew, Damian Fowkes, Neil Fielding, Toby Allen, Nick Sibbick, Laura Schofield, Hayley Brant, Gary McLoughlin
Creative Direction: Sean Millard
Art Manager: Dom Hood
Art Director: Darren Mills
Core Tech Manager: Stephen Robinson
Technical Director: Ash Bennet
Executive Producer: Pat Phelan
Studio Head: Paul Porter
European VP: Carl Cavers

With thanks to: The BBC National Orchestra of Wales

Original Theme Music: Ron Grainer
Casting Director: Andy Pryor CDG
Music: Murray Gold
Sound Effects: Matt Cox
Music Editor: Doug Sinclair
Voice Recording: Bang Post Production, Sis Live (all except 1.04), The Moat Studios
Technical Project Manager: Richard Josebury, Amanda Dahl (1.04)
Legal Manager: Ifty Khan
Production Executive: Julie Scott
Brand Executive: Ian Grutchfield (all except 1.01)
Additional Gameplay Dialogue: James Moran (1.04)
Script Editor: Lindsey Alford
Interactive Producer: Richard Jenkins
Senior Producer: Mat Fidell
Drama Producer: Brian Minchin (1.04)

APPENDIX A: THE ADVENTURE GAMES

Executive Producer, Interactive: Anwen Aspden, Charles Cecil
Executive Producer: Steven Moffat, Piers Wenger, Beth Willis

BBC Wales

**1.01 – CITY OF THE DALEKS**

Writer: Phil Ford

DEBUT RELEASE DATES

PC: 2 June 2010 (trial version), 5 June 2010 (official release); Mac: 15 June 2010

ADDITIONAL CREDITED CAST

Sara Carver (Sylvia), Nicholas Briggs (Dalek Voices)

PLOT

The Doctor and Amy arrive in London in 1963 to find the Earth ruined and under the control of the new paradigm Daleks. The sole human survivor, a woman name Sylvia, is exterminated shortly after they meet her. The Doctor deduces that the Daleks have gained the power to alter history. He takes Amy in the TARDIS to the Dalek city on their home planet Skaro. Amy begins to fade from existence, as the destruction of humanity in 1963 means she was never born, but the Doctor constructs a Chronon Blocker to slow the process. They are both captured and taken before the Dalek Emperor, who asserts that the Daleks will become the new Time Lords through the use of the Eye of Time, a bright white sphere of energy previously kept on Gallifrey. The Doctor and Amy escape by leaping into the Eye. They are transported back to a time when the Dalek city is ruined and deserted, save for an infestation of Varga plants, just before the Daleks first arrive there with the Eye. Using components found for him by Amy, the Doctor constructs a device that will disrupt the Daleks' vision. The Daleks meanwhile prepare to use the Eye to begin changing history. Amy activates the Doctor's device, allowing him to free the Eye from its restraints. They then jump into the Eye just before it vanishes. They find themselves back at the TARDIS in the future time period when they first arrived. Now, the Dalek city is still in ruins, and Amy is no longer fading from existence; the Daleks' scheme has been foiled. Using the TARDIS scanner, the Doctor and Amy see that the original 1963 has been restored and Sylvia is alive.

CONTINUITY POINTS

• The Doctor cautions Amy to be careful in the London Underground, because all sorts of things can be found there, including rats, dinosaurs and Yeti. He previously encountered dinosaurs in the Underground in 'Invasion of the Dinosaurs' (1974) and Yeti in 'The Web of Fear' (1968).

- The Dalek city is named as Kaalann.
- It is implied that Kaalann was ruined and the Daleks fled Skaro in the Time War. The new paradigm Daleks have travelled back there with the Eye of Time, which went missing from Gallifrey when the planet was destroyed, to try to rewrite history. The Doctor describes the Eye of Time as a 'natural phenomenon': 'Some say it is the heart of time and space itself; the very core of the Big Bang.'
- The spare Dalek parts that the Doctor uses to construct the Chronon Blocker are a Dalekanium Coil and a Kontron Crystal. Dalekanium is the metal out of which the Daleks' casings are made, as first mentioned in 'The Dalek Invasion of Earth' (1964). A Kontron Crystal was first featured in 'Timelash' (1985).
- Varga plants were first seen in the TV story 'Mission to the Unknown' (1965).

## 1.02 – BLOOD OF THE CYBERMEN

Writer: Phil Ford

DEBUT RELEASE DATE

26 June 2010

ADDITIONAL CREDITED CAST

Sarah Douglas (Professor Meadows), Barnaby Edwards (Chisholm), Nicholas Briggs (Cyber Voices)

PLOT

The TARDIS brings the Doctor and Amy to the Arctic in response to a distress signal. They rescue a man named Chisholm who has fallen down an ice cliff after fleeing from a nearby Geological Survey Outpost. They take him back to the base in the TARDIS. There, he is attacked by a Cybermat. The Doctor and Amy then encounter a Cyberslave – one of the base crew, converted into a Cyberman-like robot by nanoforms injected by a Cybermat – but Amy despatches it with a blast of steam from a vent. Inside the base, its commander, Professor Elizabeth Meadows, explains that all of her crew have been turned into Cyberslaves, whose purpose is to release Cybermen buried in the ice for some 10,000 years. The Doctor enlists Amy's help to reach the Cybermats' nest via the ventilation system and disable them with a sonic pulse. They hear a radio message about an incoming delivery of supplies, but Amy fixes the broken transmitter and warns them off. The Doctor synthesises a serum to reverse the effects of the Cyberslave conversion. He gives the serum to Chisholm, who then shows him and Amy how to access the underground dig via a lift. Dodging through a grid of tunnels patrolled by Cyberslaves, they find a Cyberman spaceship that crashed here before the last ice age. The Cybermen are in suspended animation. Amy is captured by two Cyberslaves and taken inside. The Doctor follows and finds Meadows, who has actually been changing into a Cyberslave from the start and deliberately lured the Doctor here. Using Amy as a hostage, she forces the Doctor to revive the

Cybermen. The Cyberleader then deletes Meadows, but the Doctor escapes and rescues Amy. Chisholm manages to destroy some of the revived Cybermen and the Doctor returns the others to stasis. He, Amy and Chisholm escape from the base before the spaceship is destroyed in an explosion. The Doctor and Amy leave Chisholm behind so he can answer any questions UNIT might have.

CONTINUITY POINTS

- When the Doctor and Amy first arrive in the Arctic Circle, the Doctor tells Amy that the TARDIS will keep her warm, for a while at least. This explains how they can move around during the rest of the adventure in their normal clothes, without being adversely affected by the extreme cold.
- When Amy mentions spiders, the Doctor says 'I'd rather we changed the subject'. This may be an oblique reference to his experiences in 'Planet of the Spiders' (1974), which led to him having to regenerate into his fourth incarnation.
- The date when the Doctor and Amy arrive is revealed to be 4 May, but the year is not given.
- Amy does not know what Cybermen are. This is despite the fact that she presumably lived through the events seen in 'Army of Ghosts'/'Doomsday' (2006). Doubtless the cracks in time are responsible for this, just as they accounted for her lack of knowledge of the Daleks in 'Victory of the Daleks'.
- The site of the survey base is said to be Zebra Bay.
- Unlike those in other new-era *Doctor Who* episodes, the Cybermen seen here have no Cybus Industries logos on their chests. This may indicate that they are from the Doctor's own universe, originating from the planet Mondas, rather than from the parallel universe where John Lumic was their creator.

**1.03 – TARDIS**

Writer: James Moran
Story by: James Moran, Phil Ford, Sean Millard

DEBUT RELEASE DATE

27 August 2010

ADDITIONAL CREDITED CAST

Sarah Douglas (Entity)

PLOT

The TARDIS gets caught in a space-time riptide. The doors open and the Doctor falls out into the void, where he is surrounded by worm-like Chronomites – mostly harmless four-dimensional creatures that live there. Through sign language, the Doctor manages to tell Amy that he cannot breathe, and that she can save him by operating red controls on the TARDIS console. She does so, and the ship's external air shell is restored. She then follows the Doctor's directions to the TARDIS drawing room and fetches a laser screwdriver, which she uses to construct a makeshift tractor beam and bring him back inside. While in the drawing room, however, she accidentally breaks a pottery flask, and fails to notice that this has released a glowing Entity from within. A lesion in time then causes the Doctor and Amy to get separated in different versions of the TARDIS control room, out of sync by 1,000 years. To fix this, the Doctor builds a tachyon feedback loop, again using parts obtained from the drawing room. He also finds the broken flask, and realises that the Entity is loose. By recording a message for Amy to receive in the future, he is able to get her to operate the tachyon feedback loop and repair the lesion, returning her to his time. The Entity wants to feed off the two travellers' time energy, but the Doctor captures it in another flask. He then releases it into the void so that it can feed forever on the energy of the Chronomites, which will be unharmed in the process. The Doctor next decides to take Amy to London after the Great Flood of the 23rd Century. They arrive in a glass tunnel in an underwater city and see a huge shark-like creature swimming above it, as if about to attack.

CONTINUITY POINTS

• The Doctor tries, unsuccessfully, to recall a holiday of his that did not go wrong, mentioning both Brighton beach – as seen in 'The Leisure Hive' (1980) – and Paris – as seen in 'City of Death' (1979).
• In the TARDIS drawing room, Amy finds lots of objects seen in the Doctor's previous adventures, including Liz 10's mask from 'The Beast Below', a Sycorax staff from 'The Christmas Invasion' (2005) and a Cyberman chest piece.
• A laser screwdriver was first seen being used by the Master in 'Last of the Time Lords' (2007).
• This game ends with a cliff-hanger leading into the next one.

**1.04 – SHADOWS OF THE VASHTA NERADA**

Writer: Phil Ford

DEBUT RELEASE DATE

22 December 2010

ADDITIONAL CREDITED CAST

Barnaby Edwards (Martin Flanagan), Sarah Douglas (Jones), Nicholas Briggs (Oswald Fox), Eleanor Matsuura (Dana Tanaka)

PLOT

The shark-like creature that the Doctor and Amy saw on arriving smashes the glass tunnel that leads to the TARDIS, but they manage to escape. They meet Martin Flanagan, who tells them that the whole of this Poseidon base is in quarantine as the crew have succumbed to a sickness. The Doctor gains access to the rest of the base by reasoning with Jones, the intelligent computer that controls the doors. They meet Oswald Fox and the base's medic, Dana Tanaka. Suddenly the lights go dim, and Martin is killed by hostile Vashta Nerada, which live in the shadows. Dodging Vashta Nerada-animated skeletons in diving suits, the Doctor and Amy make their way to the base's generator and restore the lights. The Doctor discovers that alien vortron radiation is responsible for the sickness on the base. He offers to synthesise a cure but Oswald objects, intending instead to send everyone to the surface in escape pods, despite the risk that the Vashta Nerada could be lurking inside. The Doctor convinces Dana to let him and Amy go and find the ingredients for the cure, which he then administers to her. Using the base's external scanners, the Doctor finds the source of the radiation: the shipwreck of the USS *Eldridge* from 1943. He explains that the US Navy tried to make the ship invisible, but the experiment went wrong, and although the Time Lords intervened, an unstable dimensional gateway was left open. This is the source of the base's problems. Jones helps the Doctor and Amy get back to the TARDIS via service tunnels. They then travel to the *Eldridge*, where after dodging more Vashta Nerada divers they manage to close the gateway. This sends the shark-like creature and the Vashta Nerada back to where they came from. The Doctor and Amy bid farewell to Dana and Oswald before departing in the TARDIS.

CONTINUITY POINTS

- This story takes place in 'a sub-aquatic community' at Christmastime, in a year no earlier than the 23rd Century, although the exact date is not given. The Doctor says: 'When the oceans rose, 75 percent of Earth's land mass drowned. Humanity built its own new islands, and moved onto the ocean floor to farm and mine for minerals.'
- The Vashta Nerada previously featured in the TV story 'Silence in the Library'/'Forest of the Dead' (2008).
- The Doctor escapes from being tied up by using a trick he learned from famous escapologist Harry Houdini. He previously mentioned having met Houdini in 'Planet of the Spiders' (1974).
- Although the shark-like creature is not named in the game itself, a 'Who Fact' pop-up found by examining a porthole on the USS *Eldridge* identifies it as a 'razor-toothed Zaralok'. It goes on to say that the Zaraloks were bred by the Valky clan, a sea-dwelling people on the planet Shakara, to fight an undersea war on their behalf, but turned on the Valky and ate them as well as the enemy.
- The real-life USS *Eldrich* was the ship supposedly used by the US Navy in the so-called Philadelphia Experiment around October 1943, which has since been the subject of many conspiracy theories.

# APPENDIX B
# DOCTOR WHO LIVE[47]

PERFORMANCE DETAILS

London – Wembley Arena – 8 to 10 October 2010
Sheffield – Sheffield Arena – 12 to 13 October 2010
Glasgow – Scottish Exhibition and Conference Centre – 15 to 17 October 2010
Birmingham – National Indoor Arena – 18 to 20 October 2010
Manchester – Manchester Evening News Arena – 22 to 24 October 2010
Nottingham – Trent FM Arena – 25 to 26 October 2010
Cardiff – Cardiff International Arena – 28 to 31 October 2010
Liverpool – Echo Arena Liverpool – 2 to 3 November 2010
Belfast – Odyssey Arena – 6 to 7 November 2010

Duration: Two acts of approximately 40′ each, separated by an interval of approximately 20′.

MAIN PRODUCTION CREDITS

Executive Producer and Showrunner: Steven Moffat
Executive Producer for BBC Wales: Piers Wenger, Beth Willis
Writer: Gareth Roberts, Will Brenton
Director: Will Brenton
Producer: Craig Stanley
Composer: Murray Gold
Musical Director and Arranger: Ben Foster
Producer for BBC Wales: Annabella Hurst-Brown
Brand Producer: Bethan Britton
Video Director/Offline Editor: Richard Senior
Ar Director and Costume: Keith Slote
Designer (Vorgenson), Production Designer and Lighting Designer: Mark Cunniffe
Sound Designer: Richard Sillitto
Venue Sound Designer: Rich Rowley
Illusions and SFX: Paul and Gary Hardy-Brown
Costume Designer: Ray Holman, Louise Page
Costume and Wardrobe Supervisor: Fiona Barnes
Casting Director (Vorgenson): Andy Pryor
Monster Movement Coach: Ailsa Berk
Music Associate: Dave Foster
Synthesizer Tech and Pre-record Mix: William Rice

---

[47] Credits are taken from the official programme booklet for the show.

# APPENDIX B: DOCTOR WHO LIVE

Video Programmer: David Mulcahy
Graphics: James Jackson
Animator: Oliver Smyth
Online Editor (Elstree): Steve Charles, Nathan Lindley

Theme tune music composed by Ron Grainer and realised by Delia Derbyshire

## MAIN CAST

Matt Smith (The Doctor)[48], Nigel Planer (Vorgenson), Nicholas Briggs (Winston Churchill & Players' Cast)

## OTHER CREDITED CAST

Graham Henderson (Vorgenson Understudy and Dance Captain), Adam Anderson, Charlie Adams, Claire Parrish, Graeme Henderson, Karl Greenwood, Kerry Newell, Jenny Phillips, Jon Davey, Josephine Desmond, Paul Hardy-Brown, Ross Aldred, Tarah McDonald, Vicki Davids, William Hazell (Players' Cast). Voiceover artist: Nicholas Briggs (Cyberman, Judoon, Dalek), Silas Carson (Ood), Jonathan Hart (Clockwork Robot)

## PLOT

### Act One

Vorgenson, the self-styled Greatest Showman in the Galaxy, shows the audience the various types of monsters he has captured in his Minimiser device. He plans to create a scenario to ensnare the Doctor, and to this end has kidnapped Winston Churchill. Churchill contacts the Doctor via an audience member's mobile phone, and the Doctor promises to come to his aid. Vorgenson sends Judoon out into the audience to scan for aliens, in case the Doctor has already arrived. The Judoon attempt to scan Vorgenson himself, but he tricks them into returning to the Minimiser. The Doctor contacts the audience and tells them that if at any point he shouts 'Geronimo!' they must shout it back, as this will automatically bring the TARDIS to him. He then warns that some Weeping Angels have escaped from the Minimiser, and that the audience members should not blink. Suddenly, a group of armed policemen rush in from the back of the auditorium, instructing the audience to stay in their seats. They ascend to the stage but are picked off one by one by the Weeping Angels. Vorgenson sends the Angels back into the Minimiser, joking that the police were collateral damage. The Doctor appears and warns that if Vorgenson doesn't shut down the Minimiser, he will. In a shock twist, however, Vorgenson manages to trap the Doctor himself inside the Minimiser. Vorgenson then exits, revealing to the audience that someone else is behind all this ...

---

[48] Appeared only in pre-recorded video segments.

Act Two

Cybermen descend into the auditorium, and one audience member is thrown into the Minimiser and upgraded into a Cyberman himself. Then a number of Daleks appear. They reveal that they were the ones who caused Vorgenson to construct the Minimiser, by projecting the plans into his dreams. They imprison the Doctor inside a box at the side of the stage. From the box, the Doctor uses the sonic screwdriver to send out Cybermen from the Minimiser, and they engage in battle with the Daleks. At first, it seems that the Daleks are winning, as they manage to destroy one of the Cybermen. However, the Cybermen reveal that they have upgraded their own technology, which will allow them to overpower the Daleks. Realising that they can't win, the Daleks retreat into the Minimiser. It seems that they have been defeated. The Doctor escapes from the box, and Vorgenson offers his apologies. The Doctor says that he has released all of the trapped monsters, apart from the Daleks, and sent them back to their proper times and places. He then does the same for Vorgenson too. Suddenly, it is revealed that the white Supreme Dalek managed to sneak away during the confrontation. It hovers above the stage, threatening the Doctor and the audience. However, the Doctor then calls on the audience to shout out 'Geronimo!' with him. This causes the TARDIS to appear. Energy from the TARDIS overpowers the lone Dalek, and it is banished. The Doctor thanks the audience, and leaves in the TARDIS.

CONTINUITY POINTS

- Vorgenson is the son of Vorg, the showman character seen in the TV story 'Carnival of Monsters' (1973).
- Winston Churchill tells the Doctor that the date on which Vorgenson kidnapped him was 6 June 1944, when he was organising the Normandy landings that were crucial to the Allies' war effort. The Doctor says that this was a fixed point in time, and that Churchill's removal from it could cause time and space to collapse.

PRODUCTION NOTES

- Matt Smith's appearances as the Doctor all came in the form of specially-recorded video clips projected onto screens. Karen Gillan also appeared as Amy Pond, but only in a montage of clips from the TV show.
- Monsters featured in the show included Daleks, Cybermen, Weeping Angels, Judoon, Scarecrows, Smilers and Winders, Silurians and Saturnyne vampire girls.
- In sequences where audience members became involved in the action, they were actually actors planted there.
- Various changes to the script were made during rehearsals for the show, partly for timing reasons. One sequence dropped altogether was a 1940s dance number involving Winston Churchill.

PRESS REACTION

- 'Starting out as little more than a narrator, Nigel Planer struggles to keep a sense of momentum through a succession of walk-on monster appearances. Men stomping around in character suits gets tired quickly, although the recreation of the terrifying Weeping Angels provides some genuine heart-stopping thrills. It must be hard for any single actor to hold an audience the size of Wembley in his thrall. Nicholas Briggs manages much better than Planer in his brief cameo as Winston Churchill, but the show only really comes alive when the current Doctor, Matt Smith, interjects via a series of often hilarious prerecorded video sequences.' Scott Matthewman, *The Stage* website, 11 October 2010.

- '[Nigel] Planer does his best to keep up the momentum, but on this scale, the production inevitably lacks the intimacy and fear factor of the TV show. Matt Smith's pre-recorded clips certainly get the biggest audience response as he tries hard to inject some jeopardy into the plot, but with no plausible narrative, Vorgenson's character is never much more than a device to reveal one monster after another. This, however, is what the fans have come to see, and there are some great moments of audience interaction as the monsters infiltrate the auditorium: rhino-headed Judoon scan the crowd to amusingly detect humans from "unknowns", and the show is "interrupted" by a police team whose members are picked off by the terrifying Weeping Angels. This show is certainly spectacular, and great if you have young children or are a big *Doctor Who* fan yourself – but the weak story sadly means it isn't a must-see in its own right. Overall, it's hard not to compare the viewing experience unfavourably against the show's slicker TV counterpart.' Harriet Chandler, What's On Stage website, 23 October 2010.

- 'Run, hide, scream! "The Monsters Are Coming!" So promises the first foray into the eternally risky dimension of arena-based entertainment for *Doctor Who*, a touring spectacular spearheaded by the series' current scriptwriter-in-chief Steven Moffat, who tells us he has wanted to see something like this since he was 11 years old. It may come as no surprise to anyone to learn that the resulting jamboree – dazzling, deafening and brazenly gratuitous – is probably best appreciated by 11-year-old children and younger, or indeed those with an equivalent mental age. Terror? I spent a good bulk of the first matinee showing at Wembley Arena quivering at the cost of the expedition – a pulse-raising £170 for a family of four.' Dominic Cavendish, *Telegraph* website, 11 October 2010.

- 'An excellent 16-piece band, conducted by Ben Foster, blasted through rocked-up re-arrangements of composer Murray Gold's music for the TV series, with a maniacal enthusiasm that occasionally reached the stratospheric complexity of the outer reaches of progressive rock. Highlights were the eerie Weeping Angels, who viciously saw off an entire team of "policemen" ("Be careful, policemen!" said a frightened youngster behind me before they were picked off, one by one) for a studiously unblinking audience, the imposing Cybermen and the iconic Daleks surprisingly impressive after all these years, even in their current misshapen form and hideously unimpressive new day-glo colours. The whole shebang ended with lasers, explosions and a flying Dalek, with the production managing to find ever-more-ingenious ways of making the absent [Matt] Smith more integral to the action. But the show seemed unsure what it was. Part concert, part panto, part TV episode, part monster parade, it never settled down long enough or really gathered sufficient dramatic momentum. And the overall experience was nothing like watching the TV show.' Uncredited reviewer, This is Nottingham website, 26 October 2010.

- 'Sadly there's no Doctor in person to save us, although Matt Smith ... is present on the large screen to protect and guide us. But there are loads of clips to look at as well as the charming Doctor, who pops up on screen to remind us not to blink or the Weeping Angels will get us. I'm still suffering from eye-strain! A fantastic show of this magnitude, full of stunning visual effects including a choreographed battle between Cybermen and Daleks with lots of pyrotechnics, requires music to match. That's provided by a brilliant rock band, vigorously conducted by Ben Foster, blasting out Murray Gold's fabulous score. But I wasn't prepared for the beautiful choral singing, which was the real treat for me. For older fans there were nostalgic big-screen montages of previous Doctor Who incarnations set to the various theme tunes. However, the last word should really go to the younger generation and my nine-year-old gave it 10 out of 10 and the thumbs up. As for me – I'm still trying not to blink!' Natalie Anglesey, CityLife website, 25 October 2010.

ANALYSIS

Whereas the good Doctor's TV adventures have always been cleverly tailored to a family audience, this live adaptation seemed to be aimed squarely at children. In style, it was much closer to a Christmas pantomime than to a stage play. As such, it was undeniably entertaining. However, for anyone older than about ten, the story was too slight to hold much interest, and the repeatedly-used device of a group of monsters marauding down the aisles of the auditorium before ascending to the stage and entering the Minimiser quickly became rather tired. Nigel Planer as Vorgenson was the lynchpin of the show and gave a larger-than-life performance, very much in the vein of a pantomime villain, drawing boos from the audience at appropriate points. Nicholas Briggs, the only other speaking cast member, also gave a spirited turn as Winston Churchill, as well as providing his usual excellent monster voices. However, even some of the youngsters in the audience could be heard to express disappointment that the Doctor appeared only via video clips rather than in person (which was ruled out by Matt Smith's TV commitments – a problem that could surely have been avoided if this live show had been scheduled during a break in production), and that the Daleks featured were the Teletubby-type 'Victory of the Daleks' versions rather than the iconic ones from the previous era. Two highlights of the show were the well-staged sequence where a group of armed police officers stormed onto the stage, only to fall foul of the Weeping Angels as the lights flashed on and off, and the impressive effect toward the end where the white Supreme Dalek appeared to hover in mid-air (in fact supported on a well-disguised crane arm). It was also good to be able to hear selections from Murray Gold's incidental music performed by live musicians, with Ben Foster conducting enthusiastically and appropriate clips being displayed on large screens, and to see some of the Doctor's monstrous foes 'in the flesh'. However, both of these things had been done before, and rather better, in the *Doctor Who Prom* concerts, where the music was played by a full orchestra in the same style as for

TV, as opposed to *Doctor Who Live*'s band of just 16 musicians interpreting the pieces in a rock-infused style. Admittedly the Prom concerts had the disadvantage that they were not accessible to such large audiences in venues all around the country, but to anyone who'd been lucky enough to see one of them, in this respect *Doctor Who Live* did come across as a kind of 'Prom lite'. It also did not help the atmosphere of the show that for most performances there were lots of empty seats. Reports suggested that the arena ticket prices had proved prohibitive for some families who might otherwise have attended; and it has to be said that the show did not seem to be particularly good value for money. All things considered, *Doctor Who Live* can be judged a success, especially for younger audience members, but only a qualified one.

# APPENDIX C
# DOCTOR WHO CONFIDENTIAL

As in previous years, each of *Doctor Who*'s latest run of episodes was accompanied by its own dedicated *Doctor Who Confidential* documentary. Except for the first, these had approximately the same running times as the episodes they covered. They continued to present an informative and entertaining account of various aspects of the making of *Doctor Who*, illustrated by plentiful behind-the-scenes and episode clips and supported by numerous cast and production team interviews. As usual, repeat airings generally consisted of condensed versions, each between about 10 to 16 minutes long, under the informal title *Confidential Cut-Down*. Because these shorter edits omitted the contemporary music tracks featured in the full-length ones, it was again these versions that were included in the Complete Series DVD/Blu-Ray box set released that autumn, in order to avoid potential music clearance problems and associated fees. However, anyone who missed the full-length versions on their debut screening could catch up with them, during the week that followed, via the BBC's iPlayer service or the on-demand packages offered by digital TV providers such as Virgin Media. Details are as follows.[49]

**SERIES CREDITS**[50]

With thanks to: The J Paul Getty Museum (5.10)
Narrated by: Alex Price (all except 6.00), Russell Tovey (6.00)

PRODUCTION TEAM

Graphics: Component Graphics
Title Music: Slam & Saw Productions
Space Images: NASA (5.11)
Camera: Simon Cox (5.01, 5.02, 5.03), Eric Huyton (5.01), Aled Jenkins (all except 5.04, 6.00), Steve Webb (5.03, 5.04, 5.05, 5.07, 5.08, 5.09, 5.10, 5.11, 6.00), Oli Russell (5.03, 5.06, 6.00), Dewi Davies (5.03), Steve Brand (5.04, 5.08, 5.09), Jon Rees (5.04, 5.05, 5.07, 5.08, 5.09, 5.11, 5.12, 5.13), Rhod Gray (5.05), Andy Smith (5.06, 5.08, 5.10,

---

[49] Included here are details of 'Christmas Special 2010', the *Doctor Who Confidential* episode that accompanied 'A Christmas Carol', as it had its debut transmission during the year covered by this book. However, this did not form part of Series Five – it was effectively made at the start of production on Series Six – and was not included in the Complete Series Five DVD/Blu-Ray box set.

[50] Where an episode number (or more than one) appears in brackets after a person's name in the listing, this means that they were credited only on the episode (or episodes) indicated. Otherwise, the person concerned was credited on all 14 episodes. 'Christmas Special 2010' is denoted as 6.00.

5.11, 5.13), Clay Westervelt (5.10)

Sound: Will Planitzer (5.01, 5.02, 5.03, 5.04, 5.05, 5.08, 5.09, 5.10), Jon Thomas, Johnny Stothert (5.03, 5.06), Rob Kreeger (5.06, 5.08, 5.10), Rhodri Browning (5.07, 5.10, 5.11), Cheryl Jones (5.07), Jim Siler (5.10), Steve Hoy (5.11, 5.13), Kevin Meredith (6.00), Gabriel Scott (6.00)

Runner: James Bowen (all except 6.00), Claire Riley (all except 6.00), Lee Wood (5.01, 5.02, 5.03, 5.04, 5.05, 5.06, 5.07), Ryan Simpson (6.00)

Edit Assistant: Amy McCann (6.00)

Researcher: Matthew Andrews (all except 5.02, 5.03, 5.08), Ian Osprey (5.01, 5.02, 5.03), Rob Wootton (5.03, 5.06, 5.07, 5.08, 5.11, 6.00), Stuart Laws (5.06, 5.07, 5.08, 5.09, 5.10, 5.11, 5.12, 5.13)

Assistant Producer: Tracy Comer (5.01), Paul Symonds (5.01, 5.04, 5.05, 5.10, 5.11), Hannah Williams (all except 5.06, 6.00), James Brailsford (5.07, 5.08, 5.12), Ian Hay (6.00), Donovan Keogh (6.00)

Production Team Assistant: Emma Chapman (all except 6.00), Ruby Kedge (6.00)

Production Accountant: Kevin Rickwood

Production Co-ordinator: Megan Pinches, Rhiannon Dew (5.06, 5.07, 5.10)

Production Manager: Katy Cartwright

Production Executive: Stan Matthews

Online Editor: Nick Kershaw (5.02, 5.04), Jeremy Lott (all except 5.01, 5.02), Keith Ware (5.10)

Colourist: Jon Everett (5.01, 5.02, 5.03, 5.08, 5.09, 5.10, 5.12, 5.13), Matt Mullins (5.04, 5.05, 5.06, 5.07, 5.11, 6.00)

Dubbing Mixer: Mark Ferda

Editor[51]: Gary Skipton (5.01, 5.04, 5.08), Mike Crawford (5.02, 5.03, 5.10), Anya Lewis (5.05), John Parker (5.06, 5.13), Nick Kershaw (5.07), Rahim Mastafa (5.09, 6.00), Rob Mansell (5.10, 5.11, 5.12), Lizzie Minnion (6.00)

Edit Producer: James Brailsford (5.02, 5.09, 5.13), Paul Symonds (5.03, 5.07), Tracy Comer (5.04, 5.05), Hannah Williams (5.06. 6.00), Ian Hay (5.08, 5.12), Nathan Landeg (5.10, 5.11, 5.12)

Executive Producer: Mark Cossey

Executive Producer for *Doctor Who*: Steven Moffat, Piers Wenger, Beth Willis

Producer: Zoë Rushton

Series Producer: Gillane Seaborne

BBC Wales

## EPISODE GUIDE

The episode durations quoted below are for the full versions as originally transmitted (not the shorter, *Confidential Cutdown* versions used for most repeat screenings and DVD/Blu-Ray releases).

---

[51] Role credited on 6.00 as 'Offline Editor'.

CRACKS IN TIME

## 5.01 - CALL ME THE DOCTOR

DEBUT TRANSMISSION DETAILS

BBC Three[52]
Date: 3 April 2010. Scheduled time: 7.25 pm.
Duration: 43' 44"

PUBLICITY BLURB

Behind-the-scenes look at the making of *Doctor Who*, capturing all the backstage treats from Matt Smith's first action-packed episode and giving a real 'getting to know you' taster of life as the Doctor. There's a *Cribs*-style tour of the TARDIS with Matt and production designer Edward Thomas, a glimpse of the episode one read-through and an insight into life on set as the nation's favourite Time Lord. Narrated by Alex Price and featuring interviews with Matt Smith, Karen Gillan, Steven Moffat.

## 5.02 - ALL ABOUT THE GIRL

DEBUT TRANSMISSION DETAILS

BBC Three[53]
Date: 10 April 2010. Scheduled time: 7.00 pm.
Duration: 43' 07"

PUBLICITY BLURB

An in-depth look at new companion Amy Pond and her adventures with the Doctor onboard the sinister Starship UK. Find out just what makes the sinister Smilers tick and get right in the thick of the action with actress Karen Gillan. Also, the show goes behind the mask to explore the secret of Liz 10 as Oscar-nominated actress Sophie Okonedo talks about creating this extraordinary character. Narrated by Alex Price and featuring interviews with Matt Smith, Karen Gillan and Sophie Okonedo.

## 5.03 - WAR GAMES

DEBUT TRANSMISSION DETAILS

BBC Three[54]

---

[52] 'Call Me the Doctor' was not simulcast on BBC HD. Instead, the high definition channel scheduled it for 8.40 pm the same evening.
[53] 'All About the Girl' was not simulcast on BBC HD. Instead, the high definition channel scheduled it for midnight the same evening.
[54] 'War Games' was not simulcast on BBC HD. Instead, the high definition channel scheduled it for 9.10 pm the same evening.

Date: 17 April 2010. Scheduled time: 7.15 pm.
Duration: 43' 21"

PUBLICITY BLURB

There's the paint job to end all paint jobs as the Daleks come storming back onto British TV. Writer Mark Gatiss meets the curator of the Cabinet War Rooms and Churchill Museum to see what the conditions were like at the epicentre of the British war effort. Backstage, Ian McNeice captures the essence of Winston Churchill on the screen and we find out how Mark went about writing the man behind the myth. Narrated by Alex Price and featuring interviews with Matt Smith, Karen Gillan, Mark Gatiss and Ian McNeice.

**5.04 – EYES WIDE OPEN**

DEBUT TRANSMISSION DETAILS

BBC Three[55]
Date: 24 April 2010. Scheduled time: 7.05 pm.
Duration: 43' 49"

PUBLICITY BLURB

Alex Kingston, who plays River Song, talks about the highs and lows of being suspended on wires, and there's a look back with cast and crew at the Doctor and River Song's relationship so far. The Weeping Angels get a makeover for their long-awaited comeback and Matt Smith is photographed, scanned and 'rotoscoped' for the new online *Doctor Who Adventure Games*. Narrated by Alex Price and featuring interviews with Matt Smith and Karen Gillan.

**5.05 – BLINDED BY THE LIGHT**

DEBUT TRANSMISSION DETAILS

BBC Three[56]
Date: 1 May 2010. Scheduled time: 7.10 pm.
Duration: 44' 14"

PUBLICITY BLURB

Actress Karen Gillan tells how the 'Crack in Time' series story arc fits into this episode, while writer Steven Moffat describes how the very first crack in time was actually in his son's bedroom wall. As we prepare to say goodbye (for now) to

---

[55] 'Eyes Wide Open' was not simulcast on BBC HD. Instead, the high definition channel scheduled it for 8.25 pm the same evening.
[56] 'Blinded by the Light' was not simulcast on BBC HD. Instead, the high definition channel scheduled it for 8.10 pm the same evening.

River Song, the cast and crew examine the character's shady story so far and speculate ...

## 5.06 – DEATH IN VENICE

DEBUT TRANSMISSION DETAILS

BBC Three[57]
Date: 8 May 2010. Scheduled time: 7.00 pm.
Duration: 41' 46"

PUBLICITY BLURB

The cast and crew get a trip abroad. But not to Venice, because as episode writer Toby Whithouse explains, modern day Venice doesn't really look like 16th Century Venice anymore. Instead the episode is shot in Trogir, a small medieval town in Croatia that is the spitting image of 16th Century Venice. However, Matt Smith and Toby Whithouse do take a trip to Venice and meet up with Francesco Da Mosto, who takes them on his boat and gives them a unique tour to illustrate how the world's most beautiful city works as a back drop to Toby's fiction. Narrated by Alex Price and featuring interviews with Matt Smith, Karen Gillan and Francesco Da Mosto.

## 5.07 – ARTHURIAN LEGEND

DEBUT TRANSMISSION DETAILS

BBC Three[58]
Date: 15 May 2010. Scheduled time: 7.10 pm.
Duration: 43' 28"

PUBLICITY BLURB

The TARDIS trio are thrown into two competing worlds that are not what they seem. The Dream Lord has created a dilemma to be solved, and Arthur Darvill, who plays Rory, is on hand to explain how the three companions set about finding out which world is really real. *Confidential* is on set to see Rory and Amy's future in Leadworth, complete with pregnancy, ponytails and predatory pensioners. Arthur turns stunt supremo, gliding through the air and picking a fight with an old lady. We also see the TARDIS from a safe haven to an ice-bound death trap, hurtling towards an icy end. Featuring exclusive access to the cast and crew, Arthur takes us through how an episode of *Doctor Who* is made, from read-through to wrap.

---

[57] 'Death in Venice' was not simulcast on BBC HD. Instead, the high definition channel scheduled it for 8.10 pm the same evening.
[58] 'Arthurian Legend' was not simulcast on BBC HD. Instead, the high definition channel scheduled it for 8.10 pm the same evening.

## 5.08 – AFTER EFFECTS

DEBUT TRANSMISSION DETAILS

BBC Three[59]
Date: 22 May 2010. Scheduled time: 7.00 pm.
Duration: 41' 38"

PUBLICITY BLURB

Behind-the-scenes series about the making of *Doctor Who*. Includes a journey through the production process of a *Doctor Who* episode from cutting room to living room.

## 5.09 – WHAT GOES ON TOUR …

DEBUT TRANSMISSION DETAILS

BBC Three[60]
Date: 29 May 2010. Scheduled time: 7.50 pm.
Duration: 43' 10"

PUBLICITY BLURB

The *Confidential* cameras follow the *Doctor Who* team as they travel the length and breadth of the UK to launch the new series, getting up close and personal with Matt Smith and Karen Gillan as they journey from Belfast to London, taking in emotional whistle-stop visits to their home towns along the way. There's exclusive access and personal insights from everyone involved with this unique tour. Digging deeper into the making of episode nine, there's a look at the creation of the stunning underground city and the lowdown on what it took to create the Earth-shattering climax to this epic adventure

## 5.10 – A BRUSH WITH GENIUS

DEBUT TRANSMISSION DETAILS

BBC Three/BBC HD
Date: 5 June 2010. Scheduled time: 7.30 pm.
Duration: 41' 54"

PUBLICITY BLURB

The Doctor and Amy team up with artist Vincent van Gogh, the cast and crew

---

[59] 'After Effects' was not simulcast on BBC HD. Instead, the high definition channel scheduled it for 8.00 pm the same evening.
[60] 'What Goes on Tour …' was not simulcast on BBC HD. Instead, the high definition channel scheduled it for 11.20 pm the same evening.

travel to Croatia to see if they can recreate 19th Century France in 21st Century Trogir, and actor Tony Curran takes a tour of the J Paul Getty Museum in Los Angeles to look at one of Van Gogh's most valuable paintings.

## 5.11 – EXTRA TIME

DEBUT TRANSMISSION DETAILS

BBC Three/BBC HD
Date: 12 June 2010. Scheduled time: 7.30 pm.
Duration: 43' 50"

PUBLICITY BLURB

*Confidential* gets on set and on side with James Corden as the Doctor decides it's time for a new housemate and ends up as the star of the local pub football team. Karen Gillan gets starry eyed when she visits the Royal Greenwich Observatory to meet space scientist Maggie Aderin and finds out what the time really is. Backstage, the Doctor is ready to find out what's lurking upstairs in Craig's house.

Note: This episode was immediately followed by a 30-second trailer for the first of *Doctor Who: The Adventure Games* (which is not included in the duration given above).

## 5.12 – ALIEN ABDUCTION

DEBUT TRANSMISSION DETAILS

BBC Three/BBC HD
Date: 19 June 2010. Scheduled time: 7.30 pm.
Duration: 44' 27"

PUBLICITY BLURB

The crew set out in the middle of a cold winter's night to film on the ancient site of Stonehenge, and take the ride of their lives to discover the true origin of the Pandorica.

## 5.13 – OUT OF TIME

DEBUT TRANSMISSION DETAILS

BBC Three/BBC HD
Date: 26 June 2010. Scheduled time: 7.00 pm.
Duration: 43' 26"

PUBLICITY BLURB

*Confidential* takes a closer look at the Earth-shattering action of the series finale, helping viewers to make sense of the epic series of events that unfold. And in an exciting departure, Matt Smith and Karen Gillan take a bite out of the Big Apple to help launch the new series in the USA. Featuring interviews with Matt and Karen.

## 6.00 – CHRISTMAS SPECIAL 2010

DEBUT TRANSMISSION DETAILS

BBC Three/BBC HD
Date: 25 December 2010. Scheduled time: 7.00 pm.
Duration: 56′ 04″

PUBLICITY BLURB

All the behind-the-scenes merriment of a good old-fashioned *Doctor Who* Christmas. Meet the Doctor and his companions as they set Cardiff alight and go backstage with the stars of the Dickensian Christmas special. Michael Gambon talks of swapping his wizard's wand for a taste of the Doctor's time-travelling magic and Katherine Jenkins waxes lyrical about her acting debut. Plus interviews with Matt Smith, Michael Gambon, Katherine Jenkins and Steven Moffat.

# APPENDIX D
# RATINGS AND RANKINGS

Back in 2008, Series Four of *Doctor Who* gained a superb average BBC One debut-transmission rating of 8.05 million viewers and ended on a remarkable high, its finale, 'Journey's End', attracting an amazing 10.57 million people and capturing the number one spot in the weekly viewing chart for the first time in the show's long history. The subsequent run of five specials in the 'gap year' ending on 1 January 2010 also did exceptionally well, winning an average BBC One debut-transmission audience of 11.19 million. With Series Five marking the arrival of a new lead actor and production team, a burning question for many fans – and no doubt for the new lead actor and production team themselves – was whether the show would be able to maintain such a phenomenal level of success, or whether its popularity would start to wane.

This Appendix is subdivided into five sections, revealing:

i) the facts of how the 14 episodes covered by this book – the 13 episodes of Series Five plus 'A Christmas Carol' – performed in terms of their ratings, audience shares, chart positions, appreciation index (AI) figures and other viewer reaction data;

ii) the relative popularity of the 14 episodes in terms of their ratings, AI figures and fan rankings;

iii) the comparative picture of how the figures for these 14 episodes measure up to those for the previous four full series of 21st Century *Doctor Who* (omitting the 'gap year' specials, owing to their atypical transmission pattern);

iv) the main conclusions that may be drawn from the data presented in sections i) to iii); and

v) the ratings and AI figures for the 2010 run of *Doctor Who Confidential*.

i) THE FACTS

The table below lists, for the BBC One, BBC HD [61] and BBC Three debut transmissions of each of the 14 episodes covered in this book: the estimated total number of viewers aged four and over (corrected and adjusted to include those who recorded the episode to watch within the week following transmission) in millions (RATING); percentage share of the total TV audience at the time of transmission (SHARE); chart position amongst all programmes transmitted the same day on the same channel (D); overall chart position amongst all programmes transmitted the same day on all terrestrial channels (for the BBC One transmissions [62]) or all digital channels (for the BBC HD and BBC Three transmissions) (D/O); chart position amongst all programmes transmitted the same week (Monday to Sunday inclusive) on the same channel (W); overall chart position amongst all programmes transmitted the same week (Monday to Sunday) on all terrestrial channels (for the BBC One transmissions [63]) or all digital channels (for the BBC HD and BBC Three transmissions) (W/O); and the audience AI as a percentage. The entries marked n/k are not known, as the relevant figures were too low to be recorded in the available data.

---

[61] For 'A Christmas Carol', the BBC One HD figure is given rather than the BBC HD figure. BBC One HD was launched on 3 November 2010, and all *Doctor Who* episodes from this Christmas special onwards would have their HD transmission debuts on that channel rather than on BBC HD.

[62] Includes BBC One HD for 'A Christmas Carol'.

[63] Includes BBC One HD for 'A Christmas Carol'.

| EPISODE | CHANNEL | RATING | SHARE | D | D/O | W | W/O | AI |
|---|---|---|---|---|---|---|---|---|
| 'The Eleventh Hour' | BBC One | 9.59 | 42 | 1st | 1st | 2nd | 3rd | 86 |
| | BBC HD | 0.49 | | 1st | n/k | 1st | n/k | |
| | BBC Three | 0.74 | 3 | 4th | 7th | 13th | 30th | 82 |
| 'The Beast Below' | BBC One | 7.93 | 39 | 1st | 1st | 5th | 10th | 86 |
| | BBC HD | 0.49 | | 1st | n/k | 1st | n/k | |
| | BBC Three | 0.82 | 3 | 1st | 4th | 4th | 16th | 87 |
| 'Victory of the Daleks' | BBC One | 7.82 | 37 | 1st | 2nd | 4th | 11th | 84 |
| | BBC HD++ | 0.38 | n/k | 1st | n/k | 1st | n/k | n/k |
| | BBC Three | 0.62 | 2 | n/k | n/k | n/k | n/k | 84 |
| 'The Time of Angels' | BBC One | 8.13 | 41 | 1st | 2nd | 5th | 8th | 87 |
| | BBC HD | 0.46 | | 1st | n/k | 1st | n/k | |
| | BBC Three | 0.60 | 2 | n/k | n/k | n/k | n/k | 89 |
| 'Flesh and Stone' | BBC One | 8.02 | 38 | 1st | 2nd | 5th | 10th | 86 |
| | BBC HD | 0.48 | | 1st | n/k | 1st | n/k | |
| | BBC Three | 0.67 | 3 | 1st | 10th | 10th | 30th | 91 |
| 'The Vampires of Venice' | BBC One | 7.28 | 35 | 1st | 2nd | 5th | 12th | 86 |
| | BBC HD | 0.40 | | 1st | n/k | 1st | n/k | |
| | BBC Three | 0.64 | 2 | n/k | n/k | n/k | n/k | 87 |
| 'Amy's Choice' | BBC One | 7.06 | 37 | 1st | 2nd | 6th | 13th | 84 |
| | BBC HD | 0.49 | | 1st | n/k | 1st | n/k | |
| | BBC Three | 0.63 | 2 | n/k | n/k | n/k | n/k | 89 |
| 'The Hungry Earth' | BBC One | 6.01 | 40 | 3rd | 3rd | 9th | 19th | 86 |
| | BBC HD | 0.48 | | 1st | n/k | 1st | n/k | |
| | BBC Three | 0.59 | 3 | n/k | n/k | n/k | n/k | 90 |
| 'Cold Blood' | BBC One | 7.04 | 32 | 1st | 2nd | 4th | 9th | 85 |
| | BBC HD | 0.45 | | 1st | n/k | 1st | n/k | |
| | BBC Three | 0.33 | 2 | n/k | n/k | n/k | n/k | 87 |
| 'Vincent and the Doctor' | BBC One | 6.29 | 36 | 1st | 2nd | 2nd | 17th | 86 |
| | BBC HD | 0.47 | | 1st | n/k | 1st | n/k | |
| | BBC Three | 0.54 | 3 | n/k | n/k | n/k | n/k | 86 |
| 'The Lodger' | BBC One | 5.98 | 29 | 1st | 2nd | 6th | 20th | 87 |
| | BBC HD | 0.46 | | 1st | n/k | 2nd | n/k | |
| | BBC Three | 0.47 | 2 | n/k | n/k | n/k | n/k | 89 |
| 'The Pandorica Opens' | BBC One | 6.94 | 37 | 1st | 1st | 5th | 10th | 88 |
| | BBC HD | 0.64 | | 1st | n/k | 1st | n/k | |
| | BBC Three | 0.52 | 3 | n/k | n/k | n/k | n/k | 91 |
| 'The Big Bang' | BBC One | 6.12 | 37 | 1st | 1st | 9th | 10th | 89 |
| | BBC HD | 0.58 | | 1st | n/k | 5th | n/k | |
| | BBC Three | 0.72 | 4 | 3rd | 8th | 9th | 25th | 91 |
| 'A Christmas Carol' | BBC One | 10.81 | 42 | 3rd | 3rd | 3rd | 3rd | 83 |
| | BBC One HD | 1.30 | | | | | | |
| | BBC Three | 0.59 | 4 | n/k | n/k | n/k | n/k | 83 |

++ Not simulcast with BBC One but shown later the same evening.

# APPENDIX D: RATINGS AND RANKINGS

Source for viewing figures: Broadcasters' Audience Research Board (BARB)
Source for AI figures: BBC

The full ratings statistics produced by BARB for the main BBC One transmissions (which go into too fine a level of detail to be reproduced in their entirety here) reveal that *Doctor Who* consistently scored well above the average for drama programmes under a range of viewer response headings including 'It was high quality', 'It was original and different', 'It was entertaining' and 'I made a special effort to watch'. On the other hand, it generally scored slightly below the drama average under headings including 'I learnt something new', 'It was thought-provoking' and 'It was inspiring' – although 'Vincent and the Doctor' and 'The Big Bang' were exceptions to the rule, scoring just above the drama average under all three of those headings, and 'The Pandorica Opens' also did better than average under 'It was thought-provoking'. The male/female split in the show's audience over the course of the series was almost exactly 50/50, whereas for BBC One dramas in general it averages 36/64. The biggest sections of the show's audience came in the 4-15 and 35-44 age ranges, each of which made up about 20% of the total on average. The 45-54 age range was not far behind, with 18% of the total on average. The smallest section was in the 16-24 age range, which accounted for about 9% of the total on average. This means that, on average, 71% of the show's viewers were over the age of 24. No doubt many of these would have been parents watching with children – indicating that the show was continuing to meet its family-viewing remit – although clearly, as in previous years, it also had a large adult following.

For each transmission of each TV programme on the channels it covers, BARB gives not only a final ratings figure but also an initial 'overnight' figure, which is generally available the next day after the transmission. The overnight figure indicates how many viewers watched the programme 'live' on transmission, whereas the final figure, which usually becomes available about eight days later, is adjusted to include also those who recorded it to watch within the following week. The difference between the overnight and the final ratings figures for a given programme thus shows how many people 'time-shifted' their viewing of that programme.[64] Table Two records what the time-shift was (in millions of viewers) for the BBC One debut transmissions[65] of each of the 2010 run of *Doctor Who* episodes.

---

[64] Occasionally other adjustments and corrections are made between the overnight and final ratings figures for a programme, but these are generally minor compared with the time-shift factor.
[65] Including BBC One HD for 'A Christmas Carol'

TABLE TWO – TIME-SHIFT

| EPISODE | OVERNIGHT RATING | FINAL [66] RATING | TIME-SHIFT |
|---|---|---|---|
| 'The Eleventh Hour' | 7.7 | 9.6 | 1.9 |
| 'The Beast Below' | 6.7 | 7.9 | 1.2 |
| 'Victory of the Daleks' | 6.2 | 7.8 | 1.6 |
| 'The Time of Angels' | 6.8 | 8.1 | 1.3 |
| 'Flesh and Stone' | 6.9 | 8.0 | 1.1 |
| 'The Vampires of Venice' | 6.2 | 7.3 | 1.1 |
| 'Amy's Choice' | 6.2 | 7.1 | 0.9 |
| 'The Hungry Earth' | 4.5 | 6.0 | 1.5 |
| 'Cold Blood' | 5.7 | 7.0 | 1.3 |
| 'Vincent and the Doctor' | 5.0 | 6.3 | 1.3 |
| 'The Lodger' | 4.6 | 6.0 | 1.4 |
| 'The Pandorica Opens' | 5.9 | 6.9 | 1.0 |
| 'The Big Bang' | 5.1 | 6.1 | 1.0 |
| 'A Christmas Carol' | 10.3 | 12.2 | 1.9 |
| **AVERAGE** | **6.3** | **7.6** | **1.3** |

Source: Broadcasters' Audience Research Board (BARB)

Table Three indicates how many viewers (in millions) each episode attracted not only on its BBC One[67], BBC HD and BBC Three debut transmissions[68] but also on its first BBC Three repeat and through hits within the same week on the BBC's interactive iPlayer service. This gives an overall total viewing figure – otherwise known as audience reach – for the whole period.[69] The figures for 'A Christmas Carol' are not strictly comparable to those for the other 13 episodes as, being a Christmas special, it was naturally affected by seasonal factors, and also had a BBC One repeat, nine days after its debut (i.e. just outside the seven day period usually covered here), rather than a BBC Three repeat. Nevertheless, the figures are included for completeness.

---

[66] Figures given to just one decimal place here, as the overnight ratings are available only in that form.

[67] Including BBC One HD for 'A Christmas Carol'.

[68] The BBC One and BBC HD debut transmissions were always on a Saturday evening, with the BBC Three debut transmission coming a day later, i.e. on a Sunday evening. The first BBC Three repeat was the following Friday evening, except in the cases of 'The Pandorica Opens' and 'A Christmas Carol', neither of which had a BBC Three repeat within the relevant period.

[69] General research into viewing figures has shown that the great majority of viewers who tune in for repeats are additional, i.e. that they have not already seen the programme on one or more of its earlier transmissions. Some sources suggest that the proportion is at least 90 percent.

APPENDIX D: RATINGS AND RANKINGS

TABLE THREE – TOTAL AUDIENCE REACH

| EPISODE | BBC ONE DEBUT | BBC HD DEBUT | BBC THREE DEBUT | BBC THREE REPEAT | BBC iPLAYER | ALL |
|---|---|---|---|---|---|---|
| 'The Eleventh Hour' | 9.59 | 0.49 | 0.74 | 0.57 | 1.27 | 12.66 |
| 'The Beast Below' | 7.93 | 0.49 | 0.82 | 0.53 | 1.16 | 10.93 |
| 'Victory of the Daleks' | 7.82 | 0.38 | 0.62 | 0.39 | 1.01 | 10.22 |
| 'The Time of Angels' | 8.13 | 0.46 | 0.60 | 0.34 | 1.16 | 10.69 |
| 'Flesh and Stone' | 8.02 | 0.48 | 0.67 | 0.28 | 1.08 | 10.53 |
| 'The Vampires of Venice' | 7.28 | 0.40 | 0.64 | 0.30 | 1.04 | 9.66 |
| 'Amy's Choice' | 7.06 | 0.49 | 0.63 | 0.28 | 1.27 | 9.73 |
| 'The Hungry Earth' | 6.01 | 0.48 | 0.59 | 0.39 | 1.02 | 8.49 |
| 'Cold Blood' | 7.04 | 0.45 | 0.33 | 0.37 | 0.93 | 9.12 |
| 'Vincent and the Doctor' | 6.29 | 0.47 | 0.54 | 0.40 | 0.95 | 8.65 |
| 'The Lodger' | 5.98 | 0.46 | 0.47 | 0.28 | 1.49 | 8.68 |
| 'The Pandorica Opens' | 6.94 | 0.64 | 0.52 | n/a | 1.22 | 9.32 |
| 'The Big Bang' | 6.12 | 0.58 | 0.72 | 0.68 | 1.23 | 9.33 |
| **Average over 13 episodes** | **7.25** | **0.48** | **0.61** | **0.37** | **1.14** | **9.85** |

| EPISODE | BBC ONE DEBUT [70] | BBC HD DEBUT [71] | BBC THREE DEBUT | BBC ONE REPEAT | BBC iPLAYER | ALL |
|---|---|---|---|---|---|---|
| 'A Christmas Carol' | 12.21 | 0.07 | 0.59 | 1.70 | 0.74 | 15.31 |

Source for viewing figures: Broadcasters' Audience Research Board (BARB)

[70] Includes BBC One HD.
[71] Although this episode had its HD debut on the recently-launched BBC One HD, simulcast with BBC One, it was also repeated on BBC HD on Monday 27 December 2010.

Source for iPlayer figures: BBC.

Figures for total iPlayer hits (in millions) across the duration of the whole series were as follows:

TABLE FOUR – TOTAL iPLAYER HITS

| EPISODE | DAYS AVAILABLE | iPLAYER HITS |
|---|---|---|
| 'The Eleventh Hour' | 93 | 2.18 |
| 'The Beast Below' | 86 | 1.64 |
| 'Victory of the Daleks' | 79 | 1.47 |
| 'The Time of Angels' | 72 | 1.53 |
| 'Flesh and Stone' | 65 | 1.41 |
| 'The Vampires of Venice' | 58 | 1.34 |
| 'Amy's Choice' | 51 | 1.53 |
| 'The Hungry Earth' | 44 | 1.23 |
| 'Cold Blood' | 37 | 1.15 |
| 'Vincent and the Doctor' | 30 | 1.18 |
| 'The Lodger' | 23 | 1.73 |
| 'The Pandorica Opens' | 21 | 1.44 |
| 'The Big Bang' | 14 | 1.41 |
| 'A Christmas Carol' | 14 | 0.81 |

Source: BBC

An indication of how the episodes shaped up in the estimation of dedicated fans can be gleaned from the online episode polls conducted on Gallifrey Base – the most popular *Doctor Who* fan forum on the internet – at www.gallifreybase.com. An average of 4,618 voters participated in these polls, ranging from a low of 3,834 for 'The Hungry Earth' to a high of 6,028 for 'The Eleventh Hour'. Each episode was given a mark of between one and ten by each voter, with ten being the highest. The percentages – or 'fan AIs' – in the table below have been calculated by adding together the total number of marks received by each episode (as of 2 March 2012) and dividing by the maximum that could have been achieved if everyone who voted had given the episode a ten.

TABLE FIVE – FAN APPRECIATION INDEX

| EPISODE | FAN AI |
|---|---|
| 'The Eleventh Hour' | 83 |
| 'The Beast Below' | 73 |
| 'Victory of the Daleks' | 65 |
| 'The Time of Angels' | 87 |
| 'Flesh and Stone' | 86 |
| 'The Vampires of Venice' | 74 |
| 'Amy's Choice' | 81 |
| 'The Hungry Earth' | 74 |

## APPENDIX D: RATINGS AND RANKINGS

| 'Cold Blood' | 75 |
|---|---|
| 'Vincent and the Doctor' | 84 |
| 'The Lodger' | 76 |
| 'The Pandorica Opens' | 90 |
| 'The Big Bang' | 87 |
| 'A Christmas Carol' | 79 |
| **Average** | **80** |

Source: Gallifrey Base

ii) RELATIVE POPULARITY

The total reach figures set out in Table Three above indicate that the ranking of the episodes from most-watched to least-watched was as follows:

TABLE SIX – RANKING BY TOTAL AUDIENCE REACH

| 1 | 'A Christmas Carol' |
|---|---|
| 2 | 'The Eleventh Hour' |
| 3 | 'The Beast Below' |
| 4 | 'The Time of Angels' |
| 5 | 'Flesh and Stone' |
| 6 | 'Victory of the Daleks' |
| 7 | 'Amy's Choice' |
| 8 | 'The Vampires of Venice' |
| 9 | 'The Big Bang' |
| 10 | 'The Pandorica Opens' |
| 11 | 'Cold Blood' |
| 12 | 'The Lodger' |
| 13 | 'Vincent and the Doctor' |
| 14 | 'The Hungry Earth' |

Based on the AI figures for the BBC One/BBC HD debut transmissions, the general viewing public's order of preference for the episodes, working downwards from favourite to least favourite, was:

TABLE SEVEN – RANKING BY DEBUT TRANSMISSION AI FIGURES

| 1 | 'The Big Bang' |
|---|---|
| 2 | 'The Pandorica Opens' |
| 3= | 'The Time of Angels' |
| 3= | 'The Lodger' |
| 5= | 'The Eleventh Hour' |
| 5= | 'The Beast Below' |
| 5= | 'Flesh and Stone' |
| 5= | 'The Vampires of Venice' |

| 5= | 'The Hungry Earth' |
|---|---|
| 5= | 'Vincent and the Doctor' |
| 11 | 'Cold Blood' |
| 12= | 'Victory of the Daleks' |
| 12= | 'Amy's Choice' |
| 14 | 'A Christmas Carol' |

TABLE EIGHT – RANKING BY FAN AI FIGURES

Based on the figures in Table Five, the fans' order of preference for the episodes was:

| 1 | 'The Pandorica Opens' |
|---|---|
| 2= | 'The Time of Angels' |
| 2= | 'The Big Bang' |
| 4 | 'Flesh and Stone' |
| 5 | 'Vincent and the Doctor' |
| 6 | 'The Eleventh Hour' |
| 7 | 'Amy's Choice' |
| 8 | 'A Christmas Carol' |
| 9 | 'The Lodger' |
| 10 | 'Cold Blood' |
| 11= | 'The Vampires of Venice' |
| 11= | 'The Hungry Earth' |
| 13 | 'The Beast Below' |
| 14 | 'Victory of the Daleks' |

To conclude this section, set out below, for what it's worth, is this author's own ranking of the episodes, again working downwards from favourite to least favourite – although I should perhaps add that my views on this tend to change from time to time!

TABLE NINE – RANKING BY AUTHOR'S PREFERENCE

| 1 | 'Vincent and the Doctor' |
|---|---|
| 2 | 'Amy's Choice' |
| 3 | 'The Big Bang' |
| 4 | 'The Pandorica Opens' |
| 5 | 'The Time of Angels' |
| 6 | 'Flesh and Stone' |
| 7 | 'A Christmas Carol' |
| 8 | 'The Lodger' |
| 9 | 'Cold Blood' |
| 10 | 'The Eleventh Hour' |
| 11 | 'The Hungry Earth' |
| 12 | 'The Vampires of Venice' |

APPENDIX D: RATINGS AND RANKINGS

| 13 | 'The Beast Below' |
| 14 | 'Victory of the Daleks' |

## iii) COMPARISON WITH PREVIOUS SERIES

Table Ten shows how the show's average ratings (in millions), audience shares (in percentages) and weekly overall chart placings have changed over the course of the five full series up to the end of 2010. (The Christmas specials are not included in these figures, due to their exceptional nature.)

TABLE TEN – COMPARISON OF AVERAGE RATINGS, SHARES AND CHART PLACES

| SERIES | AVERAGE RATING BBC ONE | AVERAGE RATING BBC THREE | AVERAGE TOTAL REACH | AVERAGE SHARE BBC ONE | AVERAGE CHART PLACE |
|---|---|---|---|---|---|
| Series One | 7.95 | 0.587[72] | 8.68 | 40 | 17 |
| Series Two | 7.71 | 0.63 | 8.71 | 41 | 12 |
| Series Three | 7.55 | 0.92 | 8.88 | 39 | 13 |
| Series Four | 8.05 | 1.08 | 10.54 | 39 | 10 |
| Series Five | 7.25 | 0.61 | 9.85 | 37 | 12 |

Source: Broadcasters' Audience Research Board (BARB)

Table Eleven sets out the series-by-series comparison of AI figures for the BBC One debut transmissions. (Again, the Christmas specials have been omitted.)

TABLE ELEVEN – COMPARISON OF BBC ONE AI FIGURES

| SERIES | LOW | HIGH | SPREAD | AVERAGE |
|---|---|---|---|---|
| Series One[73] | 76 | 89 | 13 | 82 |
| Series Two | 76 | 89 | 13 | 84 |
| Series Three | 84 | 88 | 4 | 86 |

[72] As for the other series, this is the average figure for the main Sunday night BBC Three transmissions. However, all bar the first four episodes of Series One actually had their BBC Three debut transmissions the previous day, in a late night slot, where they received an average viewing figure of 0.20 million, as reflected in the average total reach figure.
[73] For Series One, final AI figures are available only for the first six episodes; initial, less accurate, figures have been used for the other seven episodes.

237

| Series Four | 85 | 91 | 6 | 88 |
|---|---|---|---|---|
| Series Five | 83 | 89 | 6 | 86 |

Source: BBC

Table Twelve sets out the equivalent figures for the BBC Three debut transmissions.

TABLE TWELVE – COMPARISON OF BBC THREE AI FIGURES

| SERIES | LOW | HIGH | SPREAD | AVERAGE |
|---|---|---|---|---|
| Series One | n/a | n/a | n/a | n/a |
| Series Two[74] | 79 | 91 | 12 | 86 |
| Series Three[75] | 84 | 90 | 6 | 87 |
| Series Four[76] | 88 | 93 | 5 | 90 |
| Series Five | 82 | 91 | 9 | 88 |

Source: BBC

Lastly, Table Thirteen gives the series-by-series comparison of fan AI figures, based on the polls conducted on the forums of Gallifrey Base and its *de facto* forerunner Outpost Gallifrey. (Christmas specials are omitted once more.)

TABLE THIRTEEN – COMPARISON OF FAN AI FIGURES

| SERIES | LOW | HIGH | SPREAD | AVERAGE |
|---|---|---|---|---|
| Series One | 68 | 93 | 25 | 82 |
| Series Two | 65 | 93 | 28 | 82 |
| Series Three | 71 | 95 | 24 | 81 |
| Series Four | 72 | 92 | 20 | 81 |
| Series Five | 65 | 90 | 25 | 80 |

Source: Outpost Gallifrey/Gallifrey Base

iv) CONCLUSIONS

The main conclusion to be drawn from the figures in Table One is that, in 2010, *Doctor Who* continued to perform extraordinarily well. Over the course of Series Five, it was almost always BBC One's top-rated programme of the Saturday, and always within its top ten-rated programmes of the week. It often outstripped all of ITV's Saturday programming too, with only the hugely popular light entertainment show *Britain's Got Talent* able to give it a real run for its money. Its average weekly chart position of twelfth – with many of the higher places taken up

---

[74] Based on the 12 episodes for which figures are available.
[75] Based on the ten episodes for which figures are available.
[76] Based on the six episodes for which figures are available.

by multiple episodes of the soap operas *EastEnders* and *Coronation Street* – also showed what a huge hit it continued to be. As in previous years, the Christmas special had extremely good figures too. It was the third most-watched programme not only of Christmas Day but of the whole Christmas week. This was its top weekly chart position of the year, jointly with Matt Smith's introductory episode, 'The Eleventh Hour', which also had exceptionally good figures, as many viewers doubtless tuned in to see what the new Doctor would be like. Not only did large audiences watch the 2010 run of episodes, but they also greatly enjoyed what they saw, as demonstrated by the average AI figures of 86 on BBC One and 88 on BBC Three. [77] All in all, in Steven Moffat's first year in charge, *Doctor Who* unquestionably maintained and reinforced its position as a big-hitter in the ratings war, and one of the BBC's flagship drama productions.

As illustrated by Table Six, after the high of 'The Eleventh Hour', the overall ratings figures gradually decreased as Series Five progressed, then picked up again somewhat for the final two episodes. This mirrored what had happened in previous years, and it is indeed a typical pattern for drama series in general. A proportion of the viewers who tune in for the start of any new series are bound to find it is not to their taste and drift away, producing a dip in the figures, but often some of that lost ground is recovered over the last couple of episodes – particularly where, as in the case of Series Five, there is an ongoing element to the story – as even non-regular viewers may be curious to see how it ends.

One point brought out by Tables Six and Seven is that whereas 'A Christmas Carol' had the highest audience reach of all the 2010 episodes, it had the lowest AI figure. Again, this repeated a pattern seen previously, both in 2007 with 'The Runaway Bride' and in 2008 with 'Voyage of the Damned'. (In 2006, 'The Christmas Invasion' also had a relatively low AI figure, despite achieving the highest ratings of the year, although in that instance a couple of the regular series episodes had lower ones.) The probable reason for this is simply that the large Christmas Night audiences for these specials include a proportion of people who would not normally watch *Doctor Who* and who appreciate it rather less than regular viewers.

Some caution must be exercised in comparing the figures in Table Seven with those in Table Eight, because the BBC's official AI figures in the former reflect UK audience opinion about the quality of the episodes in relation to UK TV programmes in general, whereas the fan AI figures in the latter reflect worldwide fan opinion about the quality of the episodes in relation to *Doctor Who* in general – so, in other words, they are measuring slightly different things. That said, however, there can be seen to be some degree of correlation between the two sets of figures. 'The Time of Angels', 'The Pandorica Opens' and 'The Big Bang' come at or near the top in both tables, while 'Victory of the Daleks' comes at or near the bottom in both. (The same can also be said, indeed, of this author's own ranking of the episodes, as recorded in Table Nine.) It is therefore fair to conclude that 'The Time of Angels', 'The Pandorica Opens' and 'The Big Bang' were, overall, the most appreciated episodes of Series Five, and 'Victory of the Daleks' the least appreciated. 'Amy's Choice' and 'Vincent and the Doctor' seem to have been more

[77] Scores of 85 or over are officially considered 'excellent', and those of 90 or over 'exceptional'.

highly regarded by fans than by members of the general viewing public, whereas for 'The Lodger' the opposite is true.

One notable trend revealed by Table Ten is that the show's BBC One debut transmission viewers are making up a progressively smaller proportion of its total audience reach. For Series One the proportion was 91.6%, for Series Two it was 88.5%, for Series Three it was 85.0%, for Series Four it was 76.4%, and for Series Five it was 73.6%. This indicates that viewers are increasingly choosing to watch the episodes at times they find more convenient than on their first transmission – particularly by making more and more use of the BBC's iPlayer service, which went live on Christmas Day 2007, three months before the start of Series Four. The trend becomes even starker if one takes into account also the time-shift figures in Table Two, which indicate that on average some 17% of the viewers included in the BBC One debut transmission ratings figures for Series Five did not in fact catch the episodes live, but recorded them to watch later the same week. Although the time-shift figures for the earlier series are not given in the tables above, these have also increased significantly as the years have gone by. The equivalent average for Series One was a mere 8%.

The positive way of looking at this trend is that it simply reflects general changes in the way people in the UK choose to consume their TV programmes. Many viewers obviously enjoy *Doctor Who* sufficiently that even if it isn't convenient for them to watch a particular episode at the actual time of its debut transmission, they will still make an effort to catch up with it through other means at a later date. A more negative slant to put on the trend would be that, as time has gone by, *Doctor Who* has come to be regarded less and less as 'appointment to view' television that people make a real effort to watch 'live' at the earliest opportunity. *Doctor Who* does seem to gain consistently higher time-shift figures than other shows at a similar level of popularity, as evidenced by the fact that its weekly overall chart position tends to improve by several places between the overnight ratings figures and the final ones. It will, at any rate, be particularly interesting to see whether or not this trend continues in subsequent years.

Taken together, the figures in Tables Ten, Eleven and Twelve appear to show that *Doctor Who*'s overall popularity with the general viewing public increased slightly over the course of Series One to Four, only to fall a little for Series Five. Series Four still has the highest average audience reach, the highest average BBC One audience share and the highest average BBC One and BBC Three AI figures of all five series to the end of 2010. In all three cases, the figures for Series Five dropped back to around the same level as they were for Series Three. It would thus be fair to say that – leaving aside the 'gap year' specials of 2009/10 – Series Four represents the peak of *Doctor Who*'s general audience popularity to date.

Table Thirteen, on the other hand, suggests that, as far as the dedicated fans are concerned, Series One and Two still stand as the best so far of new-era *Doctor Who*, while Series Five brings up the rear by a small margin. 'Victory of the Daleks' joins Series Two's 'Fear Her' on an all-time-low fan poll score of 65, making these the fans' least-appreciated episodes of new-era *Doctor Who* to date, while Series Three's 'Human Nature' and 'The Family of Blood' remain their favourites, having gained impressive poll scores of 94 and 95 respectively – the latter, remarkably, a full 30 points higher than those for 'Fear Her' and 'Victory of the Daleks'.

240

## v) DOCTOR WHO CONFIDENTIAL

The ratings (in millions) and AI figures (percentages) for the debut transmissions of the fifth series of *Doctor Who Confidential* were as follows.

| EPISODE | BBC THREE RATING | BBC HD RATING | TOTAL RATING | AI |
|---|---|---|---|---|
| 'Call Me the Doctor' | 0.93 | 0.09 | 1.02 | 86 |
| 'All About the Girl' | 0.62 | 0.00 | 0.62 | 84 |
| 'War Games' | 0.62 | 0.12 | 0.74 | 85 |
| 'Eyes Wide Open' | 0.62 | 0.09 | 0.71 | 86 |
| 'Blinded by the Light' | 0.57 | 0.14 | 0.71 | 86 |
| 'Death in Venice' | 0.33 | 0.11 | 0.44 | 83 |
| 'Arthurian Legend' | 0.53 | 0.14 | 0.67 | 85 |
| 'After Effects' | 0.33 | 0.11 | 0.44 | 84 |
| 'What Goes on Tour ...' | 0.49 | 0.08 | 0.57 | 82 |
| 'A Brush With Genius' | 0.29 | 0.12 | 0.41 | 84 |
| 'Extra Time' | 0.47 | 0.14 | 0.61 | 81 |
| 'Alien Abduction' | 0.85 | 0.00 | 0.85 | 85 |
| 'Out of Time' | 0.67 | 0.00 | 0.67 | 86 |
| **Average*** | **0.56** | **0.09** | **0.65** | **84** |
| Christmas Special 2010 | 0.21** | 0.00** | 0.21** | 82 |

* Not including the Christmas special.
** Overnight figure; adjusted final rating not known.
Source for viewing figures: Broadcasters' Audience Research Board (BARB)
Source for AI figures: BBC

The performance of the show across all five full series to date is summarised in the table below.

| SERIES | AVERAGE RATING | AVERAGE AI |
|---|---|---|
| Series One | 0.54 | n/k |
| Series Two | 0.63 | 84 |
| Series Three | 0.70 | 83 |
| Series Four | 0.80 | 86 |
| Series Five | 0.65 | 84 |

Source for viewing figures: Broadcasters' Audience Research Board (BARB)
Source for AI figures: BBC

These figures indicate that – like *Doctor Who* itself – *Doctor Who Confidential* suffered a slight dip in popularity for Series Five by comparison with its peak performance in Series Four, taking it back more to the level it was at around Series Two and Series Three. Perhaps more worrying, though, was the show's slip down the BBC Three and digital TV chart placings. In fact, only one episode of Series Five actually managed to get into the weekly top ten of BBC Three programmes, and only two into the weekly top 30 of all digital channel programmes, whereas during previous series the show had featured in both charts almost every week, occasionally even capturing the number one spot. This suggests that *Doctor Who Confidential* had sadly failed to hold its own in the context of stiffer competition and much increased overall viewing numbers both on its home channel and on the digital TV landscape more generally.

# APPENDIX E
# ORIGINAL NOVELS

During 2010, BBC Books published a further six titles in their ongoing range of *Doctor Who* novels, plus the first of what was planned as a new series of special titles by acclaimed science fiction authors. All were in hardback and featured the eleventh Doctor and Amy Pond, plus in some cases Rory Williams. Summary details are as follows.

**37: APOLLO 23**

Publication date: 22 April 2010
Writer: Justin Richards
Commissioning Editor: Albert DePatrillo; Series Consultant: Justin Richards; Editor: Stephen Cole; Project Editor: Steve Tribe; Cover Design: Lee Binding; Production: Rebecca Jones

PUBLICITY BLURB

*For a few moments this afternoon, it rained on the moon ...* An astronaut in full spacesuit appears out of thin air in a busy shopping centre. Maybe it's a publicity stunt. A photo shows a well-dressed woman in a red coat lying dead at the edge of a crater on the dark side of the moon – beside her beloved dog 'Poochie'. Maybe it's a hoax. But as the Doctor and Amy find out, these are just minor events in a sinister plan to take over every human being on Earth. The plot centres on a secret military base on the moon – that's where Amy and the TARDIS are. The Doctor is back on Earth, and without the TARDIS there's no way he can get to the moon to save Amy and defeat the aliens. Or is there? The Doctor discovers one last great secret that could save humanity: Apollo 23.
This is a thrilling, all new adventure featuring the Doctor and Amy, as played by Matt Smith and Karen Gillan in the spectacular hit series from BBC Television.

NOTES

- Also released as an unabridged audiobook read by James Albrecht, by AudioGo as a download on 1 July 2010 and by BBC Audio as a CD-R set in October 2010.
- Also issued in a paperback edition in March 2011.
- A French edition, published by Milady and translated by Rosalie Guillaume, came out on 20 January 2012.

**38: NIGHT OF THE HUMANS**

Publication date: 22 April 2010
Writer: David Llewellyn
Commissioning Editor: Albert DePatrillo; Series Consultant: Justin Richards;
Project Editor: Steve Tribe; Cover Design: Lee Binding; Production: Rebecca Jones

PUBLICITY BLURB

*'This is the Gyre – the most hostile environment in the galaxy ...'* 250,000 years' worth of junk floating in deep space, home to the shipwrecked Sittuun, the carnivorous Sollogs, and worst of all – the Humans. The Doctor and Amy arrive on this terrifying world in the middle of an all-out frontier war between Sittuun and Humans, and the countdown has already started. There's a comet in the sky, and it's on a collision course with the Gyre ... When the Doctor is kidnapped, it's up to Amy and 'galaxy-famous swashbuckler' Dirk Slipstream to save the day. But who is Slipstream, exactly? And what is he really doing here? A thrilling, all new adventure featuring the Doctor and Amy, as played by Matt Smith and Karen Gillan in the spectacular hit series from BBC Television.

NOTES

• Also released as an unabridged audiobook read by Arthur Darvill, by AudioGo as a download on 1 July 2010 and by BBC Audio as a CD-R set in November 2010.
• Also issued in a paperback edition in March 2011.
• A French edition, published by Milady and translated by Laurent Queyssi, came out on 20 January 2012 under the title *La Nuit des Humains*.

**39: THE FORGOTTEN ARMY**

Publication date: 22 April 2010
Writer: Brian Minchin
Commissioning Editor: Albert DePatrillo; Series Consultant: Justin Richards;
Project Editor: Steve Tribe; Cover Design: Lee Binding; Production: Rebecca Jones

PUBLICITY BLURB

*'Let me tell you a story. Long ago, in the frozen Arctic wastes, an alien army landed. Only now, 10,000 years later, it isn't a story. And the army is ready to attack.'* New York – one of the greatest cities on 21st Century Earth ... But what's going on in the Museum? And is that really a Woolly Mammoth rampaging down Broadway? An ordinary day becomes a time of terror, as the Doctor and Amy meet a new and deadly enemy. The vicious Army of the Vykoid are armed to the teeth and determined to enslave the human race. Even though they're only seven centimetres high. With the Vykoid army swarming across Manhattan and sealing it from the world with a powerful alien force field, Amy has just 24 hours to find the Doctor and save the city. If she doesn't, the people of Manhattan will be taken to work in the doomed

asteroid mines of the Vykoid home planet. But as time starts to run out, who can she trust? And how far will she have to go to free New York from the Forgotten Army? A thrilling, all new adventure featuring the Doctor and Amy, as played by Matt Smith and Karen Gillan in the spectacular hit series from BBC Television.

NOTES

- Also released as an unabridged audiobook read by Olivia Colman, by AudioGo as a download on 1 September 2010 and by BBC Audio as a CD-R set in December 2010.
- Also issued in a paperback edition in March 2011.
- A French edition, published by Milady and translated by Rosalie Guillaume, came out on 20 January 2012 under the title *L'Armée Obliée*.

## 40: NUCLEAR TIME

Publication date: 8 July 2010
Writer: Oli Smith
Commissioning Editor: Albert DePatrillo; Series Consultant: Justin Richards; Project Editor: Steve Tribe; Cover Design: Lee Binding; Production: Rebecca Jones

PUBLICITY BLURB

*'My watch is running backwards.'* Colorado, 1981. The Doctor, Amy and Rory arrive in Appletown – an idyllic village in the remote American desert where the townsfolk go peacefully about their suburban routines. But when two more strangers arrive, things begin to change. The first is a mad scientist – whose warnings are cut short by an untimely and brutal death. The second is the Doctor … As death falls from the sky, the Doctor is trapped. The TARDIS is damaged, and the Doctor finds he is living backwards through time. With Amy and Rory being hunted through the suburban streets of the Doctor's own future and getting farther away with every passing second, he must unravel the secrets of Appletown before time runs out … A thrilling, all-new adventure featuring the Doctor, Amy and Rory, as played by Matt Smith, Karen Gillan and Arthur Darvill in the spectacular hit series from BBC Television.

NOTES

- Also released as an unabridged audiobook read by Nicholas Briggs, by AudioGo as a download on 1 February 2011 and by BBC Audio as a CD-R set in May 2011.
- Also issued in a paperback edition in March 2011.
- A French edition, published by Milady and translated by Pierre Pevel, came out on 17 February 2012 under the title *L'Horloge Nucléaire*.

## 41: THE KING'S DRAGON

Publication date: 8 July 2010
Writer: Una McCormack
Commissioning Editor: Albert DePatrillo; Series Consultant: Justin Richards;
Project Editor: Steve Tribe; Cover Design: Lee Binding; Production: Rebecca Jones

PUBLICITY BLURB

*'They called it Enamour. It turned minds, sold merchandise, and swayed elections. And it did its job far too well ...'* In the city-state of Geath, the King lives in a golden hall, and the people want for nothing. Everyone is happy and everyone is rich. Or so it seems. When the Doctor, Amy and Rory look beneath the surface, they discover a city of secrets. In dark corners, strange creatures are stirring. At the heart of the hall, a great metal dragon oozes gold. Then the Herald appears, demanding the return of her treasure ... And next come the gunships. The battle for possession of the treasure has begun, and only the Doctor and his friends can save the people of the city from being destroyed in the crossfire of an ancient civil war. But will the King surrender his new-found wealth? Or will he fight to keep it ...? A thrilling, all-new adventure featuring the Doctor, Amy and Rory, as played by Matt Smith, Karen Gillan and Arthur Darvill in the spectacular hit series from BBC Television.

NOTES

• Also released as an unabridged audiobook read by Nicholas Briggs, by AudioGo as a download on 1 March 2011 and by BBC Audio as a CD-R set in June 2011.
• Also issued in a paperback edition in March 2011.

## 42: THE GLAMOUR CHASE

Publication date: 8 July 2010
Writer: Gary Russell
Commissioning Editor: Albert DePatrillo; Series Consultant: Justin Richards;
Project Editor: Steve Tribe; Cover Design: Lee Binding; Production: Rebecca Jones

PUBLICITY BLURB

*'Why are you here? I mean – who are you, exactly?'* An archaeological dig in 1936 unearths relics of another time ... And – as the Doctor, Amy and Rory realise – another place. Another planet. But if Enola Porter, noted adventuress, has really found evidence of an alien civilisation, how come she isn't famous? Why has Rory never heard of her? Added to that, since Amy's been travelling with him for a while now, why does she now think the Doctor is from Mars? As the ancient spaceship reactivates, the Doctor discovers that nothing and no-one can be trusted. The things that seem most real could actually be literal fabrications – and very deadly indeed. Who can the Doctor believe when no-one is what they seem? And how can he defeat an enemy who can bend matter itself to their will? For the

Doctor, Amy and Rory – and all of humanity – the buried secrets of the past are very much a threat to the present ... A thrilling, all-new adventure featuring the Doctor, Amy and Rory, as played by Matt Smith, Karen Gillan and Arthur Darvill in the spectacular hit series from BBC Television.

NOTES

- Also released as an unabridged audiobook read by Arthur Darvill, by AudioGo as a download on 1 April 2011 and by BBC Audio as a CD-R set in July 2011.
- Also issued in a paperback edition in March 2011.

**S1. THE COMING OF THE TERRAPHILES**

Publication date: 14 October 2010
Writer: Michael Moorcock
Commissioning Editor: Albert DePatrillo; Series Consultant: Justin Richards; Project Editor: Steve Tribe; Editorial Manager: Nicholas Payne; Cover Design: Lee Binding; Production: Rebecca Jones

PUBLICITY BLURB

*'There are dark tides running through the universe ...'* Miggea – a star on the very edge of reality. The cusp between this universe and the next. A point where space-time has worn thin, and is in danger of collapsing ... And the venue for the grand finals of the competition to win the fabled Arrow of Law. The Doctor and Amy have joined the Terraphiles – a group obsessed with all aspects of Earth's history, and dedicated to re-enacting ancient sporting events. They are determined to win the Arrow. But just getting to Miggea proves tricky. Reality is collapsing, ships are disappearing, and Captain Cornelius and his pirates are looking for easy pickings. Even when they arrive, the Doctor and Amy's troubles won't be over. They have to find out who is so desperate to get the Arrow of Law that they will kill for it. And uncover the traitor on their own team. And win the contest fair and square. And, of course, they need to save the universe from total destruction. A thrilling, all-new adventure featuring the Doctor and Amy, as played by Matt Smith and Karen Gillan in the spectacular hit series from BBC Television written by the acclaimed science fiction and fantasy author Michael Moorcock

NOTES

- This book had the subtitle: *Or The Pirates of the Second Aether.*
- Also released on the same date as an unabridged audiobook read by Clive Mantle, by BBC Audio as a CD set and by AudioGo as a download.
- Also issued in a paperback edition on 4 August 2011.

# APPENDIX F
# ORIGINAL COMIC STRIPS

During 2010, there were three different comic strip series presenting new *Doctor Who* stories for fans to enjoy. These appeared in, respectively: Panini's *Doctor Who Magazine*, which (under various different titles) had been home to a *Doctor Who* comic strip since 1979; *Doctor Who Adventures*, a weekly comic aimed at a pre-teen audience, published by BBC Magazines; and *Doctor Who*, a US-only comic book, published by IDW.[78] At the start of the year, all three series were still rounding off their run of tenth Doctor stories – and, in fact, IDW would not move on to publishing eleventh Doctor stories until 2011. Information on the final tenth Doctor stories in all three series was given in the previous book in this range, *End of Ten* (Telos Publishing, 2010), although as the last few IDW issues had yet to be published at that point, full entries could not be included for those. Set out below are details of the eleventh Doctor stories published in *Doctor Who Magazine* and *Doctor Who Adventures* up to December 2010, and also, for completeness, details of the last few tenth Doctor issues from IDW that could not be covered properly last time. For all three series, the publication dates given are the cover dates or official publication dates and do not necessarily accord with when the issues actually went on sale.

### DOCTOR WHO MAGAZINE

#### SUPERNATURE

Story: Jonathan Morris
Pencil Art: Mike Collins; Inks: David A Roach; Colours: James Offredi; Lettering: Roger Langridge; Editors: Tom Spilsbury and Scott Gray
Publication: Issues 421-423; 26 May 2010, 23 June 2010, 21 July 2010.

#### PLOT

The Doctor and Amy arrive on an alien planet and find a group of human convicts who have been sent here as guinea-pigs in a colonisation project. A mysterious disease is causing the convicts to mutate into various strange creatures, and Amy starts to succumb too. The Doctor discovers that the disease involves different life-forms being amalgamated to form entirely new species. In the jungle that surrounds the colony, he finds an underground chamber containing the source of the problem: a gene-splicer machine that was brought here by aliens to try to speed

---

[78] IDW also publishes from time to time series of classic *Doctor Who* comic books featuring stories of earlier Doctors reprinted, with newly-added colour, from earlier incarnations of *Doctor Who Magazine*.

up evolution. The machine went wrong, and the aliens were transformed into the jungle itself. The Doctor too has started to mutate, but he uses the machine to put the process into reverse, causing everyone gradually to revert to their true forms. The machine then destroys itself. At his suggestion, the convicts send out a warning message claiming that everyone has been killed by the disease; this should ensure that they are left alone to try to make a success of their colony.

## PLANET BOLLYWOOD

Story: Jonathan Morris
Art: Roger Langridge; Colours: James Offredi; Editors: Tom Spilsbury and Scott Gray
Publication: Issue 424; 18 August 2010.

## PLOT

The Doctor and Amy arrive on a planet where everyone – including them – is frequently compelled to sing and dance as if they were in a Bollywood musical. This is caused by the influence of a sentient robot, the Muse, which was constructed as an amusement for the Maharani of Baloch. It became damaged when its ship crash-landed on this planet after an encounter with a group of Shasarak who want to steal it and use it for evil purposes, and now it is permanently activated. The Doctor repairs the Muse with his sonic screwdriver, and it then uses its influence to keep the Shasarak singing and dancing while the Doctor gets the Maharani to send a ship to take them into custody.

## THE GOLDEN ONES

Story: Jonathan Morris
Pencil Art: Martin Geraghty; Inks: David A Roach; Colours: James Offredi; Lettering: Roger Langridge; Editors: Tom Spilsbury and Scott Gray
Axons created by: Bob Baker and Dave Martin
Publication: Issues 425-428; 25 September 2010, 20 October 2010, 17 November 2010, 15 December 2010.

## PLOT

In modern-day Tokyo, the Doctor and Amy assist UNIT in investigating a supposedly intelligence-enhancing new tonic drink that is being marketed by the Shining Dawn corporation through a TV cartoon character called Goruda. The Doctor discovers that the tonic contains a 'chameleon molecule' that transforms those who drink it into Axons. UNIT estimate that at least 50,000 children have been affected. The Doctor constructs a hat-like device that will cut the telepathic link between Axos and the children, freeing them. Amy and UNIT's Major Hiraki have been taken prisoner by Axos, but they are released by a mysterious young girl named Chiyoko. Believing that Axos must be buried beneath Shining Dawn's HQ, the Doctor obtains the blueprints for the building, only to find that they are blank. The city's mayor has meanwhile been tricked into feeding power into the building, which causes it to transform: the building itself was Axos, in disguised form. The Doctor uses his hat-like device to get the children of Tokyo to use their combined mental energies to create a giant Goruda, which attacks Axos. Unable to reverse the power feed into Axos, he then broadcasts a message to every home in Tokyo, telling the residents to turn on all their electrical equipment at once. This drains Axos of power, killing it. As it dies, it accuses Chiyoko of betraying it, but she enigmatically states that its sacrifice will 'allow a greater life to come into being ...'

NOTE

• Features the Axons from the TV story 'The Claws of Axos' (1971).

## DOCTOR WHO ADVENTURES

### ATTACK OF THE SPACE LEECHES

Words: Oli Smith
Art: John Ross; Colouring: Alan Craddock
Publication: Issues 160-161; 1 April 2010, 8 April 2010

PLOT

A boy named Stephen flees when an alien spaceship crash-lands in central London and vicious space leeches emerge. The TARDIS materialises, and the Doctor and Amy meet Stephen. They realise that the leeches have left Stephen alone because he has a cold. The Doctor uses the virus to get the leeches to release their victims, then takes them into the TARDIS so that he can deposit them somewhere safe.

NOTE

• The eleventh Doctor and Amy make their debut comic strip appearances in the second part of this story.

### MADNESS ON THE M1

Words: Oli Smith
Art: John Ross; Colouring: Alan Craddock
Publication: Issue 162; 15 April 2010

PLOT

The Doctor and Amy arrive in 1959 at the Blue Boar services on the newly-constructed M1 motorway. They see three teenage Petrolions – alien joyriders – racing through the traffic on advanced motorbikes, and the Doctor determines to stop them. When the Petrolions call at a petrol station to refuel, the Doctor reverses the flow, wrecking both their motorbikes and their spacesuits and forcing them to leave Earth.

APPENDIX F: ORIGINAL COMIC STRIPS

## WINNING HAND

Words: Oli Smith
Art: John Ross; Colouring: Alan Craddock
Publication: Issue 163; 22 April 2010

PLOT

In the Trans-Vega Casino, the Doctor gambles in a game of cards with a purple alien named Hubert Crimp, the most notorious slave-dealer in the galaxy. Under cover of this distraction, Amy uses the sonic screwdriver to release all the slaves on Hubert's spaceship. The Doctor wins the card game, taking all of Hubert's money, which he vows to use to compensate the freed slaves.

## BOOKED UP

Words: Simon Guerrier
Art: John Ross; Colouring: Alan Craddock
Publication: Issue 164; 29 April 2010

PLOT

The Doctor is returning some overdue books to a disused library when he and Amy are attacked by some creatures made of books. The Doctor realises that the creatures are hungry not for people but for stories. He and Amy start to tell them about one of their adventures, then get them to finish the story themselves. The two travellers depart in the TARDIS, leaving the creatures contentedly telling stories to each other.

## BAD VIBRATIONS

Words: Eddie Robson
Art: John Ross; Colouring: Alan Craddock
Publication: Issue 165; 6 May 2010

PLOT

The TARDIS arrives in the Echo Sphere, a small, hollow world inhabited by green bird-like creatures. The echo of the TARDIS's materialisation noise gets louder and louder, causing the creatures discomfort and starting to damage the structure of the place. Amy solves the problem by using the TARDIS's fire extinguisher to cover everything in foam, muffling the sound.

251

**ABOUT FACE**

Words: Steve Lyons
Art: John Ross; Colouring: Alan Craddock
Publication: Issue 166; 13 May 2010

PLOT

The Doctor and Amy arrive on a prison spaceship and are attacked by an escapee: a tusked creature called a Charonid that can swap bodies with its victims. The Charonid swaps bodies with Amy, but the Doctor realises what has happened as her eyes have turned red. He tricks the Charonid, restoring Amy to her own body and trapping the creature in a force field.

**TRACK ATTACK**

Words: Eddie Robson
Art: John Ross; Colouring: Alan Craddock
Publication: Issue 167; 20 May 2010

PLOT

A steam train on the Northampton-Euston line in June 1885 runs out of control. The Doctor and Amy are on board, and they discover that the engine has been taken over by a ghostly orange alien, a Shift Agent, that needs to get to Euston as quickly as possible in order to dispose of some dark matter that threatens to the whole planet apart. The Doctor helps the Shift Agent to reach Euston in time and find and remove the dark matter.

**NOWHERE MAN**

Words: Oli Smith
Art: John Ross; Colouring: Alan Craddock
Publication: Issue 168; 27 May 2010

PLOT

An alien named Brox has been on a hundred-year mission in his spaceship to try to find other life-forms, but has been unsuccessful. However, his ship's faltering engines have created some small wormholes a trillion light years away in space. The Doctor takes the TARDIS through one of these, and he and Amy arrive on board Brox's ship. The Doctor realises that Brox's mission has failed because he is traversing the deserted outer rim of the universe. Amy pilots the ship in a loop-the-loop, creating a huge wormhole through which he can travel to a more inhabited region.

**MONEY TROUBLES**

Words: Steve Lyons
Art: John Ross; Colouring: Alan Craddock
Publication: Issue 169; 3 June 2010

PLOT

The TARDIS arrives in the year 40,412 inside the vault of a bank run by rat-like aliens called Ratlings. The Doctor and Amy are initially mistaken for robbers, but the bank is then stormed by the Sidewinder Syndicate – green, lizard-like alien gangsters that the Doctor has encountered before[79]. The Sidewinders accuse the Ratlings of trying to steal their money, and Amy discovers that this is indeed the case. The Doctor and Amy depart, leaving the Sidewinders and Ratlings to 'settle their own accounts'.

**FASHION VICTIMS**

Words: Christopher Cooper
Art: John Ross; Colouring: Alan Craddock
Publication: Issue 170; 10 June 2010

PLOT

The Doctor and Amy arrive in London around the 21st Century to find that everyone is wearing the same type of jackets and eye-visors. They have been compelled to do this by a green, blobby alien called a Fliis. The Fliis sends out a wi-fi signal that causes the jackets to transform into Symbiot creatures, trapping their human wearers. The Doctor tampers with the Fliis's computer, causing the fashion victims to tear off their jackets and adopt his style instead. The Fliis and the Symbiot creatures teleport away from Earth, their invasion foiled.

**THE COLLECTOR**

Words: Oli Smith
Art: John Ross; Colouring: Alan Craddock
Publication: Issue 171; 17 June 2010

PLOT

A giant creature arrives on the Nebulon Colony in the year 3415 and finds its inhabitants' peaceful way of life so beautiful that it freezes them solid to keep them as they are. 100 years later, the Doctor and Amy arrive in the TARDIS and convince the creature of the error of its ways, prompting it to thaw the citizens out again.

---

[79] In the story 'Snakes Alive!' in Issue 129 of *Doctor Who Adventures*.

CRACKS IN TIME

**THE STRAY**

Words: Eddie Robson
Art: John Ross; Colouring: Alan Craddock
Publication: Issue 172; 24 June 2010

PLOT

An old lady named Betty has taken in what she thinks is a stray dog, but is actually a parasitic Kera-Bera Beast that has just made her think it is a dog and is gradually draining her life energy. Betty doesn't believe the Doctor's warning, but when she pays a visit to the hairdresser's, Amy is able to treat her with a device that they have attached to a hairdryer. This reverses the psychic link between Betty and the Beast. She is reinvigorated, while the Beast shrinks to the size of an ordinary dog.

**MISTAKEN IDENTITY**

Words: Cavan Scott
Art: John Ross; Colouring: Alan Craddock
Publication: Issue 173; 1 July 2010

PLOT

In a dense alien forest, a law-enforcement mechanoid mistakes Amy for Egron the Flesh-Eater, a shape-shifting alien criminal it is pursuing. It tries to shoot her, and she takes refuge in what she thinks is the TARDIS. However, she has actually run straight into the mouth of Egron, who has disguised himself as the ship. The Doctor throws a rock at a patch of fungus that emits a nauseating odour, causing Egron to vomit Amy up again. The mechanoid then arrests Egron.

**FOUL PLAY**

Words: Steve Lyons
Art: John Ross; Colouring: Alan Craddock
Publication: Issue 174; 8 July 2010

PLOT

The Doctor and Amy are in the year 2050 visiting New Wembley Stadium, a space station in Earth orbit, where a company called the Chronos Corporation claims to have brought England's World Cup team of 2010 forward in time to play a match against a team of robots. In the dressing rooms, the Doctor finds a perception filter machine and switches it off. The so-called England players are revealed to be impostors: a group of purple, tentacled aliens. The Chronos Corporation are left to answer to the spectators they have tried to con.

## GATEBOTS!

Words: Christopher Cooper
Art: John Ross; Colouring: Alan Craddock
Publication: Issue 175; 15 July 2010

PLOT

The Doctor and Amy are about to leave the planet Ekthelios, having just saved it from alien conquest. The spaceport's GateBots check Amy's identity, and as she is not on any flight lists, threaten her with execution. The Doctor tricks one of the GateBots into displaying a news report on all of the spaceport's departure board screens. This proves him and Amy to be the two heroes who have just saved the planet, and the GateBots let them leave.

## BLUE SKIES THINKING

Words: Eddie Robson
Art: John Ross; Colouring: Alan Craddock
Publication: Issue 176; 22 July 2010

PLOT

The TARDIS materialises on the planet Thekla in the year 2495, where the Doctor is surprised to find a human colony. The members of the colony have been possessed by alien Aranjia, who arrived here through a wormhole and intend to use this as an advance base to mount other invasions. However, the Aranjia are repelled by the colour blue, and have banned blue items from the planet. With Amy's help, the Doctor reaches the colony's weather control mast and uses it to turn the sky from orange to blue, causing the Aranjia to abandon their human hosts and retreat through the wormhole.

## SAMURAI'S SECRET

Words: Oli Smith
Art: John Ross; Colouring: Alan Craddock
Publication: Issue 177; 29 July 2010

PLOT

The Doctor and Amy visit a village in 13th Century Japan, which is being flooded each time a dragon-like water serpent appears nearby. Amy realises that an inept Samurai named Shoju, to whom the villagers have been looking for protection, is actually the serpent disguised in human form. Shoju admits that he is an alien. He just wants to settle peacefully in the village, but he cannot maintain his human disguise for long, and when it slips, he reverts to his natural form. The floods are caused as a side effect. The Doctor uses his sonic screwdriver to fix Shoju in human form, and the villagers, believing that he has slain the serpent, welcome him into their community.

**A MESS OF TROUBLE**

Words: Eddie Robson
Art: John Ross; Colouring: Alan Craddock
Publication: Issue 178; 5 August 2010

PLOT

The inhabitants of the planet Posadis never bother to clear up their mess. Periodically, dust storms whip us, blowing all their garbage into the upper atmosphere, where the planet is also orbited by some large asteroids. Believing that they are under attack from hostile aliens, the Posadians send out a distress call, and the Doctor and Amy arrive in response. It turns out that the aliens are the inhabitants of the orbiting asteroids. They have come to Posadis not to invade but to clean up, as they are fed up with being bombarded by the Posadians' rubbish. Advising the Posadians to clean up their act, the Doctor and Amy depart.

**IN THE STARS**

Words: Eddie Robson
Art: John Ross; Colouring: Alan Craddock
Publication: Issue 179; 12 August 2010

PLOT

In Babylon in 905 BC, the Doctor and Amy meet an early astronomer named Urtaki. Urtaki has spotted some new stars in the night sky, and names this constellation the Gryphon. Suddenly the Gryphon forms into a real creature made of light, and attacks the city. Realising that it can be kept in check by reflecting it, the two travellers get the citizens to surround the creature with mirrors until the sun rises and it is deprived of its star power. The Gryphon fades away, leaving just a few electronic components, and the Doctor theorises that it was an alien terror weapon that has now lost contact with its operator. He takes the components with him into the TARDIS when he and Amy depart.

**MOST HAUNTED**

Words: Steve Lyons
Art: John Ross; Colouring: Alan Craddock
Publication: Issue 180; 19 August 2010

PLOT

Two kids named Kerri and Joe explore the supposedly haunted Harcourt Manor. They see a ghostly shape, and then meet the Doctor and Amy, who have arrived here in response to a psychic distress signal. They find a dormant alien sealed behind a wall. The Doctor revives it, and it explains that it was entombed here long ago by frightened locals after its ship crash landed. It entered a deep sleep in order to survive, but its subconscious mind has been reaching out for help – hence the ghostly apparitions. Amy says that she and the Doctor can take it home now.

## THE LIVING STORM

Words: Steve Lyons
Art: John Ross; Colouring: Alan Craddock
Publication: Issue 181; 26 August 2010

### PLOT

The Doctor and Amy are exploring the ruins of an alien city when they are assailed by a violent storm. They are then surrounded by terrifying creatures that condense from the rain and mist. Amy hears words within the thunder: 'Flee ... from ... this ... world.' The two travellers return to the TARDIS, and the storm abates, leaving only a stunning rainbow. The Doctor regrets that whatever lives in the sky here does not want to share the planet's beauty.

## THE SCARECROW

Words: Eddie Robson
Art: John Ross; Colouring: Alan Craddock
Publication: Issue 182; 2 September 2010

### PLOT

Major Luisa Suarez of the Unified South American Space Agency has been imprisoned in an atmosphere bubble on the other side of the universe, but has never seen her captors as they approach only in the dark. The Doctor and Amy suddenly arrive. The Doctor realises that they have all travelled here through the nearby Wormhole of Calibri. This is close to the planet Hazri, and it is the timid Hazrians who have imprisoned Major Suarez, to act as a 'scarecrow' in case they are paid a return visit by the Tulokon race who once attacked them. Of all the beings they have encountered, humans fill them with the most fear. The Doctor tells the Hazrians that the Tulokon are long gone, and he, Amy and Luisa are allowed to depart in the TARDIS. To reassure the Hazrians further, the Doctor leaves behind a real scarecrow, dressed up like him.

## SKY SCRAPER

Words: Christopher Cooper
Art: John Ross; Colouring: Alan Craddock
Publication: Issue 183; 9 September 2010

### PLOT

The Doctor and Amy arrive in Manchester, 2011, to find the city being evacuated as worm-like tendrils erupt from the ground. These are actually the 'fingers' of an alien creature, an Alifabe, that normally lives in hyperspace but has become ill and fallen to Earth in a nearby tower block. The RAF prepare to launch an air strike on the tower block, but the Doctor gets Amy to turn all the flats' satellite dishes to point upwards. This enables the Alifabe to make an interspacial call for help, and she is transported away just in time. The air strike is then aborted, while the Doctor and Amy enjoy a colourful sunset caused by energy from the transporter beam.

## THE PURRFECT CRIME

Words: Mark Wright
Art: John Ross; Colouring: Alan Craddock
Publication: Issue 184; 16 September 2010

PLOT

The Doctor and Amy seem to have arrived near the pyramids in ancient Egypt. They encounter what appears to be a living mummy but is really a man wrapped in bandages. This is Oliver, a security guard, who tells him that they are actually in a museum; the pyramids are just replicas. Oliver was trussed up by a group of cat-shaped aliens called Sekhmets who have come to steal the museum's prize exhibit, the Crystal Scarab. The Doctor and his friends climb up one of the pyramids in pursuit of the Sekhmets, whose spaceship breaks through the museum roof to collect them. However, the Doctor manages to retrieve the Scarab by lassoing it with one of the discarded bandages just before the Sekhmet ship departs.

## THE STEEL WEB

Words: Steve Lyons
Art: John Ross; Colouring: Alan Craddock
Publication: Issue 185; 23 September 2010

PLOT

The TARDIS gets trapped in an enormous metal spider's web. The Doctor and Amy rescue an alien who has been cocooned in the web by giant mechanical spiders. He is Heldan, a fruit farmer from the planet Pomarius. His people created the cyborg spiders to protect their beautiful orchards from attacks by fruit flies, but they ran out of control. The Doctor mixes up a noxious liquid to make the TARDIS smell like the flies. He then uses the ship to draw the cyborg spiders away from Pomarius, saving the planet. He plans to take them to an uninhabited world where they can spin their webs without harming anyone.

APPENDIX F: ORIGINAL COMIC STRIPS

**IN THE CAN**

Words: Eddie Robson
Art: John Ross; Colouring: Alan Craddock
Publication: Issue 186; 30 September 2010

PLOT

A company called Prime Soup has been using subliminal TV advertising to market its product. However, it is really a front for two walrus-like creatures who are planning to launch an invasion by using the soup cans to distribute compressed monsters. A batch of the cans has been released too early and then recalled, but the Doctor and Amy manage to intercept one and fill it with a gas that knocks out the walrus-like creatures. The Doctor disables their monster incubation tank and plans to hand them over to the galactic authorities.

**SNOW GLOBE**

Words: Christopher Cooper
Art: John Ross; Colouring: Alan Craddock
Publication: Issue 187; 7 October 2010

PLOT

The Doctor and Amy visit the Ice Age and save a Neanderthal man from being attacked by a sabre-toothed tiger. They discover that a group of aliens have used a force-wall to turn the local area into an enclosed environment that they can study in preparation for a planned invasion. While the Neanderthal frees the rest of his tribe, who have been held captive by the aliens, the Doctor deactivates the force-wall. Their invasion plans wrecked, the aliens flee from the marauding sabre-toothed tigers, while the Doctor, Amy and the tribe slip away.

**WAVE MACHINE**

Words: Trevor Baxendale
Art: John Ross; Colouring: Alan Craddock
Publication: Issue 188; 14 October 2010

PLOT

The Doctor and Amy are relaxing on the beach on the planet Smilonda, the top holiday destination of the 423rd Century. However, a green-skinned alien named Grone is annoyed that all the tourists are spoiling his peace and quiet. He unleashes a robot crab to cause chaos and scare everyone away. The Doctor uses the sonic screwdriver to hijack the robot's remote-control signal and cause it to bury Grone in the sand. The Doctor cautions Grone to be friendlier in future, and reprograms the robot to give holidaymakers fun rides in the sea.

**CELL SHOCK**

Words: Christopher Cooper
Art: John Ross; Colouring: Alan Craddock
Publication: Issue 189; 21 October 2010

PLOT

The Doctor and Amy are exploring an artificial mountain on a mysterious new planet when the ground gives way beneath them and they find themselves in a cage with a large furry creature and her cubs. The creature, Elpha, explains that they were brought here from their own world as captives. The Doctor opens the cage door with his sonic screwdriver and, exploring, discovers that they are in a planet-sized zoo. Whoever ran the place has long gone, leaving only robot security guards and automated systems behind. The Doctor closes them down and sets all the exhibits free. He agrees to take Elpha and her cubs back to their home planet in the TARDIS.

**THE TRICK**

Words: Oli Smith
Art: John Ross; Colouring: Alan Craddock
Publication: Issue 190; 28 October 2010

PLOT

The Doctor and Amy are trick-or-treating on Halloween in Texas, USA, when they meet a farmer and his son who have just witnessed the arrival of an alien spaceship. The spaceship contains four aliens who plan to launch an invasion. The Doctor, Amy, the farmer and his son put hollowed-out pumpkins with candles inside in the window of the farmhouse. This scares off the aliens by making them believe that humans hollow out the heads of their enemies and display them in an horrific ritual.

**THE LUNAR TYK**

Words: Richard Dinnick
Art: John Ross; Colouring: Alan Craddock
Publication: Issue 191; 4 November 2010

PLOT

In November 2039, two astronauts from Earth land in the Shackleton Crater on the Moon, searching for ice. The Doctor and Amy have also arrived there on the same quest, as the TARDIS's fridge is broken. When one of the astronauts shines a torch into the Crater, it provokes an attack by a vicious creature that the Doctor identifies as a light-eating Tyk. The Tyk begins to grow to giant size as it absorbs sunlight, but the Doctor tricks it into lunging at Amy's reflection in a solar panel, and it is knocked unconscious. The Doctor then launches it in a rocket into permanent orbit around the Sun, where it can get all the light it can eat.

## PENCIL PUSHER

Words: Trevor Baxendale
Art: John Ross; Colouring: Alan Craddock
Publication: Issue 192; 11 November 2010

PLOT

A young girl named Janie has found a special pencil that allows her to write 400 pages of science homework about the solar system in a single night, although her teacher is bemused to see that it contains references to the planet Speldron ... The Doctor and Amy visit the school, posing as inspectors. The Doctor seizes the pencil and uses the sonic screwdriver to free Janie of its influence. It is actually a shape-shifting criminal from Speldron named Graphon Narmolis, who is on the Shadow Proclamation's most-wanted list. The Doctor's mind is too powerful to be affected by it, and he puts it in his pocket before he and Amy depart in the TARDIS.

## THE CLEVEREST KING

Words: Trevor Baxendale
Art: John Ross; Colouring: Alan Craddock
Publication: Issue 193; 18 November 2010

PLOT

On the planet Usunru in Galaxy 57, the Doctor and Amy are seized by some strange, insect-like creatures called Kreech and taken to their nest in a giant, hollowed-out tree. There they meet Rangorr, a super-intelligent Kreech who is their Brainleader. He tells them that he longs to travel to the stars; but without him, the other Kreech would perish, so he wants the Doctor to take his place here. The Doctor challenges him to a crossword puzzle contest to see which of them is the brainiest. While Rangorr is distracted with the crossword, the Doctor and Amy escape to the TARDIS.

## SEEING THINGS

Words: Eddie Robson
Art: John Ross; Colouring: Alan Craddock
Publication: Issue 194; 25 November 2010

PLOT

In an Australian desert in 1943, the Doctor meets Sgt Brett Cooper, who has got separated from his regiment and been walking for two days. It seems he is being followed by a small pool of clear water, which he believes to be a mirage, but it is actually the reflective back of an alien creature called a Mirrorite, a nasty predator from the planet Shinnus. The Mirrorite is about to attack the Doctor and Sgt Cooper when it sees what it thinks is an easier target – Amy, 'playing possum' on the ground nearby. The Doctor tells Sgt Cooper that they must lie down too. When they do so, the Mirrorite splits into two to pursue both potential meals at once. The Doctor and Amy are then able to capture the two halves in force-nets. The Doctor plans to return the creature to its native planet – after taking Sgt Cooper home first.

## PIRATES OF THE SEVEN SEEDS

Words: Christopher Cooper
Art: John Ross; Colouring: Alan Craddock
Publication: Issue 195; 2 December 2010

PLOT

On the market planet Feltzmodo 12, the Doctor is surprised to see bunches of bananas on sale. At this point in history, the Earth is still recovering from a solar flare bombardment that has rendered it uninhabitable, and bananas should not exist. The Doctor takes Amy to a heat-ravaged Norway, where the Terran Seed Vault was built to house the seeds of Earth for future use. They find that the Vault has been infiltrated by alien pirates, Purzithroan Vagabonds from the Ambient Expanse, who are stealing the seeds and selling them to the highest bidder. The Doctor uses the Vault's climate control and security systems to project ghostly holographic images of Amy wearing a parka, scaring the pirates off.

## ROUGH WATERS

Words: Trevor Baxendale
Art: John Ross; Colouring: Alan Craddock
Publication: Issue 196; 9 December 2010

PLOT

The TARDIS brings the Doctor and Amy to a ship in the middle of the Battle of Trafalgar on 21 October 1805. One of the sailors tells the Doctor that they are being menaced by a sea monster that emerged from the fog. The 'monster' is actually a modern-day aircraft carrier that has been displaced in time by a Time Roach infestation. The Doctor finds the Time Roaches' nest and uses the sonic screwdriver to send them back into the vortex where they belong. He then rejoins Amy just before the aircraft carrier vanishes back to its own century.

## RED CHRISTMAS

Words: Oli Smith
Art: John Ross; Colouring: Alan Craddock
Publication: Issue 197; 16 December 2010

PLOT

The Doctor and Amy arrive in Hollograd on Christmas Day 1873 to find it enveloped in red psychic fog. The villagers are distraught, as their children have vanished and the night won't seem to end. However, the Doctor and Amy realise that the children are still there; the psychic fog is simply blocking them from their parents' minds. The Doctor uses the light from his sonic screwdriver to begin to disperse the fog – which is the work of the Krampus, creatures of folklore that feed on fear and sadness – but a brighter light is needed to finish the job. The Doctor materialises the TARDIS in the village square, and its roof light finally clears the fog, reuniting the villagers with their children and causing the Krampus to fade away to nothing. As they depart for further adventures, Amy wishes the Doctor a merry Christmas.

## FIRST FOOT FIRST

Words: Christopher Cooper
Art: John Ross; Colouring: Alan Craddock
Publication: Issue 198; 30 December 2010

PLOT

At midnight on New Year's Eve, a robot arrives on Earth near Edinburgh Castle, announcing that as the first visitor to set foot here in the New Year, it claims the planet as the property of the Robot Amalgamation. 24 hours earlier, the Doctor, Amy and Rory had a run-in with these robots on a vast, artificial planetoid. The robots tried to interrogate them using a neural digitiser, but the Doctor told Amy and Rory to block it by thinking of their happiest memories. Amy thought of the Hogmanay tradition of First Footing, whereby the first visitor to someone's home each year can claim a welcome gift. This is what gave the robots the idea of trying to claim Earth. However, the Doctor challenged them to a race, offering to give them all his knowledge if he lost. He has now used the TARDIS to arrive in Edinburgh before the robot, having already chased the New Year across the Earth from time zone to time zone – a concept unknown on the robots' planetoid, Robotica. The robot is forced to concede defeat, and the Doctor claims his prize: fireworks.

NOTE

- This is the first *Doctor Who Adventures* story to feature Rory as well as Amy.

## DOCTOR WHO

## DON'T STEP ON THE GRASS: OLD FRIENDS / OLD FRIENDS / WEED KILLER / DRAWING STRAWS[80]

Written by: Tony Lee
Issue 9 Cover A and RI: art: Paul Grist; colours: Phil Elliott
Issue 9 Cover B: Blair Shedd
Issue 10 Cover Regular and RI: art: Paul Grist; colours: Phil Elliott
Issue 11 Cover Regular and RI: art: Paul Grist; colours: Phil Elliott
Issue 12 Cover Regular and RI: art: Paul Grist; colours: Phil Elliott
Art: Blair Shedd; Colours: Lovern Kindzierski (9), Charlie Kirchoff (10-12); Letters: Robbie Robbins (9), Neil Uyetake (10-12); Edits: Denton J Tipton
Publication: Issues 9-12; March 2010, April 2010, May 2010, June 2010

## PLOT

The tenth Doctor, with his new companions Emily Winter and Matthew Finnegan, arrives in Greenwich in response to a phone call from Martha Jones, who is assisting UNIT in investigating reports that the trees in the park are moving and killing passers-by. The Doctor learns that Greenwich Observatory is built on top of an earlier building in which John Dee, the Elizabethan mathematician and astrologer, trapped some 'angels'. These are Enochians, energy creatures from another universe, whose ship is buried even deeper nearby and who want to conquer the Earth. The murderous trees in the park have been taken over by some escaped Enochians who no longer have clockwork bodies. The other Enochians from the ship also start to break free, and join the trees in a pitched battle against UNIT forces across London. The Doctor discovers that one of the Enochians is actually the latest guise adopted by the Gizou who previously impersonated the Krillitane Mr Finch[81]. UNIT are meanwhile joined by the Advocate[82], who says she has come to help them. The Advocate tells UNIT that the way to fight the Enochians is to destroy their ship. The Doctor, however, realises that the Advocate is actually responsible for releasing the Enochians. She admits to him that she is seeking revenge because his earlier actions inadvertently caused her to be trapped in the Time War, until she managed to escape at the same time as Davros. The Doctor tries to warn UNIT's Captain Magambo, but she has him arrested and determines to continue with the Advocate's plan. The Doctor's friends release him, and he tells Magambo that blowing up the Enochians' ship will only make matters worse, because the energy released will simply allow them to spread across Europe. Mr Crane, a man who was previously tricked into helping the Enochians, has now volunteered to carry out the Advocate's plan by placing a bomb on board

---

[80] Part One and Part Two both had the same subtitle, 'Old Friends', printed on the inside front cover of their respective issues. This was an error, and Part Two was meant to have the subtitle: 'Touched By An Angel'.
[81] In the story 'Fugitive' in Issues 3-6 of IDW's *Doctor Who*.
[82] Another character introduced in 'Fugitive', who has been secretly working against the Doctor for her own ends.

APPENDIX F: ORIGINAL COMIC STRIPS

their ship. The Doctor follows him, and manages to launch the ship. As it rises into the sky, the Enochians are forced to follow, taking them away from Earth. The bomb still detonates, destroying the ship, and Mr Crane is killed, but the Doctor is able to fly back to the ground using a pair of the clockwork Enochians' wings. The Doctor bids farewell to Martha, advising her to avoid the increasingly hard-line UNIT in future, then departs in the TARDIS with Emily. Matthew, however, decides instead to travel on with the Advocate, who has managed to turn him against the Doctor.

## GROUND CONTROL

Written by: Jonathan L Davis
Art: Kelly Yates; Colours: Phil Elliott; Letters: Robbie Robbins and Neil Uyetake; Edits: Denton J Tipton
Publication: July 2010 in IDW's *Doctor Who Annual 2010* (cover by Kelly Yates)

PLOT

The TARDIS is captured by a tractor beam and apparently brought to a space station in the year 6558. The Doctor, currently travelling without a companion, is questioned by a man named Mister K of the Safety Patrol's Interstellar Planetary Division, who wants to determine if he is a danger to the cosmos. Mister K finds archival video in the TARDIS of an incident where the Doctor and Donna narrowly escaped from a group of giant panda-like aliens called Cobalites. Unknown to them, one of the Cobalites was clinging to the outside of the TARDIS when it dematerialised, and was sent spinning into the time stream. Mister K also tells the Doctor that when he last regenerated, the energy released by the process devastated a section of the universe designated 4594A, and that he has inadvertently caused many other disasters. The Doctor is forced to admit that the TARDIS could be a weapon, in the wrong hands. However, he realises that what he has been experiencing here is an illusion. Mister K has actually been trying to distract him in order to steal the TARDIS's energy. The only thing that wasn't fabricated was the story about the Cobalite lost in the time stream, which is how Mister K found him. He takes his leave of Mister K and departs.

## THE BIG BLUE BOX

Story and Art by: Matthew Dow Smith
Colours: Charlie Kirchoff; Letters: Neil Uyetake; Edits: Denton J Tipton
Publication: July 2010 in IDW's *Doctor Who Annual 2010* (cover by Kelly Yates)

PLOT

The Doctor scares off an alien that has been chasing a man named Douglas Henderson. Douglas has glimpsed the TARDIS at various times throughout his life, and is amazed to finally meet its owner and see its impressive interior. The Doctor reveals that Douglas is not in fact human, but is an alien doomsday weapon that accidentally ended up on Earth. He has been keeping an eye on Douglas over the

265

years, trying to find a way to neutralise him safely. The TARDIS is transmatted to an alien ship in Earth orbit. Its occupants are at war with the other type of alien that tried to capture Douglas earlier. Each side wants to use the weapon against the other. Douglas detonates himself, disabling both alien fleets and giving them no choice but to return to their home worlds. The Doctor manages to save Douglas and take him back to Earth, leaving him with just enough energy to live out a normal human lifespan.

## TO SLEEP, PERCHANCE TO SCREAM

Story, Art, Colours: Al Davison
Letters: Neil Uyetake; Edits: Denton J Tipton
Publication: July 2010 in IDW's *Doctor Who Annual 2010* (cover by Kelly Yates)

PLOT

The Doctor falls asleep, and in his dream finds himself on a fire-ravaged planet where he is reunited with his former companion Sarah Jane Smith, who tells him 'They are coming back'. He sees images of many of his old adversaries, while Sarah seems to transform into various other former companions. Eventually, he encounters a small, blue-skinned alien who reaches into him and pulls out a ball of 'guilt, fear and anger'. Then he meets his own next incarnation, who tells him 'I think we are going to be fine'. The Doctor finally wakes up, speculating that the TARDIS may sometimes siphon off his bad dreams. He leaves the ship to find it has materialised on a beautiful planetscape.

## OLD FRIEND

Written by: Tony Lee
Art: Matthew Dow Smith; Colours: Charlie Kirchoff; Letters: Robbie Robbins; Edits: Denton J Tipton
Publication: July 2010 in IDW's *Doctor Who Annual 2010* (cover by Kelly Yates)

PLOT

The TARDIS brings the Doctor and Emily to a rest home on 21st Century Earth, where a frail old man named Barnaby Edwards is celebrating his birthday. Barnaby proclaims himself to a one-time companion of the Doctor's. He is delighted to see him again, and returns to him an envelope that he was entrusted to keep. However, he then dies. The Doctor does not know Barnaby, and realises that he will actually meet him in a future incarnation – one of the quirks of time travel. The envelope contains a message from his future self warning him that Matthew is in danger. The Doctor determines to thwart the Advocate's plan – whatever it might be – and save Matthew.

NOTES

• This forms an 'interlude' between the previous ongoing IDW story, 'Don't Step on the Grass', and the next one, 'Final Sacrifice'.

• Barnaby Edwards is named after the Dalek operator and *Doctor Who* audio drama director.

## FINAL SACRIFICE: EXTRAORDINARY TRAVELLERS / WHIRLED WAR, TOO / REUNION / END-GAME

Written by: Tony Lee
Issue 13 Cover Regular: art: Paul Grist; colours: Phil Elliott
Issue 13 Cover RI: art: Matthew Dow Smith; colours: Charlie Kirchoff[83]
Issue 14 Cover Regular and RI: art: Paul Grist; colours: Phil Elliott
Issue 15 Cover Regular: Regular: art: Paul Grist; colours: Phil Elliott
Issue 15 Cover RI: art: Paul Grist
Issue 16 Cover Regular and RI: art: Paul Grist; colours: Phil Elliott
Issue 16 Cover RI: art: Matthew Dow Smith
Art: Matthew Dow Smith; Colours: Charlie Kirchoff; Letters: Robbie Robbins (13), Neil Uyetake (14-16); Edits: Denton J Tipton
Publication: Issues 13-16; August 2010, September 2010, October 2010, November 2010

PLOT

In 1906, at Oxford University, Professor Alexander Hugh has constructed a time-gate using salvaged alien technology. Two agents (which we are led to believe are from Torchwood), Robert Lewis and Eliza Cooper[84], hope to use it for the British Empire. However, they, the Professor and his assistant Annabella are all transported to an alien planet 20,000 years in the future, where they meet the Doctor and Emily. Two factions on the planet, the Soul Free and the Terror Farmers, have been fighting for thousands of years. At the Soul Free base, the Doctor learns that they are led by the Gizou shape-shifter, who now calls himself Lau'tan and has turned against the Advocate. The Advocate sends agents to take the Doctor and Emily prisoner. Annabella is killed in the crossfire, but Lau'tan buys the Doctor some time by adopting his form and allowing himself to be captured with Emily. They are taken to Matthew and the Advocate, who is acting as Queen of the Terror Farmers, and she imprisons them. Emily is visited by a Tef'aree[85], who tells her that the Advocate plans to use a terraforming device to transform the planet. She is then released by Lau'tan posing as Matthew – a plan by Matthew to get her to safety. The Doctor has meanwhile taken his party to the Kol-Ne-Wah temple, where he finds a computer hard drive. From this he gleans

---

[83] Also published with a photographic 'convention exclusive' variant cover
[84] Both introduced, but not named, in 'The Time Machination', an IDW one-shot *Doctor Who* comic book published in May 2009. It is now revealed that the man 'Jonathan Smith' in that story, whom the Doctor tricked Torchwood into believing was him and assumed would eventually be released, was actually dissected by them.
[85] Introduced in the earlier story 'Tesseract', published in Issues 7 and 8 of IDW's *Doctor Who*.

the truth: the 'Soul Free', or Sol Three, and the 'Terror Farmers', or Terra-Firmers, both came from Earth, while 'Kol-Ne-Wah' is Colony One. The Advocate takes Matthew to a satellite orbiting the planet, knocks him out and uses his human DNA to activate the terraforming device. As the device starts to work, the two sides in the conflict make a truce. Lau'tan sacrifices himself to protect the others by repairing a force field sabotaged by Robert, who is killed by the terraforming process. Matthew also sacrifices himself to turn off the terraforming device, grabbing the Advocate so that she is killed by the energy released. Matthew himself however is transformed into the Tef'aree. He will now be this fifth-dimensional being throughout time. He has contrived all the adventures that the Doctor has had with Matthew and Emily, to ensure this would happen. Eliza decides to stay behind on the planet, and the Doctor and Emily return Alexander to Oxford. Emily takes the place of Annabella. As Annabella Spring, she will one day discover Archie Maplin[86]. The Doctor departs, heading for Mars.

NOTES

- This was the final tenth Doctor comic strip story.
- Torchwood is referred to only by implication and not actually named in this story. This is because the comic strip rights to Torchwood were at this point licensed to a different company, Titan.

---

[86] The film star featured in 'Silent Scream', the story that introduced Emily and Matthew, in Issues 1-2 of IDW's *Doctor Who*.

# APPENDIX G
# OTHER ORIGINAL FICTION

In addition to the novels and comic strip stories covered in the preceding Appendices, there were a number of other places where original, officially-sanctioned new series *Doctor Who* fiction could be found during 2010. Details are given below.

## DOCTOR WHO AUDIOBOOKS

In 2010, BBC Audio released two single-CD talking books of eleventh Doctor stories exclusive to the audio medium. These were as follows.

## THE RUNAWAY TRAIN

Release date: 24 April 2010[87]
Written by: Oli Smith
Read by: Matt Smith
Produced by: Kate Thomas; Project editor: Michael Stevens; Music and sound effects composed and performed by Simon Hunt; *Doctor Who* theme music by Murray Gold

PUBLICITY BLURB

Matt Smith reads this exclusive audio story featuring the eleventh Doctor and Amy. Arriving on Earth in the midst of the American Civil War, the Doctor and Amy must get a posse together to help them retrieve an alien artefact that has fallen into the clutches of the Confederate Army. The terraforming device belongs to the Cei, a race of invaders who plan to use it to turn the planet into a new home world. But neither the Army nor the aliens are keen to let the Doctor and his gang interfere with their plans, and give chase across the Wild West. The only hope of escape for the Doctor and friends is to catch the 3.25 to Arizona and race along the newly-built transcontinental railroad ... Written specially for audio by Oli Smith, with additional music and special sound, 'The Runaway Train' features the Doctor as played by Matt Smith in the acclaimed hit series from BBC Television.

NOTES

• The initial release of this audiobook on 24 April 2010 was as an advance promotional copy given away free with that day's edition of the *Daily Telegraph*. This did not have the full music and sound effects of the

---

[87] See 'Notes'.

commercially-released version, which came out on 6 October 2010, some two months after 'The Ring of Steel' (see below).

• 'The Runaway Train' was also released in the US in October 2010 with 'The Ring of Steel' as a double-CD set under the umbrella title *New Adventures: Volume One*; and in April 2011 as a library edition with 'The Ring of Steel' and the 2011 audiobook 'The Jade Pyramid' in a three-CD-R set under the umbrella title *Thrilling Adventures: Volume 1*.

## THE RING OF STEEL

Release date: 5 August 2010
Written by: Stephen Cole
Read by: Arthur Darvill
Produced by: Neil Gardner; Project editor: Michael Stevens; Music and sound effects composed and performed by Simon Hunt; *Doctor Who* theme music by Murray Gold

PUBLICITY BLURB

Arthur Darvill reads this exclusive audio adventure featuring the eleventh Doctor and Amy. When the TARDIS lands on Orkney in the near future, the Doctor and Amy arrive to find a large demonstration in progress over the construction of new electricity pylons. The Doctor tries to break things up peacefully – but suddenly the road splits open without warning and swallows police, security guards and protestors alike. Separated from the Doctor, Amy takes charge of transporting the wounded to hospital – but the rescue mission becomes a terrifying ride as the pylons come to life and begin to walk and the road rears up, erupting with boiling tarmac ... The Doctor, meanwhile, has even more than metal monsters and rebellious roads to deal with. Who is sucking the life out of the power company's employees – and just what is lurking inside the Astra-Gen headquarters? Written specially for audio by Stephen Cole and read by Arthur Darvill (Rory in the TV series), 'The Ring of Steel' features the Doctor as played by Matt Smith in the acclaimed hit series from BBC Television.

NOTE

• 'The Ring of Steel' was also released in the US in October 2010 with 'The Runaway Train' (see above) as a double-CD set under the umbrella title *New Adventures: Volume One*; and in April 2011 as a library edition with 'The Runaway Train' and the 2011 audiobook 'The Jade Pyramid' in a three-CD-R set under the umbrella title *Thrilling Adventures: Volume 1*.

APPENDIX G: OTHER ORIGINAL FICTION

## DOCTOR WHO – DECIDE YOUR DESTINY BOOKS

During 2007 and 2008, BBC Children's Books published 12 paperback *Doctor Who* books in the *Decide Your Destiny* range, aimed at younger readers than the BBC Books novels. The *Decide Your Destiny* tagline reflected the fact that these followed the 'find your fate' principle whereby the reader was given a series of options in the text that allowed them to decide which of a number of different plotlines they followed. The series was revived in 2010, when four further paperback titles were published, numbered 1 to 4. These were designed to have an interactive component, with additional information and some basic animations accessible via a website for which links were provided in the books.[88] The four titles were as follows.

### 1: CLAWS OF THE MACRA

Publication date: 29 April 2010
Writer: Trevor Baxendale

#### PUBLICITY BLURB

Join the Doctor on his travels through time and space and influence the story with your decisions. Choose a direction and let the adventures begin ... Danger and adventure await you on a school trip to a gas refinery infested by giant crustaceans! Only you can help the Doctor and Amy put a stop to the Macra's plans and save Earth! These interactive stories continue online. With links to exclusive animated scenes and an exciting online game, there's a new adventure waiting for you with every read!

#### NOTES

• Features the Macra.
• A Welsh edition, published by Rily Publications and translated by Tudur Dylan Jones, came out on 5 August under the title *Crafangau'r Macra*.

### 2: THE COLDEST WAR

Publication date: 29 April 2010
Writer: Colin Brake

#### PUBLICITY BLURB

Join the Doctor on his travels through time and space and influence the story with your decisions. Choose a direction and let the adventures begin ... You're in the TARDIS when it loses power and crash-lands in a deserted snowy landscape. Something is sucking the energy from everything that passes! Is it the Sycorax? Or something else entirely? Help the Doctor and Amy unravel the mystery, before it's

---

[88] This interactive material is no longer available.

too late … These interactive stories continue online. With links to exclusive animated scenes and an exciting online game, there's a new adventure waiting for you with every read!

NOTES

- Features the Sycorax.
- A Welsh edition, published by Rily Publications and translated by Elin Meek, came out on 5 August 2010 under the title *Y Rhyfel Oeraf*.

## 3: JUDOON MONSOON

Publication date: 2 September 2010
Writer: Oli Smith

PUBLICITY BLURB

Join the Doctor on his travels through time and space and influence the story with your decisions. Choose a direction and let the adventures begin … Bo-ro-lo-ko-sho! Giant alien insectoids are terrorising the rainy planet Betul and the menacing Judoon are wreaking havoc, too! What's going on? Only you can help the Doctor, Amy and Rory solve the mystery and restore peace! These interactive stories continue online. With links to exclusive animated scenes and an exciting online game, there's a new adventure waiting for you with every read!

NOTE

- Features the Judoon.

## 4: EMPIRE OF THE WOLF

Publication date: 2 September 2010
Writer: Neil Corry

PUBLICITY BLURB

Join the Doctor on his travels through time and space and influence the story with your decisions. Choose a direction and let the adventures begin … There's a full moon rising and an ancient evil roams the streets. The Empire of the Wolf has begun! Can you help the Doctor and Amy destroy the werewolves before being turned into one yourself? These interactive stories continue online. With links to exclusive animated scenes and an exciting online game, there's a new adventure waiting for you with every read!

NOTE

- Features werewolves, of the kind seen in the TV story 'Tooth and Claw' (2006).

APPENDIX G: OTHER ORIGINAL FICTION

## DOCTOR WHO – THE ONLY GOOD DALEK

This graphic novel, published in hardback by BBC Books, features the eleventh Doctor and Amy. It was apparently envisaged as the first of a possible series, although no others have been forthcoming at the time of writing.

Publication date: 16 September 2010
Writer: Justin Richards
Artist: Mike Collins; Colourist: Bethan Sayer; Additional Colouring: Kris Carter, Yel Zamor, John-Paul Bove, John Charles; Letterer: Ian Sharman; Script Editor: Clayton Hickman; Commissioning Editor: Albert DePatrillo; Editorial Manager: Nicholas Payne; Series Consultant: Justin Richards; Project Editor: Steve Tribe; Cover Design: Mike Collins and Lee Binding; Production: Phil Spencer

### PUBLICITY BLURB

'Station 7 is the most secret establishment in the whole of Earth-Space. Even our own people don't know it exists. It's beyond top secret. There's no way the Daleks can ever find it.' Station 7 is where the Earth Forces send all the equipment captured in their unceasing war against the Daleks. It's where Dalek technology is analysed and examined. It's where the Doctor and Amy have just arrived. But somehow the Daleks have found out about Station 7 – and there's something there that they want back! With the Doctor increasingly worried about the direction the Station's research is taking, the commander of Station 7 knows he has only one possible, desperate defence. Because the last terrible secret of Station 7 is that they don't only store captured Dalek technology –it's also a prison. And the only thing that might stop a Dalek is another Dalek! An epic, full-colour graphic novel featuring the Doctor and Amy, as played by Matt Smith and Karen Gillan in the spectacular hit series from BBC Television.

### NOTES

* This graphic novel was a replacement for one entitled The Dalek Project that was proposed some months earlier but abandoned for a number of reasons, including that it was considered to feel too much like a tenth Doctor story.
* The continuity-heavy plot features Drone, Scientist and Strategist types of the new paradigm Daleks introduced in 'Victory of the Daleks', plus a number of elements from classic-era Dalek stories, including Varga Plants, a Slyther, Robomen, Ogrons and members of the Space Security Service.

### DOCTOR WHO – THE BRILLIANT BOOK 2011

This year, there was no Doctor Who Storybook from Panini. Instead, the first in a new annual range, Doctor Who – The Brilliant Book, was published by BBC Books themselves. This featured two pieces of prose fiction – one written by science fiction author Brian Aldiss, the other recounting how the Silurians came to hibernate – the credits for which are noted below. There were also a few pieces extrapolating from the fiction of the TV episodes. Most notably, Mark Gatiss contributed *The Lost Diaries of Winston Spencer Churchill* – a UNIT archive of diary entries supposedly written by Churchill, briefly relating some of his other encounters with various incarnations of the Doctor as mentioned in 'Victory of the Daleks'.

**UMWELTS FOR HIRE**
Written by Brian Aldiss. Illustrated by Martin Geraghty.

**THE LITTLE PLANET**
Written by David Llewellyn. Illustrated by Anthony Dry.

### DOCTOR WHO – THE OFFICIAL ANNUAL 2011

The contents of *The Official Annual 2010* were, overall, a considerable improvement on the previous year's meagre offerings. However, the book still included only two comic strip stories – *Buzz!* and *The Grey Hole* – and two pieces of prose fiction – *Blind Fury* (a 'Gallifreyan fairytale' not featuring the Doctor or his companions) and *Secret of Arkatron* – credits for which are noted below. The rest of the pages were filled with factual features on the TV show and its characters – including a section on *The Sarah Jane Adventures* – plus puzzles and the like, and a free double-sided poster inside the back cover.

**BLIND FURY**
Written by Justin Richards. Illustrated by Tomislav Tomis.

**BUZZ!**
Written by Oli Smith. Illustrations by John Ross. Colours by James Offredi.

**SECRET OF ARKATRON**
Written by Justin Richards. Illustrations by John Ross. Colours by James Offredi.

**THE GREY HOLE**
Written by Trevor Baxendale. Illustrations by John Ross. Colours by James Offredi.

# ABOUT THE AUTHOR

Stephen James Walker became hooked on *Doctor Who* as a young boy, right from its debut season in 1963/64, and has been a fan ever since. He first got involved in the series' fandom in the early 1970s, when he became a member of the original Doctor Who Fan Club (DWFC). He joined the Doctor Who Appreciation Society (DWAS) immediately on its formation in May 1976, and was an attendee and steward at the first ever *Doctor Who* convention in August 1977. He soon began to contribute articles to fanzines, and in the 1980s was editor of the seminal reference work *Doctor Who – An Adventure in Space and Time* and its sister publication *The Data-File Project*. He also became a frequent writer for the official *Doctor Who Magazine*. Between 1987 and 1993 he was co-editor and publisher, with David J Howe and Mark Stammers, of the leading *Doctor Who* fanzine *The Frame*. Since that time, he has gone on to write and co-write numerous *Doctor Who* books and articles, and is now widely acknowledged as one of the foremost chroniclers of the series' history. He was the initiator and, for the first two volumes, co-editor of Virgin Publishing's *Decalog* books – the first ever *Doctor Who* short story anthology range. More recently, he has written *Inside the Hub*, the definitive factual guide book on the *Doctor Who* spin-off *Torchwood*. He has a degree in Applied Physics from University College London, and his many other interests include cult TV, film noir, vintage crime fiction, Laurel and Hardy and an eclectic mix of soul, jazz, R&B and other popular music. Between July 1983 and March 2005 he acted as an adviser to successive Governments, latterly at senior assistant director level, responsible for policy on a range of issues relating mainly to individual employment rights. Most of his working time is now taken up with his role as co-owner and director of Telos Publishing Ltd. He lives in Kent with his wife and family.

# Other Cult TV Titles
# From Telos Publishing

Back to the Vortex: *Doctor Who* 2005
Second Flight: *Doctor Who* 2006
J Shaun Lyon

Third Dimension: *Doctor Who* 2007
Monsters Within: *Doctor Who* 2008
End of Ten: *Doctor Who* 2009
Cracks in Time: *Doctor Who* 2010
River's Run: *Doctor Who* 2011
Time of the Doctor: *Doctor Who* 2012 and 2013
Stephen James Walker

The Television Companion (*Doctor Who*) Vols 1 and 2
David J Howe, Stephen James Walker

The Handbook (*Doctor Who*) Vols 1 and 2
David J Howe, Stephen James Walker, Mark Stammers

Talkback (*Doctor Who* Interview Books) Vols 1, 2 and 3
Ed. Stephen James Walker

The Target Book (*Doctor Who* Novelisations)
David J Howe

Doctor Who Exhibitions
Bedwyr Gullidge

Inside the Hub (Guide to *Torchwood* Season 1)
Something in the Darkness (Guide to *Torchwood* Season 2)
Stephen James Walker

A Day in the Life (Guide to Season 1 of *24*)
Triquetra (Guide to *Charmed*)
A Vault of Horror (Guide to 80 Great British Horror Films)
The Complete Slayer (Guide to *Buffy the Vampire Slayer*)
Keith Topping

Liberation (Guide to *Blake's 7*)
Fall Out (Guide to *The Prisoner*)
By Your Command (Guide to *Battlestar Galactica*, 2 Vols)
Alan Stevens and Fiona Moore

**A Family at War (Guide to *Till Death Us Do Part*)**
Mark Ward

**Destination Moonbase Alpha (Guide to *Space 1999*)**
Robert E Wood

**Assigned (Guide to *Sapphire and Steel*)**
Richard Callaghan

**Hear the Roar (Guide to *Thundercats*)**
David Crichton

**Hunted (Guide to *Supernatural* Seasons 1-3)**
Sam Ford and Antony Fogg

**Bowler Hats and Kinky Boots (Guide to *The Avengers*)**
Michael Richardson

**Transform and Roll Out (Guide to The Transformers Franchise)**
Ryan Frost

**Songs for Europe (Guide to the UK in the
Eurovision Song Contest: 4 Volumes)**
Gordon Roxburgh

**Prophets of Doom (Guide to *Doomwatch*)**
Michael Seely and Phil Ware

**All available online from
www.telos.co.uk**

Printed in Great Britain
by Amazon

26410093R00155